Sexual Deviance and Sexual Deviants

and

Sexual Deviance and Sexual Deviants

Edited by

**Erich Goode
and
Richard R. Troiden**

WILLIAM MORROW & COMPANY, INC.
NEW YORK 1974

Printed in the United States of America.

1 2 3 4 5   78 77 76 75 74

Book design: Helen Roberts

Library of Congress Cataloging in Publication Data

Goode, Erich, comp.
  Sexual deviance and sexual deviants.

  Bibliography: p.
  1. Sexual deviation—Addresses, essays, lectures.
I. Troiden, Richard, joint comp. II. Title.
[DNLM: 1. Sex deviation. WM610 G647s]
HQ71.G65   301.6′2   74-13344
ISBN 0-688-00280-3

Contents

v

Sexual
Deviance
and
Sexual
Deviants

I
Introduction:
The Social Side of Sex

What do pornography, prostitution, male and female homosexuality, rape, and kinky sex have in common? Probably nothing, if we were to look at the people who practice these activities, and nothing if we were to look at the activities themselves.

Rape is an act of victimization and oppression. The rapist seeks the degradation of another. Rape is the most extreme form of male domination in a society which often displays contempt for women.

Prostitution involves the participation of technically consenting adults. But it reduces sex to a cash connection—a living representation of the reduction of women to a commodity.

Homosexuality is an alternate life-style. It involves no oppression, no victimization. Nearly all of the virtues of heterosexual relationships can be embodied in homosexual relationships, in addition to virtues unique to same-sex behavior. For millions of Americans, it is a *viable* choice; they have chosen homosexuality in preference to heterosexuality.

Pornography, in its present form, often involves the degradation and humiliation of women. It often reduces human behavior and the human psyche to a single dimension. The fact that such material finds a ready market is a sad commentary on the impoverishment of the sexual lives of many of us. Highly erotic material *could be*, but apparently *is not*, produced which does not exploit women and which depicts sex in a subtle, sophisticated light. Perhaps it will be, in the future. There are signs that this is beginning to happen. Erotica has the potential for enriching our lives. The fact that it has as yet done so only on an extremely limited basis should give us pause for thought.

1

Kinky sex is an extremely broad banner under which are gathered activities ranging from mildly unusual, eccentric practices occasionally participated in by otherwise conventional people to spice up their otherwise conventional sex lives to bizarre fetishes and fixations practiced by a very small number of people who cannot become stimulated in any other way.

How is it possible to talk or write of all of these forms of sexual behavior as "deviant"? Is the term meaningless, then? The behavior we discuss ranges from the harmless to the life-threatening, from the enriching to the exploitative, from the healthy to the pathological. In what conceivable sense can one term typify them all? If these practices have no internal similarity, and if they attract people who have almost no traits in common, how can it possibly be meaningful to deal with them all in one breath?

Every civilization that has ever existed categorized things. These categories make sense if one is deeply embedded and involved in one's culture. But they may look absurd from other perspectives. They are always fraught with contradictions and inconsistencies. Few members of a society realize this. When these logical irregularities are pointed out, there are usually rationalizations and justifications ready at hand.

Deviance is such a category. It is the opposite of conventionality. Deviance is simply behavior that most people in a society think of as immoral and unconventional. It is that which conventional people get upset about, that which attracts their hostility and outrage. What is so interesting about deviance is that people get upset about the oddest things. Many people are completely indifferent about many activities which are extremely dangerous, and almost hysterical about those which present no objective threat to anyone. Thus, people may put something like masturbation or smoking marijuana on the same level as murder and rape. So, the question of justice aside, our attention has to be focused on the issue of why these quirks should rule the minds of men and women in an age and a society whose members think of themselves as rational and hardheaded.

Sex is perhaps the area of life in which these contradictions are most readily apparent. For a variety of reasons, most of us are least rational about our most intimate practices. It is in the sexual sphere that the gap between how we rationalize things and the way they appear to an outsider is most glaring. Perhaps this is one reason for focusing our attention on sexual behavior: learning about our own folly should make us wiser about the human condition.

THE SEXUAL REVOLUTION?

We live, it is said, in the midst of a sexual revolution. Some observers even go so far as to claim that the revolution has already achieved its goal: complete sexual freedom. Evidence of radical, revolutionary change is all around us. In the words of sociologists John Gagnon and William Simon, we are experiencing an ongoing *erotization of the environment* (Gagnon and Simon, 1973: 6). That which was once clandestine is now unabashedly public. The jolt of thinking what it was like on the sexual front just a few brief years ago is startling; we have come to accept as perfectly normal that which once shocked and enraged us.

That Ralph Ginzburg was imprisoned for publishing a magazine whose contents were less erotic than material which could be found on any newsstand today seems to us now an archaic leftover from a benighted and sexually repressed era.

In 1948, *The New York Times* refused to advertise the first volume of the Kinsey report. "By the middle 1960s the *Times* was carrying, without blushing, advertisements for books and films which had previously been unavailable outside the locked library cabinets of Kinsey's Institute for Sex Research" (Gagnon and Simon, 1973:7).

In the late 1960s, getting an abortion was a furtive, dangerous—or costly—matter. Today, any woman can get one, at any time, for any reason.

In the early 1960s, it was possible to view full nudity on the screen in a public theater only in bland, asexual "nudist" films, in which scenes of entire families playing volleyball seemed to be obligatory. Today, in spite of the recent unfavorable Supreme Court ruling, any adult can wander into suburban motion picture theaters around the country and witness scenes of copulation, fellatio, cunnilingus, various forms of sadism and masochism, Lesbianism, sodomy, masturbation, and orgies.

"Everybody's doing it," teenagers will explain, referring of course to premarital intercourse. "I haven't known a virgin since I was fourteen," another will say, and the wistful adult male who grew up in the 1950s thinks back to the time when "copping a feel" was a major event in his life.

Thumbing through contemporary men's magazines sold on the newsstand, such as *Oui* and *Penthouse*, reveals full-color photographic features of: a young woman exposing herself, dirty-old-man style, opening up her trenchcoat to a startled man, also in a trenchcoat, whom she obviously beat to the draw; a woman having intercourse with a swan; a model who looks like Hitler, complete with Nazi uniform and swastika armband, spanking the bare bottom of a naked woman; women clad only in steel-studded black leather outfits, dog collars and spike heels, brandishing whips; orgies involving dozens of men and women, their sprawling bodies filling up the better part of a large room.

Looking around us, it is impossible to avoid the conclusion that we have experienced a full-scale sexual revolution in the past few years. Isn't it true that "gay is good"? Isn't "swinging" the norm, almost a way of life of the affluent suburban couple? Isn't sex as easy to find as bubble gum—and just as serious? And what about the thirteen-year-old girls waiting patiently in the gynecologist's office for their supply of birth control pills? Aren't women liberated today—to seek out men who please them, or women if they wish, or free to remain celibate if that's their thing? Don't unlimited sexual options stretch before the contemporary man and woman like sands upon the beach? If everything is acceptable, then nothing is deviant. Who can possibly question the fact that *anything goes* today?

"Anything goes" is not now, nor has it ever been, the sexual way of life of any people on the face of the earth. There has indeed been a revolution on the sexual front—but it has more form than substance. Public *discussion* and *exposure* of sex is strikingly different from the past; private behavior in the sexual arena is another matter altogether.

There doesn't seem to be any doubt about the rise in premarital sex among the young. A higher and higher proportion of each new crop of young adults has engaged in intercourse before marriage. We can't have complete confidence in the polls, but they all indicate that the increase is real, significant, and that it will continue. Young people are more likely to have sex, to have it more often, to start at an earlier age, and to have it with a greater number of partners, than was true in any earlier period in recent history. The change is especially dramatic among young women. Kinsey's study found that half of all women were virgins at the point of marriage. Today's studies find this reduced to less than one-third. To marry as a virgin today is to be part of a statistically deviant minority. We can also look at women and men of different ages today and determine the extent of social change on the sexual front. One study of over two thousand married women (Bell and Balter, 1973) revealed an almost perfect relationship between age and the likelihood of having engaged in coitus before marriage. Almost exactly half of the women over forty had had premarital sexual experience, but four-fifths of the women age twenty-five and younger had had sex before marriage. This finding is verified by another recent poll involving over two thousand Americans all across the country: the younger the person, the greater the chances that he or she will have engaged in premarital intercourse. Only one-third (or 31 percent) of the women age fifty-five and older said that they had had sex before their marriage. This increased steadily as the age of the respondent went down; for women under twenty-five, it was almost exactly four-fifths, or 81 percent (Hunt, 1973).

However, what makes the figures in both of these studies less impressive than they appear at first glance is the fact that an affectionate, marriage-oriented relationship is still, as it was previously, both the ideal and the norm. In both surveys, as in Kinsey's a generation and a half earlier, about half of the women who had premarital coitus *had it with only one partner,* the man they eventually married. To be more precise, in Kinsey's sample, 53 percent of the women had limited intercourse to one partner, 34 percent had it with two to five partners, and 13 percent with six or more. In the first of the studies cited above, these figures were almost exactly the same: 50 percent had sex with one premarital partner, 36 percent with two to five, and 13 percent with six or more (Bell and Balter, 1973.) The same basic finding has been turned up in a number of different studies, the most recent being that of Kantner and Zelnick, 1972. Clearly, then, premarital sex is still a serious business. In spite of the rise in the incidence of sex before marriage, we do not seem to be living in anything like a sexually "revolutionary" age. Casual, recreational sex is, even today in our "permissive" society, the exception rather than the rule.*

---

* This might be an appropriate place to mention the methodological deficiencies of all of the surveys on sexual behavior which have ever been conducted, including the ones cited here. Kinsey's male and female samples, although huge in

*Extra*marital sex—adultery, swinging, and "open marriages"—does not seem to have increased very much in the past generation or two, in spite of the enormous place it occupies in the press and in the popular imagination. Kinsey's figures revealed that about half of the men and a quarter of the women in his sample had had extramarital intercourse once or more during their marriage. Surveys done today do not find any increase. Kinsey did not ask questions about swinging, but current surveys do not verify any stampede in this direction. *Playboy*'s national poll indicated just the opposite; of about fourteen hundred married respondents, only 2 percent said that they had ever participated in swinging, and over half of the women in this study who had, said that they had done so exactly once. Even men and women who had had extramarital sex admitted that it was less pleasurable than sex with their spouse (Hunt, 1974). If sexual deviance is on the increase, it isn't in the sphere of infidelity. Boring as it might seem, sex on the marital bed—and only on the marital bed—is overwhelmingly the norm for married couples.

It is doubtful that the incidence of homosexuality is significantly greater now than ten or twenty years ago. Public tolerance of homosexuality is unquestionably greater. Talk and writing about it has certainly increased—perhaps by as much as a hundredfold. It is probably participated in with far less guilt than before. Gay dances and clubs flourish on college campuses and in our urban centers, and any seventeen-year-old in these settings can decide, with a minimum of anxiety, that he or she may want to explore the possibility of being gay. Gay self-discovery almost certainly takes place earlier

---

number, were biased; certain groups in the population were overrepresented, while others were underrepresented. The male sample, for instance, included a far higher percentage of prisoners than there are in the general population. The female study oversampled college-educated women. The Sorensen survey of adolescent sexuality was burdened with an extremely high refusal rate, causing the researcher to wonder if the sexual patterns of those who were willing to be interviewed might be quite different from those who refused. The *Playboy* study, summarized by Morton Hunt, committed some serious blunders in interviewing technique—for instance, by interviewing some people after a group rap session, a factor which clearly could influence their answers. In the face of these and other problems, anyone interested in human sexuality has two choices: to pretend that "nothing is known," and ignore all studies that are inadequate in any way (this would invalidate nearly all survey research!) or to summarize a number of studies, each with different drawbacks, and attempt—cautiously—to reach some kind of consensus. We choose the second of these two paths.

now. Finding others who are also gay is much easier. Perhaps the frequency of homosexual intercourse, among those who are gay, has risen—just as the frequency of heterosexual intercourse is higher than it once was. All of this would seem to add up to the conclusion that many more men and women today are becoming gay than was true previously. It appeals to common sense to conclude that a much higher proportion of the population is experiencing same-sex inter-course. But in fact the proportion has not really changed very much in the years since the Kinsey surveys were done.

In a large-scale national study of the sexual beliefs and practices of American adolescents, only 9 percent had ever had an experience of "sexual stimulation or satisfaction" with someone of the same sex—6 percent for girls, 11 percent for boys; 5 percent for the younger boys (age thirteen to fifteen), 17 percent for the older boys (sixteen to nineteen), and 6 percent for girls in both age brackets (Sorensen, 1973: 285–295, 432). For most men and women—but especially for men—nearly all of the homosexual experiences they do have are confined to adolescence. Another survey found that only about one-fifth to one-quarter of all American males have any homo-sexual experience at all beyond adolescence. One in five single women and one in ten married women have a homosexual encounter at least once in their lives, and this is 10 percent and 3 percent after adolescence (Hunt, 1974).

Can it be that all of the changes we have seen in the sexual sphere over the years have been public and not private? Our toler-ance for once severely condemned behavior is far greater today. We are no longer shocked by what once enraged us. We see and read about alternatives to conventional sexuality far more than we once did. But then, the unconventional and the sensationalistic always receive a disproportionate amount of attention. Is it true that the changes are only attitudinal, and not at all behavioral? Can it really be the case that we have learned to accept a wider range of sexual behavior as normal and that's about it? Doesn't it seem impossible that this attitudinal change should not have spilled over into the arena of sexual behavior as well?

There do seem to be at least two significant trends in sexual behavior, two significant changes, two areas of behavior that were once considered unconventional and deviant, which have now ac-quired the mantle of respectability.

First, a far greater range of sexual *variety* is permitted and practiced within marriage.

Second, a much greater amount of *post*marital sex is taking place than previously.

In the *Playboy* study we mentioned above, over three-quarters of the married sample under the age of thirty-five had engaged in fellatio in the previous year, but under 25 percent of those age fifty-five and over had done so. Almost exactly the same figures held for cunnilingus (Hunt, 1973). In Kinsey's study, only 15 percent of the high-school-educated females said that their husbands used cunnilingus "at least sometimes"; for the *Playboy* sample, the figure was 56 percent. The increased incidence in the practice of oral-genital sex is perhaps more striking than any other change in marital sexuality, but almost equal changes have taken place with other activities which were almost never discussed and were very rarely practiced a generation or two ago: mildly kinky sex, anal sex, a great variety of positions, prolonged foreplay, more extended intercourse. This has probably resulted in a rise in absolute satisfaction: it is highly likely that significantly more women are having orgasms than before. But has it produced a rise in relative dissatisfaction? With a greater rate of enjoyment, has there been a rise in expectations, desires, and demands? It's difficult to say. We do know that there is far more variety in marital sex than was once true, we know that sex takes place more frequently, that it is more likely to eventuate in orgasm, and that it occupies a larger psychic space in most marriages. It is probably premature to speculate as to what larger changes these practices will bring, but it is clear that things are loosening up a good deal on the marital bed.

Divorce is now about twice as frequent as it was when Kinsey's studies were conducted. This means that there are far more people, especially in their twenties and thirties, who were once married, and who experienced the comfort and satisfaction of frequent, easily available intercourse, who are now seeking sexual partners. Most do eventually remarry, but most are also wary of marriage. Postmarital men and women have a far higher rate of intercourse, and with far more partners, than is true of premarital men and women. And postmarital men and women have sex considerably more than they did in Kinsey's time. Between 4 and 18 percent of Kinsey's postmarital men age fifty-five and under had not had intercourse at all in the year prior to the survey, and the median level of intercourse was less than once a week. In the *Playboy* study, no postmarital man of any age was sexually inactive, and the median frequency of intercourse was over twice a week. For women, the contrast was even greater. One-third of Kinsey's women, and a majority in their mid-forties, were having no sex at all, and the median frequency was once every two weeks. Only one-tenth of *Playboy*'s postmarital women were sexually inactive in the previous year, and those who had intercourse had it at a. median frequency of nearly twice a week. *Playboy*'s divorced males had sex with a median of 8 partners per year, and their divorced women, with 3.5 (Hunt, 1974). This represents an enormous increase in the total volume of sexual intercourse, as well as the total number of coital partners, for the postmarried. The day of the arrival of the sexual "revolution" seems to be *after marriage,* not before, and—excepting the variety in sex with one's spouse—not during, either.

A third trend may be in the making, although it is not so readily apparent nor is it so easily measured as number of sexual partners, frequency of intercourse, and variety of coital and noncoital sexual positions. This is the decline of the double standard. At one time it was unusual and even deviant for a woman to expect and demand the same sexual rights as a man, whereas almost unlimited premarital intercourse was permitted the man. If he engaged in intercourse with many women, he was considered virile, a stud. The young woman who had intercourse with more than one man—her future husband—was considered "loose," promiscuous.

The decay of this discriminatory ideology and behavior is suggested by a number of indicators. For one thing, the enormous discrepancies in the sexual practices of men and women are becoming smaller over time. For instance, young women are engaging in premarital intercourse at a rate that is gradually approximating that of young men. While only one-third of *Playboy*'s sample of women age fifty-five and older had had sex before marriage, four-fifths of the men their age had done so—31 percent versus 84 percent. But the gap among the under-twenty-five age group was much smaller—81 percent for the women versus 95 percent for the men. The reader might be puzzled as to how it is possible for a small minority of the women to have had intercourse with a large majority of the men in the same age bracket. If their numbers are roughly equal, how is it possible that their rates of premarital intercourse are not also equal? The answer is actually quite simple, as well as instructive. When the sexual double standard prevails, the world is divided into "good girls" and "bad girls." A large number of men prey sexually upon a small number of women who become defined as legitimate targets because of their reputation for being promiscuous. Most of these men want to marry virgins, but they also want to have sex with a number of women—whom they exploit sexually, and whom they consider beneath their dignity to marry. Although the rates of premarital intercourse for men and women are very different in the older age groups, the women who did have sex before marriage did so with a far greater number of partners than did the men. However, with the downfall of the double standard and the rise of sexual equality this good girl-bad girl distinction becomes increasingly fuzzy, and it becomes acceptable for a man to marry a sexually experienced woman. The greater the equality between the sexes, the closer are their rates of premarital intercourse.

Another indication of the growing antiquation of the sexual double standard is that a smaller and smaller proportion of young men are thinking of virginity as desirable. A small minority of young men age thirteen to nineteen—30 percent to be exact—said that they "wouldn't marry a girl who isn't a virgin at marriage." The figure was a bit more than half as high for the older adolescent (25 percent) as for the younger (38 percent), indicating that, with maturity, the double standard becomes increasingly obsolete. Also, young men who were themselves virgins were twice as likely to agree with this statement (42 percent) as were nonvirgins (21 percent), also indicating that, with experience, young men are much more likely to reject the view that it is acceptable for men to have sex before marriage, but not women (Sorensen, 1973:395).

Another sign of the death throes of the double standard is to be found in the statements made by women affirming their right to complete sexual equality. While they will grant that it is not a simple matter to find men to agree with them, and who will respect them and this right, the fact is these men can be found. While granting that the double standard still rules the minds and bodies of many men and women, one sociologist argues that its days are numbered:

> Women are not biologically monogamous, nor is monogamy congruent with woman's capacity for sexual response. Biologically woman's sex drive is probably equal to or greater than the male's. . . . Certainly, as Masters and Johnson have reported, women have more sexual stamina; they don't need a recovery period after

orgasm and one orgasm doesn't usually make them feel like turning over and going to sleep. Furthermore, women are capable of being multiorgasmic. . . . Few women are getting as much sexual activity as they are capable of enjoying. It might be reasonable to have several lovers than to expect one man to satisfy all of one's needs (Schwartz, 1973).

Which leads us to a central issue: how fixed are our sexual patterns? How much change can we expect in human sexual behavior over time? Is what we do sexually biologically determined? Or can we expect radically different sexual life-styles over the next few years? We have been told for generations that "anatomy is destiny" —that things like male dominance, the greater interest of men in sex, the greater passivity, tendency toward monogamy, and sexual conventionality on the part of women, and the high level of aggressiveness, both sexual and nonsexual, among men, are all genetically "programmed." It seems that definitions of reality such as these always follow conventional, traditional lines. What is considered "normal" is that which fits in with established ways of doing things. Whatever is declared to be "unnatural," a violation of our biological instincts, is conveniently also that which is on the unconventional side, in other words, what is seen as "deviant."

Now, with the affirmation of sexual equality on the part of independent, freethinking women, with the rise of a Women's Movement which questions the dominance and superiority of men, we are simultaneously led to question these assumptions of inherent genetic sexual programming. If it is true that women (and men) can reverse centuries-old traditions of what our gender roles are, then perhaps the notion of fixed biological drives toward specific patterns of behavior, sexual and otherwise, is completely incorrect. Perhaps we are freer to shape our sexual destiny than we think.

Perhaps it is time to ask about what our own contribution is to our sexual lives, and what is the contribution of our animal heritage.

THE SOCIAL SIDE OF SEXUAL DEVIANCE

Anything human is the proper arena of the sociologist. Sex is, perhaps, the most singularly human of all human activities. And yet it has been treated as a mere biological function by those who consider it. Who becomes labeled the "expert" on matters sexual? The physician, the biologist. As if what we did in bed could possibly be reduced to the mere friction of skin against skin, of organ inserted into organ, of hormones racing through the bloodstream. We would like to suggest that sex—seemingly a biological function—is *above all* a social activity, and that those trained in the anatomy and physiology of the human body cannot possibly understand human sexuality without a firm grounding in the sociological side of man and woman.

The late 1960s witnessed a renaissance of once-defunct genetic and biological theories of human behavior. It has, once again, become fashionable to speak of a "killer instinct," an "aggressive instinct," a "male-bonding instinct," of chromosomes as a cause of crime, of the genetic superiority in IQ of whites over Blacks, of man (but not woman?) as the "naked ape," of "sexual suicide," sexual permissiveness, and homosexuality resulting from equality between the sexes. All of these theories share with currently dominant notions of sex and sexuality the fallacy of assuming that what we are, do, and think is a simple product of our relatively fixed, inborn, congenital equipment. All biological theories of human sexuality, ranging from the conventional and commonsense notions that the man and woman on the street believe to nearly all brands of Freudian psychology, adhere to the following tenets of faith:

(1) Biological *determinism:* what we do sexually is a relatively simple function of innate drives, of animal "instincts"; culture is merely a patina shellacked onto the organism.

(2) The *strength* of the sexual drive: sex is not merely an instinct; it is a remarkably *powerful* drive which is analogous to hunger and thirst, a drive which demands fulfillment, an *importunate* drive.

(3) The *primacy* of sex: sex plays a central role in the lives of us all, either directly or indirectly; nonsexual items and activities symbolize, stand for, or inadequately stand in for sex.

(4) The inherent *destructiveness* of sex: if unchecked, our animalistic sexual needs could destroy others, as well as society as a whole; our instincts have to be controlled, sublimated, routed into the "proper" channels.

(5) The *constancy* of the sexual drive: we are all born with a fairly *fixed* need for sexual expression.

(6) The *universality* of sexual meaning: all people go through

a standard psychosexual development, face similar crises, the resolution of which determines later adaptation; behavior, organs, and thoughts mean pretty much the same thing to everyone everywhere.

It is our conviction that every one of these beliefs is false. Each one rests on fallacious assumptions. Each one fails when exposed to the facts. And yet, for nearly all of us, they are givens in the universe, taken for granted and unquestioned. Here, we would like to sketch out a radically different perspective.

What humans do sexually cannot be even remotely derived from the sexual practices of animals. In fact, far from being animalistic, far from being an exhibition of "lower," "baser" drives, sexuality as we practice it is *distinctly* human. Animals lead exceedingly *sparse* sexual lives. A cartoon in *Playboy* a few years back showed two bison trudging up a hill after intercourse; the female says to the male: "You mean that's it? A *two-minute* mating season?" Unlike animals, we can be sexually aroused at almost any time. Intercourse among animals is tightly related to fertility; the female is most receptive—and often, only receptive—when she is most fertile. This period may range from a few days to a few weeks in a given year. Among no animal species *except* the human is sexual receptivity unrelated to the likelihood of conception. Sex for fun is something we invented. *And so is sexual deviance.*

Every human being is born into a state of *sexual multipotentiality*. Put plainly, this means that we all have the innate capacity to respond to an incredibly wide range of stimuli, to enjoy and find satisfying a kaleidoscopic *range* of sexual behavior. The human sexual potential is, in fact, so broad that we never stop to consider its full extent. "Think of some of the fantastic ways in which men [and women] gain sexual gratification," writes sociologist Taylor Buckner: "homosexuality, fetishism, necrophilia, paedophilia, masturbation, oral intercourse, anal intercourse, oral-genital and oral-anal intercourse, bestiality, heterosexuality, voyeurism, exhibitionism, clusterfucks, masochism, and sadism, to name only the more direct methods" (Buckner, 1971:7).

This multipotentiality does not mean that there are *absolutely no limits at all* to human sexual expression. The number of orifices we have is finite. The number of sexual acts of which we are capable in a given hour or even day does have limits, even though they are fuzzy. The objects which turn people on are not completely random; the likelihood that a mound of earth, a toenail, or a stapler will become the agent and the target of sexual arousal is exceedingly remote. But these boundaries are generous. If we are to understand human sexuality at all, we must explore the *variations* in sexual response, excitation, and behavior; the universals are few in number and not very interesting.

And our multipotentiality also does not *justify* sexual practices which run against what most people do and believe is right. Just because homosexuality and marital infidelity are potentially "in us all" at birth does not mean that they are "right." Given the appropriate background, every one of us could have become a mass murderer, a baby-raper, a suicide, an alcoholic. The fact that a given activity is a human potential says nothing about its moral or ethical correctness, nor its viability. These are altogether different questions.

The traditional, conventional view of human sexuality is that we all have a normal, heterosexual "destiny," a destiny which can be derailed only as a result of early painful, traumatic, and pathological experiences. What is normal is dictated by how closely our sexual practices and desires correspond with this inborn biological destiny. According to this view, what is "deviant" is a departure from our biological destiny. Heterosexuality, our most common and conventional practice, becomes elevated to the status of the "normal." Anything else is branded as abnormal, pathological—deviant.

We would like to suggest a radically different view. *We have no biological "destiny."* Sexual behavior is not dictated by the body, not by our animal chemistry, but by the mind, by our human relationships, by civilization, by what has historically come to be accepted as good or bad—in short, by convention. We do what we do in bed because we have learned to do so. And what we do *could* have been otherwise; by growing up surrounded by different customs, we would have been completely different sexual beings. At birth, the possibilities for what we could do in bed—or, for that matter, out of bed, or anywhere else—are almost boundless. *We have not even begun to imagine the limits of our sexual potential, let alone practice them.*

We have no sexual "instinct." We have a sexual drive—or even better, a sexual *appetite*—which can be turned off, minimally potentiated, or strongly stimulated, after birth. We are born with the *potential* for sexual arousal, just as we are born with the potential for singing or speaking, but whether or not that potential will be realized, or what specific form that realization will take, is not inborn. It is learned.

We learn, either directly or unwittingly, to be aroused by some people and not by others. Some societies encourage homosexuality and scorn exclusive heterosexuality; in those societies homosexuality is practiced by almost everyone, and exclusive heterosexuality is almost unknown.

We learn at what age we are supposed to be capable of arousal and intercourse. Those societies that encourage prepubescent sexual activity tend to have a lot of it; those societies which savagely punish early sexual exploration tend to have very little of it.

We learn which situations are legitimate for sexual arousal. Some societies permit intercourse in view of others; many societies demand complete privacy. To us, a crowded elevator is not a sexual occasion; we tend to get upset by those for whom it is. At the same time, these definitions of proper conduct are in flux. New codes, with new expectations for when we are permitted to feel aroused, are emerging—with the subsequent effect of producing arousal in previously inappropriate situations.

We also learn, in perhaps only a semi-intended fashion, approximately what level and frequency of sexual outlet is expected. In some societies men and women are expected to engage in intercourse several times daily until well into middle age. In others, the expected frequency may be a few times a month. In prisons, where, we are told, homosexuality is "rampant" and "epidemic," the fact is that, although far more men do participate in such activity than on the outside, most engage only in desultory masturbation or discontinue sexual activity altogether. This is because most of the social cues surrounding sexual arousal are absent. Prison is not socially and culturally defined as a sexual occasion (Gagnon and Simon, 1973:235–259).

The sex drive is neither powerful nor weak; it can be almost anything we make it.

The sex drive is neither inherently beneficial nor destructive and antisocial; it can assume the functions, effects, and directions that have been assigned to it.

Sex is neither more primary than any other sphere of life, nor is it necessarily derivative; it can be either, or both, at the same time. Certainly Freud was right when he said that seemingly innocuous activities and objects can represent sex. But Kenneth Burke was equally correct in writing the opposite: that sex often stands for something else.

Sex in general, and any and all of its myriad incarnations, can mean almost anything, depending on the place it has in the fabric of a civilization, how it is translated into action, what emotional connotations surround it in everyday life.

In short, our basic biological equipment, both anatomical and hormonal, *potentiates* and *sets limits* on what we can and cannot do sexually. But it does not determine *what* we do, *with whom* we do it, *why* we do it, *when* we do it, *how often* we do it, *or even if we do it at all.*

Which brings us to a very basic question—*what's normal?*—as well as to another, its mirror image: *what's abnormal?* Sexual deviance, "deviation," or deviant behavior, has long been the province of the psychiatrist and the abnormal psychologist. They view deviance as an abnormality. This is a sophisticated version of the commonsense, conventional view of the man and woman on the street, for whom deviance calls to mind evil, degenerate, unnatural, and pathological practices. We would like to present a different view: deviance in general is simply *behavior which some people in a society find morally offensive, and which excites in these people—or would, if it were discovered—disapproval, condemnation, censure, hostility.* Deviance is immoral behavior, plain and simple—or rather, behavior that some people *think* is immoral. Deviance, therefore, is a judgment; it is a negative judgment *by* some people *about* the behavior of others. It isn't simply behavior with objective properties, but behavior which is subjectively evaluated in a negative way.

What's deviant? We can't answer this in the abstract. We have to ask the further question: *deviant to whom?* Acts (and people) are *labeled* deviant. They aren't deviant according to some abstract, universal, and absolute standard. We cannot determine whether or not some behavior is deviant in advance until we look at it in terms of certain people's actual, past, or potential reactions to it. In short, *deviance is in the eye of the beholder.* An act is deviant *insofar as it meets with social disapproval.*

This definition says nothing about abnormality. It says nothing about social harm. These are completely different questions. By some definitions of abnormality, deviant behavior is "abnormal." By other definitions it isn't. By some definitions ordinary, conventional, conforming behavior is "abnormal." Deviance and abnormality are completely independent of each other. Normality and abnormality are also judgments—although somewhat different judgments from deviance. Deviant just means "unconventional." It doesn't mean "sick." It doesn't mean "pathological." It doesn't mean "abnormal." We may like certain forms of deviant behavior. We may find others disgusting. But when we notice that a great number of people in a society also don't like that form of behavior, we enter the realm of deviance. When another form of behavior earns the approval of most people, then that behavior isn't deviant. The same goes for social harm, for the damage that one person inflicts upon another, or upon a number of others. Many forms of deviant behavior harm no one. Others are extremely harmful to many people. But the same thing holds true for conventional behavior. Taking part in a war is conventional behavior; it earns the approval of more people than refusing to kill in wartime does. Yet it is, at the same time, clearly inflicting harm on others. In this case, *deviant* behavior involves the *less* harmful of the two paths. Homosexuality is a form of behavior that harms no one. Yet most Americans find it an undesirable form of behavior; to them, it constitutes deviance. Still other forms of deviance are clearly and unquestionably harmful: rape, for example. Social harm and deviance, then, are two separate entities. We cannot define one by the other.

Whether deviance is *viable* behavior or not is also an altogether different question. Past observers, particularly psychiatrists, looked upon deviance as a kind of *disease*. They wanted to get rid of it. It was inherently undesirable. To such persons the point of studying things like homosexuality, incest, pedophilia (the erotic attraction to children), sadism and masochism, transvestism, or any other variants from what is considered "normal," was to understand them so that they could be *treated*, that is to say, *eliminated* so that ordinary heterosexual intercourse might *replace* them. To most psychiatrists, as well as to most of the public, sexual deviance is not seen as a basically "normal" variation from everyday sex. It is something that is intrinsically undesirable, something people *wouldn't practice if they were in full control of their faculties*. It is something that is *epiphenomenal*—that is, an aberration, some outward sign of an inward distress—something that will disappear when the person practicing it is normal, *something that doesn't deserve to exist*, something that would not exist in the best of all possible worlds. In other words, most people do *not* see deviance, sexual or otherwise, as viable. It is an irrational form of behavior, and therefore deserves to perish.

Everyone has his or her own conception as to what behavior is desirable and what behavior is undesirable, what should exist in a utopia, and what should eventually disappear. But we feel that this has nothing to do with whether the behavior is deviant or not. To put it another way, what the public labels as deviant is certainly closely related to what it *feels* is not viable, but this is an entirely personal matter. As sociologists, we must take note of this public feeling. We would be remiss in our duty as observers of the social scene if we did not. But we might feel quite another way. Our own personal feelings do not necessarily jibe with the public's. Our observation that the public feels negatively toward sexual deviance is unconnected with our own attitudes toward deviance, or toward different forms of it. The reader may have a different attitude altogether. The fact that the public feels a certain way—or that the majority of the public feels a certain way—toward a specific form of behavior does not make it wrong or right.

There are enormous differences between the various forms of deviant sexuality. Most people cannot handle too much complexity. They are comfortable with categories such as "good" and "bad," "black" and "white," "healthy" and "sick." The world of morality is an exemplar of this principle. Conventional people tend to stereotype deviance. They assume that a category which sounds "bad" must be characterized by other negative traits as well, and have a great deal in common with other things that sound bad. They want to link together things they put into one category, and to separate them with a wide gulf from that which they put into another category. We are saying something radically different from this conventional point of view. It is this. Behavior that is considered deviant may show *no other unconventional characteristics at all,* aside from its deviant status, aside from the fact that it meets with widespread social disapproval. Putting prostitution and homosexuality together (for example) does not mean that they are similar in all basic respects, nor in *any* basic respect, aside from the fact that they both tend to be disapproved of by most people in this society. More traditional observers—psychiatrists, for instance—have extended popular ideology by insisting that "deviant" categories share deep, fundamental characteristics, for instance, in claiming that there is a causal connection between Lesbianism and prostitution. Just because an activity is thought of as bad, or immoral, by a great many people in a society does not mean that it shares any important characteristics with other activities also thought of as immoral. The people who practice such activities may have nothing to do with one another socially, attitudinally, or behaviorally.

We would like to substitute a different view for the conventional view of deviance shared by most of the public and by more traditional perspectives such as psychiatry. This magical, dichotomous conception of deviant behavior and of the men and women who practice it hinders far more than it helps our understanding. In a sexually sophisticated age, we need sophisticated concepts.

Instead of a *dichotomous* view of sexual deviance and conventionality—based on the assumption that there are basically two categories, deviant and conventional—we suggest a *linear* view based on the proposition that the line between deviance and conventionality is not clear-cut, but gradual, subtle, blurred, almost imperceptible.

Instead of a *clinical* view—holding that deviance itself, and each type of deviant behavior, forms an almost organic entity, the existence and reality of which is indisputable to any reasonable and well-informed observer—we suggest that a more fruitful perspective is that of the *definitional* view, holding that exactly how we define deviance, and how we define its many forms, who belongs to each group and category, and what sort of behavior puts one into each group and category, is all somewhat arbitrary, and entirely dependent on the purposes at hand.

Deviance itself, and each kind of deviant behavior, is not a naturally occurring event or phenomenon. It is not classifiable in the same sense that animal and plant species are, in the way that chemicals are. It exists in the first place simply because people get upset about it; that's how it is defined. Without a feeling of moral disapproval, deviance does not exist. What we mean by deviance is morally disapproved behavior. It is this moral disapproval that *creates* deviant behavior. We know we've got our hands on deviance when we see people getting upset about something.

We also know that people get upset about different things in different settings. What is deviant here is not deviant there. Acts which seem superficially and externally the same are not necessarily the same in any other way. The fact that the participants have certain conceptions of the behavior, and that the surrounding society sees it differently, means that we are not dealing with the same form of behavior at all. We could classify all human contact between members of the same sex which leads to orgasm as "homosexual," but if it is furtive and clandestine in one case, and socially approved and even extolled in another, then for our purposes two cases are worlds apart. We are concerned with what the behavior *means* to the participants and to the society at large. To lump acts mechanically together that seem similar to us, as outside observers, is to violate the central feature of the behavior in question. Nature does not classify human behavior; people do. And different people will view the same behavior in many different ways, according to their perspective, their attitudes, their subjective views.

Past theories of deviant behavior, and especially sexual deviance, were in error for assuming that it is something existing independently of what people think of it. Early notions of deviance took it as an *objective reality*, existing in a state of nature, much like apples and oranges, cancer and tuberculosis, diamonds and emeralds. Early theorists thought of deviant behavior as a kind of *clinical entity*, a pathological phenomenon which had only to be located, identified, and classified. The scientist's classification was simply one which was presumed to mirror nature's classification. This assumption was a stupendous blunder. Naturally psychologists, psychiatrists, and sociologists thinking this way wanted to ape medicine and the natural science. They wanted to be "objective," and so they thought of sexual deviance as an "objective" phenomenon. This line of reasoning turns out to be sterile and misguided, because we cannot equate behavior with similar objective features. Deviance in general, and specifically sexual deviance, is from the very beginning a "subjective" phenomenon. *What kinds of behavior* are classified as deviant, as well as what kinds of behavior are classified as homosexuality, incest, prostitution, adultery, or anything else, is variable. Behavior defined in one society as an act of homosexuality, as an instance of incest, as prostitution or adultery, isn't defined as such within another social grouping. Acts have to be seen and categorized in a certain way. Definitions of behavior are always humanly fabricated, always arbitrary, always based on convention—and they vary a great deal from one civilization to another, from one subculture to another, and from one situation to another. Putting something into a category is always a matter of human intervention. Acts *exist* as an example of a general category because some people *think* of them as a category or group, as an entity, as a reality. *What something is* is always decided by people—and not by nature, not by the thing itself.

Even an act so outrageous as to offend the moral sensibilities of nearly all of us, such as child molestation, has to be looked upon as problematical in conception, definition, and reality. When is a given act an instance of child molestation? This can't be decided a priori, independent of the social and cultural context in which it takes place. For instance, what is a child? This varies from one civilization to another, and from one legal jurisdiction to another. It also depends on the age of the perpetrator. Two six-year-olds playing "doctor" would not be classified as an instance of child molestation by anyone. But if the man is twenty-six, then the meaning of the act changes radically for us, even though the external features of the act remain the same. We therefore put it into a completely different category. In some civilizations of the world, children are initiated into the wonders of sex by an older man or woman. No one in such a society would dream of calling what is done the sexual molestation of a child by an adult. Also, just what does a person have to do to commit an act of child molestation? Most men who are sent to prison for this charge do not have, nor do they attempt to have, sexual intercourse with their victims (Gebhard, *et al.,* 1967:71; McCaghy, 1967). Where an act stops being one of playful affection and begins to be seen as sexual aggression is a matter of definition. If we were to view all acts which are outwardly the same as belonging to the same category—child molestation—then we ignore the most important feature of that behavior: what it means to the participants, and to the society in general. This means that if we really want to understand the nature and reality of child molestation, we would have to classify acts which are externally different as belonging to the same category.

Consider incest. Isn't it forbidden everywhere and at all times to have sexual intercourse with members of one's own family? The answer is, almost—but not quite. It is true that the dominant code believed in by most members of all societies do prohibit brother-sister, father-daughter, and mother-son sexual liaisons involving intercourse *for the general population.* A very few civilizations allowed —and even insisted upon—marriages between very close kin for the royal family: the Azande of Africa, the ancient Incas in Peru, the ancient Hawaiians, and the ancient Egyptians. And, although intercourse is generally forbidden, in some societies parents may "masturbate or in some other sexual manner . . . stimulate their very young children" (Ford and Beach, 1951:112). Also, just who is defined as being part of one's own family is highly dissimilar across societal lines. For instance, first cousins are close enough in many cultures to qualify, but in others are distant enough to be fair game sexually. Also, in many societies "cross cousins" (children of one's father's sister, or one's mother's brother) are not included in the incest taboo, but "parallel cousins" (children of one's father's brother or one's mother's sister) are defined as being as close as one's own brothers and sisters. "In some cultures the interpretation of incest is so broad as to exclude as potential sex partners half the available population" (Ford and Beach, 1951:113). Also, the *degree* of public outrage generated in conventional people upon the discovery of incestuous behavior varies considerably from one culture to another, and from group to group in the same society.

It seems clear that incest cannot really be considered an act with "objective," universal features. Aristotle once wrote that a stallion which had accidentally had intercourse with his own mother committed suicide by jumping off a cliff, he was so ashamed of what he had done! This assumes that incest is a natural phenomenon, removed from time and place, from cultural context—that its horror lies in the biology of the animal, and not in social convention. This is absurd. Animals, of course, know nothing of the incest taboo; it is a human invention. And where humans invent customs, we may be sure that the reasons for their invention will vary, and hence, that the custom itself will always vary.

Knowing that the existence of deviance, and the very existence of the categories of behavior that make up deviance, are matters of custom and definition should alert us to a further insight: exactly where you draw the line between conventional and deviant behavior is a bit arbitrary. Conventional behavior *shades over into* deviant behavior. Just where behavior begins to be serious enough to get people upset is a matter of degree. Many people have deviant impulses—that is, momentary desires to commit seriously deviant acts. In fact, there are probably very few people in any society who do not have these feelings. Most married men and women lust after someone of the opposite sex who is not their spouse. All of the acts leading up to a full-fledged affair are points at which many a frightened and otherwise virtuous man and woman has stopped and retreated. Something like one married person in ten has engaged in extramarital *petting* and nothing else. At what point is extramarital sex deviant behavior? Clearly, it depends on who is looking at the behavior. And it depends on the person whose behavior is being considered; most Americans would be more lenient when thinking about the behavior of some abstract person than that of their own spouse. But it is certain that nearly all of us would think of momentary impulses as less serious than actual behavior, of an isolated instance of infidelity as less serious than an affair, of one affair as less serious than ten, and so on. Every form of deviant behavior has another, slightly less deviant form sitting next to it. Every form of deviant behavior is an exaggerated case of conventional behavior. In all conventional behavior there exists, in miniature, the possibility of deviance. Any analysis of deviance which fails to grasp its linear character is inadequate and misleading.

THE BOOK

The material in this anthology is not intended to be exhaustive, but it covers a wide range of deviant sexual behavior. We have not discussed any of the more exotic and statistically infrequent forms of behavior, such as necrophilia, transvestism, transsexuality, bestiality, and so on. There are a number of more common types of sexual deviance which we omitted simply because some sort of choice had to be exercised: incest, adultery, "open marriages," child molestation, abortion, illegitimacy. Moreover, there are some kinds of behavior which are gradually being redefined and are losing their deviant status. Certainly this is true of affectionate postadolescent premarital intercourse. Many of the rigid distinctions between what men and women are expected to do and be—our sex "roles"—are breaking down. To ignore them no longer constitutes deviance in many quarters. In short, although we have gathered together a rich and diverse collection of subjects and readings, it is necessarily and inevitably limited to those which we felt were most instructive for various purposes.

The activities had to be fairly common, rather than esoteric and exotic—yet not so common that they have become generally acceptable. They had to be sufficiently unconventional as to earn the title of "deviant." Obviously, this excluded activities which were frowned upon generations ago, but which are now more or less, or even completely, acceptable today: most premarital intercourse, masturbation, marital cunnilingus and fellatio, and so on. On the other hand, many moderately deviant activities are a kind of miniature form of others which are more severely chastised. Adolescent homosexual experimentation—two twelve-year-old boys engaging in mutual masturbation, say—is likely to be dismissed or mildly punished. Diversity in marital sex is becoming acceptable, but at what point are we discussing "diversity in marital sex" and at what point do we have "kinky"—and therefore *deviant*—marital sex? Thus, in order to discuss sexual deviance, it becomes necessary to start with *less* deviant sexual behavior. It is impossible to deal with rape in America, for instance, without stressing the point that a certain degree of sexual aggressiveness and a low estimation of women is typical of many American males who could not conceive of ever raping a woman. In many ways, deviant behavior is an extension of "normal" behavior; we cannot deal with one without the other.

Here, then, is a sampling of readings on sexual deviance. The selections bear the stamp of the editors' interests. The inclusions and the prefatory remarks cannot be said to be "objective," whatever that might mean. Over the past few years, sexuality has become politicized. We believe much of this thrust to be healthy. Too often in the past the views of one group in society became dominant, and were palmed off as objective and scientific. Just to select one area in which this sin was most glaring, until the 1970s the overwhelming majority of authors and researchers in the area of human sexuality were men, and their writings often displayed a male-centered perspective. Now that women are participating in this dialogue, and men are learning from their views and experiences, a more balanced portrait of our sexual life is emerging.

———————◆———————

Donald Marshall is an anthropologist, and author of several books on the culture, social structure, and language of various Polynesian peoples. He works for the Office of the Secretary of Defense on strategic arms limitation. John Messenger is a professor of anthropology at Ohio State University, and the author of a monograph on the ethnography of Inis Beag. Judd Marmor is a physician, and editor of several books, including one entitled *Sexual Inversion: The Multiple Roots of Homosexuality*. He is Franz Alexander Professor of Psychiatry at the University of Southern California School of Medicine.

References

Robert R. Bell and Shelli Balter, "Premarital Sexual Experiences of Married Women," *Medical Aspects of Human Sexuality,* November 1973: 111–118.

H. Taylor Buckner, *Deviance, Reality, and Change,* New York, Random House, 1971.

Clellan S. Ford and Frank A. Beach, *Patterns of Sexual Behavior,* New York, Harper and Row, 1951; Harper Colophon, 1972.

John H. Gagnon and William Simon, *Sexual Conduct: The Social Sources of Human Sexuality,* Chicago, Aldine, 1973.

Paul H. Gebhard, et. al., *Sex Offenders,* New York, Harper and Row, 1965; Bantam Books, 1967.

Morton Hunt, "Sexual Behavior in the 1970s," *Playboy,* October 1973: 85–88, 194, 197–202, 204, 206–207.

———, "Sexual Behavior in the 1970s, Part II: Premarital Sex," *Playboy,* November 1973: 74–75.

———, "Sexual Behavior in the 1970s, Part III: Sex and Marriage," *Playboy,* December 1973: 90–91, 256.

———, "Sexual Behavior in the 1970s, Part IV: Extramarital and Postmarital Sex," *Playboy,* January 1974: 60–61, 286–287.

———, "Sexual Behavior in the 1970s, Part VI: Deviant Sexuality," *Playboy,* March 1974: 54–55, 183–184.

John F. Kanter and Melvin Zelnik, "Sexual Experiences of Young Unmarried Women in the United States," *Family Planning Perspectives,* Vol. 4, No. 4 (October 1972): 9–18.

Alfred C. Kinsey, et al., *Sexual Behavior in the Human Male,* Philadelphia, Saunders, 1948.

Alfred C. Kinsey, et al., *Sexual Behavior in the Human Female,* Philadelphia, Saunders, 1953.

Charles H. McCaghy, "Child Molesters: A Study of Their Careers as Deviants," in Marshall B. Clinard and Richard Quinney, *Criminal Behavior Systems,* New York, Holt, Rinehart & Winston, 1967, pp. 75–88.

Pepper Schwartz, "Myth of the One-Man Woman," Letter to the Editor, *Playboy,* July 1973: 51–52.

———, "Female Sexuality and Monogamy," in Roger W. Libby and Robert Whitehurst (Eds.), *Renovating Marriage: Toward New Sexual Life Styles,* San Ramon, California, Consensus Publishers, 1973.

Robert C. Sorensen, *Adolescent Sexuality in Contemporary America,* New York, World, 1973.

Anthony Storr, *Sexual Deviation,* Baltimore, Pelican, 1964.

Too Much Sex in Mangaia
by Donald S. Marshall

Sex—sex for pleasure and sex for procreation—is a principal concern of the Polynesian people on tiny Mangaia, the southernmost of the Cook Islands near the geographical center of Polynesia in the South Pacific. From early puberty, Mangaians of both sexes reflect this concern in the numerous words they have for coitus, for the sexual parts and for sexual activities, and in the language of their insults.

They demonstrate that concern in the startling number of children born to unmarried parents, and in the statistics on frequency of orgasm and numbers of sexual partners. But that concern is simple fact-of-life—*not* morbid preoccupation. It is best expressed as an inclusive Polynesian philosophy in this translation of Frank Stimson's *Ode to the Gray Gull:*

> *Here he was born;*
> *Here he passed his days of*
>   *love-making;*
> *Here he grew old—*
>   *his powers waning,*
>   *dying a natural death.*

There is great directness about sex, but the approach to sex is correspondingly indirect. Among the young there is no dating, no tentative necking in the American sense. A flick of the eye, a raised eyebrow in a crowd, can lead to copulation—without a word. There is no social contact between the sexes, no rendezvous that does not

Reprinted by permission of the author from *Psychology Today*, Vol. 4, No. 9 (February 1971), pp. 43–44, 70, 74–75.

lead directly to coitus—copulation is the only imaginable outcome of heterosexual contact. The sexual intimacy of copulation precedes personal affection.

Mangaians arrive at this seeming anomaly through constant exposure to patterned ambivalence in their society and culture in the most formative childhood years. There is emphatic social division of the sexes. A cultural emphasis on sexual organs and sexual intercourse is always present—but rarely intrusive. There is sensuousness and open provocation in the local dance—which is thus banned from the villages by the Christian missionaries. Folk tales feature explicitly detailed accounts of sexual acts and sexual organs. Perfume and heavily scented flowers are much used. Yet there is a unique modesty about exposure of adult sexual organs. Mangaians are horrified at the casualness with which a European exposes his penis to other men when he urinates. There are intricate incest prohibitions, yet a Mangaian's social contacts are largely limited to his kinsmen.

In the year that I spent on Mangaia, I supplemented conventional anthropological techniques (participant observation and use of varied informants and historical records) by setting up several formal concept task groups with members from widely different segments of society. We met regularly for discussions of fundamental values, for the compilation of a Mangaian dictionary and grammar, and for detailed analysis of sexual behavior. This added another dimension to my research and enabled me to put together a picture of Mangaian sex-oriented life.

CIRCLE

The Mangaian is born, as he lives and loves and dies, in the midst of his clustered kinsmen. To bring forth her child, the mother labors in a circle formed by family members; the grandmother, the husband or father and the midwife all help her. Social warmth and approval envelop a newborn child; he is an added source of strength and power—his birth has strengthened the ties of sexual affection between his parents and extended the web of kinship.

Boys and girls may play together until three or four. Between four and five they separate into sex-age groups that will distinguish them socially for the rest of their lives. Brother and sister, sweethearts, lovers, husband and wife, mother and father, old man and old woman—except for economic activities, such pairs rarely mix socially in public, despite their intense private relationships. A six-year-old Mangaian brother and his three-year-old sister would not think of walking hand-in-hand in town, nor would the dignified Mangaian deacon and his wife walk to church together.

PLAY

The preschool Mangaian boy's bottom and penis rarely are covered except for church. There is no real shame associated with a child's genitalia (except for uncovering the glans of the penis) until he is about 12.

Small children may play at copulation, but only in private. In a somewhat different sense adult copulation never is socially acknowledged. The Mangaian enjoys an extraordinary sense of "public-privacy." He may copulate at any age in the single room of a hut that contains five to 15 family members of all ages—as have his ancestors before him. His daughter may receive and make love with a succession of nightly visitors in that same room. (This is *motoro*—the sleep-crawling tradition of Polynesian courtship in which a young man tests and socially demonstrates his courage and ardor by slipping into the family sleeping room soundless and copulating with the girl. Her parents and others in the room are theoretically asleep. But though the mother and father may listen anxiously for the sound of laughter as a sign that their daughter will be happy with her new partner, they "sleep soundly," say my informants with a smile. Parental over-vigilance might cost the daughter a husband. But under most conditions all of this takes place without social notice; everyone seems to be looking in another direction.)

A Mangaian boy first hears of masturbation when he is about seven. He discusses it with his friends and eventually, between his eighth and ninth years, he experiments with himself while off feeding the pigs or fishing.

Although parents may try to stop children's masturbation, their efforts and their punishments are both light. A traveling husband or an older boy without a girl may also masturbate, using only his hand, thinking of girls or of orgasm.

CUT

Some Mangaian boys experiment early with sexual intercourse. Such "new boys" must go to sexually promiscuous older women and widows; the younger girls won't cooperate. Most boys do not commence their sexual adventures until they are 13 or 14 and have undergone superincision. (In superincision the skin on the top of the penis is cut down through the cartilaginous tissue for almost the full length of the organ, and the skin folded back and covered with a herbal powder. Nothing is cut off or removed; the skin is rearranged so that the scar tissue will leave the glans of the penis permanently exposed.) Girls learn about sex and develop the appetite for it at 12 or 14, about the time they start to menstruate.

When a boy reaches 12 or 13 his male peers begin to press him to undergo superincision. Since he may be taunted publicly for a lack of courage or be said to have a stinking penis (the ultimate Polynesian insult), it is not long before he or his father or an uncle decides that he must submit. It is usually a kinsman who gives the idea to the boy and finds an expert to perform the operation.

The superincision expert is the most important source of the boy's formal schooling in sexual behavior—what to do with women, and how to do it. He may also arrange for a women to undertake the practical exercises when the boy's cut has healed, to provide more direct sex instruction.

Superincision of one boy or a group of them takes place in a secluded spot, preferably on the seashore or beside a mountain stream. The cut used to be made with a flake of a flintlike local stone. Most experts now prefer a straight razor. An anvil is whittled from a coconut shell to the size and shape of a tablespoon bowl, and used to protect the glans of the penis and to provide a firm working surface. When the extremely painful operation is complete the youth runs into the sea or the stream for relief, exultantly proclaiming "Now I am really a man!"

RITE

More culturally interesting than the superincision, more important to the youth than physiological treatment, is the sexual knowledge and training that the boy gets from the expert. He learns the techniques of coitus and the means of locating a "good girl." He is taught to perform cunnilingus, to kiss and suck breasts, to bring his partner to climax several times before he reaches his own climax, and to achieve mutual orgasm.

Copulation with an experienced partner follows this period of instruction. The goal in this rite of passage, some two weeks after the operation, is to remove the superincision scab by actual sexual intercourse. Obviously, an experienced woman is required. In the past she was a kinswoman; but now she may be any mature and experienced woman, perhaps the village trollop.

There is said to be a special thrill for the woman in removing the scab this way, but there are indications that some women find it objectionable. More significant to the youth, his instructress practices various acts and positions with him, and trains him to hold back until he can achieve orgasm in unison with his partner.

The newly cut penis gives a youth the cleanliness he must have to be accepted and bolsters his confidence that he can thrill his partner, make the sexual act more vigorous, and bring his partner thrice to orgasm. And, if the cut has been properly made and the scab properly removed by an experienced partner, the organ in itself is thought to be beautiful.

Thus endowed, a boy leaves off masturbation. He aggressively seeks out girls, or they seek him out. Soon copulation becomes an every-night affair.

The Mangaian girl, who also has been instructed in the ways of sex by an older woman, demands instant demonstration of sexual virility as the first test of her partner's desire for her and as a reflection of her own desirability. In one virility test, a girl requires her lover to have sexual intercourse with her while in contact with only her genitals.

ABILITY

There is a considerable technique in Mangaian coital foreplay even though the preliminary period may be brief and include little kissing or other demonstrations of intimate affection. It does include manual and lingual caressing of each other's nipples and manipulation of each other's genitalia to heighten erotic interest and arouse full passion before actual copulation.

The essential principal component of Mangaian sexual ability and interest is not the foreplay or between-play, not the nakedness, not the scene, not the props, and certainly not the position. Rather, it is the ability of the male to continue vigorously the in-and-out action of coitus over long periods of time while the female moves her hips "like a washing machine." (Nothing is despised more than a "dead" partner who does not "move.")

Although Mangaians may use a cushion under a woman's bottom in copulation, there is no indication of use of artifice or device in sex. Apparently sexual fetishism is nonexistent; there are no sexual perversions in Mangaia. Nor is there circle intercourse, orgy, or copulation by one male with more than one female at a time. Copulation with animals is not entirely unknown, but the only recorded case was obviously related to youthful experimentation.

Only during menstrual periods and in the experiments of the young do Mangaians resort to posterior positions of intercourse, intercourse with penis held between breasts, thighs, or feet, or in armpits, or other means. There is no rectal/anal intercourse. The male realizes that once he has penetrated his partner, he must keep his action continuous to bring her to climax. He may think of other things to avoid premature ejaculation, or fantasize to hasten his climax. During copulation there is talk, passing of compliments, and a good deal of moaning and sighing. There also may be strong sucking which produces a telltale red welt, evidence of sexual activity that disturbs the older members of the church when they see it in their member agemates. Biting of the partner's body is a common expression of passionate involvement in the sexual act, as is oral-genital intercourse.

ORGASM

My principal Mangaian informant says that a good man will be able to continue his actions for 15 to 30 minutes or more. Above all the man's goal is to continue the coital action—the longer one goes the more the pleasure; the man who goes only a short time does not love (e.g., want to please) his woman.

Young couples may reach climax three to five times in an evening. Mangaians see orgasm as a culminating peak of the sexual act, but not as the only goal. The interplay of copulation is the most significant part of the act and its prolongation is important. The

Mangaian says that the orgasm "feels good" and "we enjoy it." But he has not built up the elaborate concern with it that characterizes American sex folklore—perhaps because it is so universally achieved among Polynesians of both sexes. Mangaians say that a woman must "learn" orgasm and that "the good man" teaches her to have it.

A Mangaian man says he is always careful of "women's talk," so that the female will pass along his "good name." He believes that once he gives his girl the pleasure of climax she cannot keep away from him—unless another man deliberately holds her back by bettering his performance. My several informants generally agreed that the really important thing in sexual intercourse—for the married man or for his unwed fellow—was to give pleasure to his partner; that her pleasure in orgasm was what gave the male partner a special thrill, separate from his own orgasm.

NUMBERS

For many young males the premarital period is a contest to see who can copulate with the most women, and which partner is the best. If a girl tells her lover that her previous partner came to climax four or five times in one evening, the lover will try for six or seven. He may use these heroic measures to prove his admiration for a new girl, or to persuade a girl that she should marry him.

Numbers vary, but Mangaians estimate that the average "nice" girl has three or four successive boyfriends between her 13th and 20th years. But most boys are said to have at least 10 girls, and perhaps more. Some of the most active will have tested—and may have recorded in a notebook—60 or 70. (Typically, a member of this latter group will have a penis tattooed on his thigh, or a vagina tattooed on his penis.) I have never been able to reconcile the apparent male-female differences in outlet contact reflected in these figures.

Mangaian parents encourage their daughter to have sexual experiences with several men. They want her to find the man who is the most congenial—among those whose other social and material assets make them eligible. But they do not really want her to be pregnant until she finds the right man. Mangaians believe that it is continued coitus with the same man that causes pregnancy.

"BULL"

Traditionally, a male goes from female to female—leaving one when he tires or wants variety or hears that she has gone with another man. Mangaians admire the boy who has had many girls: "A strong man, like a bull, going from woman to woman." They even admired the New Zealand government official, whose wife and children were with him on the island, who went almost daily from Mangaian girl to Mangaian girl "like a bull." (Though they also laughed at the fact, reported by one of the girls delicately as "He laughed before he came to the point of the joke." While honored by his attentions, the girls preferred the abilities of their own boy friends to orgasm.) But Mangaians do *not* admire the girl who has many boys, comparing her to a pig. And although "a man must chase a woman," it is considered a great shame for a woman to chase a man, for it shows she is a "silly pig."

DEVIANCE

There is no trace of active homosexuality in either sex on Mangaia, where very nearly everything is known about very nearly everybody. Mangaians do know of homosexuals on Tahiti and on other islands, including nearby Rarotonga—but they trace this deviance to French influence from and on Tahitians.

There are a very few individuals, perhaps two or three out of a population of 2,000, who—at least socially and perhaps biologically—are intersex. These are men who enjoy doing women's work, may have feminine figures, and—to some degree—may wear their clothing in female fashion. They are well regarded socially, liked by women and girls, and frequently are called upon to assist in cooking feasts, sewing pillow cases and cutting out dresses and dress patterns. They sing in female falsetto and frequently are considered to be the best dancers in the island. But they take no sexual interest in other men. There is no sodomy.

Bastardy does not carry the social stigma in Mangaia that it does in the Western world, although the encroachment of Western law and custom now is beginning to place the illegitimate individual at a social and financial disadvantage. Because of complex kinship

and incest prohibitions a couple may have three or more children,
yet still may be refused parental permission to marry and to live
together formally. Parental consent is a principal factor, but only
one of several in the decision on who is to marry whom. A male's
interest in his potential mate's cooking and housekeeping ability now
takes second place to his concern over her appearance, particularly
her face. Sex is not a problem; tested sexual compatibility is a prerequisite, but, again, only one of several and by no means over-
riding. There are many a passionately involved couple who thoroughly enjoy each other sexually, but who do not intend to marry.
Nor is parenthood necessarily a commitment to marriage. Although
there is some social disapproval of couples who produce children
outside of marriage, the practice is common.

Infrequently a young man will come home after his first intercourse and ask his father to get the girl for his wife. This is exceptional. Similarly, a girl seldom marries the man with whom she has
her first sexual intercourse.

NUMBERS

Once he is married, the Mangaian male shifts his coital emphasis from the number of orgasms he can produce in one night to
the number of nights a week he can copulate. The emphasis on
copulation every night continues while the man is in his 20s, but
he starts to miss nights as he moves into his 30s and 40s. His virility
is affirmed publicly if his wife becomes pregnant twice in one year,
or if she becomes thin.

By consensus our Mangaian sexual discussion group analyzed
and estimated male sexual activity as follows:

approximate male age:	average number of orgasms per night:	average number of nights per week:
18	3	7
28	2	5 to 6
38	1	3 to 4
48	1	2 to 3

[Author's note: I believe the younger age estimates to be high, the older somewhat low, based upon logic (they do not allow for nature or accidents) and upon data from elsewhere in Polynesia.]

Mangaians assert that husband and wife come together only to copulate. Indeed, some men say that they need wives only to "take out the water" (semen). Certainly one observes no telling of casual stories or small talk, no public displays of affection, no calling of pet names, no hand-holding. Even money is handled separately by husbands and wives; their trading-store charge accounts are kept separate. But affection does seem to come to married partners with age, if my observations are correct.

DALLIANCE

Mangaians openly acknowledge two areas of widespread extramarital sexual activity. One is the Mangaian girl's strong inclination to return to the first man she enjoyed sexual intercourse with. Another is the general Mangaian—and Polynesian—belief that a normal human being must have a regular sexual outlet. Men who are away traveling are not condemned for taking up with other women, particularly if they select single women. Women deprived of husbandly attention are thought to have less of a problem unless the deprivation stretches out for a year or so, whereupon they are said to "go wild."

On Mangaia there is a general feeling that a local ex-pastor who had been thrown out of his job and the church on another island for adultery with his assistant's wife was harshly treated, because the assistant pastor had been away at the time of the transgression.

Today the Cook Islands Christian Church still reflects the European missionary intolerance of sexual intercourse outside of Christian marriage. The church, however, is losing some of its ethical hold, and local Polynesian pastors who replace the European missionaries are more relaxed. A young man may temporarily be put out of the church-sponsored Boys' Brigade (a kind of Boy Scouts) for fornication when the act is brought to formal public notice, or he now may be let off with a warning. Church leaders do not concern themselves with masturbation, positions used in intercourse, oral-genital contact and such.

There is some incest on Mangaia. It may include intercourse

between father and biological daughter, between first cousins, brother and sister, and—in the most usual case—father and step-daughter. None is heard of between mother and son. Social penalties once were severe and even today social discovery may lead to the suicide of a father who has copulated with his biological daughter.

USAGE

Study of sexual behavior in the Mangaian life cycle, birth through marriage and death, has led me to conclusions on sterility and impotency, homosexuality and female orgasms. Such factors as diet, venereal disease, and other biogeographic facets probably play their part in bringing about these conditions. But effects of continual usage of the organs of generation may play a major part.

The average Mangaian copulates far more frequently and much more vigorously in his youth than does the average European or the average American; some Mangaian males apparently pay a biological penalty for this activity rate. They probably are far more subject to impotency in later years than is the American male.

The Mangaian male is subject to *tira,* a condition that ranges from an initial period of insatiable desire to a final stage in which he cannot achieve an erection; his penis may actually retreat into the body. The Mangaian psychological treatment for this condition focuses upon squatting over a coconut half, with the smoke from burning herbs underneath emerging through the eyes on the top to envelop the penis. But the less frequently mentioned physiological part of the treatment includes absolute sexual abstinence for six months or so. *Tira* is attributed by old men and local medical practitioners to overindulgence in coitus.

Sterility is a concomitant problem. The concept of adolescent sterility may be particularly applicable on Mangaia. In a detailed sociocultural family census that included 474 individuals aged 14 or older it was found that not one of 30 males between 14 and 20 was a father and that only three of 29 women in that age group were mothers. Even more significant from the standpoint of sterility was the finding that 29 per cent of the 179 females over 15 were childless as were 31 per cent of the 291 males in that age bracket. Yet more significantly, 19.6 per cent of the 51 women over 50 were childless, as were 15.6 per cent of the 77 males in that age group.

In so permissive a society as Mangaia's, innate homosexuality presumably could flower unopposed. But it doesn't. And such transvestism as there is—which is very little—meets considerable social approval of the cleverness and hard-working nature of the individuals involved. Their predilections are not condemned and they play an active role in the social life of the island.

The data suggest that the proportion of homosexuals need not be a fixed characteristic of human societies and that explicit acceptance of hermaphrodism and/or transvestism may eliminate some of those social pressures that produce homosexuality in individuals who otherwise would not have moved in that direction.

Mangaian data indicate clearly (a) that the female sexual orgasm is learned; (b) that all Mangaian women do learn it; and (c) that bringing a partner to orgasm and experiencing simultaneous culmination with her are important parts of the Mangaian male's sexual pleasure. The term for the orgasm is the same as that for the achievement of perfection, pleasure and comfort.

Finally, a more general observation: among Mangaians, no man—or woman—is so maimed, so ugly, so poor, or so aberrant that he—or she—cannot find a sexual partner. This may be the most important fact of all.

Sex and Repression in Inis Beag
by John C. Messenger

Both lack of sexual knowledge and misconceptions about sex among adults combine to brand Inis Beag as one of the most sexually naive of the world's societies. Sex never is discussed in the home when children are about; only three mothers admitted giving advice, briefly and incompletely, to their daughters. We were told that boys are better advised than girls, but that the former learn about sex informally from older boys and men from observing animals. Most respondents who were questioned about sexual instructions given to youths expressed the belief that "after marriage nature takes its course," thus negating the need for anxiety-creating and embarrassing personal confrontation of parents and offspring. We were unable to discover any cases of childlessness based on sexual ignorance of spouses, as reported from other regions of peasant Ireland. Also, we were unable to discover knowledge of the sexual categories utilized by researchers in sex: insertion of tongue while kissing, male mouth on female breast, female hand on penis, cunnilingus, fellatio, femoral coitus, anal coitus, extramarital coitus, manifest homosexuality, sexual contact with animals, fetishism, and sado-masochistic behavior. Some of these activities may be practiced by particular individuals and couples; however, without a doubt they are deviant forms in Inis Beag, about which information is difficult to come by.

Menstruation and menopause arouse profound misgivings among women of the island, because few of them comprehend their physiological significance. My wife was called on to explain these processes more than any other phenomena related to sex. When they reach puberty, most girls are unprepared for the first menstrual flow and find the experience a traumatic one—especially when their mothers are unable to provide a satisfactory explanation for it. And it is commonly believed that the menopause can induce "madness"; in order to ward off this condition, some women have retired from life in their mid-forties and, in a few cases, have confined themselves to bed until death, years later. Others have so retired as a result of depressive and masochistic states. Yet the harbingers of "insanity" are simply the physical symptoms announcing the onset of menopause. In Inis Beag, these include severe headaches, hot flashes, faintness in crowds and enclosed places, and severe anxiety. Mental illness is also held to be inherited or caused by inbreeding (or by the Devil, by God punishing a sinner, or by malignant pagan beings) and stigmatizes the family of the afflicted. One old man came close to revealing what is probably the major cause of neuroses and psychoses in Ireland, when he explained the incarceration of an Inis Beag curate in a mental institution for clerics as caused by his constant association with a pretty housekeeper, who "drove him mad from frustration." This elder advocated that only plain-appearing older women (who would not "gab" to "our man") be chosen for the task. Earlier, according to island opinion, the same priest had caused to be committed to the "madhouse" a local man who publicly challenged certain of his actions. The unfortunate man was released six months later, as per law, since he was not mentally ill.

Sexual misconceptions are myriad in Inis Beag. The islanders share with most Western peoples the belief that men by nature are far more libidinous than women. The latter have been taught by some curates and in the home that sexual relations with their husbands are a "duty" which must be "endured," for to refuse coitus is a mortal sin. A frequently encountered assertion affixes the guilt for male sexual strivings on the enormous intake of potatoes of the Inis Beag male. (In Nigeria, among the people whom my wife and I studied, women are thought to be more sexually disposed than men and are the repositories of sexual knowledge; it is they who initiate coitus and so pose a threat to their spouses. Nigerian men place the blame on clitoridectomy performed just prior to marriage.) Asked to compare the sexual proclivities of Inis Beag men and women, one mother of nine said, "Men can wait a long time before wanting 'it,'

but we can wait a lot longer." There is much evidence to indicate
that the female orgasm is unknown—or at least doubted, or considered a deviant response. One middle-aged bachelor, who considers
himself wise in the ways of the outside world and has a reputation
for making love to willing tourists, described one girl's violent bodily
reactions to his fondling and asked for an explanation; when told
the "facts of life" of what obviously was an orgasm, he admitted not
realizing that women also could achieve a climax, although he was
aware that some of them apparently enjoyed kissing and being handled.

Inis Beag men feel that sexual intercourse is debilitating, a
common belief in primitive and folk societies. They will desist from
sex the night before they are to perform a job which will require
the expenditure of great energy. Women are not approached sexually during menstruation or for months after childbirth, since they
are considered "dangerous" to the male at these times. Returned
"Yanks" have been denounced from the pulpit for describing American sexual practices to island youths, and such "pornographic" magazines as *Time* and *Life,* mailed by kin from abroad, have aroused
curates to spirited sermon and instruction.

The separation of the sexes, started within the family, is aug-
mented by separation in almost all segments of adolescent and adult
activity. Boys and girls are separated to some extent in classrooms,
and completely in recess play and movement to and from school.
During church services, there is a further separation of adult men
and women, as well as boys and girls, and each of the four groups
leaves the chapel in its turn. The pubs are frequented only by men
or by women tourists and female teachers who have spent several
years on the mainland while training and thus are "set apart" (and,
of course, by inquisitive female ethnographers). Women occasionally
visit the shops to procure groceries, but it is more common for them
to send their children to do so, since supplies and drinks are proffered across the same counter, and men are usually to be found on
the premises. Even on the strand during summer months, male
tourists tend to bathe at one end and women at the other. Some
swimmers "daringly" change into bathing suits there, under towels
and dresses—a custom practiced elsewhere in Ireland which has
overtones of sexual catharsis.

It is often asserted that the major "escape valve" of sexual
frustration among single persons in Ireland is masturbation; frustra-

tion-aggression theorists, however, would stress the ubiquity of drinking, alcoholism, disputes, and pugnacity as alternative outlets. Pugnacity can also be linked to the widespread problem of male identity. Our study revealed that male masturbation in Inis Beag seems to be common, premarital coitus unknown, and marital copulation limited as to foreplay and the manner of consummation. My wife and I never witnessed courting—"walking out"—in the island. Elders proudly insist that it does not occur, but male youths admit to it in rumor. The claims of young men focus on "petting" with tourists and a few local girls, whom the "bolder" of them kiss and fondle outside of their clothing. Island girls, it is held by their "lovers," do not confess these sins because they fail to experience pleasure from the contact. The male perpetrators also shun the confessional because of their fear of the priest.

We were unable to determine the frequency of marital coitus. A considerable amount of evidence indicates that privacy in the act is stressed and that foreplay is limited to kissing and rough fondling of the lower body, especially the buttocks. Sexual activity invariably is initiated by the husband. Only the male superior position is employed; intercourse takes place with underclothes not removed; and orgasm, for the man, is achieved quickly, almost immediately after which he falls asleep. (I must stress the provisional nature of these data, for they are based on a limited sample of respondents and relate to that area of sexual behavior least freely discussed.)

Many kinds of behavior disassociated from sex in other societies, such as nudity and physiological evacuation, are considered sexual in Inis Beag. Nudity is abhorred by the islanders, and the consequences of this attitude are numerous and significant for health and survival. Only infants have their entire bodies sponged once a week, on Saturday night; children, adolescents, and adults, on the same night, wash only their faces, necks, lower arms, hands, lower legs, and feet. Several times my wife and I created intense embarrassment by entering a room in which a man had just finished his weekly ablutions and was barefooted; once when this occurred, the man hurriedly pulled on his stockings and said with obvious relief, "Sure, it's good to get your clothes on again." Clothing always is changed in private, sometimes within the secrecy of the bedcovers, and it is usual for the islanders to sleep in their underclothes.

Despite the fact that Inis Beag men spend much of their time at sea in their canoes, as far as we could determine none of them can swim. Four rationales are given for this deficiency: the men are confident that nothing will happen to them, because they are excellent seamen and weather forecasters; a man who cannot swim will be more careful; it is best to drown immediately when a canoe capsizes far out in the ocean rather than swim futilely for minutes or even hours, thus prolonging the agony; and, finally, "When death is on a man, he can't be saved." The truth of the matter is that they have never dared to bare their bodies in order to learn the skill. Some women claim to have "bathed" at the back of the island during the heat of summer, but this means wading in small pools with skirts held knee-high, in complete privacy. Even the nudity of household pets can arouse anxiety, particularly when they are sexually aroused during time of heat. In some homes, dogs are whipped for licking their genitals and soon learn to indulge in this practice outdoors. My wife, who can perform Irish step-dances and sing many of the popular folk songs, was once requested to sing a seldom-heard American Western ballad; she chose "The Lavendar Cowboy," who "had only two hairs on his chest." The audience response was perfunctory and, needless to say, she never again was "called out" to sing that particular song.

The drowning of seamen, who might have saved themselves had they been able to swim, is not the only result of the sexual symbolism of nudity; men who were unwilling to face the nurse when ill, because it might have meant baring their bodies to her, were beyond help when finally treated. While my wife and I were on the island, a nurse was assaulted by the mother of a young man for diagnosing his illness and bathing his chest in the mother's absence. (In this case, Oedipal and sexual attitudes probably were at work in tandem.)

It must be pointed out that nudity is also shunned for "health" reasons, for another obtrusive Inis Beag character trait is hypochondria. In some cases, however, it is hard to determine whether concern with modesty or health is dominant in a particular behavioral response. Fear of colds and influenza is foremost among health concerns; rheumatism and related muscular joint ailments, migraine headaches and other psychosomatic disorders, tooth decay, indigestion ("nervous stomach"), and hypermetropia are other widespread pathologies which cause worry among the folk—not to mention those of supernatural origin.

Secrecy surrounds the acts of urination and defecation. The evacuation of infants before siblings and strangers is discouraged, and animals that discharge in the house are driven out. Chickens that habitually "dirty" their nests while setting are soon killed and eaten. Although some women drink spirits privately, they seldom do so at parties. In part this is because of the embarrassment involved in visiting the outside toilet with men in the "street" looking on. One of the most carefully guarded secrets of Inis Beag, unreported in the many works describing island culture, is the use of human manure mixed with sand as a fertilizer. We were on the island eight months before we discovered that compost is not "street drippings" and "scraw," but decomposed feces. With "turf" becoming more difficult to procure from the mainland, some islanders have taken to importing coal and processed peat and burning cattle dung. The dung is prepared for use in difficult-to-reach plots at the back of the island when tourists are few in number; it is burned covertly because of the overtones of sex and poverty. Another custom that my wife and I learned of late in our research, due to the secrecy surrounding it, concerns the thickening of wool; men are required to urinate in a container and tread the wool therein with their bare feet.

Other major manifestations of sexual repression in Inis Beag are the lack of a "dirty joke" tradition (at least as the term is understood by ethnologists and folklorists) and the style of dancing, which allows little bodily contact among participants. I have heard men use various verbal devices—innuendoes, puns, and asides—that they believed bore sexual connotations; relatively speaking, they were pallid. In the song that I composed, one line of a verse refers to an island bachelor arising late in the day after "dreaming perhaps of a beautiful mate"; this is regarded as a highly suggestive phrase, and I have seen it redden cheeks and lower glances in a pub. Both step-and set-dancing are practiced in Inis Beag, although the former type is dying out. This rigid-body dancing, from which sex is removed by shifting attention below the hips, appears to have originated in Ireland during the early sixteenth century. The set patterns keep partners separated most of the time; but even so, some girls refuse to dance, because it involves touching a boy. Inis Beag men, while watching a woman step-dance, stare fixedly at her feet, and they take pains to appear indifferent when crowding at a party necessitates holding women on their laps and rubbing against them when moving from room to room. But they are extremely sensitive, nevertheless, to the entire body of the dancer and to these casual contacts, as are the women. Their covert emotional reactions (which become overt as much drink is taken) are a form of catharsis.

"Normal" and "Deviant" Sexual Behavior

by *Judd Marmor*

It is difficult to approach the topic of human sexuality with the same kind of dispassionate scientific objectivity that can be applied to functions such as speech, digestion, or locomotion. Sexual behavior is so intimately entwined with moral issues, religious and cultural value systems, and even aesthetic reactions, that those who attempt to deal with it too open-mindedly are likely to be charged by their contemporaries with being immoral or amoral, if not illegal. Sigmund Freud's efforts at the turn of the 19th century to bring the "problems of the bedroom" under scientific scrutiny caused both colleagues and friends to turn away from him in embarrassment, and even sixty years later, in the relatively enlightened second half of the 20th century, the meticulous physiological studies of Masters and Johnson stimulated cries of outrage in many quarters and titters of embarrassment in others.

Nevertheless, no discussion of human sexual behavior can be truly objective if one does not attempt to stand outside of the narrow framework of one's own cultural bias to see how the raw data of human sexual biology are shaped by and shape the infinitely varied mosaics of human experience in different places and at different times.

Historical Considerations

Even a cursory look at the recorded history of human sexuality makes it abundantly clear that patterns of sexual behavior and mor-

Reprinted by permission of the author and the American Medical Association from *The Journal of the American Medical Association*, Vol. 217 (July 12, 1971), pp. 165–170.

ality have taken many diverse forms over the centuries. Far from being "natural" and inevitable, our contemporary sexual codes and mores, seen in historical perspective, would appear no less grotesque to people of other eras than theirs appear to us. Our attitudes concerning nudity, virginity, fidelity, love, marriage, and "proper" sexual behavior are meaningful only within the context of our own cultural and religious mores. Thus, in the first millennium of the Christian era, in many parts of what is now Europe, public nudity was no cause for shame (as is still true in some aboriginal settings), virginity was not prized, marriage was usually a temporary arrangement, and extramarital relations were taken for granted. Frank and open sexuality was the rule, and incest was frequent. Women were open aggressors in inviting sexual intercourse. Bastardy was a mark of distinction because it often implied that some important person had slept with one's mother. In early feudal times new brides were usually deflowered by the feudal lord (jus primae noctis). In other early societies all the wedding guests would copulate with the bride. Far from being considered a source of concern to the husband, these practices were considered a way of strengthening the marriage in that the pain of the initial coitus would not be associated with the husband.

It was not until the Medieval Church was able to strengthen and extend its control over the peoples of Europe that guilt about sexuality began to be a cardinal feature of Western life. Even the early Hebraic laws against adultery had nothing to do with fidelity but were primarily concerned with protecting the property rights of another man (the wife being considered property). Married men were free to maintain concubines or, if they preferred, multiple wives; also, there was no ban in the Old Testament on premarital sex. The Medieval Church, however, exalted celibacy and virginity. In its efforts to make license in sexual intercourse as difficult as possible, it sanctioned it only for procreative purposes and ordained laws against abortion—laws that had not existed among the Greeks, Romans, or Jews. At one time it went so far as to make sexual intercourse between married couples illegal on Sundays, Wednesdays, and Fridays, as well as for forty days before Easter and forty days before Christmas, and also from the time of conception to forty days after parturition. (By contrast, Mohammedan law considered it grounds for divorce if intercourse did not take place at least once a week.)

Moreover, when the sexual taboos of the Medieval Church began to be widely enforced by cruel sanctions, a veritable epidemic of sexual pathology ensued—sodomy, flagellation, hysterical "possession" by witches and devils, incubi, succubi, phantom pregnancies, stigmata, and the like. In contrast, it is worth noting that in societies in which access to sexuality was open and guilt-free—the early Greeks, Europe prior to the Middle Ages and most "primitive" societies—the so-called sexual perversions tended not to be present. The homosexuality of the early Greeks, incidentally, was not an exclusive homosexuality, but part of a pattern of bisexuality in which homosexual feelings were considered to be as natural as heterosexual ones.

The ideals of romantic love and marriage for love which are taken for granted today are a relatively late development in Western history and did not make their appearance until the 12th century AD.[1] Clearly, there is nothing about our current sexual attitudes and practices that can be assumed to be either sacrosanct or immutable. They have been subject to much change and evolution in the past, and they will undoubtedly be different in the future.

Biological and Cultural Considerations

Before we can proceed, it is necessary to clarify certain fundamental questions about the nature of human sexuality that have a bearing on the problem of sexual deviation. What is the biological core of human sexuality? Is it exclusively heterosexual, or does it have a bisexual composition? Is man "naturally" polygamous? Is woman naturally monoandrous? Are most "perversions" "unnatural?" What form does natural sexuality take in children?

Zoological and cross-cultural studies in recent years clearly demonstrate that the issue of sexual behavior goes far beyond its reproductive functions. Caspari's definition of the sexual process as "the exchange of nuclear material between cells of mating types or sexes" may have validity for relatively primitive forms of life, but as we ascend the phylogenetic scale this definition becomes manifestly inadequate. Patterns of sexual behavior evolve with the species, and at higher mammalian levels there is an increasing emphasis on various sex-related activities rather than on purely reproductive ones.

Sex in human beings is usually spoken of as being an "instinct." By this we mean that it is a fundamental behavioral pattern dependent on internal biological factors but capable of being triggered by external cues. Either may create a state of disequilibrium experienced as urgency or tension; this tension then leads to behavior that has the effect of restoring the previous state of balance, with an accompanying sense of subjective gratification. It is important to remember, however, that such a reaction takes quite a different form in human beings than it does in lower animals, even though the term instinct is used equally for both. The lower in the scale of evolution an animal is, the more totally developed and less modifiable are such instinctual patterns; but as one moves up the evolutionary scale inherited instinctual patterns tend to become less preformed and more subject to modification by learning. This development reaches its highest point in man, whose instinctual patterns at birth tend to be relatively unfocused biological drives, subject to enormous modifiability by learning and experience. This is a major factor in the extraordinary range of human adaptability.

This essentially unfocussed quality of man's sexual drive in infancy is what Hampson and Hampson [2] have referred to as man's inherent "psychosexual neutrality" at birth—a neutrality that "permits the development and perpetuation of diverse patterns of psychosexual orientation and functioning in accordance with the life experiences each individual may encounter and transact." This concept of psychosexual neutrality does not, as some have mistakenly inferred, mean a "driveless" state, but rather an inborn biological drive with no specific inborn object, but with the potential for adapting its gratifactory needs to whatever objects the environment makes available to it. The term "psychosexual multipotentiality" probably expresses this more adequately than psychosexual neutrality.

In human sexual behavior, situational and learning factors are of major importance in arousal and response. In the absence of heterosexual objects, human beings (as well as many lower animals) may ultimately seek gratification in homosexual objects, or if no human object is available, in relations with animals of other species, or even by contact with inanimate objects. Even the physiological route of gratification, whether through the genitals or some other erogenous zone, or via patterns of behavior which seem to have no inherent elements of erogenicity in them at all, are subject to conditioning by specific experiences or associations. Other factors in sexual responsiveness include age, health, fatigue, nutritional state, and recency of drive fulfillment.

Freud believed that the bisexual anlage which can be observed in the human embryo is subsequently reflected in a universal bisexual tendency at a psychological level. The evidences of such bisexuality, in this view, are seen in "latent homosexual" manifestations such as affectionate feelings for members of one's own sex and in patterns of behavior or interest that are usually (in our culture) considered to be characteristic of the opposite sex. Examples of these would be artistic or culinary interests or "passive" attitudes in males, or athletic or scientific interests or "aggressive" attitudes in females.

This hypothesis was first challenged in the psychoanalytic literature by Rado [3] who pointed out that "in the final shaping of the normal individual the double embryological origin of the genital system does not result in any physiological duality of reproductive functioning." More than this, we now know that with the exception of the relatively uncommon individuals with sexual chromosome abnormalities, in almost all human beings, biological sex is clearly differentiated at the moment of conception by the XX and XY chromosomal patterns. Nevertheless, the theory of psychic bisexuality is sometimes still defended on the basis that both "male" and "female" sex hormones—androgens and estrogens—can be found in the blood of both sexes. However, although the biological activity of these hormones is essential for the growth and maturation of the primary genital apparatus in both sexes and for the development of secondary sexual characteristics, there is no evidence in humans that these hormones affect the direction of human sexuality or that they determine psychological "masculinity" or "femininity." [4] As Money has put it,

> There is no primary genetic or other innate mechanism to preordain the masculinity or femininity of psychosexual differentiation. . . . The analogy is with language. Genetics and innate determinants ordain only that language can develop . . . but not whether the language will be Nahuatl, Arabic, English, or any other. [5]

Psychological and behavioral patterns of masculinity or femininity constitute what is meant by "gender role," and are not necessarily synonymous with an individual's biological sex. As the Hampsons have pointed out:

> The psychologic phenomenon which we have termed gender role, or psychosexual orientation, evolves gradually in the course of growing up and cannot be assigned or discarded at will. The components of gender role are neither static nor universal. They change

with the times and are an integral part of each culture and subculture. Thus one may expect important differences in what is to
be considered typical and appropriate masculine or feminine gender
roles as displayed by a native of Thailand and a native of Mary-
land. . . .[2]

Opler, in the same vein, comments that

> a Navajo Indian may be a he-man, or gambler, and a philanderer
> while dressing in bright blouses adorned with jeweled belts, neck-
> laces, and bracelets. French courtiers in the retinues of effete mon-
> archs were equally philanderers, though rouged, powdered, and
> bedecked with fine lace. The Andaman Islanders like to have the
> man sit on his wife's lap in fond greetings, and friends and rela-
> tives, of the same or opposite sex, greet one another in the same
> manner after absences, crying in the affected manner of the mid-
> Victorian woman. . . . Obviously, the style of social and sexual
> behavior is something of an amalgam and is culturally influenced.[6]

> The fact is that the patterning of human sexual behavior begins
> at birth. From the moment a child is identified as either boy or girl,
> it begins to be shaped by multitudinous cues which communicate
> certain gender role expectations to it over the succeeding years. This
> results in a "core gender identity" of either maleness or femaleness,
> which becomes so profoundly fixed by the age of three, that efforts
> to reverse this identity after that time are almost always doomed to
> failure.[2]

Within every society, the process of acculturation that takes
place during these critical years begins to condition the child's behavior so as to enable it to conform to the mores of its environment
—how and what it should eat, where and when it may urinate and
defecate, what and whom it may play with, how it should think and
express itself, and how and toward whom it may express its sexual
needs. The so-called "polymorphous-perverse" sexual behavior of
young children described by Freud in his *Three Contributions to the
Theory of Sex* constitutes the normal behavior of children before
the acculturation processes of our society have funneled their sexual
patterns into "proper channels." From it we can infer what form the
"natural sexuality" of man would probably take if no cultural taboos
or restrictions at all existed in this sphere. Freud obviously was not
unaware of this when he wrote that "it is absolutely impossible not

to recognize in the uniform predisposition to all perversions . . . a universal and primitive human tendency." [7]

Developmental Factors

In his libido theory, Freud hypothesized that the sexual instinct followed a phylogenetically predestined evolutionary pathway. In the first year of life, the primary erotogenic focus was the oral zone, in the second and third years, the anal zone, and in the fourth and fifth years, the phallic zone. From the sixth year to puberty, the sexual drive then underwent an involutional process—the "latency period"—during which the "sexual energy" was deflected from sexual goals and "sublimated." With puberty, the sexual drive was again unleashed and now directed toward the ultimate adult goal of full genital gratification.

With the shift in psychoanalytic theory from an instinct-psychology to an ego-psychology, the unfolding of human sexuality may be viewed in a somewhat different light. The infant's sexual needs are seen as rather primitive and undifferentiated at birth. Such as they are, they find expression in the exercise of the child's relatively un-developed ego functions—in sucking, in body movements, and in experiencing cutaneous and kinesthetic sensations. In the course of its adaptive development the child discovers sucking its thumb and handling its genitals as special sources of somatic pleasure, and if not discouraged, will utilize these as accessory sources of gratification. Indeed, infantile masturbation may be regarded as one of the earliest experiences of autonomy in normal development. When the child discovers erogenous zones within himself that he can stimulate to give himself pleasure, he has achieved a significant step in ego mastery. Such masturbation is analogous to the behavioral patterns described by Olds [8] in his experimental rats when they discovered their ability to stimulate a "pleasure area" in their hypothalamus.

This author has never been convinced that the shift to "anal erogenicity" during the second year is either as clear-cut or as in-evitable as Freud believed. Where it does seem to occur, it may well be the consequence of the emphasis on bowel-training which takes place at this time in our culture, and which often becomes the locus for an emotionally laden transaction between child and mother. Moreover, the struggle at this point is not so much over the issue of the child's wish for anal-zone pleasure per se, as it is over the child's wish to move its bowels whenever and wherever it wishes. Thus the issue is not anality, but the broader one of the pleasure-principle versus the reality-principle—the basic battleground of every acculturation process.

It is probably not accidental also that phallic-zone interest develops when it does. The third year of life corresponds with the shift in cultural emphasis from bowel sphincter training to the development of urinary control. Simultaneously, the developing and intrusive ego of the child at this age begins to perceive, and concern itself with, the shame-ridden issues of the anatomical differences between the sexes, where babies come from, and how much fun it is to play with the forbidden genitals. This is the period of the "polymorphous perverse."

That a latency period should occur in our culture after this kind of behavior should not come as a surprise. Freud believed this period to be "organically determined," but the absence of such a reaction of latency in cultures where there are no prohibitions to the free expression of sexuality in children, clearly indicates that this is not so. Sexual latency, when it occurs, is obviously the result of repression in a culture that strongly indoctrinates the child with the conviction that its "polymorphous and perverse" sexual interests are dirty, shameful, and sinful. Under this pressure, with threats of physical punishment and loss of love (both "castration" threats), many children in our society repress their sexuality until the imperative thrust of puberty brings it to the fore again. It is worth noting, however, that there has been evidence in recent years that increasing numbers of children in their prepubertal years continue to be sexually active and interested. This is a reflection of the more accepting attitudes toward sexuality that have been emerging in our culture in recent decades.

The subsequent vicissitudes of adult sexuality also take many forms. Monogamy as a compulsory pattern of mateship, for example, occurs in only a minority of human societies—only 16% of 185 societies studied by Ford and Beach.[9] (Even in that 16%, less than one third wholly disapproved of both premarital and extramarital liaisons.) Strict monogamy, however, is not necessarily a mark of advanced civilization—some extremely primitive societies are strongly monogamous.

Patterns of monogamy and polygamy (or polyandry) are usually dependent on economic factors. Even in societies where multiple mateships are permitted, only the well-to-do usually are able to exercise this option, and single mateships, although not required, are the rule.

Rules governing premarital and extramarital relations also vary widely in different cultures. There are numerous societies in which extramarital sex is permitted and expected, and in which there is no censure of adultery. Indeed, among the polyandrous Toda of India, there is no word in their language for adultery, and moral opprobrium is attached to the man who begrudges his wife to another! It is interesting to note also that in societies that have no double standard in sexual matters and in which liaisons are freely permitted, women avail themselves of their opportunities as eagerly as men, a fact that casts serious doubts on the popular assumption that females are, by nature, less sexually assertive than males.

Definition of Sexual Deviation

How then can one define sexual deviations? It is clear from our preceding discussion that an adequate definition cannot be based on any assumption of the biological "naturalness" of any particular pattern of sexual behavior in man. What is evaluated as psychologically healthy in one era or culture may not be so in another. The normal sexual behavior of an adolescent girl among the Marquesans or Trobrianders would be considered nymphomanic or delinquent in our society. Homosexual behavior is regarded as deviant in many cultures, including our own, but was not so adjudged in ancient Greece and pre-Meiji Japan, or among the Tanalans of Madagascar, the Siwanis of Africa, the Aranda of Australia, the Keraki of New Guinea, and many others.

It is sometimes argued that this kind of culture-oriented relativistic concept of normalcy is fallacious because it fails to recognize that there is an "optimal" conception of health that transcends all cultural norms. The difficulty with this argument is that the concept of optimal itself is culture-bound. Even granting that within any culture a concept such as personality homeostasis or self-realization has validity, the content of such concepts still vary in different times and places. A definition of psychological health in psychoanalytic terms implies the ability of the "ego" to effectively handle and integrate its relationships with the "id," the "superego," and the outer world. Such a definition could undoubtedly be used cross-culturally. But again, its content will vary in different cultural contexts since the nature of the "normal" superego and of the outer world are culture-dependent.

COMMENT

It seems to this author, therefore, that there is no way in which the concepts of normal and deviant sexual behavior can be divorced from the value systems of our society; and since such value systems are always in the process of evolution and change, we must be prepared to face the possibility that some patterns currently considered deviant may not always be so regarded. The fact that we now refer to sexual "deviations" rather than to "perversions" already represents an evolutionary change within our culture toward a more objective and scientific approach to these problems, in contrast to the highly moralistic and pejorative approach of the previous generation. Perhaps some day we shall talk simply of "variations" in sexual object choice.

Such a relativistic approach to normalcy should not, however, be mistaken for a nihilistic one. We are all products of our culture, and within the context of our current Western cultural value system there are indeed certain patterns that can be regarded as psychologically optimal and healthy.

Although there is a wide spectrum of variations in human sexual motivation and behavior—most human beings, in the privacy of their bedrooms, in one way or another, and at one time or another, violate the rigid conventional standards of "proper" sexual behavior —there are nevertheless certain more widely deviant patterns of sexual behavior that in all likelihood would be considered abnormal in every society. For example, practices that involve serious injury to one of the participants in the sexual relationship could hardly be considered adaptive in any society since they would ultimately jeopardize its survival.

One way of defining a large category of sexual practices that is considered deviant in our culture is that they involve the habitual and preferential use of nongenital outlets for sexual release. The emphasis in this definition is on the terms "habitual" and "preferential," since extragenital gratification may be a part of normal sexual foreplay, or of variations in sexual experiences between perfectly normal adults. When, however, such variant activity becomes an habitual end in itself, it almost always, in the context of our culture, means some disturbance in personality functioning.

It should be noted that the above definition is a psychiatric not a legal one. Statutes in most of the United States regard any use of nongenital outlets for sexual release as illegal. Kinsey and his co-workers, after their extensive surveys of sexual practices of males and females, concluded that there are probably very few adults who have not technically violated such statutes at one time or another.

Other major forms of sexual behavior that are defined as deviant in our society involve activity that is homosexual, or sexual activity with immature partners of either sex (pedophilia), animals (bestiality), dead people (necrophilia), or inanimate objects (fetishism).

Although sexual deviations are commonly separated in terms of their outstanding clinical manifestations, in actuality they are far from discrete phenomena. There is frequent overlapping among them and it is not uncommon for an individual to present simultaneous evidence of more than one of these manifestations. Thus, a fetishist may also be an exhibitionist and a voyeur; a transvestite may also be involved in sadomasochistic practices; incest and pedophilia may be associated in the same person, and so forth.

The reason for this overlapping rests in the underlying psychodynamics that are common to all sexual deviations in our society. The deviant is in almost all instances an individual who has difficulty in achieving normal or satisfactory sexual relations with a mature partner of the opposite sex. Thus his deviant practices represent alternative ways of attempting to achieve sexual gratification; they are displacement phenomena and in many instances the displacement mechanism may operate in more than one direction. Some deviants exhibit polymorphous-perverse patterns of sexual behavior akin to that of very young children who have not yet been adequately acculturated. In this sense they may be considered to have been "fixated" at an early stage of psychosexual development, or to have "regressed" to this stage.

The choice of deviant pattern, like the choice of symptom in neurosis, is dependent on complex determinants which have to be ferreted out by a painstaking history and psychodynamic evaluation in each individual case. Disturbances in core family relationships, impairment in gender identity development, poor ego development, and specific conditioning experiences are all involved.

Apart from such clearly definable deviant patterns, human sexual relationships are often complicated by unconscious motivations of fear, hate, or guilt, which leave their stamps on the quality of the sexual transactions between partners. In our culture, a key distinguishing factor between what is regarded as healthy or unhealthy sexual behavior is whether such behavior is motivated by feelings of love or whether it becomes a vehicle for the discharge of anxiety, hostility, or guilt. Healthy sexuality seeks erotic pleasure in the context of tenderness and affection; pathologic sexuality is motivated by needs for reassurance or relief from nonsexual sources of tension. Healthy sexuality seeks both to give and receive pleasure; neurotic forms are unbalanced toward excessive giving or taking. Healthy sexuality is discriminating as to partner; neurotic patterns often tend to be nondiscriminating. The periodicity of healthy sexuality is determined primarily by recurrent erotic tensions in the context of affection. Neurotic sexual drives, on the other hand, are triggered less by erotic needs than by nonerotic tensions and are therefore more apt to be compulsive in their patterns of occurrence.

A sharp line of distinction, however, cannot always be drawn between healthy and neurotic sexuality. Since patterns of sexual behavior always reflect personality patterns and problems, and since no one in our complex society is totally exempt from individual idiosyncrasies, tensions, and anxieties, these will be manifested in sexual patterns no less than in other areas of interpersonal transactions. No human being is perfect, and nowhere is the humanity of man more transparent than in the varied patterns of his sexual relationships.

References

1. Taylor GR: *Sex in History*. New York, Vanguard Press, 1954.
2. Hampson, JL, Hampson Joan G: The ontogenesis of sexual behavior in man, in Young WC (ed): *Sex and Internal Secretions*. Baltimore, Williams & Wilkins, 1961, vol 2, ed 3.
3. Rado S: *Psychoanalysis of Behavior*. New York, Grune & Stratton, 1956, vol 1.
4. Perloff WH: Hormones and homosexuality, in Marmor J (ed): *Sexual Inversion: The Multiple Roots of Homosexuality*. New York, Basic Books, 1965, pp 44–69.
5. Money J: Developmental differentiation of femininity and masculinity compared, in Farber SM, Wilson RHL (eds): *Man and Civilization*. New York, McGraw Hill Book Co, 1963, pp 56–57.
6. Opler MK: Anthropological and cross-cultural aspects of homosexuality, in Marmor J (ed): *Sexual Inversion: The Multiple Roots of Homosexuality*. New York, Basic Books, 1965, pp 108–123.

7. Freud S: *Three Essays on the Theory of Sexuality.* J Strachey (trans, 1905), New York, Basic Books, 1962.
8. Olds J: Self stimulation of the brain. *Science* 127:315–324, 1958.
9. Ford CS, Beach FA: *Patterns of Sexual Behavior.* New York, Harper & Bros, 1952.

II
Pornography

It is practically impossible to write about any aspect of sex—pornography included—without displaying one's own prejudices in some way. Protestations of "objectivity" and "detachment" are always a lie. We all feel a certain way about, and are morally and ideologically involved in, our subject matter, although in different ways and to varying degrees.

Even so, perhaps a few cool words on pornography will help to put things in perspective.

What is pornography? And what specific works are pornographic?

As we see it, there are three *different* definitions that could be used to determine what is pornography:

(1) The *"functional"* definition: *works consumed primarily for the purpose of sexual excitation.* This definition looks at material from the point of view of the *consumers* of pornography, and primarily in terms of the responses—or presumed responses—it touches off in them.

(2) The *"labeling"* definition: *works which much of the public thinks of as obscene*—that is, material which, it is believed, excites "lustful" thoughts, and which is therefore sexually vulgar, offensive, lewd, shameful, and disgusting. This definition looks at pornography from the point of view of the (mainly disapproving) *public*. But it may also be from the *consumer's* point of view as well: many people read or look at pornography *because* they find it obscene and disgusting!

(3) The *"genre"* definition: *works which are created primarily for the purpose of arousing the lust of an audience, and which con-*

59

form to a narrow and distinct formula. The genre definition takes
the point of view of the *creators* and *producers* of pornographic
works. They assemble and manufacture and sell commercialized sex;
they want to turn on the largest number of people possible, and to
make a profit doing it.

These definitions lead us to two inescapable conclusions:

(1) *Something may be pornographic in one sense, but not in
another;*

(2) *Something may be pornographic to some people, but not
to others.* Any meaningful look at pornography must necessarily be
completely *relativistic.*

Some works can arouse sexual excitation in one audience, but
not in another. Almost anything may be sexually exciting—to some
people. And many people can be completely bored by, sexually uninterested in, and unresponsive to material that others become wildly
excited by. The nude centerfolds in *Playboy* are standard masturbatory fare for millions of adolescent boys. The reason why they
purchase *Playboy* and look at its pictures is because the material
turns them on sexually. *In this sense, and to these boys, Playboy* is
pornography. More jaded adults typically do not react in this fashion
—and so, to them, *Playboy isn't* pornographic. To still other Americans, *Playboy* is quaint, old-fashioned, prudish, and very far from
being pornographic—that is, sexually exciting. To still others, it is
a sexual turn-off, an example of male chauvinism in action. Is
Playboy pornographic? Yes—to some people. No—to others. In the
pre-*Playboy* era, when photographs of naked women were more
difficult for adolescents to lay their hands on, many young men found
photographs of nude native women in *National Geographic* to be
extremely arousing, and used them to masturbate with. So, in this
sense, the photographs appearing in *Playboy* and *National Geographic* both *are* and *are not* pornographic. They are, in the sense
that some people react to them in a largely sexual fashion. They are
not, in that others do not do so.

Likewise, the judgment of what is obscene varies from person
to person, from group to group. It is literally impossible to lay down
a universally valid definition of obscenity. Nothing is inherently
obscene—that is, everywhere and at all times, to all people. Something is obscene only *to* certain people. These two defining characteristics of pornography—sexual arousal and obscenity—are neither
mutually contradictory nor necessary to one another. People who

are excited by some work do not always and necessarily find it obscene. Those who find it obscene may not, themselves, be sexually excited by it—though many will be guilt-ridden by their state of arousal, and label what got them turned on "disgusting" for that very reason. It is this possible independence of the two, along with their possible congruence to some people, that has clouded the legal definition of pornography for decades. Here is the equation.

Pornography is sexually exciting to some people.

To some people, sexual excitation is the same thing as "lust."

Therefore, that which is sexually exciting has to be disgusting, lewd, and obscene.

Of course, by this syllogism, one's own husband, wife, or lover would be (hopefully, anyway) obscene.

Obscenity is both a social and a legal term. The courts and the law have the power to define what is obscene. The Supreme Court, in a 5-to-4 decision, laid down the following definition of obscenity in the famous *Roth* case in 1957:

> Obscene material is material which deals with sex in a manner appealing to prurient interests. I.e., material *having a tendency to excite lustful thoughts*. . . . [To] the average person, applying contemporary community standards, the dominant theme of the material taken as a whole appeals to prurient interest. . . . All ideas having even the slightest redeeming social importance—unorthodox ideas, even ideas hateful to the prevailing climate of opinion—have the full protection of the guarantees [of the First Amendment]. . . . But implicit in the history of the First Amendment *is the rejection of obscenity as utterly without redeeming social importance* [my emphasis].

In 1973, the Supreme Court rendered five important decisions on pornography, the two most central being *Miller v. California* and the *Paris Theater* case. (All of these decisions were also based on a 5-to-4 majority.) The 1973 decisions are significant because they represent a repudiation of the current trend in the direction of greater frankness and "permissiveness" in depicting sex in the media. The Court's 1973 decisions contained the following key particulars:

(1) No universal, nationally acceptable definition as to what is "offensive" or what appeals to "prurient interests" can be valid; *different states and communities may set their own standards as to what constitutes obscenity.*

(2) *The First Amendment does not apply to public showing*

of "obscene" material. Prohibiting the distribution, sale, and showing of obscenity is not an infringement of freedom of speech, and does not constitute "thought control" or censorship.

(3) *It is not necessary to demonstrate that obscenity is harmful to the individual in order to prohibit it.* "Although there is no conclusive proof of a connection between antisocial behavior and obscene material," the majority opinion reads, it is permissible *to assume* that obscenity has "a tendency to exert a corrupting and debasing impact leading to antisocial behavior."

(4) *It is no longer a permissible defense against obscenity to claim that a work contains "redeeming social value."* Material may contain it, and still be ruled obscene.

The 1973 decisions are probably unconstitutional and will eventually be overturned. In fact more recent decisions have already qualified their scope. Since many people who make the decisions equate eroticism with obscenity, anyone who wishes to understand pornography is struck with this semantic equation. Any exploration of pornography in the United States right now involves grappling with the idea that many people, and especially many influential people, still consider erotic depictions in the media shameful, disgusting, offensive, and obscene.

An issue which once concerned almost everyone in this area was just where art ended and pornography began. Most observers felt that art and pornography were incompatible; works of art could not possibly be pornographic, and vice versa. The early court decisions on obscenity—for example, on James Joyce's *Ulysses* and D. H. Lawrence's *Lady Chatterley's Lover*—drew a sharp line of demarcation between the two. Today, this distinction is widely regarded to be irrelevant. Works of art conceded to be among the greatest ever created are erotic—that is, sexually stimulating—and attract audiences largely or at least partly for this reason. And certainly a great deal of art is considered to be lewd, obscene, and vulgar by the prudish among us. True, *most* pornography is not only light years away from being artistic—it is aesthetically barren. But then so is most nonpornography as well. Most works considered to be art are not pornographic—but then neither are works which are *not* thought to be artistic. Remember, some people are stimulated or offended by almost any depiction of the human body or by routine bodily functions, activities, or behavior, whether done artistically or not.

It is also true that there is a genre of pornography, a sterile, pat formula as to what turns more people on than just about anything: lots of sex and little else. Most decidedly, this is not art. But genres are based on convention, and conventions do change over time. So what we end up with is that art and pornography do not exist in separate realms—art uncontaminated by pornography, pornography having absolutely nothing to do with art. In fact, the two are commingled. Some art is pornographic. And some pornography is art. Morse Peckham asks, in his book, *Art and Pornography,* "Can there be pornographic art?" His answer: "Yes," he says, "seems so obvious that the question hardly seems worth asking, let alone answering."

Our last definition of pornography—the genre definition—looks at works from a different angle. Most works in the pornographic genre could be called "hard core"; likewise, most (although not all) hard core is genre pornography. Hard core is easier to define than genre pornography. What distinguishes hard core from all other pornography are two things: the degree of sexual *explicitness,* and the *proportion* of sexual depictions to everything else. Hard core contains sex and little else. And its sex is out in the open; it leaves little to the imagination. In written media, sexual acts are described in extraordinary detail—with "throbbing cocks" and "gushing cunts" very much in the forefront. In visual media, the classification "hard core" is usually reserved for photographs or films showing erections, penetration, acts of intercourse, oral-genital, and anal sex. Anything else which might be included in such a work—like plot, characterization, perhaps a message—is incidental to sexual depictions and sexual arousal. Now it is probably true that *in the future,* the connection between sexual explicitness and the exclusive concentration on sex and nothing but sex will be severed. But right now, most hard core is genre pornography. And genre pornography is conventional and formulistic. What is the formula? What are the conventions? In order to pander to the sexual craving of a very large number of men, it is necessary to get to sex very quickly, without much ado. Women must be depicted as eager and extremely willing, or, if hesitant, they must be forced or persuaded into sexual acts they have been ignorant of, and learn to enjoy ecstatically. In a great deal of genre pornography, woman's function is exclusively that of serving men sexually. Her needs are beside the point; she learns to love what just comes naturally and spontaneously to men. Women are also often degraded and humiliated in hard core—and the message is that they love every minute of it. Most genre pornography describes or depicts mindless bodies rubbing against one another. The basic ingredients of sex as it can be at its best are missing: joy, ecstasy, tenderness, communication, sensitivity—even passion.

What is important in the pornography equation is not just the work, and not just the work plus an audience. We necessarily have the work, an audience, plus the social setting in which the pornography is viewed. Social setting will determine to a large degree whether an audience even *becomes* aroused by pornography. The setting must be one in which members of an audience *will permit themselves to be aroused sexually.* Otherwise, arousal will tend to be inhibited. But also remember: different people regard quite different situations as acceptable for sexual arousal. Many men masturbate in public when viewing pornography; others are horrified by the thought of such an act, and therefore become less turned on by pornography—at least in public.

Here are the main settings in which pornography is consumed:

(1) *alone,* in private, at home;

(2) *with one sexual partner,* at home;

(3) *in a sexually mixed social gathering,* like a party, in someone's private home;

(4) *at a private all-male gathering,* either of a completely informal nature (like a group of friends), or of a semi-informal nature (members of some organization—like a fraternity or some adult voluntary group or club);

(5) *in a public theater,* with a viewing audience—increasingly sexually mixed, but still predominantly male;

(6) *in an arcade,* either in a booth, behind a curtain, or in public view.

Pornography may be homosexual or heterosexual in nature. In the former case, a private all-male gathering would be exactly equivalent to the heterosexual's "sexually mixed social gathering," because one's viewing audience and one's potential sex partners are, in both cases, the same.

The changes that have taken place over the past few years in pornography have been more dramatic and significant than for any written or visual medium. This is true not only of the works themselves, but of everything that touches in any way upon the works.

Certainly the most significant of all changes in pornography is, obviously, *what is regarded* as either obscene or sexually stimulating. Material that was once smuggled back from Paris and showed proudly to friends as the ultimate in erotica would not attract a side-long glance in any pornographic bookstore today. The same adolescent boys who once resorted to *National Geographic* for sexual excitation now have *Playboy, Penthouse,* and *Oui* openly and publicly available for their pleasure; bare-breasted native women are no longer worthy of their lascivious attention. And men who peeked at "beavers"—films of naked women—in arcades a decade ago now are satisfied only with depictions of actual intercourse. The demarcation line dividing pornography from what isn't pornography is drawn at a much "stronger" and more graphic level than was true a few years ago.

Secondly, the *audience* for pornography has changed. Up until the 1960s, viewers of pornography were overwhelmingly and almost exclusively male. Now women make up an increasingly larger proportion of the viewers and consumers of pornography. At one time it was believed that women were uninterested in erotic material, and did not become aroused by it. The famous Kinsey studies suggested that, possibly, there were "basic neurophysiologic differences between males and females" which explained their different receptivity to erotica. But over a decade and a half later, the Commission on Obscenity and Pornography found that women responded just as frequently and as intensely to erotic material as men. But the gimmick is that, up until recently, pornography was written, filmed, distributed, and sold solely *by* men almost solely *to* men. Naturally, everything in it would be from a male point of view. Pornography historically represented a male fantasy world. Now women have a bit more of a hand in determining the content of erotic materials. The field is still male-dominated, to be sure, but this exclusive control is breaking down. Erotica created by and for women will look and sound different from that by men. "Women tend to get more into the emotional and psychological subtleties of sexual encounters . . . , their approach is more personal, less mechanical," writes Uta West, a keen observer of trends in erotic writing and film. Most male-created pornography, Ms. West believes, "remains rooted in the myths and moral morass of Victorianism, appealing to the man who still believes sex is dirty and that only bad girls do it and enjoy it. . . . But things are beginning to change. . . . [Readers] are growing dissatisfied with the standard fare and demanding some refinements—

more interesting stories, more believable characters, maybe even a touch of humor. Women are in the forefront of this trend to upgrade erotic fiction. Although there are relatively few lady pornographers their influence is being felt."

Georgina Spelvin, star of *The Devil in Miss Jones,* one of the most financially successful pornographic films of all time, draws a distinction between "pornography" and "erotica," to emphasize women's reactions to sexually explicit materials: "I doubt that as it stands now there will ever be a large female audience for pornography. For erotica, yes. But not for pornography, not really. Women are just more romantic. They want, you know, rose petals on the bed and satin sheets. And I think there is a great market for this which is the market I'm aiming for in my next film." But the fact is, whether we call this material "erotica" or "pornography," women can be as aroused by sexually explicit material as men. But since pornography has catered exclusively to male fantasies in the past, this fact has remained obscured. When erotic material is produced *by* and *for* women, it will arouse women sexually. But it will be quite different from pornography of the past.

Even if we look at a very narrow segment of pornography— what is now called "hard-core porn," or film depictions of scenes of intercourse, along with just about all other types of sex acts—and compare it with its counterpart of a previous generation, the "stag film," or "blue movie," we still notice significant changes.

In spite of the recent Supreme Court rulings on obscenity, "hard-core" pornography is becoming almost socially respectable. In fact, it may be because it *has* become more respectable in recent years that those who are opposed to it fear it even more than previously. In the past, almost no pornographic actress (or actor) became well known (Candy Barr is the exception). Appearing in a "stag film" was something to be deeply ashamed of, to conceal at almost any cost. It was just a step above being a prostitute. Today, the world of pornography has become almost fashionable; the ethic of "porno chic" has taken hold. Now the successful actress in pornographic films is something she never was: a star. True, she is not in the same league with actresses who star in large-scale studio-produced and distributed films—but then, who is? Linda Lovelace was only the first of a long and growing list of "new breed" pornography stars. Marilyn Chambers, in the climactic scene in *(Behind) The Green Door,* sexually services four men simultaneously, yet her face adorns millions of Ivory Snow boxes—a symbol of fresh, wholesome young motherhood. It may be a cliché, but certainly no less true, that "times have changed" as regards pornography.

Rene Bond—the subject of the interview which makes up our first selection—is an actress, the star of dozens of pornographic films. William Rotsler is a filmmaker and producer of pornographic films, and the author of the book *Contemporary Erotic Cinema*. Ron Sproat is, as he explains, the author of several pornographic novels.

Interview with a Pornographic Film Star

by Rene Bond and Winston Hill

Rene, it seems like you have a film coming out every week. How many films have you actually made?

About seventy-five.

All hardcore films?

No, not all. I've had some straight films too. But only a couple. I've only been working for a year.

And you've made seventy-five films?

Oh sure. They don't take an awfully long time to make. The average is probably about two days. It might sound like a lot of work, but it really isn't that hard, and I get to pick when I want to work. It's not hard at all working with my boyfriend, Ric Lutz. We're very much in love and working is fun. When we're apart it's kind of a drag, but we still work. It's good for us.

So you don't work with your boyfriend exclusively, then?

Oh, no.

Do you enjoy the work?

I enjoy doing the dialogue, I enjoy ad-libbing.

No, no, the sex. Do you enjoy the balling?

Wait, I was getting to that. No, I don't. Except if it's with my boyfriend. There's no way you can, because—say you're taking two hours to make just the sex scene—alright, you've got to worry about keeping the guy hard, right? You've got to keep him excited —not too excited—because if he gets too excited, you blow the whole thing.

Do you ever get excited yourself though?

With my boyfriend perhaps. Not regularly. Usually not even with my boyfriend. You have to worry about angles; you have to call the person you're working with some other name; you've got to be ad-libbing—you're saying things that aren't normal for two people making love; there's fifteen people around, and there's five hundred degrees of lights burning down on you for two hours—I mean there's really just too much. For a woman to get excited, it's a very emotional thing.

Is there any stimulation provided by being in front of the camera, or from having all these people around—I mean an exhibitionist thing?

Oh, for some people there is. But that kind of thing gets old very quick. I mean big deal, it makes no difference.

How many different guys have you worked with? A lot?

I would say so. Not an awful lot. There really aren't that many different guys. A guy will only last in the business three or four months.

Why is that?

Well, see, when a guy first gets into the business, the idea of making love to a number of different girls is exciting to him, he really digs it. But after he's been in the business a while, making love to just any girl—well, pretty soon she's got to start being a really nice person. She's got to be good looking—he's got to like her. I mean there's got to be something else besides just that she's a new chick. Because they don't get turned on. They just can't do it.

Is that why these films are plagued with the problem of guys who can't stay hard?

Well there's that, and also because it takes so long. Usually it takes at least two hours to do one sex scene. And if there's any problems, it takes longer.

You mentioned that sometimes the guy will get too excited and blow the scene. How often does that happen?

You won't believe this—this happened to me five times just last week, and it was mostly because the guys were new and didn't know what they were doing. They have to learn how to hold it. But I've had guys come when I've just touched them, before I've given them head or anything. They'll come before they even start the scene. And that's when there's problems. So besides worrying about keeping them hard—and to keep them hard you have to make them think that you like it—besides that you have to try to relax them so they don't come too soon. When I'm working with a guy that's new, I'll always try to talk to him beforehand to relax him. But this is very important, because a guy can't fake it. A girl can fake it, but a guy can't.

I noticed that in your two current films, "Devil's Little Acre" and "Good Morning Glory" you do very little sucking, or giving head, though oral sex scenes seem to be mandatory in these films. Was there a reason for that?

Well, see, in the short I didn't have to. Listen, when you're at home with your boyfriend, he's probably going to be hard at the idea of making love to you. But when he's in front of the camera, it's not the same way. You gotta give him head—unless he's new. Whether they film it or not, you've got to give him head to get him up. So if there's not very much of it, it's because I didn't have to. Now in "Good Morning Glory" I gave him head and he got hard very fast and stayed hard. I didn't have to do it anymore. They got enough of it, there was enough there.

How is the pay for this work, Rene? I've heard it can be pretty bad. Is that right?

Well, that depends on what you would consider bad. I won't usually work for less than, say, seventy-five a day. And my boyfriend figured out that between us we make what the president makes in a year. So I'm not complaining. But there are some productions that will pay maybe fifty dollars for four hours, which is not too good, considering that model pay for stills is ten dollars an hour.

Have you done hardcore stills?

Oh yeah, that's how you start out—with stills and shorts, you know, loops. And then if you're good, you can go on to features. When you're starting out the pay is worse—sometimes ten or fifteen dollars for a loop.

Is the competition really that ferocious? How do they get away with paying so little?

Well, the competition isn't bad for me in L.A. But there is a steady supply of girls. Most of the people in this business aren't models. I'm only talking about L.A. now, but most of the people are either passing through town, or they have an illness in the family —they're trying to make some quick bread, so they'll model for it.

You say there's not much competition for you? Why is that?

Because I've been in the business for a while and people know I'm reliable. Most girls don't stay at it very long, either. It's very hard to keep up with emotionally. Most people are very—well, they're full of hang-ups. They can't justify what they're doing because of the way the rest of society looks upon it. Now the people who are seriously aspiring for a career—those people are competition for me. But there aren't many of them.

Do you have any problems handling it emotionally?

No, because I believe in what I'm doing. I don't think it's wrong. I can be put in jail for it, but I really don't think it's morally wrong. Now this is it—I think that an adult should be able to see any kind of movie he wants, as long as it's not hurting anyone. I mean, in a moral issue like this, who's to say what's wrong and what's right? Now I really do think there should be an age limit. I think that's fair. But an adult should be able to see and hear what he wants.

Were you always this sure of what you were doing?

When I first started out it was because my husband was not supporting me. He wasn't making any money. So I decided, well, it sounded kind of nice, so I was going to start making stills and loops. Naturally, I was nervous—I was extremely nervous. But that didn't last long. I was working with friends, I started relaxing. But it is a hard thing to do. Society has pounded into your head how wrong it is, and that people will look down on you. You're taught to be modest all your life, and the next thing some guy's saying, "C'mon, spread your legs honey" or "We're on your face, extreme passion— you're coming, you're coming!"—things like that. But after a while it's everyday, you get used to it.

You mentioned that the people who are seriously aspiring for a career are the ones who are competition for you. Is this what you have in mind, a career?

A career in *acting,* yes. I'm in it for acting, and secondly for the money.

But how much acting do you really get to do?

Well, listen, I just finished a film called "Proposition 8." I worked for two hundred and fifty dollars, and it took a week—so we were losing money to do it, my boyfriend and I and another couple. But we took it because they promised us they would really give us the reins. And we put a lot into it—we worked hard, because they gave us a chance to really *act*. I like acting, and if they'll give me a chance to act, I'll work for less.

I'm sure you've answered this a million times, but how does your family take all this?

My parents and my family are very proud of me. And they know what I'm doing.

Are they show people?

No, they're just average middle-class—they've never had a lot of money, they're not "cool." Just middle America, you know.

And they're proud of you?

Yes they are. For doing what I believe is right. They understand my position. They may not feel the same way I do, but they respect me for going after what I think is right.

Do you plan to make more porno films?

Sure. Why not?

Contemporary Erotic Cinema
by *William Rotsler*

Why Porno?

Erotic films are here to stay. Eventually they will simply merge into
the mainstream of motion pictures and disappear as a labeled subdivision. Nothing can stop this. The history of erotic film so closely
parallels the growth of film from the silent screen onward as to be
uncanny. Man simply is gathering momentum toward freedom—
freedom of all types.

At first these sexy upstarts were not expected to last, like the
fad of airplanes or the income tax or television. Sex films were a kind
of toy, a diversion that could not possibly maintain its own against
the "biggies." In the days of silent film it was the theater that was
supposed to win out in the end. In the case of the "dirty pictures" it
would be the regular studios, but they were having trouble with
television, another bother that "wouldn't last."

But the sex films hung in there, *because they had an audience,*
in some cases a *most* devoted audience. The films became "serious"
and bigger themes were attempted, stars and directors emerged,
notice was taken.

Sound came into use, as it had with the silent film, and more
complex films were produced. As each technical level was achieved,
some practitioners were lost and new ones emerged. Artists gave
way to "investors," and "studio managers" gave way to artists again.
Thus it was in the silent film days, thus it has been in the sex film
days, though telescoped in time.

Much of the product has remained crude. This, too, has paralleled the development of the regular film. It takes time for directors, actors, writers, and cinematographers to get beyond the initial crudities of the quick, easy money-maker. Pioneers in any field are often crude in what they do. With erotic motion pictures it generally takes fairly big money investments to produce a wide range of subject matter that will appeal to various tastes. It takes time to get into the generalized distribution channels so as to reach all levels of interest.

But sex films finally reached the beginnings of a wide audience —they were noticed by the critics. People seriously reviewed pornographic movies. (In fact, they started reviewing porno films before the simulation movies.) Early sex-film pioneers, such as Russ Meyer, have already had retrospective film festivals! I predict that this is not an isolated phenomenon but definitely a trend. Some day there will be big fat books on the shelves of booksellers with titles like *Early Porno, The Love Directors, Stars of the Golden Age of Pornopix, The Films of Marilyn Chambers, How "Deep Throat" Was Made,* and perhaps even *The Golden Book of Sex.* Alex de Renzy and the Mitchell Brothers will be included in film festival tours with Hitchcock and Kubrick. The "little magazine" critics will have a field day discovering "early trends in the work of Tom Parker" and "phallic influences that motivated Pat Rocco" and formulate elaborate theories about the work of Lowell Pickett. Precious prints of early porno films will be salvaged and shown at the Museum of Modern Art. Porno-star biographies will be published with a discreet center section of selected photos.

Sure, a lot of it will be commercially whipped-up froth, but there *will* be nostalgia periods. "I remember the first time I saw a stag film. It was at the fraternity and . . ."

"There was one girl in those early split beaver flicks . . ."

"What do you want for that autographed picture of Marsha Jordan?"

"How many films did Betty Page make back in the fifties, anyway?"

"Wow! A mint press book on *Shannon's Women!*"

"You ought to see Forry's collection of lobby stills!"

But that is something to come. Right now, if you say, "I think I'll go to a sex film tonight," you will get a lot of *looks,* a lot of smirks and quips designed, usually, to cover embarrassment. But persevere. As Charles Burbee said, "The picture of a naked woman is its own justification!"

The trouble with the smirking people is that they really have no idea what they are smirking about. They haven't seen the films, or maybe they went to see one and it was one of those really bad shows, a series of grubby loops. Naturally, they were turned off. They haven't gone back but they know it all. They remind me of the people from my childhood who sneered at pulp science fiction as "crazy Buck Rogers stuff." They are, of course, the same people who later claimed to have "known it all the time" when we got to the moon and someone else found there are thirty *galaxies* for every human being alive in the world today.

But of course no one—*no one*—has seen all of the erotic films. They simply do not have the distribution around the country. Even if you lived in a "porno capital" like L.A. or San Francisco and went to them religiously, you would not have seen *all* the sex films available. So don't let *anyone* tell you he or she is an expert simply because he or she has seen 'em all. No one has, any more than one person has seen all theatrical films or all animated cartoons.

The best of the good erotic films are yet to come. *Deep Throat* and *Last Tango in Paris* and *(Behind) The Green Door* are just the beginning. As more films become fodder for the critic's mill, as more become sought-after viewing for mixed audiences of all ages, you will have at least some prior idea of what is going on. Right now erotic films are emerging from anonymity. They will soon be putting more than just the titles out front. Certain directors or production companies will be noted and featured. Newspapers will soon start to carry the titles, as for any other film. All it will take is the money to advertise. The "adult movies" ghetto that some newspapers create will disappear. Then, soon after, you will become aware of specific production companies, certain directors or producers, and certain "stars," as with mainstream movies.

If the erotic film-makers make the right movies everything will be better for the succeeding generations. If they *progress*, if they make *sensual* films, not just sensational films; if the porno-film producers *produce*, the state of the art must improve. If the sex film-makers add to the language of cinema and do not simply fall into the Repeat-*click*-Repeat-*click*-Repeat trap, then filmed pornography will progress to the point where *pornography* will be an archaic word. Right now the language of porno cinema is baby talk—but inevitably some of it will become poetry.

Just as *Deep Throat* is about fellatio there will be films that have as a central theme group sex, cunnilingus, lesbianism, anal sex, S&M, bisexuality, rape, sexual sensuality, love, and any other area of sexual specialty. Just as *(Behind) The Green Door* is an erotic fantasy about sexual awakening there will be films about triads, about sexual *gestalts,* about the aberrations that sexual deprivation generates. Just as *Bad Barbara* is about sexual boredom and sexual curiosity there will be films about every aspect of sex, of love, of conquest and submission, of shared pleasure, and even about "perversion." Just as *Black and White* is about interracial sex, films will be made that fully explore the sexual desire, curiosity, animosity, lust, and myth-making between the sexes.

It is completely logical that sex be treated at all levels of interest in one of the most pervasive communication media of our time, and as an art form. Sex as a subject has been profoundly important in the visual arts, from the most primitive sculpture to the most sophisticated Far East and Western cultures. Film is an art form that evokes an *immediate* response. It has every appearance of life, of "now," of immediacy.

Sex is part of our lives. It comes and goes. It comes and grows. It assumes fanatical intensity and dissolves to boredom. It excites and pleases and hurts. It grows in the rich soil of fantasy and blossoms in love. We cannot escape it, nor, increasingly, do we want to. It could be that the erotic film that is seen and accepted by the public at large will be the catalyst that finally breaks us loose, as a culture, from centuries of ugly repression and perversion.

Erotic films *alone* will not bring about any revolt. They are only part of the tip of the iceberg. Sex in films is a chip in a larger mosaic, but a prominent chip.

Sex films of various types and levels can teach us, they can pleasure us and arouse us and bore us—just as any art might. But they *move,* they have color and sound and *reality.* Those are *real* people and it seems like a real situation, real pleasures, real problems. Our minds merge with the fantasy on the screen. They become part of us. Their hold dissolves in time, but maybe not *all* of the film is gone. Maybe a piece remains—a single frame, a thought, an attitude revealed. We are gently pushed this way or that. We change. We grow. We respond. That causes change and growth in others.

Pornography is positive. Pornography is life-enhancing and informative. Pornography is whatever you think it is. Pornography is in the mind of the beholder, just like obscenity, love, hate, thought. But pornography *is*.

What it is is yet to be determined.

Pornography, at least in Western cultures for the past couple of thousand years, has almost always been a secret venture. It may not have been created in secret, only in solitude, but the cultures into which it was born suppressed it. Thus Victorian fig leaves were attached to pagan sculpture even as the fig leaves and all that they implied caused an amazing body of secret pornography heavily devoted to perversion. Lautrec's portfolios of whore house drawings were kept secret, the Vatican had its closed galleries, Gauguin was considered shocking, and paintings of wild orgies were given safely pagan themes and settings. Books were banned and burned. Hundreds, perhaps thousands of writers and artists never exhibited the erotic work they created in private, and virtually *every* artist has created work that might be considered pornographic by his times.

But the pressure was always there. So nice "safe" nudes were created, lodged comfortably in mythological settings, carefully censored. The exhibited "orgies" of the masters were about as exciting as a nudist camp in winter, the "straight" nudes looked like your mother, and sex—what was that?

Books used words and relatively few people could read. Those who could, didn't read "that kind of thing"—except secretly and therefore they didn't talk about it. There was a delight in just *having* pornography, however, a safe little thrill akin to having a drink at the speakeasy or lighting up a joint in your living room, or perhaps going five or ten miles over the posted speed limit.

When photography came along it was a "natural" for pornography, or at least nudes, which was about the same thing in the mind of the times. *Nudity is sex and sex is dirty.* (Deliciously dirty!) Everyone knew that. To question it was to question reality and the very foundations of culture, motherhood, the flag, and authority.

But then the photographs started to move and all hell broke loose.

No one person really invented motion pictures, or photography, for that matter. It was an idea whose time had come. *Cinema* was born and almost the first thing put on film was an erotic event: Edison's "The Kiss," which was certainly considered racy for its time.

*   *   *

Virtually every tool, every invention, every discovery or process has been taken by an artist and used, in some way, to make a work of art. Prosaic welding torches, involved electronic circuits, bent sticks, plastics, neon, negative space, laser beams, plaster, power saws, photography—all have been used to create art, or at least something someone *thought* was art.

It is quite natural, then, that one of the most flexible and versatile tools of all, the motion picture, should be used to create erotic imagery. Artists from the earliest times have depicted that which was to them, the most interesting, the most fearful or exciting, even the most forbidden. They explored the tangible and intangible. Most artists have been men, perhaps because women have had better things to do. Thus most of art has depicted what was beautiful and desirable and fearful to a man. And what is more beautiful, desirable, and fearful to a man than a woman?

Once freed from the direct inhibitions of Western religion, which has always negated the pleasures of man, art soared. New explorations were made in form, in content, in non-content, in color, in media. As the tools available to an artist increased in number and flexibility the borders of the imagination also expanded. Slowly, we have fought ourselves free of artificial, age-old inhibitions that came from people who said, "I speak to God and for God and what God wants you to do is . . ."

Tools. Tools for learning, for learning to enjoy, for escape and pleasure and knowledge. The motion picture is a tool. It's also a craft, a social event, an art, a synthesis.

They say sex is not a spectator sport and to a point, or after a point, that's true. But millions watch anyway, even if the greatest thrill is to *play* it. The kid in the bleachers, watching the pros at bat, is learning and being pleasured at the same time. So is the man or woman in the darkened porno theater.

Nevertheless, at least for most people, porno theater is different in *kind* from the porno book. Even though the theater is dark, it is a *group* experience of a feeling which most of us have been taught should be private. To break that barrier, to make the stimulation of one's sexual response occur in the presence of a group or as a public (shared) experience, has taken a massive buildup of hundreds of films combined with a basic rejection of establishment values. It is high time. A whole new world is waiting to be created and explored.

The Erotic Event.

Part of the function of this book is to help you make up your mind to go, to participate, to enjoy, to create your own events, for the best erotic events star you. Y*O*U.

DEFINITIONS

In a discussion of any new art form, or means of communication, which are the same, the first thing to get right is the terminology.

The terminology as used by many people has become quite confused. Films that are not even fairly pornographic, but that do deal with sex, are called "porno." Almost always the mistakes downgrade the motion picture. This section is an attempt to clarify the situation so that we all know what we are talking about when these words are used.

X Rated

This is an "ordinary" motion picture, usually a "Hollywood product" that might have some nudity in it and perhaps even some *non-explicit* sex. You might see anything from the glimpse of a nipple to full nudity, although at this point pubic hair is rarely shown.

R-rated films might also be included in this category. Disregard the fact that films are sometimes rated R or X for reasons other than sex or nudity. Usually, however, it is the nudity and/or sex that pulls this rating. After all, we can teach our kids to kill, but not to make love. That's the American way.

I will use X to indicate this category.

There is a somewhat less expensive version of these Hollywood-type films, often done in Europe, with all the production value these limited budgets can achieve. Strong stories, lots of action, some nudity (usually quick and fast), and even some simulated sex of a pristine nature are featured here.

Unlike the X-rated films, which may have "names" and even stars, or director-stars, this classification usually features unknowns: actors, actresses, and directors "on the way up," or a fading "name," looking for a fast buck before oblivion.

But all these films are still within the established structure of Hollywood or European film-making and distribution. There is *no* explicit sex, no "soft-core" and only some simulated sex, usually done in tight close-ups. Increasingly, there is more nudity, more suggestive situations, and violence is often substituted for action, and action for sex.

Simulated Sex Films—XX

These are the sex exploitation films, or as they are more commonly described, the *sexploitation* films. Here, the nudity is rampant, with female pubic hair shown, but not yet, at this writing, any male genitalia, except in the swiftest of glimpses. (It will be coming, though.)

At the coolest end of the scale we have nudity and mild, simulated sex. At the hottest, or *soft-core* end, we have sex scenes bordering on explicitly shown sex acts.

But the sex in *simulated* films *is* simulated, hinted at, or defused of its power in various ways. It is at this point that we move into the nonestablishment movies, even though this category has its own big producers, big distributors, and even a handful of big stars.

This category started as the "nudies" or "nudie-cuties" but has long since left that behind. The phrase "nudie film," is still around, but it is obsolete in terms of describing anything but the oldies. No one has made a "nudie" film in years, at least no one with any sense. These were the first of the "sex films" publicly exhibited and they usually had a silly, nebulous, or nonexistent story line, lots and lots of beautiful nude bodies—but no pubic hair *and certainly no cocks!* There was no sex whatsoever in these films, although that was the obvious desire of everyone in the film. These films were all fantasies, all froth and nonsense.

The nudie film died out when the "hotter" kind of film came along. While they are still exhibited in very remote or uptight areas, they constitute an extremely small percentage of the sex-film market. (I wonder what happens to these old prints. Someday the Museum of Modern Art will want to have Retrospectives . . .)

The simulated or sexploitation film has been moving up in status and in money-making on a steady curve. In 1965 *The Notorious Daughter of Fanny Hill* was considered so hot that the producers "dumped it" for $75,000 after a production budget of $25,000, and considered themselves extremely lucky. They thought they had flim-flammed the distributor who bought it, but Dave Friedman's EVI has grossed over $325,000 with it. In early 1973 it was playing drive-ins, uncut!

More and more, the "sexploitation" producer has been aiming his films toward the drive-in and the regular, or "legitimate," theaters. This category, pressed on one side by the explicit sex of the pornos, and on the other side by the budgets and technical know-how of the big boys, has been going for the low-production-budget films, with fast multiple-run exhibitions, and leaving out a lot of the nudity and sex they would formerly have put in.

So: *Simulated* films have much nudity, much simulated sex, and tend more and more to resemble low-budget Hollywood movies, but without names.

For the sake of simplicity I have labeled these XX films. Where the film is especially erotic, yet not into explicit sexual acts I call them *XX—soft core.*

Then there are the pseudo-simulation pix, sex films disguised as action movies, or documentaries, or something other than sex. But somehow there are sexual situations, whether we actually ever see anything or not. There are inevitably busty girls with lots of cleavage, lots of leg and innuendo. Many are done in New York, France, Italy, and the Philippines. They promise much by the image they project, but since they are going into general release they deliver little. The "black market" is beginning to develop a taste for this sort of film as well, and we see a lot of foxy black girls, heavy action sequences, and black triumph.

Porno Films—XXX

These you might "rate" as XXX. Sexually speaking, these are full out on everything. *Nothing* is simulated, hidden, or hinted at. At the lowest point there are the "loops," the ten-minute films, usually with no story or only a feeble premise. Then come the shorts, usually just 800 feet or twice as long as the loops. Then there are the "featurettes" of about thirty minutes, and here some premise or story line is used, and some complexity is entertained. At the "top" of this category are the features, usually sixty to seventy-two minutes, and they have real story lines, though nothing so elaborate as in the simulated films.

No term is more bandied about than porno and no term is more incorrectly used. On national TV I have seen *Myra Breckenridge* called a porno film and Russ Meyer labeled a pornographer. In book after book on the erotic cinema writers and critics constantly misuse these terms, revealing their ignorance and prejudices and confusing the reader. Russ Meyer, for example, has *never* made a pornographic movie and his latest films don't even have nudity. The brief "pornographic" scene used as such in *The Seven Minutes* was not pornographic at all, but so powerful is the Meyer touch that you *think* it is, or might be!

A porno movie shows explicit sexual acts. But porno "biggie" Jim Mitchell says, "That's not hard-core! We don't have any dogs on the screen! They're not fucking pigs! *That's* hard-core!"

Old terms: Blue movie, dirty movie, stag movie, stag action.

New terms: Porno, porn, hardcore. ("Soft-core" would be the sexploitation, the simulation cinema.)

Remember, an *X-rated* movie is not a pornographic movie. A "beaver movie" or "split beaver" is also not pornographic, though, toward the end of their popularity, they stopped simulating masturbation by the girls and "the real thing" was done, often with an amazing variety of objects.

"Porno" has nothing to do with *obscenity,* which is a legal term that has yet to be defined adequately, if at all. Pornography—or "porno," to use the hip term—is intended primarily to sexually arouse the viewer, or reader, or maybe listener.

Porno films enjoy *graphic realism.*

These are the XXX films.

The Working Day in a Porno Factory
by Ron Sproat

The ad in the Help Wanted section of *The Village Voice* read, "Writers, Staff/Free lance, must be prolific. Must spell, punctuate, and type rapidly." There was a name (Phyllis) and a phone number.

A woman answered the phone. When I inquired about the job, she said in a rather matter-of-fact voice that the firm she represented published "adult fiction." She said if I wished to apply for a job, I would have to turn up the next day with at least ten pages of erotic material. She went on to say that the job paid $120 a week, and for that sum I would be expected to write 40 pages a day, or a total of 180 to 200 pages a week.

When I hung up, I decided I hadn't heard her correctly. *Nobody* could be expected to turn out 40 pages a day, day in and day out. And producing a 200-page novel for $120 . . . well, there had to be a mistake.

Still, it was a job, and I needed one badly. Besides, my curiosity was aroused. For years I had seen paperback novels with titles like *Women in Chains* or *Whip's Women* that sold for about $2 in the less-than-reputable bookstores of New York, and I had always wondered who produced these things. I had somehow imagined they were cranked out by a small army of dirty old men and sex-crazed spinsters, all of whom, at one point or another, had taken a course in creative writing (probably by mail order) and who were now taking their various frustrations out on paper. I didn't exactly see myself as a member of their ranks. But I was extremely curious to know what these writers looked like, who they were, what motivated them to pursue this chosen line of endeavor.

So I spent the next morning writing a rather tawdry little ten-page scene about a female hitchhiker headed for a peace march and the Army lieutenant who picks her up. In reading it over, I was pleased with one aspect of it: I had borrowed heavily from Fanny Hill's synonyms, so it sounded classier and less obvious than it actually was. Or so I thought.

At four o'clock, I reported to 224 West 4th Street, the address that had been given to me by the girl over the phone. I found myself in front of a gray, institutional-looking building in the heart of Greenwich Village. The downstairs of the building housed a pizza joint. Most of the upstairs housed a gym and health club. A heavy tin door led to a flight of metal stairs that were strewn with cigarette butts. Climbing the stairs, I found myself in a long, darkened hallway with many doors, all of them unmarked, except for those that announced "Gym."

At this point, fortunately, someone came out of one of the doors and, since I apparently looked confused, asked if he could help me. When I told him what I was looking for, he directed me to an unmarked door.

Inside, I found a waiting room, sparsely furnished with a bench, a table, and several canvas chairs. Tin ashtrays on the table overflowed with cigarette butts, and the refuse can overflowed with trash. There was a Coca-Cola machine with a sign on it that said OUT OF ORDER. On the outside door was another sign that said, in childish crayoned lettering, THE LAST PERSON TO LEAVE TELLS PRODUCTION TO LOCK DE DOOR/GOT IT?

Five people were waiting . . . three men and two women. All of them appeared to be under 30, and all wore various styles of mod Village dress. All were carrying notebooks . . . or plain Manila envelopes like mine. I sat down on a bench next to a long-haired pretty girl who looked like a Vassar dropout. I wondered what *her* ten pages were like.

After a moment, a stubby blonde, who turned out to be the Phyllis of the phone call, came from the outer office and asked if we all had application forms. I said I hadn't and was given one. For the first time, I knew the name of the firm: Typographics Systems, Inc. (which, by all concerned, was known as T.S.I.). It was a routine form, asking information about previous jobs, education, and so forth, but two sentences did stand out. They were "Have you been bonded?" and "Can you be bonded?" I answered no and yes, respectively, but the questions gave me some pause. Still, I did feel a bit as if I were filling out a job application for I.B.M.

As I waited to be interviewed, I was impressed by the amount of activity that was going on. People carrying galleys and lead sheets bustled in and out of the main office, all seeming to be in a tremendous hurry. Typewriters from the inner office never stopped their clatter. The place gave me the impression of a newspaper office in one of those Warner Bros. pictures of the thirties starring Pat O'Brien and Joan Blondell.

My name was called, and I went into the inner office. It was a long L-shaped room, with three battered desks in a row. One of the desks belonged to Phyllis, who, I later found out, was the office manager (a title of which she was inordinately proud). The second desk belonged to the editor. The third was piled high with papers, and no one seemed to use it. Alongside the desks, next to the windows that overlooked the street, was a row of four typewriters on typing stands. Three men and a girl were seated in front of the typewriters, typing furiously. One man wore an ascot, and as he typed, his eyes rolled heavenward. He looked as if he were composing a Bach fugue. In the very front of the room sat an olive-skinned young man wearing a white linen suit.

The editor, whose name was Bob, motioned me to a chair next to his desk. At first glance, he was somewhat intimidating. He wore work clothes, a bandana around his neck, had a scraggly beard, and bushy black hair long enough to be worn in a bun at the back of his head. He looked not unlike newspaper photographs of members of the Manson gang.

But the moment he spoke, he dispelled this impression. He was soft-spoken, genial, and polite. It even turned out, as he examined my application, that we had gone to the same high school in Ohio.

He glanced over my ten-page scene, scanning it quickly, nodding his head as he read. When he finished, he had only one criticism. The scene wasn't "specific" enough. I was momentarily at a loss, since the scene contained enough sexual gymnastics to put the Kama Sutra to shame. Then I realized he was objecting to my choice of language. My carefully chosen Fanny Hillisms wouldn't do.

He went on to explain how his organization worked. He needed, he said, a new staff writer. Staff writers reported to the office at 9:30

in the morning and worked until 5:30. They worked on novels, the subject matter of which was assigned to them. The subjects fell roughly into three main categories: S (or straight sex), G-M (gay male), and G-F (gay female). There were, he explained, other categories such as pederasty and bestiality, but, as there wasn't much call for these books, it was unlikely I would ever be assigned to one. I would, however, be required to write 40 pages a day, or the equivalent of a novel a week, for the staggering sum of $120. Later I learned the books churned out here sold for $1.95, and Crown Productions was the publisher.

The salary, meager though it was for the work involved, didn't bother me as much as the number of pages required. I didn't think I could *type* 40 pages a day, much less write 40 pages of narrative prose. Bob assured me everyone had this fear at first, but as time went on, his writers began "spewing out their fantasies on paper," and their pages "literally flew out of the typewriter." He pointed to one of his writers and said the man was capable of writing 60 pages a day. I was still a bit dubious, since pages have not been known to fly from my typewriter, but I needed a job. I decided to give it a try.

The following Tuesday (Monday was a holiday), I reported for work at Typographics Systems, Inc., at 9:30 a.m. on the dot. As I entered the office, I noticed several changes. The first was not very startling. Phyllis, the chunky blonde, had turned into a chunky redhead. The second did surprise me, however. The other writers were not the same people I had seen before. They were all new.

Bob came in a few minutes late, and asked me if I had punched in. He said all employees of this organization were required to punch a time clock eight times a day: once on reporting to work, a second time for the allowed fifteen-minute coffee break, a third on returning from the break, a fourth time for going to lunch, a fifth for returning, a sixth time for the afternoon break, a seventh time on returning, and an eighth time on leaving for the day.

The idea of punching a time clock came as a surprise to me. I had only had to do that once before in my life, and that was when I worked nailing crates in an electric controller factory one summer during high school vacation. Bob said the time clock was in Production, which was two doors down the hall. He added that I had better punch in right now, or I would be counted as late, and the time would be subtracted from my pay check.

I found Production, which turned out to be a large but sparsely

furnished room in which people sat behind desks, apparently checking over copy while others worked at machines that were apparently
typesetters. The time clock was by the door. I found my card and
punched in.

"New here?" said a voice behind me.

I turned. A young man behind the nearest desk was addressing
me. I said I was.

"A staff writer, I suppose." I said yes.

He smiled at me and shook his head. "We have quite a turnover
of those," he said, then turned back to his work.

When I got back to the main office, Bob motioned me to his
desk and told me my first assignment would be a gay male (G-M)
novel. I was not given any kind of outline, which I had somehow
expected. I was not shown samples of the publisher's output in this
category, or even the name of the publisher, since, as Bob explained,
this information was "not available." I was simply to compose an
outline of my own and start writing a novel. Bob said I should try for
an output of 40 pages at the end of the first day.

There were, however, certain requirements: (1) each chapter
must contain a major and prolonged sex scene, and the more sex,
the better; (2) chapters should be at least eighteen pages long; (3) in
this category, homosexual sex must always be presented as pleasant,
while heterosexual sex, if any, must be portrayed as no more than
perfunctory; and, finally (4) no mention should be made of religious
or ethnic groups.

He also gave me something called the Guidesheet, which I
should refer to at all times. The top of the sheet was a glossary of
words to be used, most of them unmentionable here, except that I
was informed the word for blue jeans was to be spelled "Levi's" instead of Levis or levis, "coming" has one "m," and the product of
ejaculation is spelled in four letters instead of three.

I had vaguely, and not very originally, intended to write something about a sailor on leave in New York and the various girls he
meets. I transformed the girls to boys. At the end of the day, after
typing as fast as I could, I had produced only twenty pages. Bob,
however, said this was permissible, since it was only my first day. But
he warned me I would have to pick up speed.

As I punched out at the end of the day, I had an odd realization.
I had spoken to only three people all day long: Bob, Phyllis, and
the stranger in Production, and my contacts with them had been

perfunctory. I had been introduced to no one, and though various people had been milling around the office all day long, no one had spoken a word to me.

On my second and third days, I realized this was a fixed pattern. Though the office was crowded and noisy, often with people having arguments (arguments seemed to abound among members of the staff), no one was supposed to bother the writers. We were supposed to relate only to our typewriters. Our lunch hours were staggered, and we didn't take our coffee breaks, since we were perpetually behind in our work, so, though we worked inches from each other, we remained total strangers.

One thing soon became apparent to me: in a porno shop, it is quantity, not quality, that counts. Though Bob had been reading my copy every night, he never commented on it, except to say I wasn't meeting my quota of pages (the best I could ever do was 37 pages), and that I was going over 26 lines. (Each page was to contain 26 lines, no more, no less.)

I began, as the week wore on, to feel more and more like a literary factory worker—the punching of the time clock, the staggered shifts, the precision with which the work was to be produced (so many pages per hour, with absolutely no regard for quality).

And the people who produced the work, including me, looked as if they might be working on an assembly line. The men, with a single exception (the linen-suited bookkeeper), wore work clothes, mostly denim; the women (with the exception of Phyllis, who favored bare midriffs) wore work shirts and slacks. The unending clatter of the typewriters sounded, for all the world, like the hammering of machinery.

The books that were produced here were never seen on the premises, because they were typeset in the production office but printed elsewhere ("In Jersey," someone told me, though I cannot be certain of this). This gave me an eerie feeling of working on a product I never saw fully assembled.

Certain incidents reinforced the feeling of factory-like regimentation. The first was the Great Sandwich Dispute.

One afternoon, as I was busily pounding away at my typewriter, I heard a loud commotion behind me, even louder than the usual ones.

The man at the last typewriter, whose lunch break came late in the afternoon, had apparently gotten hungry and gone out to buy something to eat, because he was sitting at his typewriter eating a sandwich. Phyllis was standing in front of him, irate.

"Take that out of your mouth!" she was shouting.

"I'm hungry. I can't concentrate when I'm hungry," the man answered.

"There are certain rules and procedures in this office, and I'm here to enforce them!" Phyllis screamed, in a voice that could have been heard for blocks. "I am manager of this office! Everyone here is under me! You are under me! Take that sandwich out of your mouth at once!"

The man continued to eat.

"I am the office manager! I am manager of this office!" Phyllis shrieked.

The man told her she had a rather limited vocabulary, and continued to eat his sandwich.

Phyllis's position was clearly threatened now. "Get out!" she screamed. "You're fired! Get out! Leave this minute! Do you hear me?"

The man didn't say a word. He simply ended the argument by finishing his sandwich. Phyllis stormed out of the office in defeat, and didn't return until the next day.

However, that morning, the staff writers were all handed memos by Phyllis headed "Office Rules and Regulations." Besides cautioning us against the use of drugs and liquor, the memo stated that eating and drinking in the office were strictly forbidden. Under the heading "Office Dress," it said laundered jeans were permissible, but under no circumstances would shorts or hot pants be tolerated. This little touch of prudery seemed rather amusing since the only mildly provocative form of dress I had seen was Phyllis's bare midriff.

The next day we were handed another paper and told to sign it. It was not so amusing. It was a statement of our rights as employees of the company. We had to state we would produce 40 pages a day, acceptable to the company. If we didn't, we would be fired or forfeit salary for the missing pages. It stated further that until we had worked for the company for three months, we would (1) receive no increase in salary, (2) receive no sick pay, (3) receive no pay for local or national holidays or for days when the company deemed it necessary for the office to be closed, and (4) retain no rights in the work we produced as employees of the company. In other words, we had to write *twelve* full-length published novels before we could expect anything more than a minimum wage, and, furthermore, after dredging out 2,400 pages of prose, to which we retained no legal right, we could arbitrarily be replaced by someone willing to do another twelve books under the company's terms.

The company was also very protective of the work we were producing. Every night, the pages we had written that day disappeared from our desks. Only the last page was left so we could remember where we'd left off. We were never allowed to see the galleys. When a book was completed, we were instructed to write a preface, a blurb for the back jacket, and three alternate titles. We were not allowed to know what the final choice of title was. The books were published under pseudonyms, as books of this kind usually are, but we were not allowed to know what our pseudonyms were. When asked where the books were distributed, Bob said, "All over the country," but would not be more specific. Of course we were not allowed to see the final product. It was clear the company wanted to keep us as far from our work as possible, presumably in case the question of rights came up.

About this time, I realized that the words of the man in Production had been prophetic. The turnover in staff writers was remarkably high. The girl behind me didn't appear one day. An attractive and energetic black girl took her place . . . and was fired three days later for being fifteen minutes late. There was a young man who quit because he didn't like "prostituting his talents" (who did?); he was replaced by a young, bearded man. I didn't know any of these people. I was simply aware of their presence . . . and absence.

The black girl had left an unfinished novel behind her, so the Man of the Sandwich and I were assigned to finish it. We were allowed to confer for a moment. While we did, I couldn't help sneaking a look at the page in his typewriter. I felt my own writing was so off-the-top-of-the-head and thoroughly miserable that I wondered if he was doing better. A sentence caught my eye. It said, "He glared at her through clenched teeth." It answered my question.

At this point, there were only three staff writers left—the young bearded man, the Man of the Sandwich, and me. We decided to throw caution to the winds and take our coffee breaks, even if we lost a page or two in the process. I got to know something about the other two.

The bearded man, whose name was Mike, told me he desperately wanted to be a writer, and this was the only writing job he could find. We found we shared the same complaints. Aside from the forbidding assembly-line atmosphere, we hated the unending sex scenes, not because of the subject matter, but because of the numbing boredom of writing the same scene over and over again. We found we even used the same words time and again. "Throbbing" and "dripping" were the most popular. Mike decided to beat the rap by writing what was mostly a mystery novel with the sex scenes as rapidly written and minor in importance as possible. (Later Bob told him "less mystery, more sex," so he didn't beat the rap after all.)

The Man of the Sandwich was an Australian, caught, as he said, in the "unemployment crunch" (weren't we all?), and he took a more humorous view toward his work. I asked him if he liked what he was doing.

"Well," he said. "It's a long way to Brentano's."

During the almost-month I worked for Typographics, I wrote two novels and approximately half of another. I was never able to write more than an average of 35 pages and had two sick days, so my pay was prorated. The largest pay check I received was $87.

The first novel was the sailor epic. The second concerned a girl named Dot who gave her all to the superintendent of an apartment building in order to get an apartment, then proceeded to make friends with the other tenants in the building, as well as the maintenance staff. Poor Dot. The only part of her anatomy that wasn't assaulted was her nostrils, and I'm not certain about those. The third book was intended to be a homosexual *All About Eve,* but considering the way it turned out, Bette Davis should sue.

My fourth assignment was a novel about pedophilia. I was given a guideline. It said, "Emphasis on the innocence of children, lechery of adults. Boys from six to thirteen; girls from six to fifteen. Emphasize hairlessness, tiny privates, lack of tits, etc."

Below this was a guide to the art of writing about bestiality. It said the writer must remember there could be sex scenes between adults but that animals must join in at least six or seven times.

I couldn't carry out my assignment. I'd like to say it was because of moral convictions, and partially it was. My young nephew, eight years old, of whom I am very fond, had come quite close to being molested, so the subject, to say the least, didn't hold any special allure.

But that was only part of the truth. The rest was, I simply

didn't know how to write such a thing. After all, the sex scenes had to be quite prolonged, and I simply didn't know what the characters could *do*. Those little masses of hairlessness and flat-chestedness . . . how could you keep the little buggers in action for 40 pages a day? I was fresh out of sexual fantasies.

As for bestiality . . . well, I shuddered to think about attempting that. ("Woof, woof," barked Fido, beside himself with ecstasy? "Meow," she moaned, excited beyond belief?)

So I left my home-away-from-home. I was told to return for my last pay check the following week.

During that week, the Supreme Court handed down its decision on pornography, making it the right of local communities to decide what was fit and proper to print, sell, and exhibit. Porn shops all over the country would undoubtedly be closing. I wondered how this would affect Typographics—and subsequently Crown Productions.

When I returned to the office for my check, I found business going on as usual. My seat was empty, but Mike and the Australian were still there, hunched over their typewriters, grinding out pages. They didn't look up, and I didn't bother them.

I asked the bookkeeper for my check, and he gave it to me, not saying a word, not even looking at me. I left. As I walked down the hallway, I could still hear the pounding of typewriter keys, machines that mustn't stop until the time clock in Production registered 5:30 and the page in the typewriter numbered 40.

Later, much later, an enterprising friend happened upon two of the novels I had written. They were part of a "Spade Classics" series. One was called *The Chicken Sailor*, by Robert Sharp, the other *The Star's Young Boy Friend*, by Rudy Scander (neither of them my titles, of course, although the initials of my name were retained). Both stories were as terrible as I had suspected they would be. In the cover blurbs, though, I had written that they both have "surprising" conclusions. They do. At least for me. The surprise is that both novels end on page 190, leaving out the entire last chapter, so they don't end, they just stop. The copyright on both reads "Star Distributors, Ltd., P.O. Box 362, Canal Street Station, New York, New York 10013." They each sell for $1.95, and if ever anyone wants to have a book-burning party to destroy all of these things, please invite me.

The Effects of Explicit Sexual Materials

by *The Commission on Obscenity and Pornography*

The Effects Panel of the Commission undertook to develop a program of research designed to provide information on the kinds of effects which result from exposure to sexually explicit materials, and the conditions under which these effects occur. The research program embraced both inquiries into public and professional belief regarding the effects of such materials, and empirical research bearing on the actual occurrence and condition of the effects. The areas of potential effect to which the research was addressed included sexual arousal, emotions, attitudes, overt sexual behavior, moral character, and criminal and other antisocial behavior related to sex.

Research procedures included (1) surveys employing national probability samples of adults and young persons; (2) quasi-experimental studies of selected population; (3) controlled experimental studies; and (4) studies of rates and incidence of sex offenses and illegitimacy at the national level. A major study, which is cited frequently in these pages, was a national survey of American adults and youth which involved face-to-face interviews with a random probability sample of 2,486 adults and 769 young persons between the ages of 15 and 20 in the continental United States.[1]

The strengths and weaknesses of the various research methods utilized are discussed in Section A of the Report of the Effects Panel of the Commission.[2] That Report is based upon the many technical studies which generated the data from which the Panel's conclusions were derived.

From *The Report of The Commission on Obscenity and Pornography*, Washington, D.C., U.S. Government Printing Office, 1970, pp. 23–27.

A. OPINION CONCERNING EFFECTS
OF SEXUAL MATERIALS

There is no consensus among Americans regarding what they consider to be the effects of viewing or reading explicit sexual materials. A diverse and perhaps inconsistent set of beliefs concerning the effects of sexual materials is held by large and necessarily overlapping portions of American men and women. Between 40% and 60% believe that sexual materials provide information about sex, provide entertainment, lead to moral breakdown, improve sexual relationships of married couples, lead people to commit rape, produce boredom with sexual materials, encourage innovation in marital sexual technique and lead people to lose respect for women. Some of these presumed effects are obviously socially undesirable while others may be regarded as socially neutral or desirable. When questioned about effects, persons were more likely to report having personally experienced desirable than undesirable ones. Among those who believed undesirable effects had occurred, there was a greater likelihood of attributing their occurrences to others than to self. But mostly, the undesirable effects were just believed to have happened without reference to self or personal acquaintances.

Surveys of psychiatrists, psychologists, sex educators, social workers, counselors and similar professional workers reveal that large majorities of such groups believe that sexual materials do not have harmful effects on either adults or adolescents. On the other hand, a survey of police chiefs found that 58% believed that "obscene" books played a significant role in causing juvenile delinquency.

B. EMPIRICAL EVIDENCE
CONCERNING EFFECTS

A number of empirical studies conducted recently by psychiatrists, psychologists, and sociologists attempted to assess the effects of exposure to explicit sexual materials. This body of research includes several study designs, a wide range of subjects and respondents, and a variety of effect indicators. Some questions in this area are not answered by the existing research, some are answered more fully than others, and many questions have yet to be asked. Continued research efforts which embrace both replicative studies and inquiries into areas not yet investigated are needed to extend and clarify existing findings and to specify more concretely the conditions under which specific effects occur. The findings of available research are summarized below.

PSYCHOSEXUAL STIMULATION

Experimental and survey studies show that exposure to erotic stimuli produces sexual arousal in substantial portions of both males and females. Arousal is dependent on both characteristics of the stimulus and characteristics of the viewer or user.

Recent research casts doubt on the common belief that women are vastly less aroused by erotic stimuli than are men. The supposed lack of female response may well be due to social and cultural inhibitions against reporting such arousal and to the fact that erotic material is generally oriented to a male audience. When viewing erotic stimuli, more women report the physiological sensations that are associated with sexual arousal than directly report being sexually aroused.

Research also shows that young persons are more likely to be aroused by erotica than are older persons. Persons who are college educated, religiously inactive, and sexually experienced are more likely to report arousal than persons who are less educated, religiously active and sexually inexperienced.

Several studies show that depictions of conventional sexual behavior are generally regarded as more stimulating than depictions of less conventional activity. Heterosexual themes elicit more frequent and stronger arousal responses than depictions of homosexual activity; petting and coitus themes elicit greater arousal than oral sexuality, which in turn elicits more than sadomasochistic themes.

SATIATION

The only experimental study on the subject to date found that continued or repeated exposure to erotic stimuli over 15 days resulted in satiation (marked diminution) of sexual arousal and interest in such material. In this experiment, the introduction of novel sex stimuli partially rejuvenated satiated interest, but only briefly. There was also partial recovery of interest after two months of nonexposure.

EFFECTS UPON SEXUAL BEHAVIOR

When people are exposed to erotic materials, some persons increase masturbatory or coital behavior, a smaller proportion decrease it, but the majority of persons report no change in these behaviors. Increases in either of these behaviors are short lived and generally disappear within 48 hours. When masturbation follows exposure, it tends to occur among individuals with established masturbatory patterns or among persons with established but unavailable sexual partners. When coital frequencies increase following exposure to sex stimuli, such activation generally occurs among sexually experienced persons with established and available sexual partners. In one study, middle-aged married couples reported increases in both the frequency and variety of coital performance during the 24 hours after the couples viewed erotic films.

In general, established patterns of sexual behavior were found to be very stable and not altered substantially by exposure to erotica. When sexual activity occurred following the viewing or reading of these materials, it constituted a temporary activation of individuals' preexisting patterns of sexual behavior.

Other common consequences of exposure to erotic stimuli are increased frequencies of erotic dreams, sexual fantasy, and conversation about sexual matters. These responses occur among both males and females. Sexual dreaming and fantasy occur as a result of exposure more often among unmarried than married persons, but conversation about sex occurs among both married and unmarried persons. Two studies found that a substantial number of married couples reported more agreeable and enhanced marital communication and an increased willingness to discuss sexual matters with each other after exposure to erotic stimuli.

ATTITUDINAL RESPONSES

Exposure to erotic stimuli appears to have little or no effect on already established attitudinal commitments regarding either sexuality or sexual morality. A series of four studies employing a large array of indicators found practically no significant differences in such attitudes before and after single or repeated exposures to erotica. One study did find that after exposure persons became more tolerant in reference to other persons' sexual activities although their own sexual standards did not change. One study reported that some persons' attitudes toward premarital intercourse became more liberal after exposure, while other persons' attitudes became more conservative, but another study found no changes in this regard. The overall picture is almost completely a tableau of no significant change.

Several surveys suggest that there is a correlation between experience with erotic materials and general attitudes about sex: Those who have more tolerant or liberal sexual attitudes tend also to have greater experience with sexual materials. Taken together, experimental and survey studies suggest that persons who are more sexually tolerant are also less rejecting of sexual material. Several studies show that after experience with erotic material, persons become less fearful of possible detrimental effects of exposure.

EMOTIONAL AND JUDGMENTAL RESPONSES

Several studies show that persons who are unfamiliar with erotic materials may experience strong and conflicting emotional reactions when first exposed to sexual stimuli. Multiple responses, such as attraction and repulsion to an unfamiliar object, are commonly observed in the research literature on psychosensory stimulation from a variety of nonsexual as well as sexual stimuli. These emotional responses are short-lived and, as with psychosexual stimulation, do not persist long after removal of the stimulus.

Extremely varied responses to erotic stimuli occur in the judgmental realm, as, for example, in the labeling of material as obscene or pornographic. Characteristics of both the viewer and the stimulus influence the response: For any given stimulus, some persons are more likely to judge it "obscene" than are others; and for persons of a given psychological or social type, some erotic themes are more likely to be judged "obscene" than are others. In general, persons who are older, less educated, religiously active, less experienced with erotic materials, or feel sexually guilty are most likely to judge a given erotic stimulus "obscene." There is some indication that stimuli

may have to evoke both positive responses (interesting or stimulating), and negative responses (offensive or unpleasant) before they
are judged obscene or pornographic.

CRIMINAL AND DELINQUENT BEHAVIOR

Delinquent and nondelinquent youth report generally similar
experiences with explicit sexual materials. Exposure to sexual materials is widespread among both groups. The age of first exposure,
the kinds of materials to which they are exposed, the amount of
their exposure, the circumstances of exposure, and their reactions
to erotic stimuli are essentially the same, particularly when family
and neighborhood backgrounds are held constant. There is some
evidence that peer group pressure accounts for both sexual experience and exposure to erotic materials among youth. A study of a
heterogeneous group of young people found that exposure to erotica
had no impact upon moral character over and above that of a generally deviant background.

Statistical studies of the relationship between availability of
erotic materials and the rates of sex crimes in Denmark indicate that
the increased availability of explicit sexual materials has been accompanied by a decrease in the incidence of sexual crime. Analysis of
police records of the same types of sex crimes in Copenhagen during
the past 12 years revealed that a dramatic decrease in reported sex
crimes occurred during this period and that the decrease coincided
with changes in Danish law which permitted wider availability of
explicit sexual materials. Other research showed that the decrease
in reported sexual offenses cannot be attributed to concurrent
changes in the social and legal definitions of sex crimes or in public
attitudes toward reporting such crimes to the police, or in police
reporting procedures.

Statistical studies of the relationship between the availability
of erotic material and the rates of sex crimes in the United States
present a more complex picture. During the period in which there
has been a marked increase in the availability of erotic materials,
some specific rates of arrest for sex crimes have increased (e.g.,
forcible rape) and others have declined (e.g., overall juvenile rates).
For juveniles, the overall rate of arrests for sex crimes decreased
even though arrests for nonsexual crimes increased by more than

100%. For adults, arrests for sex offenses increased slightly more than did arrests for nonsex offenses. The conclusion is that, for America, the relationship between the availability of erotica and changes in sex crime rates neither proves nor disproves the possibility that availability of erotica leads to crime, but the massive overall increases in sex crimes that have been alleged do not seem to have occurred.

Available research indicates that sex offenders have had less adolescent experience with erotica than other adults. They do not differ significantly from other adults in relation to adult experience with erotica, in relation to reported arousal or in relation to the likelihood of engaging in sexual behavior during or following exposure. Available evidence suggests that sex offenders' early inexperience with erotic material is a reflection of their more generally deprived sexual environment. The relative absence of experience appears to constitute another indicator of atypical and inadequate sexual socialization.

In sum, empirical research designed to clarify the question has found no evidence to date that exposure to explicit sexual materials plays a significant role in the causation of delinquent or criminal behavior among youth or adults.[3] The Commission cannot conclude that exposure to erotic materials is a factor in the causation of sex crime or sex delinquency.

Notes

1. The study was conducted by Response Analysis Corporation of Princeton, New Jersey, and the Institute of Survey Research of Temple University, Philadelphia, Pennsylvania.
2. See also the Preface of the Commission's Report.
3. Commissioners G. William Jones, Joseph T. Klapper, and Morris A. Lipton believe "that in the interest of precision a distinction should be made between two types of statements which occur in this Report. One type, to which we subscribe, is that research to date does not indicate that a causal relationship exists between exposure to erotica and the various social ills to which the research has been addressed. There are, however, also statements to the effect that 'no evidence' exists, and we believe these should more accurately read 'no reliable evidence.' Occasional aberrant findings, some of very doubtful validity, are noted and discussed in the Report of the Effects Panel. In our opinion, none of these, either individually or in sum, are of sufficient merit to constitute reliable evidence or to alter the summary conclusion that the research to date does not indicate a causal relationship."

III
Prostitution

Prostitution is usually defined as the more or less indiscriminate granting of sexual favors for money. But exactly what acts are covered by this definition can never be determined with absolute precision. There will always be disagreement on whether this or that specific behavior is or is not prostitution. For instance, what does "more or less indiscriminate" mean? A call girl might have an extremely select list of—and have intercourse, for pay, with—only a few dozen clients. She is more "indiscriminate" than the faithful housewife, but less than the street hooker. Is what she does prostitution? What if she has only a half dozen customers? Or only one? What if the exchange is sex for gifts, not outright cash—an apartment, a car, furs, jewels? Is this prostitution? Were courtesans who were kept in luxury by a few noblemen performing acts of prostitution? Is the exchange of a movie and a dinner for sex for an evening an act of prostitution? Or the exchange of sexual favors for help in a woman's career? Does the housewife perform prostitution? When she no longer loves her husband, isn't the central difference between her and the "ordinary" prostitute simply one of numbers? Radical feminists claim that all sex between man and wife constitutes prostitution in a sexist society, because the woman, in an economically disadvantaged position, must barter her body for material comfort. Indeed, in a society in which most women are forced to seek their achievements, material and otherwise, through men, the line between conventional sex and prostitution is thin.

And another essentially unresolvable issue is this: what kinds of acts must a woman perform, and how often, in order to be defined as a prostitute? How many times does a woman have to commit

acts that we all agree are prostitution before she becomes *a* prostitute? One? A hundred? A thousand? How long does she have to
work in "the life" before we all—herself included—decide that she
is magically granted the status of *being* a prostitute? The point is,
there is a difference between "doing prostitution" and "being a prostitute." There is no clear-cut behavioral category into which acts or
women can be neatly pigeonholed. The terms "prostitution" and
"prostitute" are not real in the sense that they exist in a state of
nature, women having only to step into them to fit the description.
They are a bit arbitrary. Not everyone will agree as to what belongs
in the categories and what doesn't. What does or does not belong
is largely a matter of perspective and definition.

This means two things: first, even if everyone agrees as to what
these words mean, there will always be very profound similarities
and parallels between acts and women that *are* described by them
and those that *aren't;* and second, there will always be vast differences between and among acts and women *within* the categories
themselves.

To put things a bit simpler: there is an element of prostitution
in all heterosexual sex. And: differences among prostitutes and acts
of prostitution are often greater than similarities.

Prostitution need not, of course, occur solely between a woman
who grants sexual access and a man who seeks it and pays for it.
It may be the other way around: a woman pays a man for sex. One
of our selections describes the world of the pimp, whose motto seems
to be "A pimp keeps his dick in his pocket"—in other words, he
wants to be paid for honoring a woman with his glorious sexual
favors. The pimp prostitutes himself—to the prostitute. So men may
engage in acts of prostitution as well as women. And the character
of the gigolo is, of course, legendary: a man, usually younger, who
deigns to be in the company of, often engaging in sexual intercourse
with, a woman, usually older, and is rewarded materially for his
efforts. So prostitution can work both ways. But male-female prostitution is far, far rarer than female-male prostitution. Homosexual
prostitution is also not uncommon, although almost all of it is male-
male; it is almost nonexistent among Lesbians. However, the nature
of homosexual prostitution seems to bear the stamp of homosexuality
far more than the stamp of prostitution: in its essential characteristics, it is much more like ordinary homosexual contact than it is

like female-male prostitution. In this chapter, then, we have narrowed our focus to female prostitution.

Prostitution is often thought to be one aspect of sexual permissiveness. This is entirely false. Although in *severely* repressive societies (take Inis Beag as an example, or Puritan New England), prostitution is extremely rare, it would also be rare in societies in which true sexual freedom is the rule. In fact, sexual repression and prostitution appear to go hand in hand. This is indicated by the motives of the men who are the clients of prostitutes. Nearly all studies attempting an understanding of prostitution have sought the answers by examining the motives of the prostitute. But what about her customers? The simple fact is, prostitution is based on many men paying for the sexual favors, often of anonymous women, which they are unable to obtain noncommercially, in ordinary human relationships with women. These men are sexually deprived, not sexually free. Although prostitutes will report that some of their customers are young, attractive, and sexually desirable men, the large bulk of the men who frequent the services of prostitutes are middle-aged, and most often married. This indicates a number of things, one being that their marriages are probably sexually unsatisfying in some way.

Perhaps their wives are less than enthusiastic about performing certain sexual acts that these men want, like fellatio, or perhaps these men feel guilty about demanding such acts of their wives—who, after all, are "good" women—but not of a "bad" woman, a whore.

Perhaps they crave "variety" through intercourse with a number of women, and cannot attract women sexually unless they pay them. Or perhaps they do not wish to risk emotional commitment in a meaningful relationship.

Perhaps they have not paid too much sexual attention to their wives, and, consequently, their wives have become turned off by their lackluster performances.

Or perhaps because their wives have begun to expect sexual satisfaction—which these men feel inadequate and inept at dealing with—they seek the company of women who will put on a show of faking orgasms to bolster up the sagging male ego. Men do not feel it as necessary to apologize to a prostitute for their inability as a lover.

Perhaps these men have become successful in their careers, and have become persuaded that they are "worth" more on the sexual marketplace than their wives are. In the equation of a sexist society, a man's desirability is largely tied in with his success, particularly in the economic sphere; a woman's desirability tends to be measured by her surface physical attributes. Prostitution is one social institution designed to handle this disparity.

Or perhaps the customer comes to the prostitute as an unintended consequence of the so-called sexual revolution. A sexually deprived man will wonder, since everyone *says* that sex is easily available, why he can't get any. A painful thought like this can be partially assuaged by a visit to a woman who offers sex for pay.

Perhaps the client is starved for companionship and intimacy— for someone with whom he can say absolutely anything without fear or embarrassment. Many men do not have an "anything goes" relationship with a woman, any woman; they may be trapped in verbal, emotional, and behavioral games of masculinity—which involve bragging, lying, and pretending invulnerability. The prostitute's room may serve as a kind of confessional. As Wayland Young says about the prostitute, in *Eros Denied,* "listening next to fucking is the thing she does most of."

There are men who simply *prefer* sex for pay—either because they want things clean, neat, and uninvolved; or because they *enjoy* hiring a woman to do their sexual bidding—engaging, that is, in a watered-down version of the master-slave relationship; or because they feel that sex is basically dirty, and paying for it alleviates some of the guilt.

Of course, these do not exhaust all of the clients' reasons for visiting a prostitute. There are many men who travel a great deal— sailors, salesmen—and are frequently in a town in which they are strangers. Or there are men who work in an area which is located far from an even-sexed population—such as lumberjacks, members of the armed services, oil workers, and so on. Rather than face the prospect of an empty hotel room, or all-male companionship, or the unlikely success of a "one night stand," they seek out the services of prostitutes. Some men have just recently moved to a new location and have not yet found female companionship.

There are also the men who are physically deformed or handicapped. An anonymous letter to *Playboy* illustrates this segment of the prostitute's clientele:

> I had a severe case of polio in early childhood that left me wearing body and leg braces and necessitates the use of crutches . . . [and] the only outlet I have for sex is prostitutes. There are very few women who are not repelled by a physically handicapped male. . . . I have stopped even trying to date, because a rebuff . . . is hard on the ego. I realize that sex with a prostitute is a very poor substitute for the real thing, but it is infinitely better than nothing. Prostitution gives me both the delight of sex itself and the simple pleasure of having female companionship.

And there are what British prostitutes call "kinkies"—men whose sexual interests are so bizarre that it would be almost impossible to locate women whom they would not have to pay to take part in their requests (or men who are too ashamed to request their wives or lovers to take part in them). Sadomasochism, with the man as the "submissive" partner and the woman as the "dominant" partner, is probably the most common single form of "kinky" sex requested of the prostitute. Various fetishes—clients dressed as women, masturbating in front of the nude prostitute, a fixation on overcoats, articles of rubber, high heels and nylon stockings, and so on—also make their appearance. We have devoted a later chapter to kinky sexual practices, since they do seem to be more common than most people think.

The motives of the woman who enters into repeated acts of prostitution are probably a great deal more complex and, at the same time, more fundamental than those of her customers. Prostitution is more central to her life; it engages more of her time, more of her psychic and emotional energy, and is far more basic to her identity. Very, very few men who have visited prostitutes even frequently will walk around saying to themselves and to others, "I'm a John," "I'm a trick." But nearly all women who engage in sex for pay for more than a few dozen times will think to themselves, and say to others they are close to, "I'm a prostitute." Of course, some of this has to do with the frequency of the behavior. But much of the reason for this difference can be located in our sexist society whose double-standard rules dictate that it is morally stigmatizing for a woman to *sell* her body, but morally acceptable for a man to *hire* a woman's body. This double standard is also reflected in the application of the law. In many jurisdictions, it is against the law to sexually "solicit," but not to *accept* a solicitation, which means that the woman is the criminal, and not the man—even though they are partners in the act. In other jurisdictions, both are technically culpable, but in practice, the man is almost never arrested, whereas the woman is arrested routinely. Another indication of the stigma attached to the woman, but not the man, can be found in the fact that the number of studies, articles, and books claiming that the prostitute is mentally "sick" easily outweigh the number of works claiming that her customer is "sick" by several hundred to one.

Poverty has frequently been cited as a prime cause for impelling a woman into prostitution. It is no doubt true that prostitutes are *more likely* to be recruited from poorer segments of society, but this has to be qualified.

First of all, only a very tiny proportion of poor women become prostitutes. Depending on one's definition of poverty, between 10 and 40 percent of this nation's population is poverty-stricken. This is between twenty and eighty million people, over half of which are female, and over one-third of which are between the ages of fifteen and forty. This works out to roughly over fifteen million women who are poor and in about the right age group. But estimates of the number of women who earn, let's say, over half of their total income from prostitution run at about a quarter to half a million. (In the late 1960s and early 1970s, there were roughly a hundred thousand *arrests* in the United States per year on prostitution charges, but arrests are a very poor measure of how frequently an illegal activity takes place.) So, while poverty may be one factor in entering into frequent sex for hire, it is only a very partial explanation.

Also remember, there are many women who are not, and never were, poor, and who become prostitutes. The "blue-collar" street prostitute is far more *visible* than the middle-class, college-educated call girl. Her visibility makes it easier for her to be both arrested *and* studied. So it is easy to *underestimate* the number of women who come from a middle-class background (who are more likely to end up being semi-invisible call girls) and to *exaggerate* the number of women who come from working-class backgrounds (who are more likely to end up working on the street, and to be highly visible). Furthermore, relatively affluent women may be more likely to engage in activities which very few people would label actual prostitution, and which never officially or unofficially get *counted* as prostitution, but which are similar to it in many ways. Like marrying for money. Or receiving gifts, entertainment, and wining and dining in exchange for intercourse. The last chapter in Gail Sheehy's book on prostitution, *Hustling,* is entitled "The Ultimate Trick," and it chronicles one woman's climb to great wealth through the wise and shrewd use of her body.

It may not be that working-class women engage in prostitution more, but that *the type of sexual exchanges they make are more likely to be called* prostitution by middle-class standards. Middle-class women are, perhaps, less likely to make the leap from sex-for-gifts to sex-for-outright-cash than working-class women are because they have been more firmly convinced that the former isn't nearly as "bad" as the latter. Perhaps the difference between the two is the more hardheaded, no-nonsense, and realistic attitude on the part of working-class women. After all, most men, even today, whether they are Johns or seducers, do not respect the women with whom they have intercourse. In a sexist society, there is an element of oppression in all heterosexual contact—especially if it is specifically sexual in nature.

But there are differences as well as similarities in the sexual attitudes of working-class and middle-class men. While both could be called basically sexist, the sexist mentality is probably significantly greater among working-class men. This influences the sexual patterns of women. The "good girl-bad girl" distinction is probably stronger and more powerfully operative among working-class men. Men seek sexual conquest mainly for male peer approval and prestige more often in the working class. And the pattern of one young woman having intercourse with many young men—none of whom respect her—while many young women are virginal at marriage, or have intercourse only with their future husband, is more deeply entrenched in the working class. This "one woman, many men" pattern (still called "promiscuity" by some observers) is rarer in the middle class; here, men and women are less likely to have radically different sexual styles. The likelihood of intercourse among members of the working class is sharply different for women and for men; nearly all the men have premarital sex, but most have it with a few women who have sex with many men. But the likelihood of middle-class women and men of having premarital sex is far more equal: the typical pattern is intercourse only with one or two emotionally intimate partners, along with a far rarer incidence of the young woman who is sexually exploited by many young men.

These contrasting styles of sexuality bear directly on how women become recruited into prostitution as a way of life. Sociologists John Gagnon and William Simon explain this process:

> [There] exists a minority of females . . . primarily from working- and lower-class origins, who serve as sexual targets for fairly large numbers of males and at high rates of contact without pay. . . . Early involvement (ages twelve to fifteen) in heterosexual activity on the part of a female means, in nearly all instances, that the specific relationship will fail, that she will in large measure be "tarnished goods" to both male and female peers. For young women who have few interpersonal or familial resources during adolescence, repeated sexual contacts with males becomes a device for gaining acceptance and social status. Unfortunately, few males are capable at this age of dealing with overt sexual activity without reference to male peer group norms and standards.

It is this group of young women "who make up the largest number of women who become prostitutes."

Prostitution is one of the most alienating of all occupations. Very few prostitutes will say that they enjoy their work, and most will say that they despise it. We do not doubt the sincerity of Xaviera Hollander, in describing her adventures in whoredom in *The Happy Hooker,* but we do doubt their typicality. For every one of her, there are hundreds who have had far less pleasant experiences. Frightening, boring, painful, degrading, embittering experiences. Being a prostitute exacts a heavy emotional price. One's ordinary, nonclient relationships with men often become tainted. It is extremely easy to despise men after a few years in "the life." Although most Lesbians do not hate men, hating men is one possible avenue to Lesbianism— an avenue prostitutes often traverse. Lesbianism is common among prostitutes. Gagnon and Simon put it this way: "It is not that lesbians become prostitutes, but that prostitutes, out of their reaction to the emotional poverty of their world, seek loving human relationships." Those men who see prostitution as one manifestation of the new sexual freedom should listen to what prostitutes have to say about their experiences in the life to test out their suppositions. At the same time we should all think about how it comes to be that it is *women* who sell their sexual favors to *men*—and about what these men find lacking in their lives that makes them feel the need for this type of barter. Why is our most intimate and, at its best, emotion-drenched behavior reduced to a cold, artificial cash exchange?

Why does prostitution take the form that it does here—or anywhere? What is it about the nature of our society that produces the particular form of prostitution we have?

------◆------

Gail Sheehy is a reporter, and the author of a number of widely read books, including *Hustling,* an account of prostitution in New York City. Christina Milner is a Ph.D. in anthropology, and coauthor with her then husband, Richard, of *Black Players*—the world of the Black pimp. "J" is the designation for a former prostitute who contributed the last selection in this chapter; it was edited by Kate Millett, feminist author of *Sexual Politics* and editor of *The Prostitution Papers*.

The Economics of Prostitution: Who Profits? Who Pays?

by Gail Sheehy

Prostitution is not a business that keeps records, publishes statistics, or courts publicity. I talked with all the obvious people, police commanders and assistant district attorneys and commissioners of city agencies, and heard the stories accumulated by the tight fraternity of old-time prostitution lawyers. For six months, I fairly lived out of Manhattan's largest police precinct, following the men who had followed the same streetwalkers for years. But most of my research had to be done where this business is done: on the street.

At first my brother-in-law assisted me by alternating in the roles of John or pimp. We compared notes with the actual prostitutes and their "sweet men," followed Johns into the hotels and registered ourselves, ate badly, ran from "pross" vans, developed blisters, and soon felt as degraded and defensive as the hustlers I hoped to describe. By the second summer, having already published several articles, I found the girls were eager to teach me what I had missed the first time around. An Eighth Avenue streetwalker even allowed me to slip a tape recorder under the bed while she serviced four tricks. But the hardest job remained: linking the chain of profiteers from pimps on the street to the landlords and organized criminals safely sleeping in suburbia. No one in city government would talk about the landlords of Hell's Bedroom. After reviewing all the available real estate records, I was able to interview the landlords and catch them in their lies. They didn't like it.

For perhaps the first time, I became aware of the dimension of greed in this multibillion-dollar business which thrives on the oldest form of human degradation.

Jack, shekels, mazuma, simoleons, Mr. Green, filthy lucre—big profit is the big Why of prostitution. And profiteering in the world's "oldest profession" is now called "hustling." Surrounding the obvious streetwalker is an assorted multitude of major and minor hustlers, all of whom play their part and earn their pay directly or indirectly from prostitution. The cast extends from pimps, madams, Murphy men, knobbers, call girls, playgirls, and courtesans to preying street hustlers and hotel operators, pornographers and prostitution lawyers, politicians, police "pussy posses," and prominent businessmen, and includes, always offstage of course, the Mafia.

The stakes are high. Secrecy is stringent. Using the most current figures available, there are an estimated 200,000 to 250,000 prostitutes in the United States today. Taking the lower estimate, at only six contacts a day and at the bottom price of $20 per "trick," the millions of clients of prostitution contribute to the support of the underworld the incredible sum of between $7 and $9 *billion* annually. All of it untaxed.

The profit figure is 10 times the entire annual budget of the U.S. Department of Justice. That fact alone would seem reason enough for tax-weary Americans to look more closely, rather than snicker, at prostitution.

The class ladder of the vocation begins with the lowliest, jail-calloused street hooker and ends with the pseudo aristocratic courtesan playing in the big league for the highest stakes: wealth and social position. But before taking a climb up the class ladder, let's focus briefly on one of the key questions Americans always ask of any booming business:

WHO PROFITS?

Here is a profit-and-loss rundown of the specific and related interests:

Prostitutes

It sounds unbelievably glamorous. Come to the big city and make a minimum of $200 a night doing what comes naturally. Work six nights a week while you're young and pretty. It's the fastest way to make money in the shortest time. How else can a girl earn $70,000 a year?

There are several critical facts the recruiter fails to mention. The average *net* income for a streetwalker is less than $100 a week. "To the pimp she's nothing but a piece of meat," as one police veteran of prostitution vans puts it. And she ages very quickly. Prostitution is a physically punishing business. Right from the start a working girl begins to worry about her age. This is one profession in which seniority is not rewarded.

When, in the last few years, massage parlors and peep shows broke out all over the playing field of midtown Manhattan, I began to see Puerto Rican faces for the first time. These were inexperienced girls of no more than 21, sitting on the benches of sex parlors like scared second-stringers waiting to be called into a rough game. I noticed they were all wearing baby-doll wigs and asked why. "The wig, it gives me less age," said one skinny girl. She giggled guiltily when I asked how old she really was. "Twenty, but the men, they like eighteen."

The bottom line of the prostitute's profit sheet is this: the vast majority find themselves old at 30, bitter and broke. In 2,000 interviews conducted over 10 years for their excellent book, *The Lively Commerce* (1971: Quadrangle; 1972: New American Library paperback), Charles Winick and Paul Kinsie found no more than 100 older prostitutes who had any money left. Because prostitution is a criminal offense in many states including New York, its practitioners are generally saddled with a police record as well, which demolishes their credit rating and further diminishes their chances of finding another job. They face the future locked into a day-to-day, cash-and-carry existence. Few of them can imagine where all the money went. The lion's share, of course, went to the next profiteer.

Pimps

"He doesn't do *nothing*. But the way he does nothing is *beautiful*." That description, coming from a starry-eyed beginner in the stable of a Times Square pimp, hits the nail on the head. She sees it as a source of pride. It is her earning power that allows her "sweet man" to drive around town in glorified idleness.

For this and a few meager services, the street pimp demands his girls bring in from $200 to $250 a night. The girls rarely see more than 5 percent. The pimp pockets all and doles out "walking-around money," $5 at a time. Because of his neurotic need to prove total control, the pimp makes no allowances for a girl who can't meet her quota. One night in a driving rainstorm, I accompanied a miserable streetwalker to a pay phone while she pleaded with her man: "I can't make but a bill [$100] tonight, the rain's sent everybody home." She got one word from the pimp: "Drown."

In New York City, for example, the prostitution boom began six years ago when the state penal code was revised. In the fall of 1967, the maximum penalty for prostitution was reduced from one year to 15 days or a $50 fine. That was also the end of the Women's Court Clinic, where a doctor routinely checked arrested girls and gave prophylactic treatments of penicillin.

A hue and cry went up from midtown businessmen and the hotel lobby in anticipation of the new law. They warned, quite correctly, that New York was about to be saturated with prostitutes from other, stricter states. And, as usual, this deeply complicated social problem became a superficial political football. By the fall of 1969, a conservative legislator sponsored a bill that upped the maximum penalty to 91 days or $500—when this bill became law, prostitution was elevated from a violation to a misdemeanor, and for the first time in New York State it became a "crime."

Apart from burdening prostitutes with criminal records, the amended legislation was beside the point. Judges barely catch the names as several dozen street girls glide past the bench—"I'm a seamstress"—and taxi back to their territories to finish the night's work. Ninety percent of the loitering (for the purposes of prostitution) cases are dismissed. Only the arresting officers are held up in court, filling out reports.

Even girls who are found guilty on the more serious "pross collars" (an arrest for actual prostitution), involving a specific proposal for a specific price made to a plainclothesman, are rarely jailed. Most judges let them go for a $25 to $50 fine—and a week to pay. Any girl can work that off in an hour or so. It amounts to a license.

Word of this leniency spread with great interest through the pimp grapevine around the country. New York was wide open. Midtown became the nation's largest outdoor flesh showroom.

Despite all subsequent "crackdowns," amateur pimps are still rolling into New York from Detroit, Chicago, and even California. When local pimps have recruitment problems, they often cruise up to Montreal. A black pimp can always magnetize white *naïfs* from La Province by flashing his blistertop Cadillac.

Where does all his money go? Into "invisible investments": $15,000 custom-made cars which serve as floating country clubs (with false registration), a gypsy cab business, a home out of state, fenced clothes and jewelry, gambling at the racetrack, and to other phantom profiteers above him.

At the highest levels of pimping, very little cash changes hands. Says one white penthouse pimp, "You can buy anything with beautiful women."

Preying Street Hustlers

Prostitutes carry a lot of cash—temporarily. No one knows this better than addicts and muggers, desperate pimps and other competitive prostitutes. Murphy men make a game of selling dummy keys, for cash in advance, to customers dumb enough to believe a girl will be waiting for them in an empty apartment. Knobbers are men dressed as female hookers, who have figured out their own ripoff on prostitution. They charge the same price but offer only stand-up service, pleading monthly indisposition.

"Prostitutes are pitiful creatures really," says a captain in New York's Public Morals Division. "The trouble is, they attract all the vermin—the muggers and robbers."

Hotel Operators

Fleabag prostitution hotels are run by a diehard little band of hirelings. They have no compunction about saying, "I come with the building." The standard rate quoted by New York street girls when they nuzzle up to negotiate with potential customers is "twenty and ten." The extra $10 is for the room. This goes directly to the hotel operator when the John signs the register, no bargaining about it. No allowances for personalized service either; 10 minutes to a trick is standard operating procedure. That means the hotel operator turns over each room four times an hour on a good night, and since the smallest fleabags operate five rooms for prostitution, the smallest operator piles up his little hills of green at about the rate of $200 an hour.

That is not to mention the take in watches, rings, credit cards, and traveling cash customarily lifted from Johns once they are inside the hotel room. Depending on the specialty hustlers of the house—

from mugging to the Murphy game where a clerk or pimp bursts in pretending to be the jealous husband—the customer is lucky to leave with his clothes. It is not unusual to see a customer flying into one of the midtown police precincts naked as a plucked chicken.

Pornographers

The link between pornography and the infiltration of a new area by prostitutes is firmly established. One promises, the other delivers.

In May of 1971, the Peep Show Man was up to his ankles in sawdust on Lexington Avenue, hammering in stalls like make-do cattle pens. He looked like a hayseed Kentucky veterinarian. One couldn't have guessed he owned a string of 12 Times Square peep shows. But competition had saturated Times Square, he said, and so he followed his sixth sense to Manhattan's East Side.

"Only had three folks come by wantin' to know why I was puttin' such a thing in here," drawled the Peep Show Man that May. "Prob'ly be the first ones in to see it." And a week later there they were, one hip poking out of every stall, dropping quarters into the box to devour sexual images that have the approximate substance of shower-curtain decals.

Within a week prostitutes had followed. And what follows prostitutes is crime.

Prostitution and Pornography Lawyers

Lawyers who make their living by defending prostitutes form a small, closed, cynical fraternity. They charge what the traffic will bear. Theirs is a captive clientele. On the proceeds of prostitution they live very well, in the manner of legal pimps.

For all sorts of profiteers, 1967 was the year of the double bonanza. While New York was relaxing its prostitution law, the Supreme Court handed down a series of decisions lowering the restrictions on obscenity. Within three months organized crime had entered the midtown pornography business. Right behind them appeared another middleman, an old breed of lawyer with a lucrative new specialty—obscenity law.

What these lawyers are really defending is not the public's right to experience imaginative forms of sexual expression, but the rights of property owners and mob-connected operators to extract maximum profits from the weakness of ordinary mortals. It is not uncommon for obscenity lawyers to have their own financial interests in the sex industry. Another habit they have is writing "public-spirited" letters to major newspapers upholding the virtues of civil libertarianism, letters as transparent as a call girl's negligee.

And so, while further Supreme Court clarification of obscenity laws is awaited, sharpie lawyers do daily battle in lower courts over the delicacy of police busts and the incoherent distinctions between hard- and soft-core pornography. In the jargon of the stock market, they are "going to the moon."

Politicians and Pussy Posses

For nearly a hundred years in New York, prostitution has been used as the whipping girl for political challengers to flog political incumbents. One thing has remained constant: New York's courts levy punishment exclusively on the real victims—prostitutes—while politicians ignore the structure of commercialized vice which sustains them.

It is fashionable to blame the whole mess on the police. Politicians respond to the immediate public outcry. City Hall simply enlarges the expensive, demoralizing game of round robin played by cops and prostitutes. Their "street sweeps" last only until the courts are choked with insubstantial cases and a louder cry comes back from the district attorney's office to the police commissioner's office: cut the arrests. Meanwhile, the girls evicted from one territory simply move to another, wait for calm, and return. And then the public cries "corruption" when an investigatory commission reports that a few houses of call girls are sustained on payments to the police.

Why should a frustrated police force take the blame for a social problem that both the courts and the cream of city officialdom refuse to face squarely?

Prominent Businessmen

Landlords are the one aspect of prostitution that has been up to now almost totally ignored. It took me six months of research and roughly 50 pounds of documentation to put the names of landlords together with the properties in midtown Manhattan which housed prostitution hotels, peep shows, massage parlors, pornographic bookstores, and blue movies. And then I interviewed them.

The results were all very embarrassing. The names behind the booming sex industry belonged to a relative-by-marriage of President Nixon, several of the largest tax-paying property owners in the City of New York, respectable East Side WASPs, members of the Mayor's Times Square Development Council, Park Avenue banks . . . and at the outset of each interview, they had all lied.

Every city has these money-insulated real estate moguls. And every city to a greater or lesser degree guards them. It is hardly *comme il faut* for city officials to tattle on their peers, especially since they control much of the private capital and influence the political winds which keep a particular mayor aloft.

The Mafia

No comment on the profiteers of prostitution can overlook the shadowy but certain presence of organized crime. Who knows better the weaknesses of men and who has had more experience in harnessing them?

Prostitution was selected as a profitable racket back in 1933, when the repeal of Prohibition forced Lucky Luciano to find new employments for the Mafia. The mob has had its ups and downs in the sex industry, but 1967 was a great year. Ever since the Supreme Court eased up on sexual expression, organized criminal exploiters have been creating an almost insatiable demand for paid sex, both live and simulated. The demand still grows; it seems by now unfillable. Who are the mob's patrons? Everybody.

Prostitution, then, is many things to many people, from the street corner to the penthouse to the hidden realms of profit beyond. The one thing prostitution is not is a "victimless crime." It attracts a wide species of preying criminals and generates a long line of victims, beginning with the most obvious and least understood—the prostitute herself.

UP THE CASTE LADDER

There is probably no vocation which operates with such a fierce system of social distinctions.

The streetwalker has nothing but slurs for "those lazy flatbackers," meaning call girls. The call girl expresses contempt for the ignorant "street hooker." The madam wouldn't be caught dead with a "diseased" street girl. The independent call girl has washed her hands of the "bloodsucking" madam or pimp. And so on.

The street hooker is at the bottom of the blue-collar end of the ladder. She far outnumbers anyone else in the business.

Separate and distinct is the whore-addict who turns to prostitution for support of her own or her boyfriend's habit rather than as a vocation in itself. A persistent myth about prostitution is that most girls are addicts. This is not only untrue, but it is impossible; because a girl working at the competitive speed—running five miles a night, six nights a week, and turning six to twelve tricks daily *despite* routine rotations through jail cells and courts—couldn't keep up the pace demanded by the pimp and keep up a habit as well. If and when she begins to require enough drugs to interfere with her work, the pimp will lower her to bottom woman in the stable or drop her.

In New York, the quality and price of street girls diminish as they move westward on the city map. On the more prosperous East Side, the merchandise is sharply divided into three subclasses.

In one class are the daytimers who pull a steady blue-chip business among Grand Central commuters, which accounts for their swelling ranks. They work the office buildings like a super-hospitality coffee wagon. Score the flustered account executive in the elevator, simple! Make a date for a "noonsie" in the office while the secretary is out to lunch. Discreet accommodations of all kinds are offered for the busy executive.

Daytimers can afford to be choosy. Haughty, white, and businesslike, these are your ex-models and jobless actresses who turn a trick for no less than $60. Their ranks also include bored suburban housewives who work primarily for kicks. With a few bills in the tote bag, they'll be home to slip the frozen scampi in the wall oven before husband plotzes off the 7:02. Enterprising!

Police estimate that 10 percent of those prostitutes working the Times Square area on weekends are housewives from Long Island and New Jersey. Their husbands are mailmen or clerks on fixed salaries that don't pay the taxes on suburban homes. Since prostitutes are not fingerprinted, even with frequent arrests the married streetwalker, operating under an assumed name, can be home by 10 with a foolproof alibi (at least on the police blotter) about her weekend activities.

"Got no pimps, these daytime dames," I heard a pimp complain. "They're no dope fiends out to support a habit. These girls make big money."

The early evening girls, class two among street hookers, scuffle in and out of the grand hotels until 11 and may go home with $300, even $400 on a good night. They are still new enough, plump-fleshed and pretty enough, to pass for wives on the arms of conventioneers. Many of them also manage to work independently. By ducking home early, they avoid the pimps and escape the midnight street sweeps by police.

After midnight the frenzy begins. The tough, the old, and the desperate inhabit this third, aberrant class of street prostitutes. Pimps also send out their rambunctious new girls to prove themselves at this hour. Everyone has a gimmick. Or a habit. Or a car.

Next rung up on the prostitution ladder are rent whores, girls who turn a few tricks to buy clothes or pay the rent. They are independent but considered by colleagues lazy and unprofessional.

Massage parlors, since their export from California to every major city, offer free-lance employment that appeals to a wide range of full- or part-time prostitutes. Young, unskilled girls from Puerto Rico, Canada, and the Caribbean are drawn in for lack of alternatives; groupies pick up money to finance their star-trailing trips; runaways and college girls are attracted to the tonier parlors operated by hippie capitalists. Massage parlors offer the advantages of an indoor job on a daily contract basis. Girls pay the manager in order to work and pocket what they can in tips. But when the police pressure is on and the total earnings are in, the indoor employee of a massage parlor makes considerably less than the streetwalker. This often puts her back on the street after closing time. (A recently passed New York City law aims to regulate massage parlors by licensing them. And, for the first time, the landlord of the building and the operator of the parlor are to be penalized as well as the practitioner.)

The white-collar end of the business begins with call girls. Those managed by a madam or pimp may turn over as much as 70 percent of their income in exchange for Johns' names and an apartment in which to entertain them.

The independent call girl clears an average of $1,000 a week. She may have worked her way up, but it is not uncommon now to find young call girls from wealthy families. Many seem to have substituted for old game-playing in drugs or revolutionary politics, playing at being prostitutes—an an antipathy device. The element of risk is injected into a tediously comfortable existence. Topping off this level is the playgirl. She is a traveling parasite. Floating from country to country, executive junket to political convention, she relies on tips from the grapevine of jumbo jet hustling.

Four common factors link most of the foregoing women. Absent or inoperative parents; an early and brutal sexual experience—often with a seductive father; an early pregnancy; and their resulting attitudes toward men: fear, dependence, rage. The rage of course must be repressed. To some degree it is sublimated in the process of exerting sexual power over men who must pay. Some rage leaks out, and it fuels the violent new breed.

HAUTE CLASSE HUSTLING

Women who are in the *business* of marrying wealthy men qualify as cash-and-marry contractors. A woman who prefers to retain some freedom by moving as a mistress from man to man could be called an incorrigible courtesan. Euphemisms are very important to women who operate in the elevated circles of hustling. Although dictionary definitions of "courtesan" always include the blunt synonym "a prostitute" ("or paramour, especially one associating with men of wealth"), at least the word has the elevation of a European history.

Certainly all marriage is not prostitution, and all live-in love affairs are not courtesanships. But most of us know or read about women belonging to that exotic breed who *plan* romance only with and for men of substance.

If one wanted to chart the distinctions between obvious prostitutes and the class of courtesans, it might look like the chart below.

The thread of continuity connecting both kinds of behavior is that these women do not see themselves, nor do they require that other people see them, as people. They are willing commodities. They live their personal and professional lives by openly seeking or by cleverly insinuating themselves into a man's wallet. To the men in their lives, both are possessions. The prostitute is a temporary purchase, to be enjoyed like a bottle of wine and thrown away. The courtesan is a possession to keep (at least until he becomes bored), a sculpture to admire behind closed doors or to display as a prestige item.

It is not enough to be pretty, charming, graceful, impeccably dressed, and talented in the arts of hostessing and listening, as are all the celebrated courtesans of our day. To collect millionaires and gather from them convertible assets, these women use most imaginative devices:

Prostitute	Courtesan
Temporary encounters. She is selling her body minute by minute.	Permanent or serial relationships are the goal.
Noninvolvement of the John is required.	Commitment by the lover or husband is desired.
Demands on her are entirely *sexual*. Studies show the majority of Johns are "looking for something different."	Demands are often primarily social. The rich man wants a good hostess, an intelligent companion, a flattering accessory. He may also want to be free of sexual obligations.
Honest promiscuity: the first order of business is always to negotiate the price.	Facade of fidelity over serial promiscuity: the man cooperates; he does not want to know about her past.
Erotic presentation on the woman's part is required to excite the John. Both are playing what behavioral scientist Dr. Ray Birdwhistell calls "hyper-gender roles."	Respectable presentation is essential to protect the man from ridicule. As Sheilah Graham points out in her book, *A State of Heat* (1972: Grosset & Dunlap), "The American women who pick off the best men are careful to maintain an impeccable reputation."
The male figure, in this case the pimp, rewards quantity of sexual contacts by promoting the woman to "wife" in his stable.	The male figure, the courtesan's "protector," rewards exclusivity by providing her with a place to live, gifts, and security.
Irresponsibility: the prostitute holds herself accountable only for day-to-day survival; she leaves the planning and execution of her life goals to the pimp.	Discipline: the courtesan is capable of postponing gratification with an eye to achieving her own long-term goals.
Earnings are well over a thousand dollars a week, but she is lucky to keep $100 for herself— the pimp pockets almost all of it and doles out $5 at a time.	Material rewards are gifts, trips, homes, furnishings, and charge accounts—the sky is the limit, depending on his means and generosity, and her wiles.

Pump priming: A femme fatale well known to TV audiences often uses this technique the morning after she first allows a man to spend the night. She heads straight for Tiffany's to buy him a gold cigarette case. She has it inscribed with a sentiment both flattering and tastefully torrid, such as: "Thank you, darling, for one of the most memorable evenings of love in my life." The man receives this wildly expensive gift for doing nothing more than taking her to bed. If her pump priming works, he responds with a $25,000 necklace from Harry Winston's.

Jewelry converting: An executive salesman for one of New York's most exclusive diamond emporiums always advised cash-and-marry contractors: "Get these men to give you jewelry. If you ever fall on hard times, we'll be glad to buy the pieces back." The biggest coup was carried off by the wife of a stock market swindler. She knew, a few days before the market did, that the bottom was about to fall out of her husband's company. While he was staging a last fight to save the stock, she bounced into the diamond store and charged a half million or so worth of jewels. Her husband did go broke and fled to Brazil. She sold the baubles back to the store. But this time the trick was too blatant. The executive salesman was caught and charged with fraud, along with the acquisitive wife whose trouble was being in too much of a hurry.

Collecting tangibles: With an eye toward providing her own security in advancing age, the incorrigible courtesan taps her men for tangible, convertible gifts. Rented living quarters, no matter how sumptuous, are considered wholly undesirable. "They ask for a small *pied-à-terre*, and then shop for priceless antiques to fill it," says a Manhattan real estate agent accustomed to finding accommodations for the mistresses of her luxury clientele. "The antiques belong to them; they're salable!" Other convertible gifts are paintings, objets d'art, a co-op apartment, a piece of land, a country house.

In the process of collecting all these things on her breathtaking passage through the lives of affluent European lovers and American husbands, one envied courtesan became skilled at selling the right assets at the most propitious time. She had learned that with any less business acumen, the courtesan who is between lovers may find herself in a "sensitive cash flow position." This is not only embarrassing, but it's unattractive *and* suspicious. On reaching her mid-forties, she had consolidated all the gifts into her own estate—an exquisitely appointed home and many accumulated acres to go with it. When a super-millionaire suddenly appeared, he saw her as a member of his own rarefied circle. He offered a marriage contract settling on her a sum appropriate to her position—$10 million.

Inventing occasions: "What kind of party shall we have for my birthday?" or, "Look at the calendar, darling, we'll be married a month on Saturday!" or, "It's almost a year since our first evening together, and I'm so sentimental—how shall we celebrate?" After the marriage, a frequent visitor in the home of a former courtesan was baffled by hearing her constantly float such ideas in the presence of guests. Another wealthy woman explained. It's a way of inventing occasions for which her husband will feel obliged to buy her a present.

Name-saving: After the divorce, a lady who carried the name of an aristocratic American family revered almost as royalty, never remarried. Bystanders were baffled. She took one famous lover in the domestic film industry and drove another lover to drink himself out of the British cabinet. But she would not marry. She was not about to erase the one asset on which she could always trade—her former husband's name.

We Americans are famous for institutionalizing our social and moral hypocrisies. The polite unemployed, spongers on the rich, are called playboys; the culture-bound poor, applying for public relief, are called welfare loafers. We often acknowledge such riddles in politics, law, and ordinary business life. But we generally miss the similar deceptions when they veil the activities of people in a less familiar world—the baffling, secretive, conniving netherworld.

Excepting China, there is not a civilized country in the world without prostitution. But only in America is the prostitute punished for prostitution per se—the barter of sex for money—and she is often punished by the same men who after hours seek her favors. Very little thought has been applied to tackling, or even taxing, the real profiteers. Even less thought has been given to creative experiments in rehabilitating the prostitute.

My point is that when applied to the multibillion-dollar business of hustling, our great moral hypocrisies again break down according to class lines. Prostitutes are not laughable social deviants. They are women operating at every level of a consumer society who too often begin as a baby-sitting problem and end as throw-away human beings.

Black Players
by Christina Milner and
Richard Milner

We were inquiring strangers, anthropologists. When Christina's temporary job as a dancer in San Francisco's topless bars brought us into contact with Black pimps and their prostitutes, we decided to study their subculture in a way which had not been tried before: old-fashioned participant observation.

Books on pimps and prostitutes were full of moral judgments, clinical interviews, and breast-beating confessions, but no anthropologist had entered their subculture as if it were a village in New Guinea—to settle down and live with the people for a year or two, to observe their daily behavior and talk with their wise men, to laugh with them at their jokes and foibles, to gossip with their women, to join the men in their men's house, to attend their celebrations and play with their children. To seek to learn from them; to see if they had anything to offer which could enrich our lives and our understanding.

At the time we were both graduate students in the Department of Anthropology at the University of California at Berkeley, and were well aware in those days of social protest that the study of man begins at home. We had always thought it somewhat strange that many anthropologists who are experts in the culture of East African or Southeast Asian peoples are distinctly at a disadvantage in understanding life as it is lived in their home cities.

Perhaps people in foreign lands seem more "exotic" than the

mundane nitty-gritty of American cities, but we found the subculture of Black pimps and their prostitutes or "hos" (rhymes with "rose") to be as fascinating as any which could exist on distant shores. In their unique upside-down world polygamy (one man with several women) is the rule, men are extremely dominant but women are the economic providers, and the ideal union is between a Black man and a White woman. Among these people, a man may spend hours a day on his hair, clothes, and toilette, while his women are out working to support the household. Almost every night, many of the men gather in special houses to partake of a rare drug.

At gatherings or celebrations, the sexes rigidly separate, and the men talk only to other men while the women talk only among themselves. Yet, almost every night, these same women spend hours in intimate sexual contact with other men, most of them strangers— and towards these their own men show no jealousy. In this sub-culture, the paternity of children is often from "outside" the group, men are expected to show great style and creativity in their dress, the norm is to sleep in the daytime and to work at night, money and material objects are the idols, conspicuous consumption is more important than future security or provision for old age, and the selling of sex and fantasy is the major industry. . . .

It should be understood at the outset that a pimp is not, as the dictionary would have it, "a pander, a go-between in intrigues of love." He does not usually solicit customers for his ho, nor does he generally stay too close to the vicinity where she is working. Rather, the pimp is simply one who lives off the proceeds of a prostitute's activities. He is her man and is content to be the "manager" of his "star" of the street. . . .

For all practical purposes, a player recognizes only six categories of people: players (pimps), "hos" (the pronunciation of whores) or bitches, square bitches (women outside "The Life"), cops or "rollers" (police), "tricks" or straight Johns (the prostitute's customers), and hippies and hustlers who are not "straight" and with whom the players have certain areas of commonality (for example, drugs) but who are outside The Life. There are few people except other players with whom the pimp can feel at ease and with whom he can openly discuss his life and his profession. In addition, other players support and reinforce his value system and world view. . . .

The pimp is an aristocrat among hustlers in the Black ghetto. He is admired as a "bad" culture hero (meaning "good") because his profession incorporates all of the attributes of lower-class ghetto manhood, without its attendant poverty. He is recognized as among the best talkers or "rappers" in the hustling world, with the greatest psychological skill in "gaming off" women. He holds the reputation of a great lover, pursued by and controlling women who pay for his favors, providing him with luxuries and leisure time to drink and get high with his "partners." . . .

The Black pimp's fame and high status among lower-class Black males is assured by the fact that his income from his hos, both Black and White, originates largely from the pockets of Whitey. If "rapping," "gaming," sex, male dominance, and money to spend aren't enough, getting Whitey to foot the bill, often through the pimp's White prostitutes, is the capstone to the player's prestige.

As the profession is practiced among those players we studied and interviewed, pimping is a unique ghetto adaptation to the universal American desire for material success, without "selling out" to a "square job" for "chump change" or a way of life away from the familiar streets. Of course, there are and always have been pimps of all colors and backgrounds. But the style of Black pimps, their traditions, and the relationship of their subculture to the Black ghetto culture gives their world a special flavor. During the study we only met three White pimps, and all of them mimicked the Black style in their speech, dress, and in their adherence to "The Book," the unwritten pimp's code.

A player may have anywhere from one to twenty "ladies," although two or three is most common. While the woman is walking the streets (most prostitutes in our study were streetwalkers rather than call girls), hanging out in bars, or patrolling hotel lobbies, the player is out "on the set," moving through the "scene" of the city's night life. Usually, whether in a friend's house or a bar, his lady knows a telephone number where he can be contacted.

Late at night, players often congregate at a "jam house," a private home or apartment where players and hustlers gather to snort cocaine ("jam"). Cocaine is prestigious to use because it is so expensive; they call it the "rich man's drug." A tiny capsule sells for twenty dollars (a "twenty-cent bag"). It is not unusual for a player who is enjoying some prosperity to snort one hundred dollars' worth of "jam" in a single night, and to treat his "partners" (friends) as well. There are elaborate rituals for snorting jam. Some players carry special little gold or silver pocket knives or spoons with which to carry the powder to their noses. Often it is carried in and served on new hundred-dollar bills folded in a special way, which reinforces the luxury of the drug. One night we attended a "jam party" at which six thousand dollars' worth of cocaine went up the guests' noses. . . .

In many bars, one finds only the men *or* the women, since men don't usually frequent the same bar where their ladies are working. The reasons for this rule are that the trick is not supposed to be given any indication that the ho even has a pimp, and also that if one's woman should get "busted" (arrested), her man does not want to be implicated. Pimping is a felony whereas soliciting is only a misdemeanor. In certain cases, if the pimp were to get busted with his ho there might be no one to post bail, for some neglect their traditional obligation of placing a large sum of money into the hands of a bail bondsman beforehand.

Since pandering is virtually unheard of in this society of pimps and streetwalkers, there is no contact between pimps and the potential clients of their women. The prostitutes are entirely on their own with their "tricks" (clients). It would be impossible legally to arrest a pimp for merely being on the premises where a prostitute was soliciting unless either he were observed receiving money from her (that is, receiving the proceeds from prostitution, which they are careful to avoid), or unless she pointed him out to the arresting officer as her pimp and "signed a paper" to that effect in return for leniency, which rarely happens. Nevertheless, most pimps purposely don't follow their women around, not only to keep on the safe side, but also because they can't be bothered with the details of her working life. Their job is to prepare the woman for her nightly adventures; in the street she is on her own. It was difficult, therefore, to ascertain who belonged to whom at the beginning of the study. . . .

In any game, there must be rules and guidelines for the players. The Book is a body of tradition which contains the rules of The Game. Passed on to each new generation by word of mouth, it is the pimp's unwritten Bible. If The Book were ever written down and reduced to "commandments," the first five might look like this:

I. Man is the Lord God. He shall have dominion over women and control them; also, he shall stand with his fellow men against any bitch who puts herself before man.

II. Thou shalt have no other gods before money; for money buys affection, respect, and acceptance.

III. Thou shalt never fornicate in vain, without getting paid; for fair trade is no robbery.

IV. Thou shalt seek to avoid direct confrontation with thine enemy, and shalt trick or outwit him before resorting to violence.

V. Thou shalt not steal from thy friends. But thou shalt rob thine enemies blind. A man can't fool with the Golden Rule in a crowd that don't play fair. . . .

Essentially, The Book provides a blueprint for a male-dominated society and a rationale for wresting all control over males from women. Ironically, this condition is achieved by making woman's full-time occupation the control of men who are outside the subculture. . . . One of the basic mechanisms of control which the pimp must master in order to manage women is the discipline of his own libido. A retired pimp who was once very successful described the training required to become a pimp, that is, a "real man," in the following allegory: "Man goes out on the streets, some bitch comes up, rubs against him, he turns away. He goes out the second night some bitch rubs against him, he turns away. He goes out the third night and some bitch rubs against him and he turns away. He goes out the fourth night, he's a MAN."

⌐ A man is partially defined as one who can control a woman by mental dominance and also by physical force, if necessary, and one of the ways of gaining this control is to control one's own sexual desires. . . .

In other words, "A pimp keeps his dick in his pocket," which is a double entendre meaning (1) he controls his sexual desire, and (2) his dick is where the money is. The pimp has completely reversed the man-pursuing-woman game, which is characterized by the woman questioning the man to see if he has anything to offer *her*. . . .

There are seven principal spheres of male control: the training and guidance which a pimp provides for his woman as she becomes increasingly proficient at her trade, including setting her minimum acceptable earning per night; the maintenance of her proper role as a submissive woman by insisting on money in return for sex and affection, by insisting that she be an attentive handmaiden to his every demand, and by requiring that she show conspicuous respect for him and his friends in social situations and that she never divulge private information or behave in any way which might embarrass or show disloyalty to him; the ability to keep the peace in a stable of two or more women; the complete control of how the money is spent, what the woman's allowance is, how much will be saved and for what purpose or future goal; the decisions regarding where they will live and with whom (adults and children), and decisions about where and when his women might occasionally be sent to work outside The City (Las Vegas, Seattle, Denver, etc.); the decisions surrounding an arrest, such as which lawyer to use, which bail bondsman, how much money will be spent on the case, and whether to leave the ho sitting in jail or not; and finally, the decision whether to hire or fire a ho. . . .

According to the women, The Book says a pimp must never "chippy" (make love to a woman for the pleasure of it). Exchanging sex for money only was an ironclad rule of the earlier, orthodox version of The Book. By clinging to it the women are more conservative than the men in the face of cultural change. This is not surprising to the anthropologist, since conservatism among women is common in many societies undergoing change.

On this point the pimps are divided; some do chippy when the opportunity arises, and others never "give up any dick without being paid." . . .

If he is successful in finding a girl who wants to choose him, the pimp cements the new relationship by demanding his "choosin' money," a lump sum the woman gives him "to prove she is qualified." When a square broad is involved, the matter of "choosin' money" is especially crucial; it serves as her first major initiation ritual into The Life. Professional hos who are attracted to pimps know in advance that they cannot have sex with him unless their "money is right," and they sometimes banter about the size of the sum. "Choosin' money" is also a common topic of "high-sidin' " humor among the men. . . .

In his initial overtures to a new girl, a pimp must display absolute self-confidence and manly superiority, yet show enough interest in the girl that she doesn't think he is unattainable. The ideal pimp is a master conversationalist and psychologist who can analyze a woman's weaknesses and strengths in a short period of time, and can instantly devise a strategy tailormade to "catch" or "cop" her. . . .

"Applicants" are either square broads, women who have ho'd

before, or hos who are considering leaving their present pimp. A pimp may either turn a square broad out himself, or call upon the help of his bottom woman. Catching a square broad has its advantages and disadvantages. Chief among the disadvantages are the time and trouble it takes to acculturate her to The Life. But the advantages are very great; you don't have to undo the training of another pimp and correct the mistakes he made. . . .

⌣ Those who enter The Life already feel the whole world is against them. The Book provides them with a philosophy which neatly crystallizes this point of view, and gives them rules of behavior with which to fight back and perhaps win some of the battles. Everyone is a square outside The Life. A ho looks at all men as potential tricks or police until proven otherwise. A pimp views all women as having their price. Every friendly new face is suspected of being a con artist, informer, or a "po-lice." Life is viewed as a game in which one must get "them" before "they" get you. While The Book provides a daring offensive strategy against oppression and poverty, it most often leads to a self-destructive, self-defeating way of life from which few escape. . . .

The Life as part of the war against racism is a conscious idea in the mind of every informant, Black males and Black and White females. Their strategy is a wily one. Unlike the Black Panthers they say, "We do not put our heads in the lion's mouth; we just sneak around behind, cut off his balls, and take his wallet." . . .

The pimp or the player may be "bad" in that he ignores many rules of White and Black society, but his is a calculated "badness" which is highly respected. He values his own life and his own game, and is therefore predictable. He can be trusted not to blow his game, for he has disciplined himself to be "bad" in ways which contribute to his survival, not his self-destruction. . . .

[According to pimp philosophy, woman] embodies the principles of basic animal biology. She is by nature concerned with obtaining security for herself and her offspring, and with pleasing her man. Because part of her essence includes the role of mother she tends to be concerned with matters of basic sustenance (food, money, home life), and is therefore a natural provider.

In her pristine state, woman is only half of the completed unit. Without a man she is nothing. Her being is a vessel to nurture the thoughts and the seed which her man implants in her. Without his seed she cannot bear children, and without his Pygmalion-like efforts to shape her mind, she cannot be productive or happy. She is the natural student of man, who provides her with "direction." . . .

But woman's concern with security and rearing her children spills over into a tendency to want to dominate all men and make them her children also. However, man can resist her will to dominate by strength of mind and purpose and by sexual self-discipline. Because of the woman's basic child-bearing function, she is endowed with a much greater sexual drive than man's. Withholding sexual gratification from the female is therefore the male's trump card, which he can use to escape her domination and her desire to turn him into a child.

Although woman's natural state is to have a stronger sex drive than man, square mothers continually reverse this situation in their upbringing of children. They perpetuate the fiction that men are animals who are preoccupied with sex while women are pure and above the need for constant sexual gratification. They encourage naive girls to concentrate on obtaining a mate who will be a good provider and discourage them from forming strong sexual attractions. Square mothers also encourage their sons to regard women as sexual prizes to be treated with great deference and desire. Daughters are trained to be seductive, but only for the purpose of trading sex for a man's money and security, not for the pleasure of it. Therefore the pimps conclude that square mothers bring up their daughters to be hos and their sons to be tricks, thereby perpetuating the control of society by women. A bit later in the chapter we will explore this idea at greater length.

With both White and Black hos, the pimp exploits woman's natural drive for security for herself and her children (whether or not she has any) by keeping a money goal in the forefront of her mind. He also relies on her motherly capacity for self-sacrifice and high sex drive to motivate her further. Since all women are reflections of their men, he programs her behavior to be as lucrative as possible, while resisting her seductive domineering tendencies. In addition, much of the ho's wish to dominate and much of her sexual drive is dissipated by her mental and sexual exertions with tricks. The result is that she is always near mental and physical fatigue from maintaining dominance over her customers, and should be quite content to be docile and dominated by her man.

In an ideal, mythological state of nature, man and woman should function smoothly as a unit. Woman should please man, rear his children, help provide for them, and find her satisfaction in attaching herself to a man of great beauty and knowledge. Man should give direction and purpose to the woman, share love with her, and spend a great deal of time adorning his body and pursuing manly activities such as sports or the arts. He should not be expected to be the principal provider; it is enough that he gives the woman a reason to live and provides for her the meaning and structure of her universe.

But this ideal exists nowhere in the Western world, although several tribal peoples approximate it. Years ago, for instance, Margaret Mead reported on a Pacific people, the Tchambuli, whose men spend hours on their toilette each day and pursue artistic ceremonials, while the much drabber women work hard at fishing. Certain African cultures also approximate to the pimp's ideal. But in our own culture, where men and women have "forgotten" their essential natures, there is a constant battle of the sexes for the upper hand. Neither men nor women can be happy so long as this battle rages, since both cannot win a dominance contest. And if woman wins, she loses. . . .

Dominance-dependency games start, of course, with Momma. Most often the ho is called "Momma" affectionately by her man, and "baby" less frequently. She in turn calls him both "Daddy" and "baby," which is an indication of his dual role in relation to her. Several pimps asserted that pimping comes from Black men being supported by their mothers as kids and deciding to continue the arrangement. If Momma cannot be coerced into providing for the adolescent boy, he goes out and finds another lady who can be more easily dominated. Pimping therefore contains elements of a rebellion of the son against his mother, as well as attempts to continue aspects of her sustaining role with another lady.

Most pimps, however, believe they were raised by their mothers not to be pimps, but to be tricks. "Trick marriage" is seen by the pimps as a man's servitude to women in exchange for "her pussy." That this so-called normal and moral marriage is aberrant is proved to pimps by the many husbands who pay hos for sex they cannot get at home, which they point to as the final degradation of the American male under the heel of the almighty bitchy American wife. She not only doesn't give him what he is paying her for, but forces him to go out and also pay some other woman if he wants sex. Often he pays another woman only to have a shoulder to cry on, because the wife loses respect for a man she can dominate and is unhappy in her unnatural, unwomanly role as boss. Consequently, the man is miserable and in great need of feminine sympathy, even if it has to be bought and paid for.

The square wife who puts herself morally above a ho is therefore the object of great disdain, because she has never proved her love by complete self-sacrifice. Although merely hoing for a pimp is not enough to win his respect, personal qualities in a straight broad are not enough to merit respect either; she must ho for him as well. If she will not, then he must conclude, according to the pimp's world view, that she is trying to make him her trick, which is of course intolerable. There are only pimps and tricks in the world, and pimp lore is full of warning tales about the pimp who "got his nose opened by some square broad" and lost his entire fortune by becoming her trick. . . .

History is alive to Black pimps and its "reversal" is their deepest desire. This is one reason why Black pimps are so hated by Whitey and applauded by some Blacks: they *have* "reversed history." They dominate Black and White women ("White slavery"), they profit financially from Whitey's "slaving" because they get a part of his paycheck through their prostitutes, and they have the *compliance* of White women in putting down White men. They feel therefore that they have undermined the White man's family structure and robbed him of the respect of the women of his own race; they have also won back the respect of their own women by "putting down" the powerful White man. One major flaw in this viewpoint is that Whitey is still powerful enough to crush any pimp for life. This realization is the basis of the essentially revolutionary cry of the traditional "Pimp or die," which is akin in fervor to "Give me liberty or give me death."

But the pimp is not an organized revolutionary; he is an individual one. Boss players who thoroughly embrace their personal revolutions seek to become so respectable that Whitey can't touch their game; they intend to "pimp and live." The boss player doesn't want a fantasy of being "top dog"; he really believes that he is destined to *be* a "top dog," whereas the simple pimp believes "every underdog has his day" and when it's over, it's over. What else can an underdog expect but a moment of glory? The boss player wants that moment to last a lifetime. His new use of the Player's Book for *transcending* pimping reflects a trend in Black culture as a whole towards greater hopefulness that manly behavior will not always result in defeat, incarceration, or death. . . .

Many players say, "You must *hate* to be a pimp," even a sweet pimp. Tenderloin Tim once replied, with a big friendly grin on his face, when asked why he pimped, "I get a sadistic thrill out of getting women to sell pussy for me." In this matter the sometimes clownish Black pimp, with all his theatricality and entertaining wit, is not joking at all. Many pimps do have hatred for all women and for Whitey as well. . . .

One ho known as Birthday Cake said she worked for a pimp for four years, gave him a new Cadillac every year, and one night came home from work with her money "funny" and got the beating of her life. She walked in and handed over her money; he counted it and said, "That's all right, honey," drew her a bath, laid her down afterwards on the bed, went to the closet and got a tire iron and beat her senseless with it. She showed us the long scars which required hundreds of stitches and demonstrated her permanent slight limp. Horrifying as this seems, it should be noted that Birthday Cake continues to find herself with men who specialize in physical punishment, and often tells hair-raising stories about such incidents with a matter-of-fact "ain't I soulful" air. The other girls like her and listen politely to her stories, although they think "she crazy." . . .

(Every American major institution, from the law courts and the business Establishment to the Armed Services, is viewed by the players as a pimping situation. They see society itself as a network of people gaming off each other for money, power, or some kind of ego-gratification. The preacher is a pimp gaming off his congregation, the politician is a pimp gaming off his constituents, the law-enforcement system pimps the lawbreakers, the wife is a ho gaming off her husband who is her trick, the employer games off his workers, the Whites pimp the Blacks, and the federal government pimps everybody!) This view, widely held throughout the ghetto, has recently found expression in the writings of Black militants and is one of the few areas in which pimps and Panthers seem to be in perfect agreement.

The player conceives of himself as a small businessman within the capitalist tradition of free enterprise and considers himself to be no more corrupt in his methods than the legitimate businessman trying to get ahead in a ruthless, competitive, materialistic economy.

"J," "The Life"
(Interview and Editing
by Kate Millett)

The way that I got into it was like this. I was just broke and I had never liked to be in debt to anyone. I have a thing about it—being in debt. I've never liked to be financially dependent on anyone. I've always had this thing. What happened was I borrowed ten dollars from someone, and then I realized, after I borrowed it, that I couldn't pay it back. I had no way of knowing that I'd ever be able to pay it back—it was a man that I'd slept with too. So that's how I got into it. I just decided fuck it, man, I'm not going to be poor any more. I'd never been poor and I wasn't used to it. . . .

So I just went on the street. The thing that broke the ice had actually happened years before at a concert of Miles Davis. Davis was playing in a club, and someone outside wanted to take me. You know, asked me if I wanted to go in. And I knew that if I went in with him I'd have to sleep with him. But I figured it was worth it; I wanted to see Miles Davis. I had no feeling for this guy; I just wanted the ticket to get in there. I realized I'd whored—there was no way of denying the truth to myself. So when the time came a few years later and I was absolutely broke, I was ready.

I had talked to somebody and gotten a connection. I was living in an S.R.O.* over on Ninety-fifth Street, and there was this woman and one night she came down the hall and she said, "I'm going out hustling tonight." I couldn't have started by myself if I hadn't had a connection. And you make connections very fast if you're into it or want to get into it. She said she'd take me out and show me what to do, how to watch out for the cops, everything.

* Single room occupancy.

135

I didn't know I'd make really good money. But she told me to ask for fifteen dollars, "take ten dollars if you have to, and if you're really broke, go down to seven dollars." So I started off kinda slow, down Seventy-second Street, in high heels, and I must have looked inexperienced because no one made an offer. I walked until four in the morning and ended up in a coffee shop, exhausted. I'd walked all the way from Ninety-fifth Street down to Seventy-second. . . .

Then I felt I ought to go back on the street and make some money. I'd gotten all dressed up and I had decided to do it. So I started to walk back. This guy came up in a gray car, and I got in. I was a little scared getting in the car. I didn't know what he would do. I think I brought him back to my place, and I think he offered me ten dollars. I might have asked for fifteen dollars. I don't remember how it went down. But he was very nice. . . .

I can never remember one job from another, but I do remember the first two. They all merge in a gray mass. . . .

There are guys who come back time and time again because they can't afford to keep a call girl. They can only afford the ten or twenty dollars a week, so they come back because they can't afford anything else. I don't think they want all that, you know, a mistress. It becomes like a business relationship, time after time—a relationship like you might have with someone at the corner grocery.

There was one guy who wanted to pay me to beat him. It turns me on just to talk about it. I never thought I wanted to beat somebody, but when I did it, I felt I really liked it. I learned something that way—I learned that I really got pleasure from it. It wasn't sexy —it was not a sexual excitement at all. I guess I was getting back at all the men who'd done me wrong. I never get sexually excited in any relationship with a john. I've never made love with another woman. Now I guess I'm sort of neuter. I don't have sexual relationships now with anyone. . . .

If you're on the street you have to take anybody who comes along, no matter what they look like—as long as they are reasonably clean. I didn't walk the street after that first time. I don't have to take just anybody. And if someone asks me to do something I don't want to do, I can refuse. I can refuse anybody because there were so many people. New York is crawling with johns. And, what's very important, I wasn't dependent on any one man.

I was always scared to get into a car with somebody. I knew, second or third hand, of women who have been hurt by sadists, but

I never got that kind. And I've seen women with marks and bruises that they got from their pimps. But I never knew anyone who was beaten up by a john. Of course it's different on the street. On the street you take anybody. On the street it's anything and anybody and, to a certain extent, whatever his sickness is, you're at his mercy. . . .

When prostitutes put down other women, women like housewives, it's really only out of self-defense. Prostitutes feel that housewives are very moralistic people who even know that their husbands are cheating on them. While they're cheating on them they're seeing us. We're really not a threat to them; not at all. I wouldn't mind if I had a husband who went to see a whore. It wouldn't bother me. But then, if he had an affair with somebody, that would bother me —if he loved someone, if he got involved, then that would be a threat. The difference between being a prostitute and being a wife is the security a wife's got. But it's also the difference in having a lot of men versus having just one. If you have a lot of men—like if you have ten a day—then you're not dependent on any one of them. They can always be replaced; if one of them gives you trouble, you can just say "fuck you." But you can't do that if you're married and you can't do that if you're being kept. . . .

A lot of them wondered—they want to take you out to dinner, want to talk to you; they wanted to mimic the behavior of lovers. Maybe that's what they want. Some of them really do want that— to be lovers. They fall in love with you. That's very hard to take. I never liked that. Because that was crossing the boundary—it wasn't business any more. And this was business; it wasn't love.

Johns are full of self-pity. They come on with this line about their wife doesn't understand them, and we follow right along with it. Or they turn us on to being good sports. And, you know, that made me feel great—that they'd say I was a good sport. They make you feel for a moment that you're somebody special, not a whore. When they would tell me I was special, I wanted to say; "Baby, I'm just a plain whore. Forget that crap." And the old line about "How could a nice girl like you get into a business like this?" That's really said a lot. It's said a lot, especially by people who seem educated or middle class. And then sometimes they tell you that you aren't really a whore. I had a guy who I was seeing—about a month ago—I actually couldn't take it any longer. I saw him every week or every two weeks; he gave me a lot of money. Every time

I saw him he gave me about sixty dollars, and I would see him for about an hour. He was a very, very old guy—about sixty-seven. He was in love with me, and he would keep telling me, "You're not a whore." He was so hung up. Poor man. You have to feel sorry for someone who's that screwed up.

Johns go into this whole thing like, "I want to leave her, but if I divorce her, she'll take all my money." And they come on screaming and yelling about their alimony. I don't believe in alimony, but I certainly believe in child support. When you look into it, that's usually all they're paying, if that. And the wife, who's stuck taking care of the children, is doing him a service. In waiting on the child she's doing his work too because a child is something between two people.

You wouldn't have prostitution in a utopia. But you might still have it somewhere halfway between what we have now and a utopia. Prostitution might even, in a certain sense, be a reasonable service to be sold—sexual attention. But as it is now, I see it as a symptom, a symptom of the kind of sex we have here now. I think as long as you're going to have compulsive marriage and compulsive families, I think you're going to have prostitution. If I had a husband who wanted variety, it would be better if he had prostitutes than lovers. That's my hangup: I'm very possessive. I have this demanding possessiveness and insecurity. I wish I weren't so hung up on monogamy myself; I think it's idiocy. Monogamy and prostitution go together. There are lonely women all over New York, women sitting in bars, who would go with a guy, take him back to their place, make it with him, treat him well too—and be glad to do it. But instead men go to prostitutes on Seventh Avenue, Fifty-Seventh Street, and Broadway, because there are no strings attached to a whore. And if you're married, that's a consideration. There isn't even that much chance that she'll be clean if she's from the street. But there are no strings attached.

I don't know why they go with girls from the street, unless they don't have connections. And there's always the chance of getting rolled. I really don't know why they go to the street. I think that it must be because there is nothing asked of them, even so far as spending the night. And then there are no games. You don't have to play seduction or anything. It's right on the table. And if they're worried about their masculinity, well, they're taking a chance with a girl if she's going for free. You don't know if she'll let you get laid or not.

You might have to go through a lot of changes to get laid. And you might have to spend money and spend time. And a prostitute can't say, "Well, I don't suck," whereas another woman might. She's got to do what he says or the deal is off. A pickup doesn't have to. You make the deal with her when you pick her up, you may do it without even speaking of it. But if she's chicken, well, you lose the whole thing—the time and effort. But with a whore, there's no risk, no gamble. Somehow you always pay for what you get, one way or another.

But what they're buying, in a way, is power. You're supposed to please them. They can tell you what to do, and you're supposed to please them, follow orders. Even in the case of masochists who like to follow orders themselves, you're still following his order to give him orders. Prostitution not only puts down women, but it puts down sex—it really puts down sex. Often I really couldn't understand the customer, couldn't understand what he got out of this, because I really felt I was giving nothing. What he got was nothing. I could never see myself in his position, doing what he was doing. I would think it would be humiliating to buy a person, to have to offer somebody money. I felt the poor guy's gotta buy it; I felt sorry for him. He's really hard up. But then I remember he could be not so hard up as to have to buy, really; he wanted instead to have something so special you gotta buy it. I did not always see the gesture of buying someone as arrogance because I did not feel that controlled by the customer. I felt I was the boss because I could say no to the deal. I didn't want even the involvement of being a kept woman because then it's control again. When you're living with someone—when I was living with someone, that's when I really felt controlled. Then you can't refuse. People I've lived with, men I've lived with—I really felt that they had power because I couldn't say no to them. Because then I could lose them and, if I did, I would lose my whole life—lose my whole reason for living.

I felt freer of men as a prostitute than I would as a wife or a mistress or a beloved. Because he isn't there all the time—the john. Like for half an hour and that's all. And then someone else comes in. They really can't control you very much. You don't have the oppression that comes because you love the person and are so afraid of losing them. When you're a whore and somebody rejects you and says they want to see another girl, well, that's just part of the business. That's the reason he's coming to you in the first place—

because he wants variety. It's much safer to do it for money, much safer. . . .

I don't think you can ever eliminate the economic factor motivating women to prostitution. Even a call girl could never make as much in a straight job as she could at prostitution. All prostitutes are in it for the money. With most uptown call girls, the choice is not between starvation and life, but it is a choice between $5,000 and $25,000 or between $10,000 and $50,000. That's a pretty big choice: a pretty big difference. You can say that they're in this business because of the difference of $40,000 a year. A businessman would say so. Businessmen do things because of the difference of $40,000 a year. Call girls do go into capitalism and think like capitalists. But you can't say, even of the call girl, that she has so many other ways to earn an adequate living. Even with an undergraduate degree, chances are that she couldn't do better than earn $5,000 or $6,000 a year, outside of prostitution. Because it's very hard for women to earn an adequate living and so we do not have much economic choice—even the call girl. And the minority woman on the street—the poor woman—she has no choice at all.

For white women you usually can't say that there's no choice but prostitution. There is. But the choice itself is a choice between working for somebody else and going into business for yourself. Going into business for yourself and hoping to make a lot of money. There's that choice. Prostitution on those terms is a kind of laissez-faire capitalism. But it's also slavery, psychologically. And it's also feudalism, where the protection of a pimp is offered in return for services. Unless you're starving so bad you literally have no choice —as some women do—the choice is between a lower-middle income and a really good one, lots of money. Lots of whores are on junk: it's expensive. A junkie has very little choice. For the junkie the only choice is getting off junk, a tough thing to do. Then too, a junkie off junk wouldn't be a junkie anymore. Prostitution is a kind of addiction too. It's an addiction to money. I felt that.

The worst part about prostitution is that you're obliged not to sell sex only, but your humanity. That's the worst part of it: that what you're selling is your human dignity. Not really so much in bed, but in accepting the agreement—in becoming a bought person. When I really felt like a whore was when I had to talk to them, fucking up to them really while only talking. That's why I don't like to go out to dinner and why I don't like to spend the night. . . .

That's when I really felt that I was a whore. That's the most humiliating thing—having to agree with them all the time because you're bought.

That's why it's not as easy as just saying "prostitution is selling a service." That's why it's selling your soul and not selling a service. In business people sell their souls too, and that's why business destroys people—how would you feel about selling encyclopedias to poor people? But there's a special indignity in prostitution, as if sex were dirty and men can only enjoy it with someone low. It involves a type of contempt, a kind of disdain, and a kind of triumph over another human being. Guys who can't get it up with their wives can do it with whores. They have to pay for it. For some of them, *paying* for it is very important.

But a lot of them didn't make me feel degraded. Most of them didn't. If they had, I wouldn't have stayed. . . .

And they've got to use all the words—all the words they can't say to their wives, covering you with the language of their shame. And their anger. That was another thing I didn't like either. When you're doing prostitution—if only in order to cope—you've got to have tremendous defenses. You've just gotta turn off, somehow. Drugs or will power, you've got to cut yourself off.

I think that the conviction that females are dirty, that their genitals are dirty, really sticks to us. I think that's why I don't like men to go down on me. Because I think I'm dirty. I just don't like it because I think I must be dirty—and I think they're not. . . .

Here I go, thinking about all the things I don't like. And now I'm really getting into it. I know I didn't like it and I don't want to get into it again. One of the worst things about it was the faking. You had to fake orgasm. They expect it because that proves their masculinity. That's one of the worst things about it. That's really being a whore, being so dishonest. I don't know how they believe it—johns. Some of the ones I've had were even bachelors—good-looking guys with a lot of money, eligible young men. Very good-looking with a lot of money, didn't want to marry, wanted to go to whores. They had a tremendous fear of getting involved because that's giving something. . . .

I think the worst thing about prostitution was the way it spoiled my relationship with men. It's very hard to be common property like that, hard to find a man who'll put up with it. They either want you to quit or they want to take all your money, and there're very few men who don't fall into either one of those categories. Most of the ones I'd like would want me to quit. The other ones want my money. The only exceptions I've been able to find are gangsters. And the guys who want you to quit, they want you to be true, like they feel you're cheating if you're whoring. Very few men will understand that when a woman screws for money, she has no involvement at all. Yet they can just go out and get laid and feel no involvement. But they don't understand how you can do it for money and feel nothing. They think you're cheating and they can't take that. And the guy who wants you to quit: he's seeing you as property; he's changing you, from like currency, which passes from hand to hand, to something like real estate. *Real* property. There's an *owning* thing about wanting you to quit, especially if the guy is poor.

And I don't want to be kept. I don't care how much I love somebody, I don't want to be kept. Because anyone who keeps me has power over me. To ask someone for money to buy something, that would be so demeaning. I couldn't do that. I'll tell you what it is with the money and not wanting to be kept. If I loved someone and were dependent emotionally, then to be economically dependent too would be terrible. At least let me be financially independent because I'm so dependent emotionally. I have a tremendous thing about this; I had it with my parents too. I'm getting a little better about it with them. Because I feel so helplessly at someone's mercy.

Yet dating, for example, I found so much more humiliating. It's the same thing as prostitution—they're buying you, but they're doing it indirectly. And we're all pretending that this isn't happening. You see I can't pretend. Because I know what it's about; that's why I can't do it.

Men think that sex once is sex always, on demand. If you go out with them and make it, you're their thing. Maybe you haven't got laid in six months, but they don't consider that. It's a terrible disappointment. I feel like sleeping with somebody sometime. Then he turns out to be a real son of a bitch—like he'll introduce me to friends. His friends I don't feel like sleeping with; I just want to say "fuck off." But the friend is so sure he's going to get laid because you slept with his pal—as if they felt they could loan us or "fix us up." And if you don't put out, they call you a lesbian or else they'll say, "Are you prejudiced because I'm black?" You're getting cornered all the time. But when you whore, at least you're getting something back—you're getting cash. So in a sense whoring is less oppressive. And with the cash you can do anything that you want to. Cash—you can get it from a southern racist and give it to the Black Panthers; you can do what you want to with it. With the dinner and the date, what can you do? Just get fat. And they force you to eat a lot or drink too much so they can lay you.

I would so much rather turn a trick with somebody than go out on a date. Turning a trick is not anxiety-producing. But going out on a date, I just freak out. Of course, on a date you may kid yourself that it's your personality they like. But when you're whoring, it's sometimes your personality they like too. There's one guy who . . . gives me ten dollars just to talk to me. . . .

When I think, how did the john get the money he pays me? By exploiting another woman—a secretary, or someone like that, a wife. The boss is likely to sleep with his secretary on the side. She's doing it for nothing and that's really horrible. Secretaries and women in sweat shops—places like that—are put in the position where they feel that if they don't put out, they'll lose their job.

I don't feel that I'm a whore now, but the social stigma attached to prostitution is a very powerful thing. It makes a kind of total state out of prostitution so that the whore is always a whore. It's as if— you did it once, you become it. This makes it very easy for people to get locked into it. It's very hard to get married; then too, most of the people who do it are not that well educated, not that many of them could do any other job. You get locked into it simply because you get hooked on luxuries. You can get hooked on consumerism, or even just on living decently. You can get hooked on a certain kind of freedom, where you can go where you want to without being beholden to someone who supports you. For me prostitution didn't even offer good hours 'cause I had this work hangup. I worked about twenty-four hours a day—I was into making so much money— obsessive about it. I can also see how people could be trapped in it because it's so hard for them literally, objectively so difficult to do anything else, let alone to do as well economically.

But however underpaid a woman factory worker or a typist may be, she still has something the whore doesn't have. Even I wanted to have a legitimate front. I had to do something else too. Lots of call girls have done secretarial work from time to time. I don't put women down who have straight jobs. I wanted a straight job more than anything and I'm going into a straight job. I'm not going to make any more money. I may even, as an intern, make less than the average secretary and a great deal less than I made when I was in the life. Yet I'm looking forward to it. Because you are selling a *lot* when you are being a whore. You're giving up a lot. One thing you're giving up is a chance to have a normal relationship with a man.

As a prostitute you're alienated, isolated even, not only from yourself but from the rest of society because you can't talk to people about it. And when I was doing it, I only had friends that I could tell about it, people in the life. For the power of straight society to oppress prostitutes—for that to—disappear—prostitution has to be legalized. Right now you can't even tell people because of the law. And the cops are very scary, very hard to spot. Ugliest bastards in the world driving around in old Plymouths. They are frightening because they can pick you up. If you were able to tell people, that that's what you do, if it weren't assumed that that's what you're always going to do, you would be able to leave it and do something else. Imprisoned in it—you shouldn't be imprisoned in it all the rest of your life. Having done it now prevents you from doing anything else in the future. . . . Yet you ought to be able to go straight whenever you want to.

Funny—that expression, "go straight"—same expression that's used for gay people. I wonder what's the opposite of going straight. Crooked? I wonder what is synonymous with going straight—being perfect, I guess. It's funny that both those worlds should use that expression. The underworld too—"going straight." All three groups are outsiders.

If you tell me that being in the life is beating yourself up psychologically, I can't help but resent that. Because psychologically I've suffered so much more in other situations, been humiliated much more in other situations. I think the money had a lot to do with my feeling freer. I didn't feel I was taking nearly so much shit when I was in the life as I do now that I am a teaching assistant. As a teaching assistant I am really put down and I don't make nearly as much money. True, it carries a certain social status that's a lot higher than that of a prostitute, but you pay for it, you really pay for it. I worked long hours for little money and I took shit. I was in tears so much more in graduate school, infuriated and sick. I didn't get an ulcer when I was a prostitute. That happened when I was in graduate school.

And I'll tell you, I have not cried nearly as much being a prostitute as I have being a student. It's different somehow. When I was a prostitute it wasn't me somehow. I didn't get put down in the same way. I didn't feel it as much. You just don't get that put down in the same way. Maybe because you're down so far, you just can't get put down any further when you're a prostitute. The street is the street and you expect nothing from it. The academic world I did expect something from. You're always defensive with johns. You never invest your ego with them. But I did with the university. After all, this was going to be my profession. The university was going to be my way out from the street—from being a prostitute. What a disappointment. School just doesn't have to be that way—they just don't have to humiliate you that way. They should just treat you with respect, for God's sake. All I want is respect, for God's sake. I don't want unconditional love, just respect.

As for me, I feel better about being a prostitute than being married to somebody I can't stand and being locked into that. If I were the slave of a pimp and getting beat up all the time, I would see that not as prostitution but as another kind of marriage. It's very hard to find a prostitute who hasn't got a pimp, and so I'm not really representative of prostitutes. I not only didn't have a pimp, but my education also makes me unrepresentative. . . .

I'm terribly messed up as far as sex is concerned—that's why I could become a prostitute. I've always been messed up as far as sex is concerned. Now I don't relate to men at all. It's easy to go along with what most people say about prostitution 'cause they read it all in a book. But I'm not going to say it's true unless I feel it. And I do hate prostitution—I do hate it. That's why I'm not doing it now. I spent all these years in school just to get out of it. If I liked it I'd be there now. At the time I was so numb that I felt nothing. I hate it now because now I feel. I just can't stand it now when people touch me. I just can't stand being put there. Here I've had all these years of education and I should still have to do this and I'm still expected to put out. And now it's for a lousy dinner. Even with my Ph.D. Now I hate it but I won't project about how I felt about it then or failed to feel. I did, I must have hated it then. But I wasn't aware of it or I couldn't admit it. I think I'm getting better now, now that I realize that I hated it so much. But now I'm getting so I hate men. I'm getting so that I avoid men. What I am is I'm becoming aware of how much I always hated it. And I know now how it has ruined all my relationships with men. We are so afraid to say that we hate men. So the prostitute finds a pimp and says this is the one man I can love. And he treats her like dirt. I've become aware of hating men, and I've been afraid to say it for a long time. I'm becoming aware of how the whole experience just freaked me out. They put you down for what they have made of you. I learned this lesson too well—first when I got put down in school, then you get put down for having done prostitution so you learn the lesson all over again. Say you come out and do it honestly and sell yourself for money. And then you're put down for that.

When I became a prostitute I didn't feel my will being broken. To become a prostitute was just the easiest thing in the world—I was ready for it. Because sex had never meant much to me at all. So I could make money with it; might as well use it for that. Most of the time it just didn't mean anything at all: I guess that's what made me ready. And that didn't change when I was in the life. I felt nothing, a lack of feeling in sex. Except with special people. And with the special people there was this terrible emotional dependency which is really the way a prostitute is—although she doesn't feel anything when she's out hustling. And they're just hung up and depend on their pimp—so I was into that. That I could screw all kinds of guys and not care. Screw. Maybe get screwed by is the right word.

Long before I got into prostitution I would go to bed with guys, because I thought I owed it to them, because I'd "led them on" or some bullshit. I let them con me into that. And when that happens you just lay back and say "Okay, I got myself into this. Go ahead, I don't care—do it. Go ahead, do your thing." Passive. Even being passive is a way of resisting. It says, yes, you can have my body, but you won't get me excited. Neither angry nor sexually excited. The scary thing about it is the way I put myself out, asleep inside. Now if you're actually making love to a guy you get tired, use up energy. But if you're passive as I was, you use up little, you suppress it all. When I was a whore I never got tired, never exerted myself.

I could anesthetize myself so that I didn't suffer that much. But a lot of whores can't. They're really in conflict all the time. . . . I didn't have a pimp. To organize prostitutes the hardest thing about it will be to get around the pimp. You're gonna have the pimp down on you; after all, his livelihood and his interests are threatened. . . .

Pimps really do nothing. They don't get you dates. They provide no service at all and do nothing at all all day. They gamble, they drink, they beat you up. They ride around in them Cadillacs. They look pretty. They stink from perfume. Pimps don't do a damn thing for you. They spend all your money. That's what they do for you. They'll bail you out of jail only 'cause you're their money. But you can bail yourself out of jail and you can keep your own money. You don't need a pimp. . . .

I may have hated prostitution but I had the *right* to do it. I don't like people telling me not to do it. Gets me mad, when they tell me not to do it—that I'm too good for it and so on and so forth. I feel that's a "superior" kind of attitude, morally superior. I get very tired of the people with that "healthy" nonsense—the argument that prostitution's not psychologically healthy. They have a double standard about prostitution, you know. I could be doing all kinds of self-destructive things and they wouldn't mind. They wouldn't criticize me for self-destructiveness if I were just as compliant or masochistic outside of prostitution, as a girl friend or wife. I could be doing much worse things to myself, and they would approve. When they tell me, "You shouldn't do it, it's bad for you." I hear, "You shouldn't do it, it's bad." And I hear them saying, "I'm superior, what a wonderful person I am to speak to you and lift you up, you fallen woman."

I like to believe I have some kind of free choice. Some choice in my life. That I chose a lesser evil. I wanted to do it. And somehow I want that to be respected. I wanted to do that. Somehow their pity deprives me of my freedom of choice. I don't want to be saved; saved by the Christians or saved by the shrink. Whatever the rationale is, it's the same: condescending, patronizing. Something in me just resents this moralism, their uplifting. I'd like so much to have the illusion that I had some freedom of choice. Maybe it's just an illusion, but I need to think I had some freedom. Yet then I realize how much was determined in the way I got into prostitution, how determined my life had been, how fucked over I was to have no confidence in myself. But I had to get myself out of it somehow. So I believed I'd chosen it. What's most terrifying is to look back, to realize what I went through and that I endured it.

When I look back on prostitution, I have so much ambivalence. I'm not even sure how I feel about it. It's not all negative. In remembering it, I was so afraid to come off with the ready answers the shrink had demanded. It's really more complex. So there was much that I denied, because it was only too painful to remember. Also I had seen how much conformity there was in the therapist's way of regarding it so I resisted that kind of pat answer. I denied at first what I can remember feeling—how in the beginning I just hated the men, just wanted them to stop touching me. To just get away.

IV
Male Homosexuality

Like any other area of human life, homosexuality is in large part a matter of definition. Put plainly and simply, there is no possible definition of who is a homosexual, or even what is homosexual behavior, that will satisfy everyone. It is more fruitful to examine different *dimensions* of homosexuality—dimensions which are often, but not necessarily, found together. Past observers have attempted to attach a precise label to specific people and specific acts, thinking that they could be unambiguously classified as *either* homosexual *or* heterosexual. Anna Freud—Sigmund Freud's illustrious daughter—wrote that the ultimate criterion of sexual orientation was the sex of one's masturbatory fantasies. While this might be one of a number of useful criteria, we would like to suggest something quite different.

First: that there is no such thing as a "homosexual."

And second: that there is no such thing, strictly speaking, as "homosexual behavior."

By these statements I do not mean that homosexuals and homosexuality do not exist.

Merely that who and what falls into these categories is arbitrary, not absolute, fixed, or final.

That such categorizing depends on selecting specific criteria for defining people and their behavior.

That these criteria cannot be justified scientifically—they can only be justified according to what one or another observer considers important.

That the nature of one's sexual commitment changes over time, sometimes drastically.

That there are many dimensions of homosexuality; most people

149

will be classified as "homosexual" according to some of them, but not according to others.

And lastly: that homosexuality is a matter of *degree*. There is a *spectrum* from complete homosexuality, through mixed homosexuality, to complete heterosexuality. The two polar types are rare; most of us fall in between them.

Let's look at a few examples to show what we mean.

A young man is unhappily married, and has intercourse with his wife only two or three times a month. But several times a week he visits public urinals knowing that other men will be there who will fellate, or "blow" him. He also masturbates regularly, but always fantasizes intercourse with women when he does. He has no friends who consider themselves homosexuals, is not part of a homosexual subculture, and does not think of himself as a homosexual. While most of his behavior would be technically classified as homosexual in nature, by no other criteria can he be considered a homosexual. Perhaps in time he will have an extramarital heterosexual affair. Perhaps he and his wife will eventually divorce. But right now, his *identity* is heterosexual, his *subcultural involvement* is heterosexual, his *masturbatory fantasies* are heterosexual—but his *behavior* is predominantly homosexual. Is he a homosexual? That depends on how you want to define it.

An adolescent boy is thought by his peers to be effeminate—a "pansy," a "fruit." The boy thinks that he is, perhaps, a homosexual. He begins to frequent homosexual bars. He is sexually excited by pictures, and even the thought, of handsome, muscular men. Yet, he has not, as yet, engaged in sexual behavior with another man; he has, however, had intercourse with two girls with whom he maintains a close emotional friendship. Is this boy a homosexual? Again, the only accurate answer that could possibly be given to this question is: it depends on what you mean. He is in some senses, but not in others.

A man has been in prison for several years. Prior to his imprisonment, he had intercourse only with women. As a prisoner, he is engaged in a long-term liaison with a younger man. Our man is the "active" partner—that is, he is fellated by the other man, and he inserts his penis into the other man's anus in intercourse. He does not assume the "passive" part in intercourse, ever. Our man thinks of his behavior as masculine—and of the behavior of the other man as feminine. The other man agrees. Among fellow inmates, our man is considered supremely masculine, not by any means a homosexual.

Now, his behavior is technically homosexual in the sense that it involves organ contact with a member of the same sex. But it isn't homosexual in the sense that it isn't *regarded* as homosexual by anyone in the social group in which it takes place. The behavior of the "passive" partner in this alliance, the man who is the object of sexual contact, *is* thought to be homosexual. Those of us outside the prison community would think of *both* as homosexual. Prisoners wouldn't agree. Which is it? Is our man engaging in "homosexual behavior" or not? Again, it's a question of perspective, not a solid, indisputable fact.

Alfred Kinsey, in his *Sexual Behavior in the Human Male*, first published in 1948, took a giant step in this area by looking upon sexual orientation as a *continuum*. He devised a "heterosexual-homosexual rating scale," which classified men from 0 to 6 in their degree of being one or the other. This scale was based on: (1) "physical contacts which result in erotic arousal or orgasm," and (2) "psychic response." The 0s were exclusively heterosexual, and 6s were exclusively homosexual, and the 1s through 5s were, in varying degrees, in between. Commenting on the scale, Kinsey wrote:

> Males do not represent two discrete populations, heterosexual and homosexual. The world is not to be divided into sheep and goats. Not all things are black nor all things white. It is a fundamental of taxonomy that nature rarely deals with discrete categories. Only the human mind invents categories and tries to force facts into pigeonholes. The living world is a continuum in each and every one of its aspects. The sooner we learn this concerning human sexual behavior the sooner we shall reach a sound understanding of the realities of sex.

One of the most often cited statistics in the social science literature is from Kinsey's research: over one-third, or 37 percent, of all American males have at least one homosexual episode which results in orgasm from the onset of adolescence to old age. In addition, about 60 percent of all preadolescent boys engage in some sort of homosexual activity. About 6 percent of the total of all of Kinsey's subjects' orgasms were derived from homosexual contact. About four males in one hundred could be regarded as exclusively homosexual—they had never had any sexual contact with women, and were not aroused by them. About 50 percent of the sample were exclusively heterosexual: they had never had any sexual contact at all with another man, and had never been aroused by one. Clearly, *most* men with some homosexual contact had had very little of it; most of it was adolescent experimentation, it took place very infrequently, and was discontinued fairly soon after its inception. Only about one man in eight (13 percent) had engaged in more homosexual contact than heterosexual—that is, were 3s, 4s, 5s, and 6s on Kinsey's rating scale.

Although Kinsey's research and analysis represented a considerable advance over the literature prior to 1948, today we realize that the situation is even more complex than his scheme allows. To begin with, Kinsey did not consider *self-identity* as a crucial dimension of homosexuality. How a man defines his own gender preference has an enormous impact on his behavior, his sense of ease with his life, his social relations with others, what he thinks, how he feels, his experiences both internal and external. This is not to say that a man who *doesn't think* he is a homosexual, but who is in all other respects, *therefore isn't a homosexual*. All it means is that this particular dimension is lacking in his makeup. *In the sense of self-identity,* he isn't a homosexual; in other respects, he may be. If we fail to consider this dimension, our analysis is necessarily shallow and incomplete.

A second crucial dimension any careful observer of the sexual scene must consider is *subcultural involvement*. This means association with others who are homosexuals—who consider themselves as such, and who practice homosexual behavior. Subcultural involvement refers to one's immersion in a specific social "scene." Like any category of humanity, homosexuals do not form a tightly knit group —but they are a kind of group nonetheless, a "quasi group," or a "near group." Think of any social category: policemen, the very rich, marijuana smokers, bird watchers, people with red hair, Quakers, residents of Chicago. Some of these categories will form the basis for group cohesion; others will not. In speaking of a group or a subculture, we mean that: (a) its members interact with one another more frequently and more intimately than they do with members of other social categories; (b) its members' way of life, and their beliefs, are somewhat different from members of other social categories; (c) its members think of themselves as belonging to a specific group, and they are so defined by those who do not share this trait. In these three senses, then, homosexuals do form a subculture, or group. *But not all men who practice homosexual behavior are involved in the subculture.* In fact, men are *differentially* involved, some almost to the complete exclusion of "straight" people, others absolutely not at all. The degree to which a given man who practices homosexual behavior is involved in and with the homosexual subculture determines many crucial facets of his life, both sexual and nonsexual. To ignore this dimension would be suicidal.

A third crucial dimension of homosexuality often lacking in past analyses is the subjective *meaning* which both participants and nonparticipants attach to behavior, people, and roles people play. By "subjective meaning," I mean simply *whether or not homosexuality is considered part of what's going on*. This isn't dictated by the formal properties of what people are or do; it grows out of certain definitions and judgments which vary from place to place, from time to time. Recall the prisoner we discussed a few pages back: what he did was not considered "homosexuality" by him, by his partner, or by his fellow prisoners. The same goes for our married man who engages in transitory, easily available same-sex oral-genital contact in public lavatories. If these two men were asked, "Have you ever engaged in homosexual behavior?", each would probably answer in the negative. Many young men "hustle" homosexuals for money. They allow themselves to be fellated, but they never reciprocate. They do this only if they are paid, and they maintain a rigid emotional barrier between themselves and the men who fellate them. To break any of these rules would threaten their masculinity, and invite being defined as a homosexual. But within the boundaries of what they do, they do not see their behavior as homosexual. Most have girl friends and eventually drift out of hustling to get married.

In short, technically homosexual behavior—that is, genital contact to the point of orgasm—does not necessarily entail the *subjective meaning* of homosexuality for all involved. We may not all agree on what we see as "homosexual behavior"; conceptions as to what constitutes homosexuality follow different rules. And each perspective has to be examined separately, in its own right.

In order to make our investigation complete, it is necessary to look at *sexual preferences*. Now, it is never the case that everything is equal. No one is faced with the alternative of two sexual partners who are exactly the same except for gender. So we have to visualize gender preference as hypothetical rather than real. We all encounter many people during the course of our day, some of them men, and some women. How does it come to pass that we end up in bed with a member of one or the other sex? Is it because of *availability?* Men in prisons do not choose the gender of their partners; it is forced on them by circumstance. If they had the power of choice, many, perhaps most, would have intercourse with women, not men. It is relatively easy to find willing male sex partners in an urban center after a few minutes of "cruising" in the right place; talking women into bed is generally much more difficult. Many men *prefer* the sexual company of women, but don't want to be subject to the "hassle" it would entail. They end up having sex with men because men are far more readily available. On the other hand, many men prefer to abstain from sex altogether than have intercourse with other men. So we have a spectrum along the dimension of same-sex preference: from the *preferential* homosexual, the man who, in the face of almost unlimited options available, consistently chooses men over women; through the *situational* homosexual, who engages in same-sex intercourse only where women are not to be found, or where men are far more readily available than women; on over to the *confirmed heterosexual,* who prefers no sex to sex with men. Certainly sexual preferences—especially taking existing social context into account —comprises an absolutely crucial dimension of sexuality.

Also, *romantic preferences,* or the potential for becoming *emotionally* involved with men or women, should be considered in any definitional scheme. The ability to fall in love with someone of the same sex affectionately and sensually must be counted as one out of a number of ways of determining sexual orientation. Some men can be said to be *homoemotional.*

Likewise, the ability to be *turned on* physically is important: whether or not one becomes sexually *aroused* by men or by women has to be taken into account in constructing a complete picture of homosexuality. Men who are *homoerotic* are homosexual along this particular dimension. We agree with Anna Freud in this respect: the gender of the object of one's masturbatory fantasies, which fuel sexual excitement, is basic in deciding whether one is homosexual or heterosexual. But again, it is only one dimension out of a number of important dimensions.

And lastly, the public definition of one's sexual role and preference cannot be ignored when understanding the phenomenon of sexual orientation. This does not mean that if anyone else thinks you are a homosexual, therefore you are. But it does mean that being *labeled* as a homosexual will make a great deal of difference to your sexual life, and to your life in general, in a large number of ways.

The secret homosexual and the overt homosexual do not lead the same sorts of lives; likewise, the man who is falsely thought to be a homosexual by everyone in a community will not lead the same sort of life as the one who is correctly assumed to be "straight." By itself, the public labeling of our gender preference will have an impact on many other things we consider important. At the very least, it is crucial in influencing one's self-identity and definition. It is not, however, the whole story by itself.

Perhaps the main point to emerge out of this discussion is that *no single dimension of homosexuality alone determines a man's sexual orientation.* A man may be "a homosexual" in a number of *different* ways. And secondly: *these dimensions are not necessarily found together in the same person.* In other words, a given man may be a homosexual in one way, but not in another. Although these dimensions are *often* found together, and are generally correlated with one another, it doesn't *always* happen. We have to examine various *combinations* of characteristics, and the kind of consequences these combinations have for people's lives, both sexual and nonsexual. Too often, one or another of these dimensions has been ignored in the past, or one dimension has been reduced or absorbed into another, or has been thought absolutely and unequivocally to cause the other. Thinking this way is to think in simplified stereotypes. The real world is much more complex.

As with any other area of human sexuality, particularly sexual deviance, the debate on homosexuality can become rancorous and even hostile. We might have supposed that, after centuries of writings on homosexual behavior, some sort of consensus about its nature would be emerging. This appears not to be the case. Perhaps still the most vigorously contested question is whether or not homosexuality is *normal* or *abnormal*, an alternative life-style or a manifestation of psychic pathology, a viable form of behavior or a mental illness. On one side, taking the "pathology" position, are many—perhaps, even now, most—psychiatrists, other physicians, such as endocrinologists, some psychologists, and, of course, most of the public. On the other, we have younger psychiatrists, some other physicians, and most behavioral scientists—anthropologists, psychologists and sociologists principally. The second faction would hold to the "alternative life-style" notion.

Even the most rigid of the sexual pathologists makes a distinction between *exclusive,* or "obligatory," homosexuality (sometimes called *"true"* homosexuality), and episodic, temporary, or *situational* homosexuality. However, exactly where the line is drawn between these two groups isn't altogether clear. Irving Bieber, perhaps the foremost spokesman for the pathology position, and an author of the influential book *Homosexuality: A Psychoanalytic Study,* whose views are as exemplary of the pathology position as anyone's, stated: "An isolated homosexual experience doesn't define a man as homosexual; *but if he has one such experience every year, he would have to be considered homosexual"* (my emphasis; the quote is from the *Playboy* panel on homosexuality, published in April, 1971). This means that a heterosexually active male, *1* percent of whose experiences are homosexual, 99 percent of which are heterosexual, would be considered homosexual at least according to this view.

Writings on homosexuals have tended to focus more or less entirely on the man (or woman—although actually, far, far less has been written on the Lesbian than on the male homosexual) who chooses to remain a homosexual in the face of heterosexual options. A more or less equal desire for both sexes, usually referred to as bisexuality, or "ambisexuality," is not admitted as a possibility by most orthodox psychiatrists. They see the two categories as mutually exclusive.

The first premise of the pathologists is that obligatory homosexuality is the manifestation of a psychosexual *disorder,* equivalent to a disease. They do not say merely that *many* homosexuals are neurotic, or that homosexuals are *more likely* to be sick than heterosexuals. They say that exclusive homosexuality is *always* and *by definition* a sign of disordered sexuality.

Irving Bieber put it this way, in a debate with another psychiatrist before the American Psychiatric Association:

> The central question is: Is homosexuality a normal sexual variant, that develops like left-handedness does in some people, or does it represent some kind of disturbance in sexual development? There is no question in my mind: Every male homosexual goes through an initial stage of heterosexual development, and in all homosexuals, there has been a disturbance of normal heterosexual development, as a result of fears which produce anxieties and inhibitions of sexual function. His sexual adaptation is a substitutive adaptation.

Bieber goes on to make a medical, or pathology, analogy: *"What you have in a homosexual adult is a person whose heterosexual func-*

tion is crippled like the legs of a polio victim." While denying that homosexuality *is* a mental illness, Bieber claims that it is the *manifestation of a psychiatric disorder.* (Some may feel that the distinction is one of form rather than of substance.) In an interview with *Playboy,* as part of a panel of experts on homosexuality, Bieber states: "Heterosexuality is part of normal biosocial development, while homosexuality is *always* the result of a disordered sexual development. . . . It is not normal for a man to make love to a man. It doesn't disorder sexual development for two men to make love to each other. It is merely evidence that their sexuality is already disordered. . . . I should like to underscore the point that it isn't easy to sidetrack a male from a heterosexual destiny. It takes a lot of trauma. . . ."

Pathologists reject the idea that homosexuality is culturally defined, that it is acceptable in one place and "deviant" in another only because of the historical accident of culture. Homosexuality, Bieber says, "is maladaptive because it is based on fears that are not realistic, and not because of cultural unacceptability. It would be no less abnormal if it were culturally accepted." Homosexuality, according to this view, "is a type of heterosexual inadequacy." It "is *never* unrelated to fears and inhibitions associated with heterosexuality." It is totally incorrect "that normalcy can only be culturally defined and that homosexuality would not be pathological in a society that accepted it." This implies "that if our society accepted it, homosexuals wouldn't suffer any more psychological problems than heterosexuals. During the Victorian era, frigidity was regarded as normal. Can we therefore assume that frigidity created no psychological problems for a woman or for her husband because it was culturally defined as normal? I think not." (This interview appears in the April, 1971, issue of *Playboy.*)

We believe these views to be archaic. They are refuted by the available evidence.

First: the assumption as to the inherent desirability of heterosexuality is merely, solely, and exclusively *a value judgment,* couched in the form of a pseudoscientific medical fact. It is a judgment which anyone is free to accept or reject, according to one's personal feelings and taste.

Second: while pathologists decree that homosexuality represents a kind of inadequate or disordered heterosexual functioning, they never consider the opposite—that heterosexuality represents an inadequate or disordered *homosexual* functioning. Male homosexuality is no more a fear or a hatred of women than heterosexuality is a hatred or a fear of men. If obligatory male homosexuals exclude half the available population from their sexual scope—that is, all women —then obligatory male heterosexuals do likewise: they refuse to consider sex with any and all males. And the faithfully married couple represents the most restrictive of all forms of sexual behavior—aside from celibacy. The least restrictive sexual pattern would be displayed by the bisexual—or better yet, the "polymorphous pansexual," the man or woman who is willing to entertain the notion of sex with anyone, or even anything.

In fact, we could make a third point by taking this argument a step further: men and women who are self-designated homosexuals as a general rule *have had far more heterosexual contact* than heterosexuals have had homosexual contact. The overwhelming majority of homosexuals have at the very least given heterosexuality a try; relatively few heterosexuals, at least after adolescence, have experimented with homosexuality. We might, therefore, see heterosexuality as "compulsive," and homosexuality as freely chosen!

Fourth: there is no evidence whatsoever that there is anything like a "heterosexual destiny." Many sexual pathologists will say that sexual instincts do not necessarily dictate gender sexual choice, but they invoke a "male-female design . . . , anatomically determined," the result of an inexorable "evolutionary development." Homosexuals "are unable to form a healthy sexual identity in accordance with their anatomical and biological capacities," to quote Dr. Charles Socarides, another outspoken proponent of the pathology viewpoint. But exactly what this all means in precise terms can never be determined. At one time, to be sure, it was in the interest of human survival to reproduce. Certainly heterosexual intercourse was adaptive in an evolutionary sense. Now, of course, the opposite is true: it is in the best interests of humans to maintain the population, rather than to increase it. The anatomic equipment of men and women certainly *permits* heterosexual intercourse—but it does not dictate it. Likewise, the anatomical equipment of men permits homosexual behavior: hands, the mouth, and the anus are as capable of sexual stimulation and satisfaction as is the vagina. And the same may be said of the anatomical equipment of women. Male and female homosexuality is as anatomically "rational" as is heterosexuality.

Fifth: just how the personalities of homosexuals are "disordered" is not altogether clear. Psychologist Evelyn Hooker subjected a number of homosexuals and matched heterosexual controls to personality tests, and then asked a panel of psychiatrists and clinical psychologists to pick out which were which on the basis of their test scores. The panel did not do any better than guessing—indicating either that the tests couldn't tap whatever personality differences these two groups supposedly displayed, or that there were no such differences. Of course, it is always possible to declare *by fiat* that adequate heterosexual functioning is a necessary definition of mental health. Then homosexuality is by definition a sign of a disordered sexuality. But statements which are true by definition don't help us understand the world at all, since literally anything may be declared to be true by defining it that way.

Sixth: if homosexuals actually are sick, and if homosexuality actually is a manifestation of a psychosexual disorder, *psychiatrists would be the last of all researchers to know it.* In order to bolster up their expertise in this area, psychotherapists claim that their patients represent a cross section of all homosexuals, that whatever ailments they complain of are characteristic of homosexuals in general. But some thought renders this claim invalid. It is only homosexuals suffering from psychic distress who seek help of psychiatrists in the first place. What about those who are happy, well adjusted, satisfied with their lives? Why should they seek psychotherapy? The fact is, they wouldn't. And psychiatrists would not know of such people, of how typical they might be, or how atypical their own patients. And their theories do not take this simple fact into account. They reason solely and exclusively from their own patients. Imagine if a psychiatrist tried to claim that all shoe salesmen suffer from mental illness. When pressed for evidence, the reply is: "Because all of my patients who are shoe salesmen suffer from mental illness!" Of course; that's why they see a psychiatrist in the first place! Absurd as this whimsical example is, it corresponds exactly to the quality of evidence that has been presented when the personalities of homosexuals are described. Psychiatric descriptions and explanations of homosexuality are almost without exception based on this fundamental methodological fallacy.

For nearly all heterosexuals, the inherent superiority of heterosexuality is unquestioned, taken for granted. Psychiatric theories and evaluations are little more than a formalization of these popular prejudices. Most of us do not stop and consider just how ingrained these prejudices are.

When the issue of a male homosexual teaching adolescent boys is considered, most heterosexuals will raise the question of whether he will seduce his students. The fact that this possibility holds equally for male heterosexual teachers of adolescent girls rarely enters the minds of most heterosexuals.

Lesbian mothers are often asked if they "brainwash" their daughters to become Lesbians. The fact is that heterosexuals are engaged in an almost daily, nonconscious campaign to "brainwash" their children to become heterosexuals.

When the question of repealing the laws against homosexuality is debated, a cry often goes up that this will open the doors to homosexual assaults upon young boys. Consider this diatribe published in the *Humbard Christian Report* in 1972 (not 1872), quoted by John W. Petras in *Sexuality in Society:*

> Here in Youngstown, we are shocked by a terrible crime against a young boy by a sex pervert which resulted in the boy's murder, yet our lawmakers passed a bill legalizing this crime. . . ! What insanity! This is giving a green light to more and worse sex crimes. This is bringing out into the open what the law and moral standards have always condemned. . . . This bill, if it passes the Senate, will open a Pandora's box of crime and filth unparalleled in the history of the United States.

Why one case of homosexual violence should be any more typical of homosexuality in general than one case of a heterosexual rape-murder is of heterosexuality in general is not clear. But the fact that this equation is taken seriously by many heterosexuals emphasizes that the same sort of logic does not apply to the two forms of behavior.

The conceptions and theories which have been used in the past have served only to stigmatize homosexuals and to rationalize the superiority of heterosexuality. It is time, we believe, to look at homosexuality from a fresh perspective.

———◆———

John Reid is the pseudonym of the author of the book *The Best Little Boy in the World Has a Secret.* Barry M. Dank is an assistant professor in the department of sociology at California State University at Long Beach; he wrote a research monograph on homosexuality. Richard Troiden teaches sociology at the Miami University at Oxford, Ohio; he is at work on a full-length book on the development of a homosexual identity.

The Best Little Boy in the World Has a Secret

by John Reid

June is college reunion month, and I will probably go to mine. True, I am not the mindlessly rah-rah post-game party-goer that I was, or pretended to be, a few years ago as an undergraduate. But then, I haven't exactly abandoned the Establishment, either. As the alumni association computer fondly notes in sizing me up for a contribution, I was one of a tiny proportion of my class to go straight from college into the business world. I like wearing a tie and jacket into the Yale Club, and I hope they keep the rule.

By and large, I had a great time in college, and in high school, too, for that matter, though I did spend an inordinate amount of time worrying about sex. That should have made me feel consummately normal, I suppose, but it didn't. I was thinking thoughts I thought the best little boy in the world shouldn't think, so I kept them to myself. And kept thinking them, for hours on end, day after day. In retrospect, it all seems to have worked out pretty well, I'm happy to report; but it sure took long enough.

It was hazy and vague, age eleven. But I had gone off to camp the previous summer and was about to enter junior high school. I was being jolted into thinking a little. I no longer just looked at the picture of the Golden Gloves boxer in *Sports Illustrated* and liked it —I began to wonder *why* I liked it. And whether I was supposed to like it. And if not, whether I would stop liking it.

I was going through a stage. Sure enough, young boys all knew:

one of these days a little hair would start to grow in odd places (it did); the clerk would stop calling you "Miss" when you phoned in a grocery order (he did); muscles would begin to bulge all over your body (they did); and those little girls you had been ignoring would begin to drive you wild. I was waiting for those girls to start driving me wild, but I was very skeptical.

By the age of thirteen I was poignantly aware of what I was. Me, the best little boy in the world. But though I had found out about myself, no one else would ever find out as long as I lived. That stigma and keeping it a secret were the fundamental core of my mind, from which all other thoughts and actions flowed.

I would somehow cope. I would somehow enjoy hour after hour of cosmic depression, day after day, year after year. I knew what was happening now, and I spent most of my time writing programs for my defense department computer. The guns of Navarone were like water pistols in a shoebox compared with the fortress that guarded my secret. You would never catch *me* spilling the beans in my sleep. You would never catch *me* electing art instead of science, playing Hamlet instead of playing tennis.

One ingenious defense was to remain as ignorant as possible on the subject of homosexuality. The less I knew, I reasoned, the less chance that I would start looking like one or acting like one. I *wasn't* one, God damn it. Those people I saw on the streets with their pocketbooks and their swish and their pink hair—they disgusted me as much as they disgusted everyone else, probably more. I would sooner have slept with a girl, God forbid, than with one of those horrible people. Do you understand? I wasn't a homosexual, I just desperately wanted to be Tommy Roth's best friend. God, how I wanted to be *like* him, to do the same mischievous, self-assured things he did, to have muscles and blond hair and a smile like his. Nothing in our relationship would be disgusting, nothing unmentionable. Just to be like the Hardy Boys, two blood brothers, two cowboys . . . that's it: two cowboys.

So I never read anything about homosexuality. The F.B.I. would never catch *me* at the "HO" drawer of the New York Public Library card catalogue. Bachelor J. Edgar Hoover and his all-male army would have to be a lot more clever than that to trip me up.

My most important line of defense on a practical day-to-day basis was my prodigious list of activities. "Highly motivated; a self-starter," the teachers would write on my character reports. You're damn straight I was motivated! No one could expect me to be out dating on Saturday nights if the school paper was going to be on the stands on Tuesday. No one could expect me to be partying over Christmas vacation when I had a list of seventeen urgent projects to complete—I would be lucky to find time to open my presents, let alone go to parties or date, for crying out loud.

In high school it had been enough to learn to check out attractive girls on the street: look them up and down, leer a little, nudge my companion (naturally I only bothered with this nonsense when there was someone else around), maybe sigh or pant a little, or mutter something dirty . . . and then go back to noticing the boys.

Noticing attractive girls was not as easy to learn as it sounds. There was no department in my subconscious responsible for spotting pretty girls out of the corners of my eyes, as there was in the subconsciouses of my friends. I had to consciously remind myself to look, or else suffer the embarrassment of being reminded by a friend's poke to *catch those legs—ooooWEEEE!* But I ran a significant risk in leering and nudging: as I was attracted by boys, not girls, I had to use the most mechanical techniques in deciding which girls were "attractive." While others would have a simple groin reaction, I would nervously rush through a little checklist. I knew girls in laced shoes or combat boots were out. I knew legs were important, and had heard someone talk scornfully about a girl with "piano legs," so I tried to avoid those. I would ignore any girls whose heads did not at least come up even with the parking meters, as well as those whose heads brushed the bus stop signs as they walked by. Frizzy redheads, for some reason, were out. Girls who looked like boys, except with pony tails, were out. The hardest part, especially under winter coats, was to determine whether a girl was "built," or just fat. There was nothing whatever to be gained by leering and chortling over a dog. One slip like that and my cover would be blown: *You're not really attracted to girls!* YOU'RE JUST FAKING IT!

My back-up defense in such situations was myopia. I purposely kept my glasses off—they weren't very strong anyway—so that any omitted or mistaken leers and nudges could be blamed on my ophthalmologist.

That was all very well and good for high school. But in college you had to do more than just leer and chortle. You had to date.

Maybe you didn't have to if you were ugly, and maybe you didn't have to if you weren't worried about your normality. But if you were me, you had to date.

Not counting high school parties and camp dances, where everyone had to go by the busload—more like holding class in the evening or a special dancing lesson than a date—I can remember having had three dates prior to entering Yale.

The first was when I was seven. It was with Holly Frye, who would cry at the slightest provocation. She was unbelievable. She would cry if the teacher squeaked chalk against the blackboard. She would cry if cookie crumbs got on her dress. She would cry when she heard anyone else crying. I certainly didn't like her, but for some reason I found her one afternoon with my mother and her mother in our car, picked up from school, on the way to MY ROOM, of all places.

It was a disaster. We started playing with my chemistry set, the litmus paper bit, and she used an entire piece of my litmus paper to test—I don't know what it was, probably some lemon juice or something of equal scientific significance. Well, any fool knows you are only supposed to use just a tiny corner of the litmus paper! The whole piece! My God, she used the whole piece! I didn't hit her. I just said something nasty and then ignored her. Which was hard to do, as she immediately began to wail and cry and scream and howl, and was finally taken home, much to my relief.

Dumb girl. Ukh.

My second date, I think I was fourteen or fifteen. I can't remember this girl's name, but I remember that she was a regular at the dances I would force myself to go to. She had a four-inch chin, but was otherwise attractive for a fourteen-year-old girl, as best I could tell. I was infatuated at the time with a genuine preppie, who only flew into the city for vacations, and who suggested we double. My eagerness to be cowboys with this preppie knowing no bounds, I got a date.

We doubled to a double feature, my first movie date. I just spent the four hours watching what the preppie did, and doing as much of it to my date as I could bring myself to do. That is, I put my arm around the back of her chair. And once, by mistake (I had lost all feeling and control in that arm), I think I brushed her shoulder. Maybe it was the back of her chair.

The problem was, I felt nearly as uncomfortable *not* doing anything to her as I would have felt doing something. I wanted to want to do something, the way the preppie did, but all I could do for hours was wonder what it was that made me different. What was I going to do when it came time to get married?

My third date was also when I was about fifteen, my last summer in camp, and Tommy Roth's. Tommy was dating a counselor at our sister camp. I had to be dating somebody, so I was dating Hilda Goldbaum, from Queens. She was weighed down by two of the most enormous, terrifying, yes, nauseating breasts I could imagine. We had happened to pair up the first night they took a busload of us seniors out to the sister camp for a dance, so it was Hilda and me for the summer.

Brother-sister camp dances, as you may know, are very risky affairs that send camp directors' hearts aflutter. Once, in 1932, a girl got pregnant, possibly as a result of one of these dances, and the sister camp went out of business then and there. Since 1932, the state militia had been called out to guard the exits at all of our brother-sister camp dances, and the only way you could possibly hold your head up in the bus on the way back to camp was if you had been *missed*—that is, if you and your girl had been missed at some point during the course of the evening. Maximum points were scored by the couple who could turn up under the yellow circle of a flashlight—down at the rifle range. Where they have mattresses.

So Hilda and I *had* to be missed. Yet this was one test of my manhood I was just going to have to fail. I couldn't bring myself to seduce Hilda into the dark piny woods. I would just have to blame it on the security guards and change the subject when people asked me.

As it happened, Hilda had different ideas. She led me through a maze of piled tables and chairs, through the kitchen and the dishwashing apparatus, to an unguarded ratty old warped sinful-looking screen door, and out into the dark piny woods. She was hot, she said, why not go for a walk? I stopped after a few yards to try to marshal my resources for some kind of brilliant excuse. When I got older I planned to use the one about having had my thing shot off in the war. I started to open my mouth, in a hesitating sort of way because I was not sure what I would say, and Hilda grabbed me as though I had just sent her an engraved invitation. She pressed her lips hard against mine. I gritted my teeth and held my breath.

It was awful. The kiss itself, my first on the lips, could have been worse. It was just like pressing your lips against something squishy. Nothing more, nothing less. But knowing that it was nothing more, when it should have been; and, far worse, knowing that when this kiss was over (it was dragging out for an excruciatingly long time), Hilda and the world would have discovered that I didn't know how to kiss—that was awful. What are you, a weirdo?

Finally she loosened her grip and moved her face away, and I prepared for the worst. I had just stood there, after all. Whatever kissing is, however they do it in the movies, I had just stood there. My major achievement had been to repress the natural impulse I had to wrinkle up my nose. But do you know what she said? She said, "Oooow, that was *wonn*derful. It's been a month since I had a man!" She actually said that.

Newly self-confident as I was, I said in my deepest, most leader-ship kind of voice, "I think we'd better get back before they miss us."

She dutifully followed her man back to the dance.

Shortly thereafter, Hilda and Kathy somehow contrived to get over to our camp to see Tommy and me. Tommy was delighted, and after lunch (I remember it was ravioli) he commandeered an empty tent for us. He put the flaps down. I kept trying to protest about the grave risk we were taking, but Tommy had had the flaps down be-fore. He started making out with Kathy, lying on top of her, kissing her, putting his hands all over her. I made some very awkward at-tempts, with more help from Hilda than I wanted, to do roughly the same things, hoping against hope that some counselor would come along and break it up. Even being sent home would be better than this. And by now, all things considered, it might not have been altogether bad for my image at home to be sent back for this. My parents weren't pushing, but they let me know I would be more than welcome to start bringing girls home, to start dating under proper circumstances, to go to more dances—and whom was I planning to take to the Junior Prom?

But no counselor came along. Hilda, meanwhile, was getting ready to go all the way. It was time to French-kiss. She pried open my mouth with her crowbar tongue and stuck it in. Agh! Germs!

Germs, hell: ravioli. I don't mean to be vulgar, but her breath smelled like ravioli, and I felt like puking. Or running, or passing out. But there was Tommy, whose respect meant more to me than anything, making out gleefully with Kathy.

End-of-rest-hour was bugled out over the loudspeaker, which, thank God, was the call for retreat. It was over. I went for a gargle in the lake.

That was the sexual experience I brought with me to Yale. And now I had to date in earnest. I was in the majors. A few people were even thinking about getting *married,* for crying out loud.

The first thing I did that year was subscribe to *Playboy.* Like a blind man at a silent movie, I would religiously thumb through my monthly *Playboy,* forcing myself to check out, leer, and nudge my roommate, Roger. I liked *Playboy* because I didn't have to worry about chortling over a dog by mistake. I would hang the centerfold on the wall over my bed for all to see.

It was obvious to me in a theoretical, mathematical sort of way that I could not be the only straight-looking, athletic young man in search of someone to be cowboys with. Yet it was equally obvious to me in a very real, practical sort of way that it would be impossible for me to find the right buddy. Because he, too, would be pretending with all his might; he, too, would refuse back rubs and look girls up and down and leer. Even if one in ten boys really did have "tendencies," who was going to risk everything on a one-in-ten chance?

I guess I was never more tempted to take a chance than with Roger. We shared the same room, beds a few feet apart, and he frequently would laugh and say, "Hey, roomie! Wanna jump into bed with me?"

Tempting? But he was kidding. He *had* to be kidding. He laid his girlfriend twice a week in that bed, so he had to be kidding. He was so sure of his masculinity that he could even afford to joke about being queer. Maybe he had doubts about me and was trying to trap me. I would accept one of those invitations to bed, he would get nauseated and violent, and then he would call the dean and say he wanted a new roommate because I was a homosexual.

Yale would not expel me. They would give me a private room; daily therapy. And they would call my parents for permission for the therapy, and send them a letter confirming that their son was a queer . . .

*   *   *

Sophomore year you got to choose your own roommates for the next three years. Roger and I parted on friendly enough terms (well, friendly enough for him, anyway) and I roomed with several guys, including Hank. I was hopelessly in love with Hank, though of course I couldn't let on.

In writing honestly this way, I don't want to give you the wrong impression. It may rub you wrong to read about guys loving other guys. Perhaps you instinctively picture me as having been, at best, the assistant-soccer-team-manager type tagging along with the Big Man On Campus, wearing very thick glasses, and getting nosebleeds at the slightest exertion. *Real* guys don't love other guys, right? Perhaps so. But at least to all outward appearances, I was a real guy, and something of a Big Man On Campus, myself. True, where I was good-looking, Hank was downright charismatic. And though I could beat him in tennis and could swim better, he was clearly the better athlete. But if anything, I spent less time studying than he did; and the little extracurricular empire I ran was at least as noteworthy as Hank's. I even got my face in *Time* once (way in the back, a small picture). So we weren't exactly Wild Bill Hickok and Andy Devine, if you know what I mean. If only I could have told Hank that I loved him.

My room that year was so small, I had to suspend the bed like Brooklyn Bridge over the wardrobe closet and bookshelves. Of course, I had arranged the room this way, and failed to build any kind of ladder, to keep all but the most vigorous of pole vaulters out of my bed. And I was careful not to date pole vaulters.

I was sneaky, but I had to be. Hank and I would frequently go out hunting for a little action. Girls always travel in pairs and, fortunately, the pair is always a beautiful girl and a dog, for obvious ego-boosting reasons. Hank was better looking than I was, so I would simply say: Oh, wow! Sure, let's make it with those girls! Yeah! I'll take Kathy, you can have Gladys. Hank, of course, would no sooner have gone to bed with Gladys than with the Creature from the Black Lagoon. But, to his everlasting credit, he was too considerate of his best friend to say Go Screw, or even to go home with Kathy and leave me to fend for myself.

So, while I am not particularly proud of having aborted so many of Hank's copulations, I always managed to make it home with my image of normality intact.

Almost always. One summer we went to Europe together. We were in Tossá, on the coast of Spain. The inevitable Kathy and Gladys, British birds this time, came into view, and we spent the customary hour walking around with them, looking for a place to dance, telling them about Yale and about our nifty hotel room. Then, while they went off to the bathroom to reconnoiter, Hank and I went through our little ritual. Wow, those chicks are dynamite! They're dying for it, too! Yeah, let's screw 'em! I think they'll come back with us! Yeah, wow! *"I'll take Kathy, if that's okay with you, Hank."* *"Yeah, okay, what the hell,"* Hank said, obviously drunk out of his mind, and the world caved in.

The girls came back; my head was awash in adrenalin. Hank asked them if they wanted to come back to the hotel. Sure they did. Hank took Gladys's arm and Kathy and I followed. Gladys was chewing gum, obviously delighted. Kathy was less than delighted—yes! she would find a way to avoid sleeping with me!—but, while I wasn't Hank, I was apparently, to my dismay, good enough. I was silently going bananas.

Hank and I, of course, were sharing a double hotel room. Not one of those where we slept together in the same double bed, though there had been many of those. (Can you imagine sleeping like that and not being able to touch?) This room had two single beds, and was ample for the four of us. But whatever was going to happen with Kathy, it simply could not happen in the same room with Hank. I could accept death. I could not accept torture.

I said I liked privacy when I slept with a girl—a little lame, but reasonable. It was so late at night the front desk was deserted, so I couldn't rent another room, even if there had been one. I went downstairs to the desk, behind the desk, and stole one of the keys hanging by an empty postbox—hoping that it was indeed the key to a vacant room, and that no one would be returning even later that night to use it.

The best little boy in the world actually stole the key. Kathy and I adjourned to the vacant room. I immediately went to the bathroom and locked myself in, water running madly to drown out any thoughts that might otherwise be overheard.

I emerged from the bathroom. Kathy was sitting on the bed.

Kathy was no Hilda Goldbaum. She was one attractive girl, as even I could tell, and she was not about to do my work for me. But I wasn't up to it, either.

I'm sure my unhappiness and discomfort showed, and that sort of thing is contagious. I doubt Kathy was much happier than I was. I took off my clothes, except for my shorts; and, as it was two in the morning and no one was helping Kathy take off hers, she had no logical alternative but to take them off herself. We got into bed together. Luckily, a fairly wide bed. I put my arm around her and after a little while I muttered something about being sorry, that it wasn't her, that I was sorry, and I was dead tired, and would she like to go to sleep? Yeah. I turned over on my stomach and lay motionless— as far from sleep as anyone could possibly be, of course—for about three hours until there was a faint suggestion that the sun was on the rise. I rustled enough to wake Kathy and said that since I had stolen the key to the room, maybe we had better leave before they found us. I would walk her back to her hotel room.

I lay on the beach watching the sun rise, feeling awful. I waited a few hours and then rejoined Hank at the hotel. Hank smiled. I tried to smile. How was it? I asked. "Good, but I think I caught a cold."

"As long as you didn't catch anything else," I managed out of my pretend-normal vocabulary of words and expressions I didn't really understand. He smiled.

"How was it?" he asked.

"Good," I said.

The dates I had in college were almost always friends of Hank's girlfriends. I had no black book of my own. I got along with them okay. One in particular I saw on and off during a whole year, and she would come to all the mandatory football weekends and college parties. I felt bad about "using" her as a cover, but I needed a cover. Her name was Hillary and she was Hank's girl's best friend.

She was not unattractive, she was bright, considerate, and best of all, something of a prude. I could make all kinds of advances, trying to get my arm from around her shoulder (a position that I had mastered and that she allowed) over and around her breast. She would never let me touch her there, or down below, which was a wonderful arrangement. She could go back to Vassar and tell Hank's girlfriend about my advances; Hank's girlfriend would tell Hank; Hank would think I had normal inclinations, if less than normal success.

Of course, I began to wonder why Hillary wouldn't let me do anything. Not that I wanted to, but I wanted to know what was wrong with me. That is, what other people perceived as being wrong. The bad-breath syndrome. Hillary explained that she liked me well enough, but she just couldn't let herself go with me *because she thought I was only interested in her body*.

Hank would usually get home from these evenings around three, and for all he knew, I had come in only a few minutes earlier. Sometimes I would wait up for him. "How was it, Hank?" "Good." "How was it?" he would ask. "Good." (If you are wondering why Hank came home at all, as well you might, I have to say, first, that sometimes he didn't, but second, and mainly, try to remember how much different things were just a few years ago. Short hair, no dope, all-male schools . . . a very few years ago.)

I didn't enjoy always getting home before Hank. Why did I have to be the social cripple? What were he and my other roommates going to think if I always got home before they did?

How could I keep up my game? Surely I would slip sooner or later. What about after college? How would I explain not getting married? How would I explain to my parents that I never brought girls home? How would I explain to my colleagues, in whatever field it happened to be, why I was still a bachelor? What girls would want to date me, by that time, if I didn't *do anything,* for crying out loud?

The future looked bleak. I had vague notions of two years in the Peace Corps. A series of letters home talking about this girl I had met in Nairobi, a picture or two sent; a sudden marriage which, for fear they would not approve of my marrying a Nairobian girl, we decided to hold there without family or friends (read: witnesses). A year of letters about how happy we were and what we were doing. And then tragedy. She was bitten by a snake, or leukemia—whatever seemed more plausible. I would be so grief-stricken I would not be able to remarry for years, maybe ever.

One evening, I decided it was time for me not to be the first one home. I was walking back from Hillary's hotel. Instead of going back to the dorm—looking first to see that no one was watching me, and feeling tremendously guilty—I ducked into another hotel and asked for a room. "No luggage, sir?" No luggage, I gulped, feeling exposed, guiltier still; but determined.

I went up to the room and tried to sleep, with only moderate success. There was no clock or radio in the room, and no phone. When the sun in the window woke me Sunday morning, I had no idea what time it was. I waited in bed as long as I could, and then went out into the street—again stealthily, to be sure no one saw me.

The clock above the newsstand said seven-fifteen. I walked around feeling guilty for two hours and then went to make my grand unshaven entrance in last night's wrinkled clothes, hoping my room-mates might possibly have waked by this time and noticed that my bed was made, and no me anywhere in sight. Of course, they were asleep, so after turning on the lights in my room for extra effect, I went stealthily back out and walked around for another hour.

At quarter past ten they were still asleep. I hadn't slept much myself, and was exhausted by my ridiculous fraud. But I had invested $12 and lots of energy in it, and had to have it go as planned. Finally, on my fourth attempt, just before noon, I walked in and saw that my roommates were up and reading the Sunday *Times*. I walked past them into my room as nonchalantly as I could, with a simple, "Morning." I waited a minute for the applause, or at least for a question or two. After all, we had been living together for nearly two years and this was the first time I had ever stayed out all night with a girl. My best friend Hank should have had something to say.

Hank kept reading the paper. I took off my tie and jacket and sat down with them to read the paper. Nothing.

A couple of days later I broke down and asked Hank, "Hey, didn't you notice that I didn't come home Saturday night?"

"Oh, yeah?" he asked. "How was it?"

"Good."

"Good."

We were nineteen years old then. When I told Hank four years later that I had just had sex for the first time in my life, aged 23, and that it had been with a boy, not a girl, and that for the past twelve years and as long as I had known him I had been homosexual, though entirely chaste—his reaction was somewhat more animated.

Now I am 25, going into my third year of being relatively honest and relaxed (read: out of the closet). I have told all my straight friends and several of my business associates what I told Hank. To my relief, it only made us closer friends. I have made hundreds of gay acquaintances—waiters, construction workers, writers, students, drop-outs, bankers, pro athletes, pianists, piano tuners, priests, models, secretaries, hairdressers, West Point cadets, interior decorators— and I have made a handful of close gay friends. One was a Senate page when he was a kid and is a Washington lawyer now. One was president of his student body in college and is at Harvard Business School now. One periodically appears on local TV (not in New York) representing "The Youth of Today." One is vice president of a large conglomerate. Lance Loud, though I respect his right to be, look and act as he wants, is not one of my friends.

The Homosexual
by Barry M. Dank

INTRODUCTION

Don is thirty-three years old and is of Mexican American background. He is a buyer for a large department store, and he feels that he has been occupationally successful. Don lives with Leslie in a modest home in a white middle-class suburban community.

Don and Leslie have been married for seven years. They feel that their marriage represents a lifelong partnership. They emphasize the fact that their marriage represents a sexual commitment of faithfulness, and neither has had a sexual relationship with another person since they began living together.

Don and Leslie's life style is one that is overtly similar to the dominant life style of American society. They are indistinguishable from millions of other couples who live in suburbia except that they are male homosexuals (or in the traditional language of our society, they are "perverts," "mentally ill," "sick," "child molesters," "criminals," "effeminates," "sodomites," "fags," "queers," etc.) and they commit a "crime" that has been regarded with such horror, such revulsion, that it has been literally regarded as "the unspeakable and abominable crime against nature." Don and Leslie living their overtly indistinguishable lives in suburban America are outsiders, living beyond the mores of Western Christian civilization and beyond the laws of most states of the United States.*

Who are the homosexuals? What percentage of the American male population do homosexuals represent? † Unfortunately there are no definitive answers to these questions. The whole subject of homosexuals and homosexuality has been shrouded in an aura of silence and fear and consequently ignorance. Sociologically and statistically, the homosexual couple that was just described and others like them virtually do not exist. There have never been any studies on homosexually married couples, and the probability of couples like Don and Leslie being included in surveys on homosexuality has been very low. For example, many persons like Don and Leslie have never been arrested, never seen a psychiatrist, do not frequent gay bars, do not frequent private or public meeting places of homosexuals, are not members of formal or informal organizations of homosexuals, and may very infrequently, if at all, engage in sexual relations with another male.

Probably the most quoted study as to the percentage of homosexuals in our society is that of Kinsey et al. (60). Kinsey found that 37% of his sample had at least some overt homosexual experience leading to orgasm between adolescence and old age, and that another 13% had experienced some homosexual contact but not to the point of orgasm. In addition, Kinsey constructed a seven-category heterosexual-homosexual behavior scale with category zero representing those who are totally heterosexual in behavior and attraction, 3 representing those who are equally homosexual and heterosexual, and '6 representing those who are only homosexually oriented. Employing this scale, Kinsey found that 4% were 6s or exclusively homosexual throughout their lives; that 25% had more than an incidental history of homosexual behavior for at least three years, and that 10% were more or less exclusively homosexual throughout

* Much of the material that is presented in this chapter is based on a study of various homosexual communities as they exist in the Los Angeles metropolitan area. This research began in the fall of 1968 and is still continuing. The research methodologies employed have been in-depth interviews and questionnaire surveys of self-identified male homosexuals; and that of "participant observation" in which the researcher as researcher became integrated into friendship networks of homosexuals. The researcher was introduced to one of these friendship networks by one of his homosexual students, who presented the researcher as a heterosexual who was interested in studying the gay community.

† This chapter will not include material on female homosexuals. For information on female homosexuality see references 9, 10, 23, 30, 43, 58, 69, 84, 85, 90, 91.

a period of at least three years (20). This data was the first indication that homosexuality is more than a rare phenomenon in our society and that many millions of men are to some degree involved in such behavior (20, 110). However, Kinsey's study cannot be accepted as necessarily representing an accurate estimate of the "homosexual" population since he worked with a nonrandom sample and only with volunteer subjects (49).

The problems confronting the researcher who attempts to estimate accurately the extent of homosexuality in our society are essentially insurmountable. He can only work with volunteer subjects, and therefore have a nonprobability sample. Many different variables influence whether a homosexually oriented individual will become part of his research project. Numerous researchers have recognized that the size of the homosexual population or the volume of homosexual behavior is unknowable. For example, Schur has stated that "there are no satisfactory statistics regarding the prevalence of homosexuality. . . . Estimates by individual homosexuals are not likely to be very accurate. . . . Many homosexuals have a psychological stake in exaggerating their number" (87, p. 75). And Westwood has observed, "An attempt was made to obtain information about the incidence of homosexuality but the answer to these questions are very unsatisfactory. . . . Homosexuality has existed in Great Britain . . . and in all other European countries, but it is impossible to tell if the incidence has increased at different periods" (111, p. 62). Although the specific volume of homosexuality in our society is unknowable, it is known that many millions of men engage in homosexual behavior and that a significant percentage do so with a high degree of regularity (35, 41, 42).

In approaching the study of homosexuality, or sexual behavior in general, we can employ five basic concepts that will enable us to obtain a clearer understanding of this complex subject. These concepts are (*a*) sex, (*b*) gender, (*c*) sexual behavior, (*d*) sexual attraction, and (*e*) sexual identity.

The concept of sex is a dichotomous one and refers to the physical characteristics of the individual. Almost always an individual is male or female and we can differentiate male from female by the structure of the sexual organs or by taking a genetic skin test and determining whether the individual is male (XY) or female (XX). There are those rare cases in which an individual is born with physical characteristics of both sexes (the true hermaphrodite) or characteristics that *appear* to be of both sexes (the pseudohermaphrodite) or with a chromosomal abnormality (67). In this chapter, however, we will not be concerned with those individuals who are born with, or develop, physical sex anomalies.

In contrast to the concept of sex, gender is a psychological variable that we may think of as being on a continuum (96). Gender ranges from the very masculine to the very feminine. Masculinity-femininity refers to behaviors, mannerisms, feelings that our society associates with one sex versus the other. Recently there has been much controversy over what should be considered to be "really" masculine or "really" feminine. From a sociological viewpoint it becomes problematic what behaviors are to be regarded as masculine or feminine; i.e., what the individual thinks is masculine, is masculine for him or her. However, in our society there is some shared agreement concerning what is masculine or feminine, although the content of these concepts may change over time.

The fact that the concept of masculinity is culturally associated with the male, and femininity with the female, does not mean that in reality we cannot have different relationships between gender and sex. As well as having the feminine female we can have the masculine female or the feminine male. Some persons' gender may be so directly opposite from their sex that they feel they must seek a sex-change operation in order to make their sex consistent with their gender. Such persons are referred to as *transsexuals*. The male transsexual seeks the operation in order to physically appear as a female and be accepted as a female. After the operation the person's gender would still be the same, but the physical anatomy would be changed (12, 45, 96). Other persons whose sex and gender are not consistent may not seek out this operation and may be content to dress in the clothes of the opposite sex. Such persons are generally referred to as *transvestites* (97).

Our third concept is sexual behavior. We can view this concept as being on a continuum, with the *heterosexual*, who has sex relations only with persons of the opposite sex, on one end. In the middle is the *bisexual*, who has sex relations equally with both sexes; and at the opposite end is the *homosexual*, who has sex relations only with persons of the same sex.

What is extremely important to remember is that gender is not necessarily indicative of sexual behavior. A masculine male may be behaviorally heterosexual or bisexual or homosexual. In addition, some feminine men may dress in women's clothing, and are therefore transvestites, but may still be heterosexually oriented (17, 76). In fact, there is a national organization for heterosexual transvestites led by Virginia Prince (a male), who is also the editor of *Transvestia,* a publication written by and for heterosexual transvestites (106).

Our fourth concept is sexual attraction. Sexual attraction is also on a continuum, with the heterosexual, who is only attracted to persons of the opposite sex, on one end; in the middle is the bisexual, who is equally attracted to both sexes; and finally homosexual persons, who are attracted only to persons of the same sex.

Just as there is no perfect relationship between gender and sexual behavior, so there is no perfect relationship between sexual behavior and sexual attraction. Males who are sexually attracted only to men may be behaviorally 100% heterosexual. As we shall see, it is no rare phenomenon to have heterosexually married men being behaviorally heterosexual or predominantly heterosexual, but being sexually attracted to males (26, 81). Married men in such situations may think or fantasize about men during their sexual relationships with their wives (26). This highlights the fact that sexual attraction is in one's thought, in one's mind, and may not be reflected in one's behavior. How should we classify the sex relationship of the male who, while he is having sex with his wife, thinks about men?

It is also possible for the person who is predominantly or only homosexual in behavior to be attracted solely to persons of the opposite sex. For example, it is quite clear that homosexual behavior is widespread in many prisons in the United States but that these prisoners remain overwhelmingly psychologically heterosexual (21, 29, 39, 43, 98, 105, 107).

Our fifth concept is sexual identity. Sexual identity refers to how a person regards himself sexually. In our society there are basically three different sexual identities available: heterosexual, bisexual, and homosexual (25). A person may be behaviorally or psychologically homosexual, but still consider himself heterosexual. On the other hand, a person may be behaviorally heterosexual and still be willing to say to himself, "I am a homosexual." It is important to note that it is not always possible to predict sexual identity from knowledge of behavior, from knowledge of attraction, or from knowledge of gender.

Given the presentation of these concepts, the following questions logically follow: Who are the homosexuals? How are we to define the homosexuals? Who is really homosexual? My response to these questions is that there is no need for me as a social scientist, or for other social scientists, to answer these questions. I do not think it is the function of social scientists, including psychiatrists, to define other people, particularly when these other people have not asked or do not want to be defined by us. For research purposes and for purposes of this chapter, a homosexual is regarded as a person who identifies himself *to himself* as being a homosexual.

Pertinent questions that concern definitions of homosexuals are of the following nature: Why do some persons who are behaviorally homosexual define themselves as heterosexuals while others do not? Why do some persons who are psychologically homosexual define themselves as heterosexual while others do not? Why do some persons at one point in time regard themselves as heterosexual and in spite of the same sexual behavior and attraction at a later time regard themselves as homosexual? What are the social and psychological consequences for an individual as a result of a change in his sexual identity? What is the nature of the social and psychological processes that lead a person to decide that he is a homosexual? *

THE DILEMMA OF THE HOMOSEXUAL

Coming Out

Persons who come to define themselves as being homosexual do not go through a period of anticipatory socialization in order to prepare themselves for an adult homosexual role. Homosexuals almost always grow up in heterosexual families with a parent or parents who expect them to be very much like themselves. Such ideas are communicated to the child as part of the parents' definition of their child. In this sense, homosexual minority groups differ radically from other minority groups. They differ because racial and ethnic minority-group parents communicate to their children what it means and what it is like to be black, a Jew, a Polish Catholic, etc. These parents know, or believe they know, who their son really is. Jewish

---

* These questions logically follow from the symbolic interactionist or labeling approach to the study of deviant behavior. This approach is particularly concerned with studying the processes that are associated with the development of a deviant identity (22, 44, 62, 64, 65, 82, 83).

parents know that their son is Jewish, the son knows he is Jewish, and at the age of fifteen the parents and the son do not suddenly discover he is a Polish Catholic. However, for the homosexual, the parents and the son may discover at fifteen that he is really not like them at all, that he is really quite different since he is homosexual.

Given a population of young male adolescents with sexual desires toward persons of the same sex, the problem that confronts many of these young people is how they are to make sense of their sexual feelings or their sexual behavior. What meaning are they capable of attaching to their behavior? To themselves? Traditionally in our society it has been quite probable that these young people would receive no information at all concerning homosexuality, or if they were to receive and information concerning homosexuality it was likely that it would be quite negative. This has been the case because there has been a taboo in our society in reference to speaking about homosexuality. Hoffman has characterized this situation in the following manner:

> Society deals with homosexuality as if it did not exist. Although this situation is rapidly changing, the subject was not even discussed and was not even the subject of scientific investigation until a few decades ago. We just didn't speak about these things; they were literally unspeakable and so loathsome that nothing could be said in polite society about them. . . . (50, p. 195)

Such a lack of information does not provide the young person with an acceptable vocabulary to explain his behavior to himself. If the young person has never heard of the category of homosexual, he cannot identify himself as being homosexual or interpret his behavior in terms of that category. If the young person has heard of the homosexual category in negative terms such as "pervert," "fag," "effeminate," etc., he is likely not to be able to readily put himself in that category. His decision *not* to put himself in the homosexual category functions to preserve his own sense of self-esteem (25).

For example, I have asked self-identified homosexuals how they would have honestly responded to the question "Are you a homosexual?" at the time they just graduated from high school. Following is a typical response:

> Truthfully I wouldn't have known what a homosexual was. . . . There was this kid who I was attracted to, and I made a pass at him, and he was a good enough of a friend to say: "What's wrong,

are you a homo?" And I didn't even know what he was talking about. I heard kids at school use the expression "homo" and I didn't know what it meant.

And below is a typical response of an individual who interpreted his own sexual behavior in a manner completely unrelated to his image of the homosexual category:

> I really didn't know what a homosexual was. [Did you know what a "queer" was?] No, because in the back of my mind, my definition of homosexual or queer was someone who wore girls' clothing and women's shoes because my brothers said this, and I knew I wasn't.

Self-identified homosexuals often refer to the identity change to homosexual as the "coming out" of the individual (9, 25, 38). When an individual states, "I came out at twenty-five," this could very well mean, "I decided I was homosexual at the age of twenty-five." (However, it would be wise to ask the individual to define his terms, since the meaning of gay * terms vary from region to region, and within regions.) The coming-out process often involves a change in the symbolic meaning of the homosexual category for the homosexually oriented individual. The meaning of the homosexual category is transformed in such a way that the subject can place himself in this category but yet preserves a sense of his own self-esteem. What for him was previously a category for the mentally ill, perverts, etc., now becomes a socially acceptable category. This transformation of meaning often occurs in one-sex environments in which the individual discovers some new, favorable information concerning homosexuality (25). Some individuals come out when they first discover the existence of a gay bar:

> I knew that there were homosexuals, queers and what not; I had read some books, and I was resigned to the fact that I was a foul, dirty person, but I actually wasn't calling myself a homosexual yet. . . . And the time I really caught myself coming out is the time I walked into this bar and saw a whole crowd of groovy, groovy guys. And I said to myself, there was the realization, that not all gay men are dirty old men or idiots, silly queens, but there are just normal looking and acting people. I saw gay society and I said, "Wow, I'm home." (25, p. 187)

---

* The term *gay* is currently preferred by self-identified homosexuals in referring to themselves. *Eds.*

The age for the development of a homosexual identity varies greatly. For example, in a questionnaire survey conducted by the author of a population of 386 self-identified homosexuals, the mean age for homosexual identity development was twenty-one, and the age distribution was as follows: 12% between ages eight and fourteen; about 35% between ages fifteen and nineteen; about 31% between ages twenty and twenty-four; and about 22% age twenty-five or older.

What might explain this variation in the age of coming out? The age of coming out may be related to the nature of one's early socialization. For example, individuals who were raised in highly restrictive religious backgrounds may tend to come out later than others, since they would find it more difficult to neutralize or transform the traditional societal definition of the homosexual.

In addition, Weinberg (108) has recently presented data indicating that younger homosexuals are, on the whole, not as well psychologically adjusted as older homosexuals. This finding may be interpreted as reflecting the fact that many younger homosexuals still do have doubts about their self-identity. As the individual ages, he becomes more secure in his self-identity.

Closet Queens and Heterosexual Marriage

Some persons may go for lengthy periods of time with strong homosexual desires and possibly engage in homosexual acts but yet do not have a homosexual identity. Such persons are often referred to as "closet queens" by persons who have already developed such a homosexual identity. Closet queens truly find themselves in a dilemma, since their sexual attraction and sexual identity are not consistent. There are a number of possible adaptations to this dilemma, one of which is heterosexual marriage.

Since closet queens still have some continuing identity with heterosexual men, it is quite likely that such persons will consider heterosexual marriage (26, 81). In a questionnaire survey by the author it was found that 25% of a self-identified sample of homosexuals had been previously married and that these formerly married men tend to be ex-closet queens.

These heterosexual marriages represent one of the greatest problems of homosexual life. I have found that, when "homosexuals" marry women, generally these men suffer from great feelings of guilt, loneliness, and fear, and at times experience severe conflicts within the marriage (26).

Closet Queens and T-Room Queens

Closet queens also tend to be "t-room queens," individuals who frequent men's rooms for fast, impersonal, sexual gratification. For the heterosexually married closet queen, t-rooms may represent his major or only homosexual outlet. Humphreys (55), in a study of t-room habitués in a midwestern city, found that the majority of the men in his sample were heterosexually married. One of the chief problem areas concerning homosexual behavior has been such behavior in men's rooms, but interestingly enough the situation appears to be predominantly the result of the behavior of persons who do not accept themselves as homosexual.

Closet queens, particularly long-term closet queens, may also play a significant role in advocating antihomosexual ideas and attitudes and therefore contribute to the continuation of the antihomosexual prejudice in our society. In organized homosexual worlds, it is a widely shared belief that many of those who are strongly antihomosexual are attempting to hide their own homosexual feelings. Humphreys found that many of his t-room closet queens protected themselves in a "breastplate of righteousness," advocating traditional moralistic positions. For example one of his interviewee's comments on homosexual activities was, "This moral corruption must be stopped"(55, p. 141). Humphreys noted that his data suggest "the ironic possibility of a type of moral entrepreneur who contributes to hs own stigmatization" (55, p. 141).

Stereotyping and Homosexuals

The sociopsychological adjustment of homosexually oriented individuals is intimately related to the nature of the societal stereotype of the homosexual (89). Homosexuals have been a much-stereotyped group in our society, since information that might combat these stereotypes has traditionally not been allowed to circulate. Persons might believe that all homosexuals are, say, child molesters or hairdressers, and never have any of these stereotypes been challenged at any time.

Basically, ideas become widely accepted stereotypes because of their advocacy by prestigious leaders of society—by recognized experts and by those who have "authority." These individuals are believed because it is felt that their training or their success gives them special access to the "truth." In reference to outsiders and minority groups, these stereotype leaders define these groups for society. They tell society what drug users, or mental patients, or homosexuals are "really" like.

Those "experts" who have specialized in defining homosexuals have been religious leaders, psychiatrists, police and other legal authorities, and, to a lesser degree, social scientists. Historically, religious leaders have played the major role in defining homosexuals, and their definition has been essentially that of sodomites and sinners. In effect these religious leaders have held homosexuals to be beyond the pale, to be saved only if they give up their sinning. Space does not permit a detailed analysis of the religious evaluation of homosexuals, although there have been several historical and critical analyses of the religious evaluation of homosexuality (8, 13, 20, 57, 102, 112, 116).

During most of the twentieth century psychiatrists have played the major role in stereotyping the homosexual. In the guise of applying a value-free medical model of behavior, many psychiatrists have translated the rhetoric of religion, which treated homosexuals as sinful and evil, to the rhetoric of mental health and mental illness, thus regarding homosexuals as mentally ill. In the 1968, revised edition of the American Psychiatric Association's *Diagnostic and Statistical Manual,* homosexuality is defined as a mental disorder and assigned code number 302.0 (6).

Szasz has brilliantly analyzed the concept of mental illness as it applies to homosexuality (101, 102) and other so-called "deviant" behaviors (99, 100). He has demonstrated that the mental health rhetoric functions to disguise the ethical and moral issues surrounding homosexuality with the jargon of medicine. As it is employed now, the statement that homosexuals are mentally ill only functions to degrade the homosexual and to assert that homosexuals are inferior to heterosexuals because "health" (heterosexuality) is superior to "illness" (homosexuality). As a result of this modern-day psychiatric position, the psychiatrist most often offers, and sometimes insists, that the homosexual adopt the role of sick patient. In psyciatric terms this is progress, since previously the homosexual was regarded as simply being a sinner.

Probably the most vociferous psychiatric advocate of the viewpoint that homosexuals are mentally ill has been Charles Socarides.

Socarides differs from most other psychiatric writers in that he has attempted to give the reasons why homosexuals should be considered mentally ill:

> After detailed exploration the Committee on Public Health of the New York Academy of Medicine reported its finding that homosexuality is a mental disorder whose only effective treatment is psychotherapy. The committee, totaling 30 members, consisted of several deans of medical schools, prominent representatives of the medical specialties, including six psychiatrists, the then commissioner of the police of the city of New York as well as members of the judiciary. The 1964 report recognized homosexuality as an illness of social proportions, national significance and serious portent. (93, pp. 1200–1)

In other words, homosexuals should be considered mentally ill because prestigious persons think they are mentally ill. Of course, other prestigious persons do not consider homosexuals to be mentally ill. For example, in 1970 the National Association of Mental Health issued a position paper on homosexuality which included such statements as, "[homosexual] behavior does not constitute a specific mental or emotional illness," and "there is no evidence either in empirical research or in the experience of other countries that homosexual behavior in itself endangers the health of the individual or of society" (68, p. 131).

In order to preserve self-esteem or self-pride homosexuals must generally neutralize this "mental illness" stereotype. In the gay worlds one usually finds that homosexuals do not regard themselves as being mentally ill. A typical homosexual reaction to the idea that homosexuals are mentally ill is:

> Being a homosexual does not label a person as sick or mentally ill. In every other capacity I am as normal or more normal than straight people. Just because I happen to like strawberry ice cream and they like vanilla, doesn't make them right or me right. (25, p. 190)

Some psychiatrists have contributed to the reinforcement of other stereotypes of the homosexual. For example, Abrahamsen reinforces the effeminate stereotype of the homosexual in the following classic statement:

> A typical homosexual, although not always so, may be described thus: he is thin and has slender limbs, his cheeks are flushed, his face soft, and his appearance and manners pleasant. Hair on the

chest, axilla and pubes rare. He behaves like a girl, walks like a girl and smiles like a girl. He may like to cook and sew, . . . he may start to dress like a girl, perhaps take a girl's name, "marry" a man, and pose as "his wife." (1, p. 169)

The most recent psychiatric effort to stereotype the homosexual in a degrading manner has been that of David Reuben in his best-selling-book, *Everything You Always Wanted To Know About Sex (But Were Afraid To Ask)*. Reuben presents the homosexual in an almost totally sexual manner:

> The usual homosexual experience is mutual masturbation. It is fast, easy, and requires a minimum amount of equipment. The chaps simply undress, go to bed and manipulate each others' penises to the point of orgasm. (79, p. 132)
>
> The majority of gay guys, when they cruise, dispense with courtship. They don't even have time for footsies or love notes on toilet paper. Homosexuality seems to have a compelling urgency about it. A homosexual walks into a men's washroom and spots another homosexual. One drops to his knees, the other unzips his pants, and a few moments later, it's all over. No name, no faces, no emotion. A masturbation machine might do it better. (79, p. 133)

Such stereotyping increases the *tendency* toward promiscuity in the gay world since such definitions tend to become part of the homosexual's own self-definition. Hoffman clearly recognized this situation when he stated, "To put the matter in its *most* simple terms, the reason that males who are homosexually inclined cannot form stable relations with each other is that society does not want them to" (50, p. 176).

Gay Communities

The world of self-identified homosexuals is often referred to as the "homosexual community," "gay community," or "homosexual subculture." Such words as *subculture* or *community* used in the singular are misleading because they give the impression there is *one* or *a* gay community or subculture. I prefer to speak of gay communities or subcultures or friendship groupings since these terms are indicative of one of the most important sociological aspects of homosexual life styles—diversity, heterogeneity, variability.

It would be naive to expect to find the existence of a unitary, cohesive gay community, since homosexuals come from such diverse social backgrounds (20, 42, 52, 86, 111). The fact that homosexuals have a sexual identification in common does not erase their economic, political, religious, ethnic, and educational differences. Gay life styles are the product of both the individual's own unique social background and personality, and the nature of his interaction with other homosexuals.

Gay "Marriages"

There is a type of life style that has not been previously studied by social scientists and psychiatrists, and is nonexistent according to such authorities as Reuben. I am specifically referring to men who are involved in long-term homosexual "marriages."

Men involved in homosexual "marriage"-type relationships may or may not refer to these relationships as marriages and, of course, most likely have not gone through a religious wedding ceremony. They are married in the sense that they feel they have a permanent love and sexual and social commitment toward each other, and in the sense that they regard themselves as a couple and prefer to be regarded by other homosexuals as a couple. Such couples live together and reach different types of agreements concerning how their everyday tasks should be managed. The idea of the relationship consisting of one masculine and one feminine partner may or may not be applicable to any one marriage.

The social milieu in which such marriages are located varies greatly. Space does not permit a thorough review of these different types of marriages. One such type of marriage consists of the couple who predominantly associates with other gay married couples. Their gay social activities take place in the privacy of their homes, and they are only rarely found, if ever, in the public places of gay life. Before their marriage they most likely had some involvement with the gay-bar scene or other meeting places. But after they decided to live with each other they gradually decreased their gay social contacts. Often these couples have great commitment to sexual fidelity.

Many couples do not break off their contacts with single homosexuals after they begin to live together, and may still remain a part of the gay-bar scene. Such couples face the problem of promiscuity which was alluded to before. Their marriage may not be taken seriously by other gay people in the sense that they are considered fair game sexually. In fact, at times homosexually married couples become more sexually attractive precisely because they are married. They often become a challenge—a sexual challenge—that single gay men do not represent to other single gay men. These couples may also be employed to prove a point which has been stated to me in the following manner: "See, they really weren't that serious. Their marriage is just one big lie."

Couples in such promiscuous settings make a number of different adjustments. They may break up. Or they may reach various types of sexual agrements—e.g., having "extramarital" relations only with a third person, whom they share; agreeing to let each individual have one night out per week; going to the baths together or alone; never having sex with the same person more than once; never talking about their outside sexual relationships; etc. An individual couple may go through a number of these different agreements, and although some may reach a successful agreement, it is my impression that most ultimately fail. Hoffman (50) has referred to this as the problem of paired intimacy in the gay world. And, as previously stated, I agree basically with Hoffman that the problem of promiscuity in the gay world is ultimately the result of the homosexual's acceptance of the societal definition of himself as being inferior, and the lack of social and cultural support for such relationships. However, I believe that even if there were a change in these factors, there would still be certain structural factors in gay marriages that would militate against a high degree of success. For example, there is the absence of children. Since homosexuals do not have children, their emotional relationships are more focused and consequently more fragile than those found in heterosexual marriages with children. The only bind in the gay marriage is "spouse-to-spouse" and *not* the multiple emotional-affective binds that are often found in heterosexual marriages (mother-father, mother-daughter, father-daughter, father-son, etc.).

High-Status "Passers"

There are numerous self-identified homosexuals who, because of the nature of their occupation, may have only peripheral contact with organized gay communities, although they may have a significant identification with gay communities. These include high-ranking military officers, high government officials, those with top-secret government security clearances, police officers, ministers, teachers, and other persons in similar occupational positions.

The contacts of these persons with the gay world may be purely sexual, such as contacts with hustlers (77), or contacts in t-rooms or YMCAs, or visits to male houses of prostitution (75). Contacts may be to some degree social through visiting distant gay bars while on business trips or vacations or through having a few trusted gay friends. In order to be successful "passers," their lives must be carefully structured and planned (88). The arrest of Walter Jenkins, an adviser to President Johnson, in a YMCA men's room may have represented an unsuccessful attempt at passing.

The Trade Seeker

There is another type of self-identified homosexual who may be considered peripheral to the gay worlds. Although this person may be a part of gay friendship networks and on occasion frequent gay bars, he is not sexually integrated into a gay community. Rather he seeks a young, straight, masculine sex partner. The men he seeks may at times be referred to as "trade" (young "hustlers" who do not consider themselves to be homosexual and play the passive role in oral copulation). He may purposely seek out "rough trade" (individuals he knows may physically brutalize him or steal his money). The life of the trade seeker is characterized by extreme promiscuity—an almost continual prowling of the streets for the appropriate sexual contact, and a revolving door in and out of the hospital.

Public Meeting Places of Homosexuals

"Gay bars" are the major meeting places for homosexuals. These bars function as sexual marketplaces and as a center for one's leisure social activities (2, 50, 52, 53). The emphasis on sexuality may vary from one gay bar to the other, with some bars fulfilling the social functions of a neighborhood tavern and others functioning almost exclusively as sexual meeting places.

Bars can be differentiated according to the nature of their clientele. There are bars that cater to the leather set, or to the sado-masochistic group, or to the younger college crowd, or to drag queens (transvestites) and feminine homosexuals, etc. There are a number of bars that tend to have customers of the same social class, and others that cater to certain racial groups, particularly bars that cater to blacks. These more specialized gay bars coexist with a number of bars in which one can find all the different social strata of the gay world present.

Homosexual bathhouses are also prominent meeting places for

some homosexuals (50). These bathhouses are usually almost completely sexual in their functions. The typical bathhouse consists of a
steam room, separate cubicles in which individuals can have sexual
relations, and what is commonly called an "orgy" room. Some bathhouses have purposely attempted to present a less impersonal, more
relaxed atmosphere in which there is a significant degree of nonsexual social interaction. For example, one prominent bathhouse in
Los Angeles has a special room that is referred to as the "rap room,"
in which one can have coffee, engage in conversation, or simply
watch television.

Some residential areas having heavy concentrations of homosexuals also serve to facilitate social activities. Several parts of Los
Angeles have such areas, although the overwhelming majority of
homosexuals in Los Angeles do not live in these areas.

Many summer resort areas become known as gay vacation
spots. Along the coast of California there are numerous gay sections
of beaches. Probably the most famous gay beach-resort town on the
West Coast is California's Laguna Beach. Here even the naive
observer can tell where the gay section of the beach begins by the
sudden appearance of a heavy concentration of persons only of the
same sex.

There are many other settings in metropolitan areas that become meeting places for homosexuals: men's rooms, men's clothing
stores, coffee shops, restaurants, particular street corners, certain
sections of parks (78), movie theatres, etc. may function as meeting
places. Formal homophile * organizations that cater to the needs
of homosexuals have increasingly functioned as social centers for
their members. This has particularly been the case for Metropolitan
Community Church of Los Angeles, a Christian church for homosexuals, and the Society for Individual Rights (SIR) in San Francisco.

The homophile newspaper *Advocate* has had a tremendous impact on the nature of homosexual life, particularly in Los Angeles.
The *Advocate* presents both local and national news items relevant
to gay life. The *Advocate* also presents news of local gay events
and carries ads for many of the local gay establishments and homo-

---

* The term *homophile* refers to those, either homosexual or heterosexual (or, for
that matter, bisexual), who are sympathetic toward and supportive of homosexuals,
their problems, and the gay community at large. However, in this chapter it is
frequently used interchangeably with the term *homosexual. Eds.*

phile organizations. In a sense, the *Advocate* is bringing various disparate gay communities together, since it provides a medium of communication between these communities.

Masculinity-Femininity

In the gay worlds masculinity is a valued commodity, an asset in the sexual marketplace (51). I believe that the high value put on masculinity cuts through most of the different segments of the gay world. If there is a consensus on any subject in the gay world, it is that masculinity is better than femininity. The norm in the gay world is that one should be masculine. One should "be a man" and not "a sissy." Statements such as, "Those nellie queens make me sick," are typical.

This preference for the masculine involves not only the area of sexual attraction, but other social areas as well. In the friendship groupings and homophile organizations that I have studied, I found that status differentiation within these groups is highly related to masculinity-femininity, with the most masculine being nearest the top of the status hierarchy.

One of the major problems that exists in gay communities is the problem of prejudice toward femininity in general, and toward feminine homosexuals in particular. This situation leads many gay men to hate or to reject their own femininity. They often attempt to follow the norm of being overly masculine in spite of the fact that they feel feminine. Many homosexuals refer to this phenomenon as "butching it up." A person may butch it up only part of the time while in the presence of other gay people, or it may occur all of the time so that one's gay associates may regard the person as being his masculine self. Such persons who are able to have a continuing effective masculine presentation of self may have gone through long periods of masculinity rehearsal or training:

> The real change came when I went to the Playhouse school. There I learned acting in combination with psychology. The acting taught me what to do about my actions, and I proceeded to change them. I changed the way I walk, the way I dress, the voice, posture, mannerisms. Before I went to the Playhouse I wouldn't have considered myself masculine. . . . I worked at developing the masculine mannerisms.

In the gay worlds it is often impossible to know a person's gender by observing his overt behavior. Such role playing may lead to a feeling of tension or cognitive dissonance (34). "Camping behavior" (the display of feminine behavior in a humorous manner) may function to reduce this cognitive dissonance, for the individual can say: "Oh, that's not really me, I was just kidding, being campy." Also, drag shows and drag balls * may function as an outlet for one's femininity. Halloween in the gay world is somewhat analogous to New Year's Eve in the sense that traditional norms are suspended on Halloween and one can come out and be one's feminine self. This does not mean that all feminine behavior displayed on such occasions reflects one's inner femininity. There are definitely those who engage in feminine behavior to mock straight society, but do feel genuinely masculine.

Not all homosexuals who feel feminine accept the masculine norms of the gay worlds. Some individuals flaunt their femininity or simply behave as they feel—feminine. The individuals often form their own friendship groupings in which they know they are with those who are like themselves. For example, there are gay bars in most major cities in the United States that specifically cater to drag queens. Some overtly feminine homosexuals are even fortunate enough to find a homosexual who is sexually attracted to feminine men.

Jealousy

Another problem that I have found to be widespread among homosexuals is the problem of jealousy (80, 110), not of heterosexuals but of other homosexuals. Intense jealousy in the gay world often leads to what are called "bitch fights," which consequently often lead to the dissolution of informal friendship groupings and even of formal homophile organizations. Such jealousy, at times, may lead to threats of blackmail or to simply directly informing an employer that one of their employees is a homosexual (110). It can be hypothesized that, if systematic data were available on successful and unsuccessful blackmail attempts against homosexuals, these data would demonstrate that homosexuals are blackmailed more often by other homosexuals than by heterosexuals.

It can also be hypothesized that the intense jealousy displayed by many homosexuals is a result of their inability to completely emancipate themselves from the societal definition of themselves as

---

* *Drag* = dressing up as a member of the opposite sex. *Eds.*

being inferior. Since these homosexuals have not completely accepted themselves as homosexual, they may become extremely jealous
of other homosexuals' success. Based on my observations of the
internal politics of a number of different homophile organizations,
I have formulated the hypothesis that individual success is predictive
of failure—that is, the more successful the homophile leader, the
greater the willingness of others to take actions against the leader.
It is only the rare homophile leader who can avoid the pitfalls of
being successful.*

APPROACHES AND POSSIBILITIES
FOR RESOLVING THE DILEMMA
OF THE HOMOSEXUAL

The Law and the Police

Consenting sexual relations between adult persons of the same
sex in public or in private are illegal, as of 1972, in forty-five of
the fifty states of the United States. (The five exceptions are Illinois,
Connecticut, Colorado, Oregon, and Hawaii.) The felony laws of
California regulating such behavior are fairly representative of the
forty other states. California's two basic laws are 286A (sodomy)
and 288A (oral copulation):

> Sodomy: Every person who is guilty of the infamous crime against
> nature, committed with mankind or any animal, is punishable by
> imprisonment [for] not less than on year. (40, p. 674)
>
> Oral copulation: Any person participating in an act of copu-
> lating the mouth of one person with the sexual organ of another is
> punishable by imprisonment in the state prison for not exceeding 15
> years or by imprisonment in the county jail not to exceed 1 year.
> (40, p. 677)

Although such laws are rarely enforced against individuals who
privately engage in these acts, these laws nevertheless function to
degrade the homosexual and are used to justify the legal harassment

* In addition, the homophile leader may suffer from a significant degree of insecurity. In this case the homophile leader's own insecurity may motivate him to
take actions that tend to degrade his followers. Such actions often arouse even
greater jealousy in the followers and reinforce their desire to take actions against
the homophile leader.

and discrimination that is directed against the homosexual. These laws are symbolic in the sense that they communicate to society what behaviors are acceptable and not acceptable, which are legitimate and not legitimate (46). Most leaders of the homophile movement recognize the symbolic importance of these laws and emphasize the importance of their removal.

The symbolic nature of these laws was illustrated in June 1970 in Los Angeles when, after the homosexual leader Rev. Troy D. Perry, pastor of Metropolitan Community Church, requested a permit for a parade along Hollywood Boulevard demonstrating for homosexual civil liberties, Los Angeles Police Chief Edward Davis publicly responded in the following manner:

> We would be ill-advised to discommode the people to have a burglars' or robbers' or homosexuals' parade. (4, p. 1)

Legislative efforts to repeal these laws have almost uniformly failed. When they have succeeded, the laws were repealed in a context in which there was a general reform of the penal code, and little or no publicity was attached to the laws regulating homosexual conduct.

Efforts to declare these laws unconstitutional via the courts have also essentially failed. No case involving the constitutionality of these laws has been reviewed by the Supreme Court. Recently the California Court of Appeals rejected an attempt to declare the California oral-copulation law unconstitutional. Judge Mildred L. Lillie gave the following rationale for her decision.

> In the exercise of the police power, each state has the right to enact laws to protect public health, safety, morals and welfare. . . . Penal statutes proscribing illicit sexual contacts constitute a legitimate and proper exercise of that power. . . . The making of unnatural sexual relations a crime is embedded in the history of the common law, and finds its sanction in the broader base of the settled mores of western civilization. (5, p. 1)

The most recent case that invoved homosexuality to come before the Supreme Court was *Boutilier* v. *Immigration and Naturalization Service* in 1967. Boutilier had emigrated to the United States in 1955, and several years later it was discovered by the U.S. government that Boutilier was engaging in homosexual acts and that he had engaged in such acts prior to entry. Invoking the Immigration and Naturalization Act of 1952, the government ordered Boutilier deported on the grounds that, according to the Act, "Aliens afflicted with psychopathic personality, epilepsy or a mental defect . . . shall be excludable from admission into the United States" (102, p. 246). The Court upheld the deportation of Boutilier in a five-to-four decision, declaring that Congress had intended the term *psychopathic personality* to include homosexuals.

In 1969 there was a significant legal breakthrough that involved the dismissal of a U.S. Civil Service employee because he was homosexual (73). In the case of *Norton* v. *Macy* the Federal Appeals Court for the District of Columbia ruled that a governmental agency could not dismiss an employee without presenting evidence that his homosexuality in some manner interfered with his work. However, this decision is not necessarily legally applicable to other Federal Court districts, and consequently the U.S. Civil Service is still firing employees simply because they are homosexual.

Decisions such as *Norton* v. *Macy* will not become effective unless they are accompanied by significant attitudinal change on the part of the employer. The fact that a California court recently ruled that homosexual schoolteachers cannot be fired because they are homosexual did not cause the homosexual schoolteachers I have met to be any less fearful of discovery.

The bulk of the homosexuals' involvement with the law is in the form of some contact with the police. Arrests of homosexuals are most often made under misdemeanor laws that make illegal the acts of solicitation, disorderly conduct, or indecent behavior. These arrests tend to occur in the public meeting places of homosexuals, such as gay bars, public restrooms, parks, etc. (40).

Police methods of operation vary (66). In public restrooms police often operate as decoys, loitering about, using the sink or urinal or commode for long periods of time with the hope of obtaining a solicitation. Use of the decoy method becomes illegal entrapment if it can be demonstrated that the intent to commit the crime originated in the mind of the police officer (40). In reality, entrapment is almost impossible to prove, and in suspicious cases the judge or jury is much more likely to believe the arresting officer. A UCLA Law School study (40) found that entrapment practices definitely exist in Los Angeles. This coincides with the widespread belief in the

Los Angeles gay communities that such practices are far from rare.

Police tactics in gay bars vary widely, from engaging in lengthy conversations with customers with the hope that they will eventually make a solicitation, to entering the bar and making random arrests, to heavy patrol of bars, to frequently entering bars and checking identification of customers (40). Police harassment of gay bars also tends to be episodic. For example, Garden Grove, California, traditionally has had a very liberal attitude toward gay bars, with the consequence being the heaviest concentration of gay bars in Orange County. During the first part of 1971, the Garden Grove bars experienced a number of arrests. The reasons for this change in policy remain unknown.

By far the most serious charge involving police behavior is that of physical police brutality. The impression that one receives in many gay communities is that the police are not at all hesitant about employing brutality against homosexuals. Charges of police brutality are of course extremely difficult to document. The *Advocate* has reported numerous cases of alleged police brutality in Los Angeles. Probably one of the most infamous cases involved a police raid of the Black Cat, a Los Angeles gay bar, at midnight on New Year's Eve 1967. The resulting panic led to the police beating several patrons.

Police enforcement practices are undoubtedly the result of police attitudes toward homosexuals, and it is my impression that the police tend to be more antihomosexual than most other occupational groups. I am aware of no police training or education programs that emphasize the civil liberties and/or humanity of homosexuals. A vice control textbook that is widely employed in police science courses in California treats homosexuals in the following manner:

> Many do-gooders and other misinformed people have been asking for more social and official tolerance of homosexuals. . . . The truth of the matter is that these "Hollywood" and "Greenwich" village "cannibals" are constantly on the lookout for "new stuff" —persons who are not homosexuals. . . . Homosexuals are constantly seeking recruits and prefer young boys and young men to older men and older queers. The contaminating influence they exert can be reduced to a minimum by tough, relentless law enforcement. (114, p. 27)

With "education" such as this, it is not surprising that police officers are generally the most adamant opponents of homosexual-law reform at legislative committee hearings.

The New Awareness

Presently we are in the midst of a true revolution with regard to the societal treatment of the homosexual. This revolution has taken the form of a communications revolution, of a new willingness in our society to talk about homosexuals and homosexuality. As long as the societal taboo of not talking about homosexuality was effective, there could not be any recognition that homosexuals or the treatment of homosexuals represented a social problem and that some action should be taken to ameliorate this social problem.

This communications revolution has taken place in mass-circulation magazines, movies, newspapers, radio, and television. Probably the most significant and trend-setting action was taken by *Time* magazine (104) in 1969 when they ran a front-cover story on "The Homosexual in America." The article departed from previous articles in mass-circulation magazines in that it did not present homosexuals in a uniformly negative context, but rather emphasized the humanity of homosexuals. This *Time* article set the basis for an amazing article that appeared in the "American Family" edition of *Look* magazine (95) in 1971. The article described, with words and pictures and in a nonevaluative manner, a homosexually married couple.

During the period from 1969 to 1971 many local television stations and newspapers became significantly more liberal in presenting information on homosexuality. Television station KNBC of Los Angeles was given an Emmy award by the Hollywood chapter of the National Academy of Television Arts and Sciences for its documentary "Out of the Shadows." Television documentaries on homosexuality were also accompanied by interviews with self-admitted homosexuals, and the first nationally televised interview with publicly admitted homosexuals occurred on the Dick Cavett Show in 1970. *Victim!* in 1961 became the first movie in which the term *homosexual* was employed (74), and subsequently Hollywood produced a number of movies that overtly dealt with homosexual themes, although most of these movies presented homosexuals in a rather depressing manner. However, movies such as *Women in Love* and *Sunday Bloody Sunday* reflect a new willingness to present this subject in a more favorable and enlightening manner.

The Homophile Movement

Movements for the improvement of minority-group members cannot obtain a mass following until the leaders of the movement have the ability to communicate with group members and with each other, and until the group members and leaders believe that there is the potentiality of their group exerting power because of their large numbers. The communications revolution has provided these factors for the homophile movement. Most importantly, it has provided many homosexuals with the opportunity to say, "I am not alone," or, "We are not alone."

The *Advocate,* the national homophile newspaper based in Los Angeles, has played a crucial role in facilitating communication among homosexuals and homophile leaders. The *Advocate* provides a vehicle through which leaders can present their views and recruit members to their organizations. It provides news of the activities of the homophile movement in cities throughout the United States and therefore leads to a greater feeling of national unity. It may indeed be no coincidence that prior to the *Advocate,* formal homosexual organizations were essentially small in numbers, local in membership, and nonpolitically oriented.

The crucial role of the *Advocate* and other communications media was clearly demonstrated in the phenomenal growth of Metropolitan Community Church (MCC) and the rise of its pastor, Rev. Troy D. Perry, to the status of being the only national leader within the homophile movement. Perry, a Pentecostal minister, formed MCC in October 1968 in order to serve the religious and social needs of homosexuals in Los Angeles. Attendance at the first meeting was twelve, and grew only slowly during the next few months. In 1969 the *Advocate* ran a story on Perry and his church; attendance soared. Soon other communications media ran stories on the church (28, 36, 70), and not only did attendance continue to increase, but requests for permission to form other MCCs poured in from all over the country.

Presently the Los Angeles congregation has an attendance of five to six hundred every Sunday and a church building of its own. A national denomination of the Universal Fellowship of Metropolitan Community Churches has been formed, with churches and missions in many cities in the United States. Perry has led demonstrations for homosexual civil liberties throughout the country and, in 1971, led marches on the state capitals of New York and California. Perry has appeared on numerous television programs, and these appearances may be functioning to significantly change heterosexual images of the homosexual, since Perry presents himself as a masculine clergyman who espouses a traditional Christian rhetoric—except on the subject of homosexuality.

Meanwhile, on the East Coast, in June 1969 police raided a gay bar in Greenwich Village in New York City. For the first time there was active resistance by customers to a police raid on a gay bar. This resistance quickly turned into a riot. News of the event was effectively communicated by the *Advocate,* and the "Christopher Street riot" became a symbol for new gay militant groups, often calling themselves "gay liberation fronts" (103).

The growth of the gay liberation movement has united a part of the homophile movement with the "radical left" and "hippie" movements. For example, in 1970 Los Angeles Gay Liberation Front (GLF) members tended to be young (average age about twenty-three) and to wear hippie-type clothing, beards, and long hair. Given the association of college-age youth with the new "counterculture," it is not surprising that GLF groups have been formed on many college campuses.

The basic assumptions of many GLF groups, particularly GLF-Los Angeles, appear to be the following: (*a*) only homosexuals can publicly discuss homosexuality; (*b*) the hippie counterculture is the only valid life style; (*c*) only GLF speaks for the homosexual; and (*d*) every homosexual must liberate himself or herself at once.

Some GLF groups are willing to resort to tactics that moderate homophile groups are not willing to employ. Such tactics were employed in 1970 when a GLF group disrupted meetings of the National Association of Mental Health and the Conference on Behavior Modification in Los Angeles.

The emergence of the radical gay liberation movement significantly widens the disunity within the homophile movement. The depth of this disunity was illustrated by the disruption, in August 1970, of the North American Conference of Homophile Organizations (NACHO) meeting in San Francisco by various GLF factions. The conference ended in a state of chaos and turmoil. Some reactions by conservative homophile leaders to GLF tactics were the following:

With the gay militants there is another element involved. As I watched them and listened to them, and tried to argue with them (it's impossible to really communicate with them), I was suddenly shocked to realize that these people do not accept themselves. They are so full of feelings of guilt and self-hatred that they have to scream and kick at the rest of the world, demanding that we accept them so that they can accept themselves. (18, p. 14)

We watch the activities of the most disruptive gay militants with fascination. We try in vain to detect some rationale in their tactics and in their philosophy. . . .

But it becomes more and more apparent that these so-called gay militants are not so much pro-gay as they are anti-Establishment, anti-capitalist, anti-society. They lash out in all directions, destroying everything in sight—gay or straight. (31, p. 18)

The dilemma of the homophile movement is reflected in the very heterogeneity of its members. The fact that homosexuals come from such varied backgrounds makes unity within the movement and even within particular homophile groups extremely difficult. This problem is further compounded by the status insecurity that was discussed earlier in this chapter. Although Humphreys (56) sees the possibility of a figure such as Troy Perry unifying the homophile movement, the probability of this occurring is extremely low, as evidenced by the fact that Perry's presence at the San Francisco NACHO conference could not bring the various warring factions together.

It is the opinion of this writer that the continued growth of the homophile movement is dependent on the ability of group leaders to recognize that there are a number of homophile movements and that no one group represents all homosexuals. Unless there is a recognition of and tolerance of pluralism within the movement, the probability of the homophile movement's being destroyed from within is very great.*

Governmental Policies

In spite of the increasing nationwide discussion of homosexuality, governmental actions aimed at changing or ameliorating

* I do not mean to imply that there is no degree of unity within the homophile movement. All homophile groups are dedicated to improving the social and legal status of the homosexual, and for varying periods of time are able to work together. For example, homophile groups have been able to effectively work together in organizing activities for Gay Pride Day, June 27, which in effect has become a gay national holiday.

problems associated with homosexuality have been few. Probably the most significant action involving a government unit on the national level was the 1969 Final Report of the Task Force on Homosexuality (35). This task force was appointed in September 1967 by Dr. Stanley Yolles, director of the National Institute of Mental Health, and consisted of many leading authorities on homosexuality. Some of their recommendations were: that legal penalties be no longer imposed for homosexual acts conducted in private between consenting adults; that a reassessment be made of employment policies dealing with homosexuals; that sex-information programs be made to include information on homosexuality; that special training be instituted for law-enforcement personnel who deal with homosexuals; and that high priority be given to research projects that study homosexual behavior. Governmental reaction to these proposals has been essentially one of silence. The U.S. Government Printing Office apparently considered this document to be of such little significance that it did not merit publication!

Governmental policies on the local level may be influenced by the power of the homophile movement to unify homosexuals behind specific political candidates. During the 1969 Los Angeles City Council election campaign, a number of homophile groups vigorously campaigned for Robert Stevenson, who opposed incumbent Paul Lamport. In an upset election Lamport was defeated, with the deciding factor seemingly being the homosexual vote. Lamport summarized his defeat in the following manner: "I'm inclined to think that the final vote was the vote of 3,000 homosexuals who're probably pretty pleased that they were able to defeat me. I think that the *Free Press* and *Advocate*, and the slimy newspapers of the lower levels of our city assisted" (3, p. 5).

The major issue involving governmental policies has been the repeal of state felony laws regulating homosexual behavior (19). In spite of the fact that Illinois repealed these laws with no apparent harm to their populace as of 1972, only four other states have followed suit. U.S. government bodies also have knowledge of the repeal of these laws in England (57, 115) and Canada without any apparent harm to these two nations. Obviously, the belief in this country that sexual morality should be reflected in the law continues to be widespread, and consequently the probability of the large-scale repeal of these laws remains rather low.

Educational Policies

Efforts to include objective information on homosexuality in sex-education programs in the public schools are not likely to meet with success. In fact, opponents of sex-education programs sometimes cite the existence of information on homosexuality as reasons for abolishing such programs. Sex-education programs are more likely to miseducate than educate when the teachers of sex education have attitudes of the following nature: "At the heart of sex education classes is the concept that sex is normal for mature men and women. By sheer definition sex connotes heterosexuality" (16, p. 27).

Efforts to introduce courses dealing with homosexual behavior on the college level have met with somewhat more success. In the fall of 1970, the first two college courses for credit to deal totally with homosexuality began: a graduate interdisciplinary seminar taught by Professor Louis Crompton at the University of Nebraska and an undergraduate course entitled "Sociology of Homosexual Behavior" taught by this writer at California State College, Long Beach. As might be expected, the Nebraska course received a great deal of opposition from local politicians, and consequently the course was abolished at the end of the academic year. The California course met with no opposition and was well received by the academic and non-academic communities. What was significant was that at least one of the courses did survive; such success may facilitate the introduction of courses on homosexuality in other universities and colleges.

Changing educational policies have also been reflected in the official recognition of gay student groups by a number of different colleges. Changing attitudes within academe were most clearly reflected in 1971 with the election of a publicly admitted homosexual as president of the University of Minnesota student body.

Psychiatric Attitudes

Contemporary psychiatric attitudes on homosexuality still tend to be conservative, most often viewing homosexuality as a mental illness, albeit a behavior that should not be criminalized. The most significant departure from this traditional position was taken by the National Association of Mental Health (68) in 1970, when they issued a new position paper on homosexuality in which they stated that homosexuals are not necessarily mentally ill, that psychotherapy

offers no definite assurance of change from homosexual to heterosexual behavior, and that homosexual acts should not be criminalized. Individual psychiatrists such as Hoffman (50) and Szasz (101,
102) have played a significant role in challenging traditional psychiatric thought on this subject.

Religious Attitudes

The new awareness of homosexuality has influenced a few
Protestant denominations in recent years to modify their positions
on homosexuality. Such modifications have occurred in the United
Presbyterian, Lutheran, and Unitarian churches. However, in spite
of these changes the predominant religious viewpoint still is that
homosexuality is the "unspeakable crime against nature." The continuation of such an attitude has led to the creation of special
churches essentially for homosexuals, as Metropolitan Community
Church and the American Orthodox Church of New York City.

Research and Treatment

Research on homosexuality has traditionally focused on the
etiology of homosexual behavior. Those who have conducted such
research have generally had a correctional interest in homosexual
behavior. Their hope has been that if the causes of homosexual behavior could be determined, then methods of conversion would also
be more likely to be discovered (15).

These etiological studies have been characterized by faulty
methodologies and highly biased samples (59). More recently, however, rather diverse studies are producing data that point to the
importance of early family relations and that particularly highlight
the importance of the combination of a psychologically absent, distant, or hostile father and a warm, affectionate, close mother in the
etiology of homosexual behavior (7, 11, 14, 15, 27, 33, 37, 54, 72).
Some researchers are increasingly emphasizing the role of the father
(15, 27, 110), since the type of behaviors demonstrated by these
fathers would not be expected to facilitate a strong masculine
identification in their sons.

Evidence of successful conversion therapies have not been
produced. Although there have been numerous claims of success by
therapists, these claims are not supported by systematic scientific
studies (15, 48, 92). Even the claims that are based on relatively
large samples do not contain extensive follow-up studies and suffer

from lack of control groups.* Some therapists assert that homosexuals can be changed if they *really* want to change (47); such assertions function to cover up the failure of the therapist, since if the therapy fails it becomes the patient's fault and not the therapist's or his choice of therapy.

Recently, a number of researchers have abandoned this etiological-treatment emphasis and have conducted research that views the adult homosexual in his various social contexts. These research efforts attempt to view the homosexual in his everyday life and to understand the nature of the problems that he is likely to encounter (2, 25, 26, 38, 50, 51, 52, 53, 55, 61, 63, 81, 108, 113).

PROSPECTS FOR THE HOMOSEXUAL

In spite of the new awareness of homosexuality and in spite of some attitudinal change in our society, it would be naïve to assume that the antihomosexual prejudice in our society will not continue to exist. The predominant attitude still is that homosexuals are in some sense unacceptable or inferior to heterosexuals. The continued widespread use of the word *queer* to refer to homosexuals is indicative of this fact.

Although much of the antihomosexual prejudice is a result of cultural tradition and the norm of silence, there is another very important factor that promotes its continuation. Heterosexual parents desire their children to be like themselves. As long as homosexuals are produced by heterosexual parents, parents will tend to fear those who they feel could lead their children from the heterosexual path. It should therefore not be surprising that one of the most common stereotypes of the homosexual in our society is that of the child molester.

In one of the most revealing essays on the nature of the antihomosexual prejudice, Joseph Epstein, a literary critic, attempts to understand why he dislikes homosexuals. After extensively exploring his own views, Epstein concludes with the following:

> One can tolerate homosexuality, a small enough price to be asked to pay for someone else's pain, but accepting it, really accepting it,

---

* I do not mean to state that no individuals have ever changed from being predominantly homosexual to predominantly heterosexual in the context of psychotherapy. Unquestionably there have been such cases. What is being questioned is the assertion that there is evidence that the therapy caused the change.

is another thing altogether. I find I can accept it least of all when I look at my children. There is much my four sons can do in their lives that might cause me anguish, that might outrage me, that might make me ashamed of them and of myself as their father. But nothing they could ever do would make me sadder than if they were to become homosexual. (32, p. 51)

The prospects of the heterosexual majority completely accepting homosexuals as equals remain dim. As long as our society permits relatively freer communication on this subject, the prospect of continued *greater* acceptance of homosexuals by heterosexuals and by themselves is favorable. The fact that the future social status of the homosexual has now become problematic represents a revolutionary departure from the traditional societal rejection of the homosexual.

References

1. Abrahamsen, D. *The psychology of crime.* New York: John Wiley, 1961.
2. Achilles, N. The development of the homosexual bar as an institution. In J. Gagnon and W. Wimon (eds.), *Sexual deviance.* New York: Harper & Row, 1967, pp. 228–44.
3. *Advocate,* August 1969.
4. *Advocate,* July 8–21, 1970.
5. *Advocate,* Feb. 3–16, 1971.
6. American Psychiatric Association. *Diagnostic and statistical manual of mental disorders,* (2nd ed.) Washington, D.C., 1968.
7. Apperson, L. B., and McAdoo, W. G. Parental factors in the childhood of homosexuals. *Journal of Abnormal Psychology,* 1968, *73,* 201–6.
8. Bailey, D. S. *Homosexuality and the Western Christian tradition.* London: Longmans, Green, 1955.
9. Bell, R. B. *Social deviance.* Homewood, Ill.: Dorsey Press, 1971.
10. Bene, E. On the genesis of female homosexuality. *British Journal of Psychiatry,* 1965, *111,* 815–21.
11. Bene, E. On the genesis of male homosexuality. *British Journal of Psychiatry,* 1965, *111,* 803–13.
12. Benjamin, H. *The transsexual phenomenon.* New York: Julian Press, 1966.
13. Benson, R. O. D. *In defense of homosexuality.* New York: Julian Press, 1965. (Republished as Benson, R. O. D. *What every homosexual knows.* New York: Ace, 1970.)
14. Bergler, E. *Neurotic counterfeit-sex.* New York: Grune and Stratton, 1951.
15. Bieber, I., et al. *Homosexuality: A psychoanalytic study of male homosexuals.* New York: Basic Books, 1962.
16. Blaufarb, E. Making sex education relevant. *School Health Review,* 1971, *2*(1), 27–28.

17. Buckner, H. T. The transvestic career path. *Psychiatry,* 1970, *33,* 381–89.
18. Cervantes, M. They don't accept themselves. *Advocate,* Jan. 6–19, 1971, p. 14.
19. *The challenge and progress of homosexual law reform.* 1968. (Available from Society for Individual Rights, 83 6th St., San Francisco, Calif. 94103.)
20. Churchill, W. *Homosexual behavior among males: A cross-cultural and cross-species investigation.* New York: Hawthorn, 1967.
21. Clemmer, D. *The prison community.* New York: Holt, Rinehart, 1958.
22. Clinard, M. B. *Sociology of deviant behavior.* New York: Holt, Rinehart, 1968.
23. Cory, D. W. *The lesbian in America.* New York: Citadel Press, 1964.
24. Dalrymple, R. Vice laws and the Bible. *Los Angeles Herald-Examiner,* January 23, 1971, Religion section.
25. Dank, B. M. Coming out in the gay world. *Psychiatry,* 1971, *34,* 180–97.
26. Dank, B. M. Why homosexuals marry women. *Medical Aspects of Human Sexuality,* in press.
27. Dank, B. M. Homosexual siblings. *Archives of Sexual Behavior,* 1971, *1,* 193–204.
28. Dart, J. Church for homosexuals. *Los Angeles Times,* Dec. 8, 1969, part 2, pp. 1–3.
29. Davis, A. J. Sexual assaults in the Philadelphia prison system and sheriffs' vans. *Trans-action,* 1968, *6,*(2), 8–16.
30. DeMartino, M. F. *The new female sexuality.* New York: Julian Press, 1969.
31. Editorial: Not right on. *Advocate,* Sept. 30–Oct. 13, 1970, 18.
32. Epstein, J. Homo/hetero: The struggle for sexual identity. *Harper's,* 1970, *241*(9), 37–51.
33. Evans, R. B. Childhood parental relationships of homosexual men. *Journal of Consulting and Clinical Psychology,* 1969, *33,* 129–35.
34. Festinger, L. *A theory of cognitive dissonance.* Evanston, Ill.: Row, Peterson, 1957.
35. *Final report of the task force on homosexuality.* National Institute of Mental Health, 1969. (Available from One Institute, 2256 Venice Blvd., Los Angeles, Calif. 90006.)
36. Fiske, E. B. Homosexuals in Los Angeles . . . establish their own church. *New York Times,* Feb. 15, 1970, section 1, p. 58.
37. Freund, K. & Pinkava, V. Homosexuality in man and its association with parental relationships. *Review of Czechoslovakian Medicine,* 1961, *7,* 32–40.
38. Gagnon, J., & Simon, W. Homosexuality: The formulation of a sociological perspective. In M. Lefton et al. (eds.), *Approaches to deviance.* New York: Appleton-Century-Crofts, 1968, pp. 349–61.
39. Gagnon, J., & Simon, W. The social meaning of prison homosexuality. *Federal Probation,* 1968, *32,* 23–29.
40. Gallo, J. J., et. al. The consenting adult homosexual and the law: An

empirical study of enforcement and administration in Los Angeles County. *UCLA Law Review,* 1966, *13,* 644–832.

41. Gebhard, P. Incidence of overt homosexuality in the United States and Western Europe. Background paper submitted to the Task Force on Homosexuality (see 35).
42. Gebhard, P., Gagnon, J., Pomeroy, W. B., & Christenson, C. *Sex offenders: An analysis of types.* New York: Hoeber-Harper, 1965.
43. Giallombardo, R. *Society of women: A study of a women's prison.* New York: John Wiley, 1966.
44. Goffman, E. *Stigma: Notes on the management of spoiled identity.* Englewood Cliffs, N.J.: Prentice-Hall, 1963.
45. Green, R., & Money, J. (eds.). *Transsexualism and sex reassignment.* Baltimore: Johns Hopkins Press, 1969.
46. Gusfield, J. R. Moral passage: The symbolic process in public designations of deviance. *Social Problems,* 1967, *15,* 175–80.
47. Hadden, S. B. A way out for homosexuals. *Harper's,* March 1967, pp. 107–20.
48. Hatterer, L. J. *Changing homosexuality in the male: Treatment for men troubled by homosexuality.* New York: McGraw-Hill, 1970.
49. Himelhoch, J., & Fava, S. F., (eds.). *Sexual behavior in American society.* New York: W. W. Norton, 1955.
50. Hoffman, M. *The gay world: Male homosexuality and the social creation of evil.* New York: Basic Books, 1968.
51. Hooker, E. An empirical study of some relations between sexual patterns and gender identity in male homosexuals. In J. Money (ed.), *Sex research: New developments.* New York: Holt, Rinehart, 1965. Pp. 24–52.
52. Hooker, E. Male homosexuals and their "worlds." In J. Marmor (ed.), *Sexual inversion: The multiple roots of homosexuality.* New York: Basic Books, 1965. Pp. 83–107.
53. Hooker, E. The homosexual community. In J. Gagnon & W. Simon (eds.), *Sexual deviance.* New York: Harper & Row, 1967. Pp. 167–96.
54. Hooker, E. Parental relations and male homosexuality in patient and non-patient samples. *Journal of Consulting and Clinical Psychology,* 1969, *33,* 140–42.
55. Humphreys, L. *Tearoom trade.* Chicago: Aldine, 1970.
56. Humphreys, L. New styles in homosexual manliness. *Trans-action,* 1971, *8*(5-6), 38–46, 64–66.
57. Hyde, H. M. *The love that dare not speak its name: A candid history of homosexuality in Britain.* Boston: Little, Brown, 1970.
58. Kenyon, F. E. Studies in female homosexuality: IV—Social and psychiatric aspects; V—Sexual development, attitudes, and experience. *British Journal of Psychiatry,* 1968, *114,* 1337–50.
59. Kepner, J. Dr. Bieber's enormous carrot. *Tangents,* 1968, *2,* 13–19.
60. Kinsey, A. C., Pomeroy, W. B., & Martin, C. E. *Sexual behavior in the human male.* Philadelphia: W. B. Saunders, 1948.
61. Kitsuse, J. I. Societal reactions to deviant behavior: Problems of theory and method. *Social Problems,* 1962, *9,* 247–56.
62. Lemert, E. *Social pathology.* New York: McGraw-Hill, 1951.

63. Leznoff, M., & Westley, W. The homosexual community. *Social Problems,* 1956, *3,* 257–62.
64. Lofland, J. *Deviance and identity.* Englewood Cliffs, N.J.: Prentice-Hall, 1969.
65. Matza, D. *Becoming deviant.* Englewood Cliffs, N.J.: Prentice-Hall, 1969.
66. Mitchell, R. S. *The homosexual and the law.* New York: Arco, 1969.
67. Money, J. *Sex errors of the body.* Baltimore: Johns Hopkins Press, 1968.
68. National Association of Mental Health. Homosexuality. *Mental Hygiene,* 1971, *55,* 131–32.
69. Nemy, E. The woman homosexual: More assertive, less willing to hide. *New York Times,* Nov. 17, 1969, p. 61.
70. *Newsweek* article: The homosexual church. Oct. 12, 1970, p. 107.
71. Oberholtzer, W. D. (ed.). *Is gay good? Ethics, theology, and homosexuality.* Philadelphia: Westminster Press, 1971.
72. O'Connor, P. J. Aetiological factors in homosexuality as seen in Royal Air Force psychiatric practice. *British Journal of Psychiatry,* 1964, *110,* 381–91.
73. Parker, W. *Homosexuals and employment,* 1970. (Available from Society for Individual Rights, 83 6th St., San Francisco, Calif. 94103.)
74. Phillips, G. D. Homosexuality in the movies. *Sexual Behavior,* 1971, *1*(2), 18–23, 37.
75. Pittman, D. The male house of prostitution. *Trans-action,* 1971, *8* (6), 21–27.
76. Prince, C. V. The transvestite and his wife. Los Angeles: Chevalier Publications, 1967.
77. Rechy, J. *City of night.* New York: Grove Press, 1963.
78. Rechy, J. *Numbers.* New York: Grove Press, 1967.
79. Reuben, D. *Everything you always wanted to know about sex (but were afraid to ask).* New York: David McKay, 1969.
80. Romm, M. E. Sexuality and homosexuality in women. In J. Marmor (ed.), *Sexual inversion: The multiple roots of homosexuality.* New York: Basic Books, 1965.
81. Ross, H. L. Modes of adjustment of married homosexuals. *Social Problems,* 1971, *18,* 385–93.
82. Rubington, E., & Weinberg, M. (eds.). *Deviance: The interactionist perspective.* New York: Macmillan, 1968.
83. Rubington, E., & Weinberg, M. (eds.). *The study of social problems.* New York: Oxford University Press, 1971.
84. Saghir, M. T., et al. Homosexuality: IV—Psychiatric disorders and disability in the female homosexual. *American Journal of Psychiatry,* 1970, *127,* 147–54.
85. Saghir, M. T., & Robins, E. Homosexuality: I—Sexual behavior of the female homosexual. *Archives of General Psychiatry,* 1969, *20,* 192–201.
86. Schofield, M. *Sociological aspects of homosexuality.* London: Longmans, Green, 1965.

87. Schur, E. *Crimes without victims.* Englewood Cliffs, N.J.: Prentice-Hall, 1965.
88. Scott, M. B., & Lyman, S. M. Paranoia, homosexuality, and game theory. *Journal of Health and Social Behavior,* 1968, *9,* 179–87.
89. Simmons, J. L. Public stereotypes of deviants. *Social Problems,* 1965, *13,* 223–32.
90. Simon, W., & Gagnon, J. Femininity in the lesbian community. *Social Problems,* 1967, *15,* 212–21.
91. Simon, W., & Gagnon, J. The lesbians: A preliminary overview. In J. Gagnon & W. Simon (eds.), *Sexual deviance.* New York: Harper & Row, 1967. Pp. 247–82.
92. Socarides, C. W. *The overt homosexual.* New York: Grune and Stratton, 1968.
93. Socarides, C. W. Homosexuality and medicine. *Journal of the American Medical Association,* 1970, *212,* 1119–202.
94. Sonenschein, D. The ethnography of male homosexual relationships. *Journal of Sex Research,* 1968, *4,* 69–83.
95. Star, J. The homosexual couple. *Look,* Jan. 26, 1971, pp. 69–71.
96. Stoller, R. *Sex and gender.* New York: Science House, 1968.
97. Stoller, R. The term transvestism. *Archives of General Psychiatry,* 1971, *24,* 230–37.
98. Sykes, G. M. *Society of captives.* Princeton: Princeton University Press, 1958.
99. Szasz, T. The myth of mental illness. *American Psychologist,* 1960, *15,* 113–18.
100. Szasz, T. *Law, liberty, and psychiatry.* New York: Macmillan, 1963.
101. Szasz, T. Legal and moral aspects of homosexuality. In J. Marmor (ed.), *Sexual inversion: The multiple roots of homosexuality.* New York: Basic Books, 1965.
102. Szasz, T. *The manufacture of madness.* New York: Harper & Row, 1970.
103. Teal, D. *The gay militants.* New York: Stein & Day, 1971.
104. *Time* article: The homosexual in America. Oct. 31, 1969, pp. 61–62, 64–67.
105. Tittle, C. R. Inmate organization: Sex differentiation and the influence of criminal subcultures. *American Sociological Review,* 1969, *34,* 492–505.
106. *Transvestia.* Chevalier Publications, Box 36091, Los Angeles, Calif. 90036.
107. Ward D., & Kassebaum, G. *Women's prison: Sex and social structure.* Chicago: Aldine, 1965.
108. Weinberg, M. S. The male homosexual: Age-related variations in social and psychological characteristics. *Social Problems,* 1970, *17,* 527–37.
109. West, D. J. Parental figures in the genesis of male homosexuality. *International Journal of Social Psychiatry,* 1959, *5,* 85–97.
110. West, D. J. *Homosexuality.* Chicago: Aldine, 1967.
111. Westwood, G. *A minority: A report on the life of the male homosexual in Great Britain.* London: Longmans, Green, 1960.
112. What about homosexuality? *Social Progress,* 1967, *58* (whole issue).

113. Williams, C. J., & Weinberg, M. S. Being discovered: A study of homosexuals in the military. *Social Problems,* 1970, *18,* 217–27.
114. Williams, J. B. *Vice control in California.* Beverly Hills, Calif.: Glencoe Press, 1964.
115. *The Wolfenden report.* New York: Lancer Books, 1964.
116. Wood, R. W. *Christ and the homosexual.* New York: Vantage Press, 1960.

Homosexual Encounters in a Highway Rest Stop

by Richard R. Troiden

The highway rest stop provides a site for two types of activities: respectable and deviant. As a respectable place, the rest area provides the weary traveler with a place to stop and take a nap, if tired. Or a place to walk, stretch, and loosen muscles cramped as a result of too many hours spent behind the wheel. Or a place for families and couples to picnic. A place where litter may be disposed of. Or a place where one may relieve oneself—either in the restrooms provided, or, failing that, in the bushes.

But rest stops also harbor a netherworld, a world completely unanticipated by those who designed, paid for, and built them. A *sexual service* is provided by these seemingly innocuous places: they are the site of transitory homosexual liaisons.

Shortly after five o'clock on a weekday late one spring, a 1971 gold Camaro eased out of the heavy traffic flow on a major, commuter-choked expressway on the distant outskirts of New York City, slowed down as it entered the approach road to a rest stop, and coasted to a halt in a designated parking space some fifty feet into the rest area. The driver emerged from the car. As he straightened up, he loosened his tie, removed his sports coat, dropped it onto the back seat of the car, then yawned slowly and stretched. While doing so, he cast a momentary glance in my direction. I sat—relaxing and smoking a cigarette after a long drive—at my vantage point, a picnic table some twenty-five feet away. The man was roughly six feet tall, about thirty years old; a blond, with short hair—the clean-cut, good-looking salesman image, I thought. Rather slender, but well built—

no gut. He somehow seemed too casual, though, and his nonchalance appeared to be too studied as he approached me. "Hi, my name is Ed," he said with a smile, as he extended his hand.

I noticed his wedding band as I shook his hand, saying, "My name is Rick."

"Do you live around here?" he asked.

"No," I replied, "I don't. I'm on my way to visit friends."

"You're lucky—not having to live around here, I mean," he said.

"Why?" I asked.

Before answering me, he pointedly looked toward the weeded area directly behind me, returned his gaze to me, and said, "Well, you know, there's not very much in the way of fun and games around here. I would really like some excitement. I often find myself wishing that something exciting would happen, you know?"

"Yes, I know what you mean," I replied, before adding, "but I think that most people feel that way at one time or another. I guess you can't always get what you want."

"I guess not," he replied.

Despite the "nothing-unusual-is-happening" tone of the conversation, I was, in fact, being propositioned—that is, subtly invited to engage in homosexual activity. Ed's cultivated attitude of nonchalance, his pointed interest in the wooded area directly behind us—evidenced by his periodic glances in that direction—coupled with his openly admitted search for "fun," "games," and "excitement," are tactics that are frequently used to initiate homosexual activity in highway rest stops. My response—"You can't always get what you want"—is but one of several standard techniques of indicating lack of interest. I might have said nothing, walked away, or mentioned that it was time for me to get going. Most propositions are couched in the rhetoric of play or the game—"Looking for some fun?", "Is there any action around here?", "Looking for excitement?", "Do you play around?", "Are you interested in having some fun and games?"—and are thus euphemisms for sexual activity.

Men who seek homosexual activity in highway rest areas may be called "players"—players of a special and complicated game.

The wooded grounds surrounding many of the rest stops that are strung along the nation's highways serve as settings in which every year thousands of men—both married and unmarried, those who see themselves as homosexual, as well as those who see themselves as uncompromisingly straight—seek out and engage in same-sex contact.

What's their game? Any one, or any combination, of the following: active or passive oral sex, active or passive anal intercourse, often after, before, or during masturbation, usually mutual, although sometimes one-sided. The combinations are almost limitless, but as we shall see, some are more popular than others.

Rest stops, like the bushes in parks and the balconies of movie theaters, by their very definition are *public*—that is, nearly everyone may enter. A public setting has no entrance requirements. This allows for easy physical entry. The rest stop offers the advantages of public settings in other ways as well: it is highly *visible;* easily *recognized;* and easily *accessible*—that is, in close proximity to a highway, therefore easy to get to; and is *used by large numbers of the public.* But the rest area has its private side, too: the woods surrounding some rest stops afford their users a certain measure of privacy should this be desired. The sheltering brush provides a potential occasion for the expression of intimacy in the midst of a very public, impersonal place.

So subterranean are transitory homosexual activities in public and semipublic places—although so easily observed if one knows of their existence—that very little previous research has been conducted on them.

While conducting a participant observation study, Laud Humphreys (1970) found that large numbers of otherwise heterosexual urban males seek out "tearoom sex," or easily obtainable oral-genital sex, with other men in public urinals; over half were married and living with their wives—who were unaware of their tearoom activity—in unions which do not appear unstable. Very few participants thought of themselves, or were labeled by others, as homosexuals. Tearooms are "closed regions" (Cavan, 1966); they are *not* centers of sociability—patrons are almost never accessible to one another for conversational encounters—that is, participants almost never exchange words. Physical involvement is also minimized in most tearoom encounters; often the only physical contact that occurs between partners involves the mouth or anus of the insertee and the penis of the inserter. The lack of emotional involvement, limited physical contact, and "sheltering silence" coalesce to create the aura of impersonality that surrounds tearoom encounters, an atmosphere that makes "instant sex" or sex for fun—that is, sex without any involvement or commitment whatsoever—more easily obtainable.

Two elements of play or recreation of tearoom encounters—*inconsequentiality* and *unseriousness* (Cavan, 1966)—reinforce the casual attitudes of the participants.

Meredith R. Ponte (1974) observed men as they attempted to initiate homosexual encounters in a city beach parking lot in Southern California. He did not, however, actually witness any concrete instances of homosexual activity. He mainly focused upon one feature of the parking-lot "pickup" process—the ways men indicate or express sexual interest in other men while in public places.

Ponte's observations disclosed that two distinctly different groups of men—which he designated "parkers" and "society"—frequent the parking lot. "Parkers" are predominantly middle-class, middle-aged married men looking for sexual action. "Society" men were younger and involved in the gay subculture. "Society" saw "parkers" as sexually unappealing, unattractive, dirty old men. "Parkers" were almost exclusively interested in the sexual side of the parking lot. "Society" tended to emphasize its social side as well—a place where gossip is exchanged, invitations to parties issued, and social events planned.

Parkers "cruise" the parking lot. In the homosexual argot, cruising can refer to either of two activities: the act of seeking out or looking for potential sex partners, and the means of conveying sexual interest, usually visually, by first catching the attention of a desirable partner. Often the latter will entail gazing pointedly, steadily, and intently directly into his eyes without looking away; this may involve letting the gaze noticeably waver between the other man's eyes and crotch. The individual who is being cruised may express a shared interest by returning the look, or he may indicate a lack of interest or distaste by looking or walking away. The exchange may alternatively be predominantly verbal. Sexual attraction is indicated when one individual approaches another and strikes up a conversation, using a well-known and standardized expression or "line"—instantly recognizable as such to anyone who is at all familiar with the homosexual subculture. Common examples are available; phrases such as "Do you have the time?", "Got a match?", "Anything happening tonight?", or "Do you live around here?" are frequently used.

The rest stop that I observed was pointed out to me by a student who was a regular player. During the summer months, I conducted systematic observations almost daily—at four randomly chosen times, between the hours of 10:00 A.M. and 9:30 P.M.—for intervals lasting thirty minutes.

On one of my first days in the field, I struck up an acquaintance with "Ralph": a short, pudgy, balding, middle-aged man who was then unemployed. "Ralph" had worked at a skilled trade for nearly twenty-five years in a company that had recently gone out of business.

Ralph, who had seen me recording the ongoing activities of a few players, decided to approach me to find out what I was up to. When I told him that I was conducting a research study, he was incredulous. But as the summer progressed and we continued to encounter each other almost daily, he finally decided that I was "for real" and not just "another young number playing hard to get." He then volunteered his assistance, as he had "nothing better to do" while he waited for an "interested" party to arrive on the scene. I gladly accepted his offer, and asked him if he would introduce me to any players he thought might be willing to discuss the "game." He agreed.

Ralph's help proved to be invaluable. He had been a player for eleven years, and claimed that as far as he knew, no one else had frequented this particular rest stop for as long a period of time. Possessed of an incredible memory for detail, Ralph knew something—if not name, then occupation, or marital status, or sexual preference, or car—about nearly everyone who frequented the rest stop for sexual purposes more than two or three times. In fact, he often referred to certain men in terms of these specifics. For instance, there were: "Lousy Blow Job," "The Shrink," "The Major," "The Fabulous Fuck," "The LTD," "The Throat," "The Dong," "Henpecked," "Super-Stud," "The Electra," "The Castrated Husband," "The Doctor," and "The Capon." And if a "new face" started to appear on "the scene," Ralph lost no time in collecting from other players whatever information they possessed regarding the biography of the "stranger."

Because he was well known, Ralph's word that I was "all right" put most of the players at ease. In fact, I did not have enough time to speak with all of the men who expressed a willingness to discuss the game with me. Even so, I conducted 50 informal interviews. In addition, Ralph and I observed a total of 207 rest stop encounters which culminated in sexual activity. In each instance, we noted: (1) the number of persons involved in each episode; (2) the approximate ages of the partners; (3) whether the players spoke or exchanged words; (4) the age of the partner who "initiated" the encounter;

(5) the type of sexual activity in which the partners engaged; (6) where the activity occurred—in the woods or in a parked car; (7) any displays of affection, such as hugging, kissing, or caressing.

Like Humphreys (1970), I fulfilled the participants' need for a *lookout* or, in the homosexual argot, "watchqueen," while I conducted this research. I performed the dual role of "observer-lookout" while sitting on the bench of a picnic table just outside the patch of woods in which most of the sexual activity took place. I was expected to walk into the woods and inform the players of the arrival of "outsiders" such as a family, or of the presence of small children, the appearance of a car filled with teen-aged boys who might be "fag-hunting"—that is, looking for homosexuals to beat up and rob, or of unexpected police incursions into the area. Since the "lookout" role uniquely fitted my own research purposes—that of "observer"—I decided to perform in this dual capacity. In so doing, however, I was acutely aware of the fact that I had willingly chosen to become a witness to a criminal activity, and, as a "lookout," perhaps even an accomplice.

While I did not take great pains to indicate the fact that I was conducting a study, I did nothing to actively conceal this from my informants, or to mislead them in any way. In dealing with the players, I tried, at all times, to be forthright, honest, and candid.

Of the 207 rest-area encounters, to the best of my knowledge each episode involved different partners. Ralph witnessed 141 of these interactions; I saw 66. Very few men who served as informants were also observed partaking of sexual activity.

Since most sexual contacts were struck up in and around the stretch of boulevard on which my lookout post was located, or in the vicinity of nearby cars, I was able to overhear the conversations that took place between most of the players that were on the scene while I was observing. Much of the sexual activity took place roughly thirty feet into the woods, about five feet off the path that entered the underbrush directly behind the picnic table on which I sat. I could observe these encounters by walking down the path about twenty feet. If players became aware of my presence and moved further back into the brush, I did not follow them. Nor did I pursue those partners who walked the full length of the trail to its end at the fence which served as a boundary marker. I dared not leave my lookout post for any extended period of time, and I felt it unwise, insensitive, and unjust to continue to follow a couple who very probably had moved further into the woods in order to preserve their own privacy by avoiding me. As a consequence, I was unable to view thirty-nine episodes through to their completion. As a player himself, Ralph was under no such constraints, and followed the players he was observing wherever they went, but always at a discreet distance. He would remove himself even further away—about twenty-five feet —once sexual activity commenced. Sexual activity which occurred in and around cars was easier to observe—and probably for this reason, less often practiced.

This study was conducted during the summer months, and thus the effects of seasonal variation on rest-stop activity remain unknown. In addition, these observations apply specifically to the daylight hours; evening might, for the obvious reason of lack of visibility, be characterized by different patterns of activity.

Out-of-door sexual activity usually occurs within the patch of woods—approximately fifty yards in length—that is encountered upon leaving the approach road and entering the rest stop itself. Sexual activity, then, is accomplished in the wooded area most greatly removed from the open clearing that attracts heterosexual couples and families. As many as thirty-five cars can be parked in the designated spaces in front of the "boulevard" which spans the entire length of the rest stop. In addition, five 50-gallon trash cans and five picnic tables are scattered at varying intervals along the boulevard. I used a picnic table on the far right as my lookout post.

To the conventional member of society, the rest stop holds no special attraction. It is a location that is basically taken for granted; a place for travelers to stop when need be, and then to leave within a short period. An understanding of the "normal" activities of "normal" users might well enable us to discover—by way of contrast— the types of rest-stop activity most likely to be *judged* or *evaluated* as "deviant." If, for instance, "legitimate" users spend little or no time at all exploring the wooded grounds surrounding a rest area, then presumably the "illegitimate" user will break this pattern.

In the particular highway rest stop described in this study, there is a group of men—rest-stop players—who, unlike nonplayers, almost never leave the area within a reasonable period of time. On the contrary, some stay for hours—sitting in or walking around their cars, pacing up and down a slice of the boulevard that parallels the woods, or lounging about the picnic table that sits in close proximity to the wooded section of the rest area. At periodic intervals, a man will casually stroll into the woods; within a minute or two, someone else will follow closely behind. Later, both men reappear. Each emerges from the underbrush on a separate trail. Each walks briskly to his car, gets in, and drives off. Several aspects of this pattern of social interaction inform the observant rest-stop player that this rest area is "active"—that is, a place in which homosexual contacts can be established. These features are: (1) the noticeable absence of women; (2) the protective covering provided by the weeds; (3) men alone—sitting in cars or leaning against them, pacing upon the boulevard, or sitting at a picnic table; (4) the subtle but discernible flow of human traffic, rarely in pairs or in twos, into and out of the sheltering weeds. The same patterns of interaction tend to occur in and around active tearooms (Humphreys, 1970). And, over a period of time, many players grow quite attached to certain "active" rest stops, a type of behavior that Humphreys also observed on the part of many tearoom participants.

Regular players often refer to the wooded setting in which "the games" take place with expressions of fondness and affection. In fact, many assume something of a proprietary manner when they reminisce about past events that occurred in "their" section of the rest stop. The "regulars" have, in a sense, appropriated this space as a "home territory" or base from which to launch their sexual activities. But this "colonization" is far more symbolic than real; the players, like the patrons of tearooms, cannot ignore, let alone deny, the public character of their territory and its surrounding environs. And although the invasions or incursions by "outsiders" into the area are resented, the "aliens" are ignored rather than repelled. To defend the home territory against these encroachments would entail too great a risk; the illicit purposes to which this slice of "public space" is put might be made apparent. Indeed, the continued existence of the game would seriously be endangered if a request for police intervention was to be lodged by an indignant, morally outraged "outsider." For this reason, then, the claims of outsiders to the unencumbered use of public space are almost never challenged by members of either "deviant" group. But who are the players and what are they like? Why does a man become a player?

Through informal conversations with fifty rest-stop players, I was able to gain information that sheds some light on the social characteristics of the men who frequent rest stops for sexual purposes. Two important dimensions of homosexuality form the basis along which I ranked rest-stop players: (1) *sexual identity*—that is, an individual's conception and designation of his own sexual preference as heterosexual, homosexual, or bisexual; (2) *participation in the homosexual subculture,* or the degree of social contact a person has with others who share his sexual interests. The men with whom I spoke roughly conformed to the same categories that Humphreys (1970) uses to classify tearoom participants: (a) Ambisexuals; (b) Trade; (c) Gay Guys; (d) Closet Queens. It should be stressed, however, that the line separating the members of one category from the partners of another probably becomes blurred over time due to the drift of men between groups.

Ambisexuals: Twenty-four of the fifty men I interviewed saw themselves as being essentially *bisexual.* All of these men are married, and twenty-one out of the twenty-four are fathers. Their wives are unaware of their rest-stop activities. All have attended college for at least a year; two-thirds work at white-collar jobs, while the other third are professional men. They see themselves as "oversexed," as well as erotically attracted to both men and women. They view rest stops as a way in which these impulses may be satisfied. All rate their marriages, as well as their heterosexual relations in general, as being quite satisfactory. All engage in all of the forms of homosexual activity: active and passive, oral and anal sex.

Trade: Seven of my informants conceive of themselves as being essentially *heterosexual.* Four are married, and the other three are either engaged or have a steady girl friend. None attended college; all are skilled manual laborers—five out of seven, in fact, are truck drivers. These men have no homosexual subcultural involvement whatsoever, other than their rest-stop encounters. All keep their rest-stop involvements a secret from the women in their life. Indeed, it is to these women that the "trade" attribute the necessity of seeking rest-stop sex; their wives and girl friends are unwilling to have sexual relations as often as these men would wish. Rest-stop sex, then, *supplements* their heterosexual activity. Their main interest is in obtaining "instant sex" easily, quickly, and in as impersonal a manner as possible. In general, "trade" are unwilling to engage in "active" oral sex, or "passive" anal intercourse—the threat to their masculine self-images is too great.

Gay Guys: It is this group of men that is most commonly referred to as "homosexual" by both professionals and the lay public. These men lead what are, essentially, homosexual lives. That is to say, these are men whose *self-image* is a homosexual one, whose *sexual activity* is predominantly, if not exclusively, confined to same-sex members, and whose *friends* are *primarily homosexual*. Fourteen of my informants are best described using this category. Virtually all of these men frequent the rest stop only because there are no "gay bars" in the immediate vicinity in which they could locate potential sex partners. Most of these men appear to be in their mid-twenties. Half are college students; the rest are college graduates who hold white-collar positions. Not one of these men has ever married.

Closet Queens: Although these men have arrived at homosexual self-definitions, and their sexual activity is predominantly, if not exclusively, confined to same-sex members, the scope of *their involvement in the homosexual community is extremely limited*. Unlike the "gay guys," "closet queens" have very few homosexual friends, frequent "gay bars" very rarely, if ever, and derive most of their sexual gratification from tearoom and rest-stop encounters. Five out of the fifty informants are of this type. None has ever been married. Three of these work at skilled trades and have had no college. The other two hold white-collar jobs and have graduated from college. These men appear to be roughly in their mid-thirties.

Observation of 207 rest-stop encounters indicate a number of similarities between the patterns of homosexual activity that occur in rest stops and those which take place in tearooms. Over four-fifths of the participants appear to be more than thirty years old. In the rest stop, as in the tearoom, the older partner usually approaches or propositions the younger: this happened in almost two-thirds of the encounters we saw. In roughly half of the cases, however, the age span between partners appears to be no greater than ten years, and in approximately a quarter of the episodes, the ages of the partners seemed about equal. As in tearoom encounters, fellatio is the most frequently (77%) performed sexual activity. Fellatio occurs more often outside, in the woods, than in a parked car, whereas for anal intercourse, it is the reverse. And, like their tearoom counterparts, insertees masturbate themselves as they fellate their partner. Although no sexual episodes involving more than two partners were directly observed, informants claim that multiple-partner encounters—"daisy chains"—do occasionally take place, usually under the cover of darkness, which greatly diminishes the probability that a venture of this magnitude will be observed. The sexual activity after dark in a rest stop is reported to be more similar to that of tearoom activity than is the case during the day. Contacts are more impersonal—conversations are limited or nonexistent. And last, both the rest area and the tearoom are capable of handling a large volume of traffic; in principle, a participant could, if he wished, have sexual relations with several different men in succession, or sexual relations with more than one partner simultaneously.

Differences also exist between tearoom and rest-stop episodes, however.

Sexual encounters in rest stops differ significantly from those in tearooms in two major ways: (1) partners speak or exchange words in a majority (69%) of these encounters—that is, an atmosphere of "sheltering silence" *does not* surround rest-stop encounters. Indeed, the rest area is an "open region"—individuals are accessible to one another for conversational encounters (Cavan, 1966); (2) displays of affection—caressing and sometimes kissing—are evident in a majority (86%) of rest-stop episodes. The woods provide an opportunity for privacy that encourages these displays of warmth.

Rest stop-tearoom differences might also be accounted for by the norms or rules which guide men's-room behavior in general. Most "respectable" men view the public restroom as a somewhat undesirable location, to be used only when necessary, and to be left as quickly as possible. In addition, the norms of men's-room deportment dictate that any others in the situation be accorded *civil inattention* and *noninterference*—that is, each person's presence is to be acknowledged, but great care taken to convey the attitude that no single individual is the object of undue interest or design (Goffman, 1963). In short, staring is prohibited. Since most men's rooms are small and physically confining, especially when crowded, patrons are generally extremely sensitive to any form of physical encroachment, which, along with any form of verbal communication to a stranger, is to be avoided if at all possible (Cornwell, 1973). When examined within the context of "normal" men's-room behavior, the primary features of "tearoom encounters"—lack of emotional involvement, limited physical contact, and "sheltering silence"—are *logical extensions of,* not departures or deviations from, the norms that dictate *appropriate men's-room behavior.* Thus the norms governing tearoom behavior illustrate the principle that "deviance" can be an extension of "normalcy." The same principle appears to apply to rest-stop encounters as well, where many of the techniques that rest-stop players use to carry on their deviant activity also assume, at least outwardly, characteristics usually associated with "proper" rest-area behavior.

Perhaps the four most outstanding features of highway rest-stop encounters are: the visibility of the tactics used to initiate the encounter; the extreme reliance placed upon verbal and nonverbal communication and meaning in conveying sexual interest; the displays of warmth expressed between players during the sexual episode itself; the element of risk—the potential for being arrested, robbed, beaten up, or even blackmailed.

The sexual contact itself is often originally initiated quite openly and visibly in the parking lot or on the boulevard when a player approaches another man and engages him in conversation. Since he is attempting to establish potential contacts in a public place, however, the player must limit his conversations to only those topics deemed appropriate for discussion between strangers, namely, small talk. Nevertheless, it is through the medium of social discourse or conversation, and not through silence, that these encounters are established.

The initiation of small talk provides the player with an opportunity to determine whether the other individual also "plays," and if so, whether he would be interested in making a "game." During these seemingly trivial discussions, the player who initiated the conversation looks for verbal as well as nonverbal signs of interest from the other party. A player may resort to small talk after he has received nonverbal cues from the other individual—a glance, a slight nod of the head, or a smile—which lead him to suspect that the other person is sexually interested. Or, the player might initiate a conversation in order to subtly indicate his own interest, and in hopes of eliciting signs that the other individual is attracted as well. Either way, the player finds himself confronted by the following paradox: to satisfy the norms which govern behavior in public places, he must give off the impression that he is a conventional and respectable man; to satisfy his own goal, that of locating an interested player, he must indicate that he possesses unconventional interests. Thus, while acting "as if" he is a conventional man, the player must try to somehow simultaneously convey his actual, unconventional intentions.

Rest-area encounters are open regions (Cavan; 1966)—participants are open to one another for conversational encounters. The greater sociability and the physical features of the rest stop might well account for the greater displays of warmth between players. Sexual experience, of necessity, almost always occurs in the relative privacy of a parked car, or in a secluded patch of brush within the woods surrounding the rest area. The trees and underbrush can be used as relatively private settings, of limited visibility, in which an atmosphere can be created that is conducive to open shows of playful, casual affection or warmth.

As might be expected, feeling constrained to manage "a respectable front" might occasionally prove to be a source of tension or anxiety, but rarely does it greatly decrease the player's chances of locating a sexual partner. It should be remembered, however, that a player can never be exactly certain of the extent of another individual's involvement in the scene. It is not uncommon for a heterosexual to lead a player to suspect that he is interested in making a game. This impression is usually fostered quite unintentionally when the heterosexual unknowingly responds in a favorable manner to the verbal lines and the nonverbal signs of sexual attraction that the player is directing toward him. Indeed, the player can't even be completely certain of the nature of the other individual's motive after physical contact is initiated and seemingly welcomed. The possibility still remains that the person might be a plainclothesman who will arrest him immediately after the actual sexual activity has taken place, or a potential robber or blackmailer. Every encounter, then, is fraught with a certain amount of risk.

Players can usually be distinguished from nonplayers in a number of ways; the player's entrance into the scene is distinctly different from the "nonplayer's" in a manner immediately apparent to the "seasoned gamester," but not so distinctive as to capture the interest or attract the attention of most people that are present. The player who is cruising out-of-doors tends to use a delaying tactic after he emerges from his car. "This involves a minute pause, necessitated by some small task in which the individual engages himself; the pause provides him with a few additional seconds within which to assess his surroundings" (Lofland, 1973:101). Informants told me that they will usually pause for a moment before they walk in the general vicinity of the woods; during the pause most men either deposit litter in one of the trash cans, or open the trunk of their car and pretend to be looking for something. In either case, this brief pause allows them to get an idea of "what's available" and "what the action is like." By way of contrast, the *heterosexual* resorts to the use of a "beeline" tactic as he (or she) approaches the woods. "With eyes focused on the desired site, he moves straight toward it, rapidly, purposefully, not turning his body, head, or eyes in any other direction" (Lofland, 1973:105). The "nonchalance" of the player, then, distinguishes him from his businesslike, nonplaying counterpart.

The nonplayer does not usually loiter. He completes his task, whatever it may be, and leaves. The player remains for an inordinate length of time, and acts as if he is killing time. Some men lean against the side of their car; others pace back and forth on the patch of the boulevard that lies in front of the woods; still other men sit in their car, taking great pains to be clearly visible at all times, as they survey the patterns of activity that are unfolding before their eyes. Occasionally one of the men sitting in a car will step on his brakes, or flick on one of his turning signals, or switch on his emergency "flashers" for a very short period of time; the brief glow of the lights informs any interested party of the driver's player status. Car lights are used both during the day and at dusk as a means of locating potential partners. The use of *headlights* as a signaling device, however, is thought to be in extremely poor taste; it is viewed as much too obvious a means of announcing one's availability, and as such, its use risks making apparent to outsiders the previously unnoticed sexual service that the rest stop provides. By way of contrast, those nonplayers that remain in their cars for any length of time are most likely to be found sprawled out on the front seat sound asleep, only visible at close range. And among nonplayers, even the accidental flashing of lights occurs so rarely as to be an almost unwitnessed phenomenon. Potential players, then, can be located or distinguished from nonplayers in roughly *three* ways: (1) by their entrance style; (2) because players generally appear to be killing time in or around their cars, or nearby, or within a patch of woods that covers part of the rest stop; (3) by the periodic and unwarranted use of a car's signal lights.

The inextricable tie that exists between "deviant" and "normal" behavior is perhaps nowhere more clearly expressed than in our everyday speech or social discourse. Conventional words are used to do far more than simply describe deviant behavior. Everyday language is also used to convey a willingness, or desire, or an intention to engage in some form of forbidden behavior. Some types of deviance, such as homosexual activity, however, require the joint participation of a partner in order to be successfully accomplished. As a method of communication, then, the language of "respectable" or conventional society can be used as a means to attain legitimate as well as deviant or unconventional goals. The rest-stop player often uses *conventional words,* or small talk, *for an unconventional purpose*—that of subtly conveying a sexual interest that would almost certainly be labeled deviant or "immoral" if openly expressed.

Consider for a moment the following conversational gambit often used by players when they are cruising out-of-doors: "Do you have the time?" The meaning which is assigned to this question depends upon the social context—as perceived by the person being asked the question—in which the question is asked, and upon the past experience of the individual who is questioned. On its face, the question seems innocent enough, and would probably be taken as such by a man who has not engaged in homosexual activity as an adult, and is unfamiliar with cruising techniques. In all likelihood, our man will also fail to notice the watch which our "questioner" purposely wears *to discredit the credibility of his own request*—attempting thereby to convey to the potential partner the actual reason which prompted the question: sexual attraction. And even if our man noticed the watch, there is no guarantee that he would attach any sexual significance to the question; he might see it as a sign of absentmindedness; as an overture to his being mugged; or as a lonely guy's attempt at striking up a conversation. A seasoned player would immediately recognize this statement for what it is. He views the rest area as a place in which homosexual liaisons can be entered into, and his past experience has sensitized him to the nuances of the game. Our man, on the other hand, probably sees the rest area—if he thinks about it at all—as a relatively "neutral" setting, to be used when the need arises, but otherwise to be taken for granted. Other players intentionally undermine their credibility by asking someone for a match, making sure that he later observes them lighting their own cigarette with a lighter. Two other frequently used outdoor cruising "lines" are: "Anything happening?" or "Do you want some fun?" Some out-of-door cruisers use nonverbal means to express their sexual interest. Eye contact is most frequently used to show sexual attraction; the player catches the attention of a potential partner, and then gazes steadily and directly into his eyes. Or, a man might follow someone he is interested in—always remaining visible, but at a discreet distance of approximately fifty feet, where he awaits an encouraging gesture—a smile or a slight nod of the head—which indicates that the attraction is mutual and that he may approach.

If a player "car cruises"—that is, approaches someone who is sitting in a car—the approach itself telegraphs his interest. His initial questions and statements are usually quite trivial. If the driver makes an obvious effort to keep his end of the conversation going, he is probably interested. At this point, the man who approached will probably ask the driver one of two stock lines: "Do you want some fun or company?" or "Would you like me to join you for a while?" The drivers of two cars will often cruise one another and convey this interest nonverbally by flicking on turn signals, parking lights, or brake lights. If the other party is interested, he will return the flash.

In the rest stop, as in other settings in which homosexual contacts are pursued, a high premium is placed on youth and physical beauty. Young men—in their late teens or early twenties—are the "hunted"; the older men, the "hunters." (These terms are employed by the players themselves.) An older man, then, is usually expected to *approach* a younger man, *and strike up a conversation*. This weakens his bargaining position; he invests both ego and effort in the encounter before the "hunted" has expended any energy at all. Furthermore, the type of sexual activity in which the two men engage is usually determined by the "hunted," and is aimed at gratifying his preferences. The sexual activity is usually initiated by the older partner as soon as both men recognize that the sexual attraction is mutual. The initial behavior usually involves touch, especially in the area of the upper body, but soon becomes centered in and around the area of the genitals. The major norm that guides and organizes rest-stop behavior might best be referred to as "No means No." That is, if a person says or indicates to another that he is not sexually interested, the "hunter" is expected to honor this claim immediately. Most players judiciously abide by this rule.

Commitment of oneself to a "deviant" course of activity in the rest stop, then, appears to occur in roughly three stages: walking up and down the boulevard or sitting in one's car can be easily accounted for; actually striking up a conversation with a potential player, or responding to his conversational gambit, involves a greater commitment; the claim of "idle conversation," however, can still be used to convincingly explain away the accusation of deviance; obviously, a more critical commitment is made at the point of actually partaking of homosexual activity. In such a circumstance, small talk is very useful: it conceals one's intentions until the last possible minute, minimizing greatly the risk involved in homosexual encounters in highway rest stops.

As my study indicated, "ambisexuals" and "trade" *do not define or conceive of themselves as homosexual,* while "gay guys" and "closet queens" do. Only the "gay guys" are deeply involved in the homosexual community, and lead what are, essentially, "homosexual lives." "Ambisexuals" and "trade" professed no interest whatsoever in becoming *emotionally* involved with another man, while "gay guys" and "closet queens" possess a same-sex romantic preference. And last, both the "gay guys" and the "closet queens" are predominantly, if not exclusively, attracted to and sexually aroused by members of the same sex. Despite these differences, however, rest-area players, as members of a social category, constitute a kind of "primitive" or quasi subculture. However tenuous the ties might be, a link nevertheless exists between all players: *all partake of deviant activity* —that is, all breach moral rules which, if discovered, would stand a high probability of being condemned by "respectable" members of society.

But this "deviant" activity is neither as anonymous nor as cold and impersonal as the tearoom encounters which Laud Humphreys (1970) observed. Indeed, the players might best be described as assuming "postures of intimacy" as they accomplish their sexual activity. That is, the trees and ground cover within the rest area offer some of the advantages of a private setting: decreased visibility, an opportunity to display warmth and affection, and an occasion to engage in sexual activity. The shelter provided by the woods allows the players to create their own, private social worlds, within which, through shows of warmth and affection, they can invest their sexual encounters with great meaning and importance—however brief these episodes might be.

References

Cavan, Sherri, *Liquor License,* Chicago, *Aldine,* 1966.

Cornwell, David A., "The Management of Tensions Between Conflicting Usages of a Public Place," *The Sociological Review,* Vol. 21, No. 2 (May 1973): 197–210.

Goffman, Erving, *Behavior in Public Places,* New York, The Free Press, 1963.

Humphreys, Laud, *Tearoom Trade: Impersonal Sex in Public Places,* Chicago, Aldine, 1970.

Lofland, Lyn H., "Self-Management in Public Settings: Part I," *Urban Life and Culture,* Vol. 1, No. 1 (April 1972): 93–108.

Ponte, Meredith R., "Life in a Parking Lot: An Ethnography of a Homosexual Drive-In," Jerry Jacobs (Ed.), *Deviance: Field Studies and Self-Disclosures,* Palo Alto, California, National Books, 1974, pp. 7–29.

V
Lesbianism

Lesbianism has only recently become a controversial and highly sensitive social issue in American society. Prior to the reemergence of the feminist movement and the birth of gay liberation—both undoubtedly outgrowths of the turbulent atmosphere of political dissent and social unrest that spanned the decade of the 1960s—Lesbians and Lesbianism were largely ignored and rarely studied. National consciousness came to be riveted upon the topic of female homosexuality when radical Lesbians—as women first, and gays second—adopted Women's Liberation as their primary point of identification. We suggest that it is against the backdrop of our sexist, male-dominated society that the most salient features of Lesbian life, Lesbian sexuality, and Lesbian identity are most obviously and vividly etched.

There are enormous differences between male and female homosexuals and homosexuality. In fact, one of the most serious blunders of past observations on Lesbianism—few though they were—was the assumption that what was said about males automatically applied to females.

However, there are parallels as well as differences. Some of the previous generalizations about what constitutes male homosexuality and male homosexuals apply equally to Lesbianism and Lesbians.

Namely:

That there is literally no meaningful and objective definition of who is a Lesbian, or even what sort of behavior constitutes female homosexuality, that will satisfy everyone.

That it is therefore more worthwhile to examine different *di-*

mensions of female homosexuality; many women will be classified as Lesbian according to some of them, but not according to others.

That female homosexuality is a matter of *degree.* There is a continuum which runs from complete homosexuality, through mixed homosexuality, to complete heterosexuality.

That Lesbian love and sexuality *is distinctly feminine in both form and expression.*

That societal reactions toward Lesbianism provide us with a strong indication of the generally inferior social status that women in this society occupy relative to that of men.

Definitions of who is a Lesbian or what constitutes Lesbianism differ. They do so mainly according to the purposes and perspectives of those who devise or formulate the categorizations.

Thus, a psychiatrist will probably think of a Lesbian primarily in *therapeutic* terms: as being possessed of a condition, circumstance, or state of mind that is characterized by a "misdirected" choice of sexual object and is something to be remedied, eliminated, eradicated, or "cured."

The psychologist, however, might look at a Lesbian largely in terms of her *adjustment potential:* as someone who engages in a form of unconventional sexual behavior, which in some cases might hinder self-awareness and adjustment, but in no way precludes this possibility in most.

And a sociologist will usually see the Lesbian primarily in social and cultural terms: as a participant in an atypical but harmless alternative sexual life-style that is both potentially viable and rewarding.

The man in the street, however, might well see the Lesbian mainly in *sexual* terms: as a sexually unawakened woman who needs only a "good stiff prick" to "straighten" her out, or as a sexual object upon whom he can enact his own (chauvinistic) sexual fantasies of conquest and domination—with the supposed aim of "converting" her to heterosexuality.

The woman on the street will generally look upon the Lesbian chiefly in terms of her *unmarried status:* as being devoid of maternal "instinct," and failing to fulfill her "natural" destiny of childbearing.

The pornographer will often see the Lesbian principally in terms of her *erotic potential:* as the practitioner of a form of sexual expression about which many men fantasize and will gladly pay to see. (Lesbianism is a common fare in pornography. Men are aroused by the sight of women making love; they do not feel threatened by it because, in their male-centered world, no woman could challenge their sexual invincibility.)

But the young political radical will probably look at the Lesbian primarily in *ideological* terms: as a fellow traveler who is also reacting against or attacking "the system" by resorting to unconventional behavior.

There are, of course, countless other ways of defining or examining Lesbianism or Lesbians. In each of the instances just cited, the Lesbian is viewed somewhat differently. Which view is correct? The answer is, of course, none of them. What is stressed here is that *any definition is, at rock bottom, arbitrary—influenced* far more *by* matters of *personal taste* and *judgment* than by cold, hard, immutable scientific fact. Past investigators have focused almost exclusively upon the sexual activity itself—thinking that sexual behavior alone could be used to unambiguously classify a woman as *either* Lesbian *or* heterosexual. Very few of these studies detail just exactly what it is that the Lesbian does when she is not acting out her "deviant" commitment—which is most of the time. Sexual behavior is but one of several useful criteria. An analysis based upon sexual activity alone is, then, necessarily shallow and incomplete. We would like to suggest something different.

Since there are no universally agreed upon definitions of what is a Lesbian and what kinds of activity constitute female homosexuality, we suggest that, as with male homosexuality, it is more worthwhile to examine different *dimensions* of same-sex relations— dimensions which are frequently, but not necessarily, found together —in order to better understand the phenomenon as a whole. In addition to the frequency and number of *same-sex* contacts to the point of orgasm, at least four other key dimensions of Lesbianism should be considered: *self-identity,* or how a person defines her gender preference; *subcultural involvement,* or the degree of one's immersion or participation in the homosexual "scene"; *romantic preference,* or the potential for becoming emotionally involved with men versus women; *sexual arousal,* or the ability to be "turned on" physically by members of either or both sexes. Thus it is possible for a woman to be "Lesbian" in terms of some of these dimensions, but not in terms of others. And it is possible that the dimensions along which a person falls will vary from one point in time to another. There is nothing fixed, absolute, or final, then, about a person's sexual commitment; these criteria simply provide us with a means by which we can describe the complexity of such commitment.

In his study *Sexual Behavior in the Human Female,* Alfred Kinsey viewed sexual orientation as a continuum, as he did in the volume on the male. He also used once more the "heterosexual-homosexual rating scale" to classify women from 0 to 6 in terms of the extent to which they were straight or gay. The 0s were exclusive heterosexuals, and the 6s exclusive homosexuals, and the 1–5s fell, in varying degrees, between the two extremes. The results he obtained regarding the sexual activity of American women were not nearly as dramatic as those he elicited in his pioneering study of males. Nevertheless, it was found that 13 percent of all American females had at least one homosexual experience to orgasm from the onset of puberty to old age. An additional 7 percent of the female population had engaged in one or more homoerotic episodes after adolescence, but without ever achieving orgasm. Roughly 2 or 3 females in 100 could be regarded as exclusively homosexual—they had neither had sexual contact with men, nor were they sexually aroused by them. Their only sources of sexual contact and arousal had been other women.

Even today, Kinsey's research on the human female is one of the very few sources from which any meaningful information regarding the incidence and frequency of Lesbian behavior can be acquired. We now realize, however, that more is involved in female homosexuality than his classification allows. Although he did consider the criterion of same-sex activity and sexual arousal—or the ability to be "turned on" physically by members of either or both sexes—Kinsey did not consider the following three dimensions: *self-identity, romantic preference, or subcultural involvement.* Each of these is a salient feature of Lesbian love and sexuality.

In her social, emotional, and occupational behaviors, the Lesbian, contrary to the popular imagination, most often fits neither the stereotype of the "counterfeit man"—that is, behaving as if she were a man "trapped" within a woman's body by affecting the gestures, mannerisms, and dress of a male—nor does she correspond to the image of the heterosexual "reject" who is, as popular culture would have it, so ugly that she is at a complete disadvantage in the competitive "rating and dating" social world of the young heterosexual "singles," and is therefore forced to turn to other women for the love and sex that she cannot get from men. Nearly all Lesbians have dated men, and the overwhelming majority have had a sexual relationship with one or more men. Far from being rejected by men, Lesbians tend to be unsatisfied by them. The fact that their erotic and emotional life is with women is the result of an active choice. They have chosen women over men; they *prefer* women to men. It is difficult for men to understand this, because such a choice would represent a threat to their desirability. The only explanation most would find acceptable would be one that relegates such a choice to the twilight world of psychiatric pathology, an explanation which is ideological—based on a masculine fear—rather than scientific.

Moreover, most straight people would not recognize a Lesbian if they saw one. Most Lesbians are indistinguishable from their straight sisters. In fact, Lesbians are socially less visible than are the members of many groups, and certainly less so than male homosexuals. This is true for a number of reasons.

First, those who wish their sexual preference to remain by and large unknown have usually so carefully cultivated a heterosexual "front" or "image" that the behavior comes to be an integral and characteristic part of the self.

Second, the norms governing body contact and the open display of emotion in public places grant women a greater latitude for deviation than they do men—open displays of affection such as hugging and kissing can frequently be observed to occur between women, and any "slipups" a woman might make which could possibly reveal her Lesbian identity are just as likely to be unnoticed or, if observed, thought of as trivial or unimportant.

Third, most gay women become aware of their same-sex interest at a later age than do gay men; most Lesbians are in their late teens or early twenties when they recognize this attraction. For occupational reasons—namely job security—she may exercise a greater degree of discretion in revealing her homosexual preference than her male homosexual counterpart, who usually discovers his sexual preference at an earlier age—before he has made a professional commitment—which allows him to be somewhat more indiscreet with respect to the people to whom he reveals his homosexuality.

Fourth, most women usually discover their *romantic preference,* or ability to become emotionally involved with another woman, as a consequence of finding themselves in the midst of an intense, affectionate relationship. An awareness of a romantic preference often facilitates the acquisition of a Lesbian identity—that is, the defining of one's self and sexual interest as essentially Lesbian. A very close and warm friendship, with a gradual progression toward the sexual, usually characterizes Lesbian relationships, and usually aids a woman at arriving at a self-definition or *self-identification* as Lesbian. And, in most instances, sexual activity follows rather than initiates the development of emotional ties between partners. The relationship itself, however, is very private and nonvisible. Lesbians don't usually "cruise"—that is, seek out sexual partners in public places such as gay bars—as do their gay male counterparts.

Fifth, even the *subcultural involvement* of the Lesbian tends to be of a somewhat private nature. By subcultural involvement we mean association with others who are Lesbians—who consider themselves as such, and who practice Lesbian behavior. Many Lesbians establish stable, monogamous and long-lasting relationships with the same partner. It is not surprising, then, that the primary focus of leisure-hour activity is likely to consist of informal, loosely organized gatherings between friends or groups of friends in private homes or apartments. Participation in the more public sector of the homosexual community, such as gay bars, is extremely limited. Indeed, in comparison with the male homosexual bar—a major institution within the world of gay men—the Lesbian bar tends to play only a minor role in the lives of many, if not the majority, of gay women.

As we have seen, then, Lesbian love and sexuality bears a close resemblance to that of her heterosexual counterpart: relationships grow out of intense, emotional involvements; sexual activity grows out of, rather than initiates, the relationship. The relative invisibility of Lesbianism itself, however, does not adequately explain why the Lesbian is accorded better treatment in our society than is her male homosexual counterpart.

On the whole, the social condemnation of Lesbians appears to be much less harsh than that reserved for male homosexuals for several reasons—all of them sexist.

Just in terms of sheer numbers, fewer women than men engage in same-sex relations to orgasm in the course of their lives, which increases the likelihood that Lesbianism will be viewed more as a "rarity" than as a "social problem."

Lesbianism is also harder to detect than male homosexuality. A lot of what passes as "normal" behavior between two women—hugging, kissing, and other overt displays of affection—might well be homosexual. Such behavior, however, is usually cause for alarm if engaged in by two men.

Many men find the Lesbian to be sexually titillating—a challenge to be met, conquered, overpowered, dominated, and forced into revering the "power of the prick." Still other men see the Lesbian as sexually unawakened and inexperienced, in need of but one sexually satisfying relationship with a man (to be read as "a large penis") to be "converted" to heterosexuality. Either way, the Lesbian is definitely *not* seen as someone whose sexuality is to be taken seriously, while male homosexuals are seen (erroneously) as imitating what is, by male-dominated standards, an "inferior" role—that of woman. They therefore earn the scorn of the average straight male. The Lesbian is thought (again, incorrectly) to be imitating a "superior" role. She therefore does not generate quite so much hostility from conventional Americans.

In a society such as ours, organized as it is in accordance with the principle that woman is inherently inferior to man, homosexual acts between men—particularly "passive" anal intercourse, where one partner is wrongly believed to simulate the coital function of the female—are construed as intolerable normative violations, a rejection of a central Western value—*machismo*. By way of contrast, the Lesbian merely rejects a drab lifetime of domestic and sexual servitude.

Within the context of our society's sex roles, tremendous pressures are brought to bear on a person to prove his "manhood" or her "womanhood"—this inevitably entails the rejection of any "fag" or "dyke" characteristics in oneself or others. That this process is more readily observable in the case of men is yet another indication of the low esteem, relative to that of men, in which women are held. Indeed, in terms of their sex-role training and socialization, men are perhaps even more rigorously and narrowly programmed than are women. From their early childhood, males are told to "be a man"; it is continually impressed upon them that they must be "little men" at all times: decisive, strong, dominant—the guardians and keepers of those weaker than themselves, namely female peers and even younger children. To the extent that they can successfully meet these demands and fulfill these role expectations, they are viewed as "real men." To the extent that they fail—by exhibiting "feminine" traits of submissiveness, fear of violence, or timidity—they are "womanly"; unworthy of respect. A sort of grudging, even though gratuitous, admiration is paid those women who exhibit so-called masculine qualities—aggressiveness, self-confidence, and independence. Even among little children, however, "tomboys" are more acceptable than "sissies." The division of behavior into "masculine" and "feminine" traits is arbitrary and culture-bound—that is, relative to a given time and place. Men are almost as arbitrarily and narrowly conditioned and programmed as women. And it is safe to say that if the traits of submissiveness, shyness, timidity, and fear of violence were culturally valued attributes believed to be "naturally" associated with the masculine role, most men would exhibit these behaviors. What is or is not masculine or feminine is decided by us—by our civilization. And in this society, to be "womanly," or to exhibit behaviors thought to be associated with feminine role behavior, is to court social stigma.

The Lesbian bears the burden of two social stigmas—her sexual gender and her commitment to unconventional sexual activity—both of which have conspired to place her in a social status that falls somewhere near the bottom of the heap. As such, Lesbians occupy a uniquely marginal position in the social structure: they have nothing to lose in rebelling against a sex-role power structure that supports heterosexual male supremacy. But even more important, Lesbians have achieved a sense of independence from men. They are no longer dependent on male approval for a sense of personal worth, and can therefore serve as testimony that a successful and rewarding life independent of men is possible—if equality between the sexes can be obtained in no other way; that dependency on men as the primary sources of identity, self-esteem, and social status is something that women learn instead of inherit and therefore is something that can be unlearned, a dependency that can be severed.

The affiliation of gay women with Women's Lib was inevitable. Both Lesbians and their heterosexual counterparts reject the long-established condition of "woman as second-class citizen"; members of both groups identify themselves first and foremost as women—differences in sexual object choice are given only secondary consideration; all strive to develop self-respect and self-worth, which necessitates withdrawing themselves from the potentially oppressive influence of any relationships with chauvinistic, heterosexual males; Lesbian love and sexuality is as distinctly feminine as that of her heterosexual sister. Indeed, as we have seen, Lesbians have far more in common with their straight sisters than with their gay brothers. But the women's movement is nevertheless one with which male homosexuals can also readily identify. No one need tell a gay man about the unpleasantness of being viewed as a sexual object only —he learned this soon after he entered the homosexual subculture. Gay men can appreciate the position of women in yet another way: most have themselves been victimized by the players of the *macho* role, and realize that each time the self-respect and dignity of a woman is undermined simply because of her sexual gender, so too, only more indirectly, is the self-worth of the gay man, who occupies a similarly disadvantaged position in the social structure. Unlike women, however, most male homosexuals have also suffered because they themselves have been forced to enact the *macho* role at least for a time; a role whose requirements exceed the capabilities of most men—gay or straight; a role that is emotionally crippling, unsatisfying, and self-alienating.

Our brief discussion of the social position of the Lesbian relative to that of her straight sister and her male homosexual counterpart was undertaken in order to underscore the point that socially and culturally determined sex roles of "masculine"/"feminine" govern the staging, balance, and direction of social interaction between persons or groups—always inviting and often forcing one group of people to oppress and exploit the members of another.

◆

Del Martin and Phyllis Lyon are the feminist authors of *Lesbian/Woman,* and the founders of The Daughters of Bilitis. William Simon and John H. Gagnon are sociologists, the authors of *Sexual Conduct,* and the editors of *The Sexual Scene* and *Sexual Deviance.* They were both previously affiliated with the Institute for Sex Research; Simon is now a researcher at the Institute for Juvenile Research, and Gagnon is a professor of sociology at the State University of New York at Stony Brook. Denise Cronin is a graduate student at Stony Brook, and is at work on a large-scale study of Lesbianism. Pepper Schwartz and Philip Blumstein are assistant professors of sociology at the University of Washington in Seattle.

Lesbian Love and Sexuality
by Del Martin and Phyllis Lyon

So little is known about lesbians that even we ourselves are caught up in the myths and stereotypes so prevalent in our society. These stereotypes are based upon the false assumption that the lesbian is first and foremost *sexual* in all her thoughts, desires, and actions. What people fail to realize is that being a lesbian is not merely indulging in physical acts of lovemaking. For the woman involved, it is a way of life, encompassing her whole personality, one fact of which is, of course, her sexuality. For her it is the expression of a way of feeling, of loving, of responding to other human beings.

A lesbian is a woman whose primary erotic, psychological, emotional, and social interest is in a member of her own sex, even though that interest may not be overtly expressed. At a time when women, the forgotten sex, are voicing their rage and demanding their personhood, it is fitting that we emerge from the shadows. Like her heterosexual sister, the lesbian has been downtrodden, but doubly so: first, because she is a woman, and second, because she is a lesbian.

We are lesbians. We have lived together as lovers for 19 years. We also helped to found the Daughters of Bilitis in 1955. Over the years in which we have been deeply involved in the homophile movement, we have talked to, counseled, socialized with, and been friends with thousands of lesbians. We have lived the experiences that we are writing about.

When we first started living together as a couple, we knew practically nothing about female homosexuality. We only knew that we loved each other and wanted to be together.

From *Lesbian/Woman*, Del Martin and Phyllis Lyon, Glide Publications, 1972.

Del had read a few books. She had been to a number of gay bars, which was always a twitchy experience, since police raids were commonplace then. She had met a few lesbians and had had one previous affair.

Phyllis had been vaguely aware of homosexuality, but the possibility that she and her roommate had been thrown out of their college dorm due to implied homosexuality had never occurred to her until years later. Although she liked men, dated them, and even once went so far as to become engaged, Phyllis still had reservations about taking that final step down the aisle. She had always maintained a number of close friendships with women.

That's about where we were. Hardly the ideal background from which to launch a lesbian "marriage," which is the way we thought of our relationship. The only model we knew, a pattern that also seemed to hold true for those few lesbians we had met, was that of the mom-and-dad, or heterosexual, marriage. So Del assumed the role of "butch," while Phyllis, being completely brainwashed in society's role of woman anyway, decided she must be the "femme."

In the course of our 19 years together, we have learned that many lesbians in our age group (late forties) went through the same kind of role-playing. While a few became trapped in this butch-femme pattern, most come in time, as we did, to the realization that they are both women and that's why they are together.

Although she is most often seen solely as a sexual person by straight society, the lesbian has as many sexual problems as her heterosexual sisters. For she is caught in the same morass of sexual suppression as other women. By and large, she is raised to prepare herself to become wife and mother and helpmeet to her male mate. She is still taught that woman must save herself sexually for her husband—the nice girl doesn't play around. She is taught that woman is not aggressive—at least not obviously—but rather uses devious (feminine) means to achieve her ends. She is taught, more often than we would like to think, that sex is something evil or dirty and not, heaven forbid, something which is pleasurable and joyous.

It is not at all strange, then, that the lesbian often grows to adulthood denying her sexuality, afraid of her sexual feelings, and in many instances unaware and unknowledgeable of what they mean and how to cope with them. You can imagine the chaotic state of mind that a young lesbian may suffer: not only is she, like every woman, basically ignorant about the real meaning of sexuality, but she is also faced with the horrifying fact that the sexual feelings surfacing in her are directed toward another woman. It is little wonder, then, that a percentage of lesbians find themselves frigid (or nearly so), that many lesbians are completely passive and cannot bring themselves to reciprocate and make love to their partners, and that a number of lesbians never have any sex at all.

To understand the lesbian as a sexual being, one must understand woman as a sexual being. Until about the end of World War I in America, a woman was considered nonsexual by men and by herself. It seems incredible now, but prior to that time it was considered totally "unladylike" for a woman to enjoy sex. So heavy was this pressure that some women had operations for clitoris removal, so that they would not act in such an unseemly manner. From this background, women started the long and still not completed fight to regain control of their own bodies, the fight to be considered full, natural sexual beings.

Imagine a young woman 18 years old finally sorting out her feelings, her emotions, her sexual responses only to find that they all point toward the fact that she is a lesbian. At the same time she will find that she is considered illegal, immoral, and sick; a man-hater, a woman-seducer, masculine, and hard.

Further, considering that most young women of 18 in this country are very naïve about sex, either theirs or anyone else's, it follows that our young woman probably hasn't the foggiest notion of how to go about making love to another woman. In fact, she probably hasn't any idea of how to go about meeting another woman of like persuasion. Depending on her background, she either feels that sex is a good thing, a bad thing, or just a thing. These values will be with her as a lesbian, just as they would have been with her had she been heterosexually oriented. Fate will have something to do with the outcome. Her first sexual contact may be with an experienced lesbian, in which case at least she will have some idea of what goes on; it may be with someone as inexperienced as she. If this is the case, much will depend on the attitudes of both women toward sex.

A third possibility for our 18-year-old is that she may have had her first introduction to sex with a man. According to a study on "Sexual Behavior of the Female Homosexual" done by Drs. Marcel T. Saghir and Eli Robins, more than three-fourths of the lesbians interviewed had experienced heterosexual intercourse. For the majority, this occurred between the ages of 20 and 29 and was primarily done in a spirit of experimentation rather than because of strong sexual arousal.

We mentioned earlier that many lesbians are frigid, a concept that blows the minds of most straight persons who have always thought of lesbians only as sexual beings. It shows, too, that heterosexual women do not have a corner on the frigidity market.

There is nothing mysterious or magical about lesbian lovemaking (except, perhaps, for the two people involved). The body goes through certain physiological changes during the sexual cycle whether the initiator of the cycle is you, a partner, or an inanimate object. The mystery and the magic come from the person with whom you are making love. Everything that one woman does to another can be done also by a man, but for a lesbian that would change everything. It isn't the actions or the act: it is the woman involved who makes it more than just "physiological changes."

What do lesbians do sexually? We do very much the same thing a man and a woman (or a man and a man) do, with the exception that there is no penis present. There are many ways that two women can seek and find sexual gratification together, ways limited only by the imaginations of the persons involved.

The three most common techniques used in lesbian lovemaking are: mutual masturbation, cunnilingus, and tribadism. Mutual masturbation consists of manipulation of the clitoris, caressing the labia, and/or penetration of the vagina by the fingers until sexual excitation or orgasm occurs. This can be done simultaneously by the partners or in turn. Cunnilingus is the stimulation of the clitoris, the labia, and sometimes penetration of the vagina by the tongue of the partner. Again, this can be done by one to the other or, in the "69" position, by both at the same time. Tribadism, on the other hand, involves one woman lying atop the other, followed by up-and-down rhythmic movements to stimulate the clitoris of each. It is a technique which takes time to master but which may fulfill the butch-femme fantasies of male-and-female sexual role-playing. Whatever the variations of position, satisfaction comes from stimulation of the clitoris by the friction of movement against the body of the partner.

Two other methods by which two women may achieve sexual gratification seem to be relatively rare in practice. One is the use of penis substitutes or dildos (usually a rubber apparatus shaped and colored to look like a penis). While this idea tickles the fancy of most men who cannot imagine women enjoying or being satisfied sexually without a penis, the dildo's most prevalent use is by heterosexual women in masturbation. But the truth is that the great majority of women, whether lesbian or heterosexual, have never seen a dildo. Women who feel the need for inserting a penis substitute in the vagina to fulfill their heterosexual fantasies are more apt to improvise and use a candle, a banana or a cucumber. However creative these intercourse devices may be, it is important to emphasize that a penis (or penis substitute) is not necessary for a woman's sexual gratification.

In all studies (and there haven't been that many) about lesbian sexual practices, one unanimous finding has been that the use of penis substitutes is relatively rare. We are sure that most lesbians have tried something at one time or another, but for continuing satisfaction in sex there is nothing like a living, breathing, responding person. As one lesbian declared during a discussion one evening, "If I wanted a penis for sex, I'd go find a live one, not a fake."

The remaining technique is anilingus, use of the tongue in and around the anus. The finger of one partner may also be used to stimulate the anal region, which is an erogenous zone.

As in the case of any sexual communication between two people, full knowledge and prowess come only by practice. Further, there are a number of possible variations on these basic techniques. Foreplay (embracing, kissing on the mouth and other parts of the body, breast fondling and sucking, nibbling at the ear, and touching and stroking various erogenous zones of the body) is important in lovemaking.

These, then, are the techniques, open to much variation by individual women. They have been listed in books before, primarily in those of a scientific or pseudoscientific nature. This has been helpful to many a young lesbian. Not so long ago, about the only way she could educate herself was to go to a gay bar and pick up (or be picked up by) someone more experienced than she was.

Although the great majority of lesbians make love to one another, there are some who either refuse to make love to their partners or who refuse to be made love to. The former is usually a woman with one (or all) of three problems. She has been brainwashed into thinking that women are passive in sex; she is new at the game and afraid she won't perform correctly; or she really feels sex is dirty and can't bring herself to action. Given half a chance, with the right partner, she can overcome all three of her blocks.

But the woman who won't let anyone make love to her, who can only be the aggressor, has a much deeper problem. Mac, very much the sophisticated businesswoman during the day, metamorphosed into very much the "male" and "husband" when she was at home. Her "wife," who didn't work, literally brought Mac her slippers and pipe. "I can't let Jan touch me sexually," she explained. "It would destroy the illusion. Besides, the man should be the aggressive one." It was unfortunate she hadn't discussed the matter with Jan, for Jan didn't have any illusions that Mac was a man. She loved *her* and would much have preferred a woman-to-woman relationship. Jan had tried discussing the matter with Mac early in their relationship, but had run into a mammoth wall of stubbornness and had given up.

The gay terminology for a couple like Mac and Jan is butch and femme. Why did the butch-femme idea arise, and why has it lasted? For one thing, it isn't difficult for women, regardless of their age, to look around and see that it is an advantage to be a man. It seems fairly logical, also, that if you are sexually attracted to a woman, you should play the "masculine" role. Especially if what you have in mind is getting yourself a wife. Two women setting up housekeeping have only the model of the heterosexual marriage: the division of labor along strictly sex-role lines.

The stereotype of the dyke is an extreme of the butch. A young woman who has decided she is a lesbian may know only this stereotype: a masculine-looking woman *à la* Stephen Gordon in *The Well of Loneliness*. So she dresses and acts the part she thinks she must as she makes her first tentative forays into homosexual society. In some lesbian circles, she is likely to find herself pressured into declaring herself either butch or femme, and she is then expected to conform in matters of dress, speech, and action to the prevailing mode of the group she hopes to join.

There are also lesbians who truly believe they are more "masculine" than "feminine" and that they were born so. One assumes that they equate the masculine role with aggression, power, and superiority, while they feel that the feminine means passivity, inferiority, and softness.

Those women who feel that they are "born butch" tend to ape all the least desirable characteristics of men. In this case, one may say to these butches, "Up against the wall, male chauvinist pigs!" For to consider oneself a heterosexual; to stress that male and female are opposites which presumably attract, is to accept the entire male-imposed doctrine that woman's place is indeed in the home serving the male. Much of the polarity between men and women has centered around procreation. But the sex act itself is neither male nor female: it is a human being reaching out for the ultimate in communication with another human being. The roles men and women (or butch and femme) play in our country are only acting, not honest and equal relationships between two human beings.

We can't stress too strongly that the great majority of lesbians think of themselves as women and are looking for (or have found) another woman with whom to share their lives. Many go through the butch stage for the identification factor. If you look like any other woman on the street, how in the world are you going to find other lesbians, or, more to the point, how are you going to find you? So stereotyping yourself may be a plus factor at the beginning of one's gay career. Thankfully, the vast majority of those now proudly fighting their "butchhood" in gay bars and meeting places around the country will shift to their true identity as women as they become older, wiser, and more sure of their identity as people.

We have found some interesting anomalies in the butch-femme pattern over the years. One which crops up rather consistently is women—usually divorced and, we suspect, not lesbian at all—who pair up with butch lesbians. In these partnerships the entire male-female dichotomy is acted out to the nth degree. The femmes insist that their butches wear only male clothing and that they appear and act as nearly like the stereotyped male as possible.

Most of these femmes have been divorced more than once. Their only knowledge of a relationship is that of man to woman, so they fashion their own "man" out of the woman they can relate to. It does not make for a happy situation for either party, and usually the twosome doesn't last very long. Most lesbians, whatever their life-style, are striving today for more egalitarian relationships.

We have watched the gradual decline of the butch-femme concept of a relationship for 16 years, though the stereotype has not yet vanished. As a life-style it has many disadvantages. One is the jealousy which invariably creeps in. Jealousy of one's partner, especially obsessive jealousy, indicates an uncertainty of the relationship and bears witness to the fact that the two partners feel possessed like chattel, by one another. If you are sure of your partner's love, if your partner is a person and not a thing, then jealousy either doesn't exist or is extremely minimal.

While there is a certain amount of jealousy among lesbian couples, as much as there is between heterosexual couples, the Saghir-Robins study previously mentioned indicates that jealousy ranks last as a reason for relationships breaking up. Further, many women who break up their relationship as lovers remain fast friends. This wouldn't be possible if the split had come over jealousy rather than a change in, or loss of, emotional attachment—the reason given for most "divorces."

Much change has taken place in the way all women (straight or gay) in this country think about sex roles and personal relationships. There appear to be three strong influences: 1) a questioning of religious dogma, exposing myths and reexamining taboos, thereby developing a new code of sexual and social ethics; 2) research on human sexuality, opening up avenues to more widespread sex education, and discovery of the Pill; and 3) the various liberation movements, which all decry the use of labels to separate people and which raise the question of what it really means to be human.

The homophile thrust for freedom and equality has forced some clergymen at least to recognize that love and sex between two persons of the same sex can be, and is, equal to and as valid as that between two persons of the opposite sex. Such a realization leads inevitably to a reevaluation of the sacred institution of marriage. If the church recognizes love between two homosexuals, it cannot very well continue to condemn love between two heterosexuals who have not bothered to "sanctify" their love through wedding vows. Theologians are presently wrestling with these problems.

Those naturalists who have condemned homosexuals not only point to Adam and Eve, but to lower animals as proof that our true nature is to be heterosexual. Biologists, however, have observed homosexual contacts in widely varied species of mammals, and anthropologists have found homosexual activity in creatures as diverse as hamsters and horses or porcupines and pigs.

More recently, Dr. Albert Ellis, sexologist and executive director of the Institute for Rational Living in New York City, has stated that those persons who are either exclusively heterosexual or exclusively homosexual are neurotic. The Kinsey studies verify that American men and women are not necessarily as exclusive in their private sexual behavior as they pretend publicly.

As Dr. C. A. Tripp, psychologist, pointed out, most human sexual behavior is *learned*. It is only in the lower animals that it is totally instinctive. The higher on the evolutionary scale you are, the less instinctive are your sexual relations. So our life experiences "teach" us our sexuality, which may turn out to be hetero, homo, or bi. The Kinsey staff, in *Sexual Behavior in the Human Female*, pondered the fact that, given the physiology of human sexual response plus our mammalian background of behavior, "it is not so difficult to explain why a human animal does a particular thing sexually. It is more difficult to explain why each and every individual is not involved in every type of sexual activity." At least three-fourths of the lesbians we have known have had heterosexual intercourse more than once. For the majority of these women, the experience was good erotically; that is, orgasm was achieved, and there was a pleasurable feeling. But there was not the emotional involvement which was present in a lesbian sexual relationship.

And that is what makes the difference.

Loving Another Woman
by *Anne Koedt*

Question. *You said you had been friends for a while before you realized you were attracted to each other. How did you become aware of it?*

Answer. I wasn't conscious of it until one evening when we were together and it all just sort of exploded. But, looking back, there are always signs, only one represses seeing them.

For example, I remember one evening—we are in the same feminist group together—and we were all talking very abstractly about love. All of a sudden, even though the group was carrying on the conversation in a theoretical way, we were having a personal conversation. We were starting to tell each other that we liked each other. Of course one of the things we discussed was: What is the thin line between friendship and love?

Or, there were times when we were very aware of having "accidentally" touched each other. And Jennie told me later that when we first met she remembered thinking, "abstractly" again, that if she were ever to get involved with a woman, she'd like to get involved with someone like me.

The mind-blowing thing is that you aren't at all conscious of what you are feeling; rather, you subconsciously, and systematically, refuse to deal with the implications of what's coming out. You just let it hang there because you're too scared to let it continue and see what it means.

"Loving Another Woman" was written for and first appeared in NOTES FROM THE THIRD YEAR: WOMEN'S LIBERATION. It was also reprinted in *Ms.* Copyright © 1971 by Anne Koedt. The following is an interview with a woman who had recently begun her first love relationship with another woman. The article honors their request for anonymity.

Q. *What did you do when you became aware of your mutual attraction?*

A. We'd been seeing a lot of each other, and I was at her house for dinner. During the evening—we were having a nice time, but I remember also feeling uncomfortable—I became very aware of her as we were sitting together looking at something. There was an unusual kind of tension throughout the whole evening.

It was quite late by the time we broke up, so she asked me whether I wanted to stay over and sleep on her couch. And I remember really being very uptight—something I certainly wouldn't have felt in any other situation with a friend. Yet, even when I was uptight and felt that in some way by staying I would get myself into something, I wasn't quite sure what—something new and dangerous—I decided to stay anyway.

It wasn't really until I tried to fall asleep, and couldn't, that all of a sudden I became very, very aware. I was flooded with a tremendous attraction for her. And I wanted to tell her, I wanted to sleep with her, I wanted to let her know what I was feeling. At the same time I was totally bewildered, because here I was—not only did I want to tell her, but I was having a hard time just facing up to what was coming out in myself. My mind was working overtime trying to deal with this new thing.

She was awake too, and so we sat and talked. It took me about two hours to build up the courage to even bring up the subject. I think it is probably one of the most difficult things I ever had to do. To say—to in any way whatsoever open up the subject—to say anything was just so hard.

When I did bring it up in an oblique way and told her that I was attracted to her, she replied somewhat generally that she felt the same way. You see, she was as scared as I was, but I didn't know it. I thought she seemed very cool, so I wasn't even sure if she was interested. Although I think subconsciously I knew, because otherwise I wouldn't have asked her—I think I would have been too scared of rejection.

But when I finally did bring it up, and she said she felt the same way, well, at that point there was really no space left for anything in your mind. So we agreed to just drop it and let things happen as they would at a later time. My main, immediate worry was that maybe I had blown a good friendship which I really valued. Also even if she did feel the same way, would we know what to do with it?

Q. *When you first realized that you were possibly getting involved with a woman, were you afraid or upset?*

A. No. The strange thing is that the next morning, after I left, I felt a fantastic high. I was bouncing down the street and the sun was shining and I felt tremendously good. My mind was on a super high.

When I got home I couldn't do any kind of work. My mind kept operating on this emergency speed, trying to deal with my new feelings for her. So I sat down and wrote a letter to myself. Just wrote it free association—didn't try to work it out in any kind of theory—and as I was writing I was learning from myself what I was feeling. Unexpectedly I wasn't feeling guilty or worried. I felt great.

Q. *When did you start sleeping with each other?*

A. The next time we were together. Again, we really wanted each other, but to finally make the move, the same move that with a man would have been automatic, was tremendously difficult . . . and exhilarating. Although we did sleep together, it wasn't sexual, just affectionate and very sensual. After that evening we started sleeping together sexually as well.

I guess it was also a surprise to find that you weren't struck down by God in a final shaft of lightning. That once you fight through that initial wall of undefined fears built to protect those taboos, they wither rapidly and leave you to operate freely in a new self-defined circle of what's natural. You have a new sense of boldness, of daring, about yourself.

Q. *Was it different from what you had thought a relationship with a woman would be like?*

A. Generally, no. Most of the things that I had thought intellectually in fact turned out to be true in my experience. One thing, however, was different. Like, I'd really felt that very possibly a relationship with a woman might not be terribly physical. That it would be for the most part warm and affectionate. I think I probably thought this because with men sex is so frequently confused with conquest. Men have applied a symbolic value to sex, where the penis equals dominance and the vagina equals submission. Since sensuality has no specific sex and is rather a general expression of mutual affection, its symbolic value, power-wise, is nil. So sex with a man is usually genitally oriented.

Perhaps I wasn't quite sure what would happen to sexuality once it was removed from its conventional context. But one of the things I discovered was that when you really like somebody, there's a perfectly natural connection between affection and love and sensuality and sexuality. That sexuality is a natural part of sensuality.

Q. *How is sex different with a woman?*

A. One of the really mind-blowing things about all this has been that it added a whole new dimension to my own sexuality. You can have good sex, technically, with a woman or a man. But at this point in time I think women have a much broader sense of sensuality. Since she and I both brought our experiences as women to sexuality, it was quite something.

Another aspect of sexuality is your feelings. Again, this is of course an area that has been delegated to women; we are supposed to provide the love and affection. It is one of our duties in a male-female relationship. Though it has been very oppressive in the context that we've been allowed it, the *ability* to show affection and love for someone else is, I think, a fine thing—which men should develop more in themselves, as a matter of fact. Love and affection are a necessary aspect of full sexuality. And one of the things I really enjoy with Jennie is this uninhibited ability to show our feelings.

Q. *Is the physical aspect of loving women really as satisfying as sex with a man?*

A. Yes.

Q. *You've been together a while now. What's your relationship like?*

A. Once we got over the initial week or so of just getting used to this entirely new thing, it very quickly became natural—natural is really the word I'd use for it. It was like adding another dimension to what we'd already been feeling for each other. It is quite a combination to fall in love with your friend.

We don't have any plans, any desire, to live together, although we do see a great deal of each other. We both like our own apartments, our own space.

I think one of the good things we did in the beginning was to say: Let's just see where it will go. We didn't say that we loved each other, just that we liked each other. We didn't immediately proclaim it a "relationship," as one is accustomed to do with a man—you know, making mental plans for the next ten years. So each new feeling was often surprising, and very intensely experienced.

Q. *What would you say is the difference between this relationship and those you have had with men?*

A. Well, one of the biggest differences is that for the first time I haven't felt those knots-in-the-stomach undercurrents of trying to figure out what's *really* happening under what you *think* is happening.

I think it all boils down to an absence of role-playing; I haven't felt with Jen that we've fallen into that. Both of us are equally strong persons. I mean, you can ask yourself the question, if there were going to be roles, who'd play what? Well, I certainly won't play "the female," and I won't play "the male," and it's just as absurd to imagine her in either one of them. So in fact what we have is much more like what one gets in a friendship, which is more equalized. It's a more aboveboard feeling.

I don't find the traditional contradictions. If I do something strong and self-assertive, she doesn't find that a conflict with her having a relationship with me. I don't get reminded that I might be making myself "less womanly," And along with that there's less *self*-censorship, too. There's a mutual, unqualified, support for daring to try new things that I have never quite known before.

As a result, my old sense of limits is changing. For example, for the first time in my life I'm beginning to feel that I don't have a weak body, that my body isn't some kind of passive baggage. The other day I gritted my teeth and slid down a fireman's pole at a park playground. It may sound ordinary, but it was something I had never dared before, and I felt a very private victory.

Q. *Given the social disapproval and legal restrictions against lesbianism, what are some of the external problems you have faced?*

A. One thing is that I hesitate to show my affection for her in public. If you're walking down the street and you want to put your arm around someone or give them a kiss—the kind of thing you do without thinking if it is a man—well, that's hardly considered romantic by most people if it's done with someone of your own sex. I know that if I were to express my feelings in public with Jennie, there would be a lot of social intrusion that I would have to deal with. Somehow, people would assume a license to intrude upon your privacy in public; their hostile comments, hostile attitudes, would ruin the whole experience. So you're sort of caught in a bind. But we have in fact begun to do it more and more, because it bothers me that I can't express my feeling as I see fit, without hostile interference.

Q. *What made you fall in love with a woman?*

A. Well, that's a hard question. I think maybe it's even a bit misleading the way you phrased it. Because I didn't fall in love with "a woman," I fell in love with Jen—which is not exactly the same thing. A better way to ask the question is: How were you able to *overcome* the fact that it was a woman? In other words, how was I able to overcome my heterosexual training and allow my feelings for her to come out?

Certainly in my case it would never have happened without the existence of the women's movement. My own awareness of "maleness" and "femaleness" had become acute, and I was really probing what it meant. You see, I think in a sense I never wanted to be either male *or* female. Even when I was quite little and in many ways seemed feminine and "passive"—deep down, I never felt at home with the kinds of things women were supposed to be. On the other hand, I didn't particularly want to be a man either, so I didn't develop a male identity. Before I even got involved with the women's movement, I was already wanting something new. But the movement brought it out into the open for me.

Another thing the movement helped me with was shedding the notion that, however independent my life was, I must have a man; that somehow, no matter what I did myself, there was something that needed that magical element of male approval. Without confronting this I could never have allowed myself to fall in love with Jennie. In a way, I am like an addict who has kicked the habit.

But most important of all, I like her. In fact I think she's the healthiest person I have ever been involved with. See, I think we were lucky, because it happened spontaneously and unexpectedly from both sides. We didn't do it because we felt compelled to put our ideological beliefs into reality.

Many feminists are now beginning to at least theoretically consider the fact that there's no reason why one shouldn't love a woman. But I think that a certain kind of experimentation going on now with lesbianism can be really bad. Because even if you do ideologically think that it is perfectly fine—well, that's a *political* position; but being able to love somebody is a very personal and private thing as well, and even if you remove political barriers, well, then you are left with finding an individual who particularly fits *you*.

So I guess I'm saying that I don't think women who are beginning to think about lesbianism should get involved with anyone until they are really attracted to somebody. And that includes refusing to be seduced by lesbians who play the male seduction game and tell you, "you don't love women," and "you are oppressing us" if you

don't jump into bed with them. It's terrible to try to seduce someone
on ideological grounds.

Q. *Do you now look at women in a more sexual way?*

A. You mean, do I now eye all women as potential bed partners? No. Nor did I ever see men that way. As a matter of fact, I've
never found myself being attracted to a man just because, for example, he had a good physique. I had a sexual relationship with whatever boy friend I had, but I related to most other men pretty asexually.
It's no different with women. My female friends—well, I still see
them as friends, because that's what they are. I don't sit around and
have secret fantasies of being in bed with them.

But there's a real question here: What is the source, the impetus,
for one's sexuality? Is it affection and love, or is it essentially conquest
in bed? If it's sex as conquest in bed, then the question you just
asked is relevant, for adding the category of women to those you
sleep with would mean that every woman—who's attractive enough
to be a prize worth conquering, of course—could arouse your
sexuality. But if the sexual source lies in affection and love, then the
question becomes absurd. For one obviously does not immediately
fall in love with every woman one meets simply because one is *able*
to sleep with women.

Also, one thing that really turns me off about this whole business
of viewing women as potential bed mates is the implied possessiveness
of it. It has taken me this long just to figure out how men are treating
women sexually; now when I see some lesbians doing precisely the
same kinds of things, I'm supposed to have instant amnesia in the
name of sisterhood. I have heard some lesbians say things like, "I
see all men as my rivals," or have heard them proudly discuss how
they intimidated a heterosexual couple publicly to "teach the woman
a political lesson." This brings out in me the same kind of intense
rage that I get when, for example, I hear white men discussing how
black men are "taking their women" (or vice versa). Who the hell
says we belong to anyone?

Q. *Do you think that you would have difficulty relating to a
man again if this relationship broke up? That is, can you "go back"
to men after having had a relationship with a woman?*

A. It's an interesting thing that when people ask that question,
most often what they're really asking is, are you "lost" to the world
of what's "natural"? Sometimes I find myself not wanting to answer
the question at all just because they're starting out by assuming that

something's wrong with having a relationship with a woman. That's usually what's meant by "go back to men"—like you've been off someplace wild and crazy and, most of all, unsafe, and can you find your way home to papa, or something. So first of all it wouldn't be "going back."

And since I didn't become involved with a woman in order to make a political statement, by the same token I wouldn't make the converse statement. So, sure I could have a relationship with a man if he were the right kind of person and if he had rejected playing "the man" with me—that leaves out a lot of men here, I must add. But if a man had the right combination of qualities, I see no reason why I shouldn't be able to love him as I now love her.

At a certain point, I think, you realize that the final qualification is not being male or female, but whether they've joined the middle. That is—whether they have started from the male or the female side —they've gone toward the center where they are working toward combining the healthy aspects of so-called male and female characteristics. That's where I want to go and that's what I'm beginning to realize I respond to in other people.

Q. *Now that you've gotten involved with a woman, what is your attitude toward gay and lesbian groups?*

A. I have really mixed feelings about them. To some extent, for example, there has been a healthy interplay between the gay movement and the feminist movement. Feminists have had a very good influence on the gay movement because women's liberation challenges the very nature of the sex role system, not just whether one may be allowed to make transfers within it. On the other hand, the gay movement has helped open up the question of women loving other women. Though some of this was beginning to happen by itself, lesbians made a point of pressing the issue and therefore speeded up the process.

But there is a problem to me with focusing on sexual choice, as the gay movement does. Sleeping with another woman is not *necessarily* a healthy thing by itself. It does not mean—or prove, for that matter—that you therefore love women. It doesn't mean that you have avoided bad "male" or "female" behavior. It doesn't guarantee you anything. If you think about it, it can be the same game with new partners: On the one hand, male roles are learned, not genetic; women can ape them too. On the other, the feminine role can be comfortably carried into lesbianism, except now instead of a woman being passive with a man, she's passive with another woman. Which is all very familiar and is all going nowhere.

I guess to me, at this point in my life, feminism, naturally incorporates the possibility of sleeping with and loving women; but it is only one of *many* elements of what I define as radical feminism—that is, the elimination of sex roles. The main point of feminism is still to understand that we as women are a political group living on the margin of a male society, that sex roles define our inferior "place" for us, and that radical feminism means the ultimate destruction of that role system. Within that perspective, sleeping with and loving women is only one possibility, and becomes a purely personal solution to living within a sexist society unless it is seen in the larger light of destroying sex roles altogether.

The confusing of sexual *partners* with sexual *roles* has also led to a really bizarre situation where some lesbians insist that you aren't really a radical feminist if you are not in bed with a woman. Which is wrong politically and outrageous personally.

Q. *Did the fact that lesbians pushed the issue in the women's movement have a major effect upon your own decision to have a relationship with a woman?*

A. It's hard to know. I think that the lesbian movement has escalated the thinking in the women's movement, and to that extent it probably escalated mine.

But at the same time I know I was slowly getting there myself anyway. I'd been thinking about it for a long time. Because it is a natural question; if you want to remove sexual roles, and if you say that men and women are equal human beings, well, the next question is: Why should you only love men? I remember asking myself that question, and I remember it being discussed in many workshops I was in—what is it that makes us assume that you can only receive and give love to a man?

Femininity in the Lesbian Community
by William Simon and
John H. Gagnon

For some time now it has been our conviction that studies in deviant behavior frequently have been overimpressed with the "special," or "exotic," character of the populations or groups studied. Many students of deviant behavior have been vulnerable to the temptations of a kind of intellectual "hipsterism," delighting in familiarity with esoteric argots and the ease with which they can display their "cool." One almost senses a reluctance to engage seriously more general conceptions—conceptions traditionally applied to the behavior of conforming populations—lest exotic behavior be transformed into pedestrian behavior, thus denying to the student a sense of special engagement. Consequently, for example, a good deal is known about the homosexual bar or tavern, but very little about the ways the homosexual earns a living, finds a place to live, or manages relations with his family. Similar to the larger society's reaction, there has been a tendency to be too exclusively preoccupied with the manifest deviance, and a failure to observe or report upon the conforming behavior which frequently accounts for the larger part of a deviant's time and energy—and provides the context for deviant performances as well as often giving meaning to such performances.

Similarly, studies of deviance tend to be overly preoccupied with failures in socialization. To be sure, deviance that becomes a major individual commitment represents, from the societal point

A revised version of a paper presented at the Sixteenth Annual Meetings of the Society for Social Problems, August 26–28, 1966, Miami Beach, Florida. This research was supported by USPHS Grant MH-12535.

Reprinted by permission of the publisher from *Social Problems,* Vol. 15, No. 2 (Fall 1967), pp. 212–221.

of view, inappropriate socialization at the very least. Being homosexual, for example, is never the desired outcome of the childrearing process. The concern for explaining this undesired and unanticipated outcome, however, becomes the sociologist's version of the etiological question that too exclusively preoccupies the psychiatrist. Indeed, while the language of socialization failure or inappropriate socialization is itself appropriate, it is extremely unlikely that one can talk about total failures in socialization or socialization that is totally inappropriate. There has been a tendency to avoid the complex processes that represent the meshing of both conventional and unconventional forms of socialization resulting in an excessively narrow focus upon deviant adjustments and a corresponding neglect of conventional patterns of adjustment. Where there have been concerns with conventional adjustments, these were scrutinized simply to see how they reflect the deviant commitment; rarely is there concern with the ways in which deviant adjustments reflect conventional commitments.

The lesbian represents an excellent example of the need to integrate our understanding of both deviant and conventional developmental processes. Where, one may ask, is the research literature that reports upon the attributes and activities of the lesbian when she is *not* acting out her deviant commitment? The answer is that there is virtually none. As a result, the present paper must rely upon an exceedingly thin scientific literature,[1] an examination of the literature generated by female homophile organizations,[2] the general literature on the processes of the development of feminine identifications

[1] See Anonymous, "Some Comparisons Between Male and Female Homosexuals," *The Ladder*, 4, 12 (1966), pp. 4–25; Virginia Armon, "Some Personality Variables in Overt Female Homosexuality," Unpublished Ph.D. dissertation, University of Southern California, Los Angeles, 1961; Donald Webster Cory, *The Lesbian in America*, New York: Citadel Press, 1964; Helene Deutsch, "Homosexuality in Women," *International Journal of Psychoanalysis*, 14 (1933), pp. 34–56; Sylvan Keiser and Dora Schaffer, "Environmental Factors in Homosexuality in Adolescent Girls," *Psychoanalytic Review*, 36 (1949), pp. 283–295; Brian Magee, *One in Twenty. A Study of Homosexual Men and Women*, London: Secker & Warburg, 1966; Marijane Meaker (Ann Aldrich, pseud.), *We Walk Alone*, New York: Fawcett, 1955; J. D. Mercer, *They Walk in Shadow*, New York: Comet Press, 1959; Lionel Ovesey, "Masculine Aspirations in Women: An Adaptational Analysis," *Psychiatry*, 19 (1956), pp. 341–351; Joseph C. Rheingold, *The Fear of Being a Woman*, New York: Grune and Stratton, 1964, pp. 372–380; C. B. Wilbur, "Clinical Aspects of Homosexuality," in Judd Marmor, (ed.), *Sexual Inversion: The Multiple Roots of Homosexuality*, New York: Basic Books, 1965, pp. 268–281.

[2] *The Ladder*, published by the female homophile organization The Daughters of Bilitis, is useful and often insightful reading, as is the publication of the Minorities Research Group in England, *Arena 3*.

and role patterns,[3] a series of exploratory, depth interviews conducted with a relatively small number of lesbians,[4] and a reanalysis of some of the data gathered by Kinsey and his associates. What follows, then, is a tentative attempt to piece together from disparate sources of information and theory an organizing perspective; its major justification is that it might serve as an effective basis for systematic research.

The lesbian differs from other women in the gender of the object that engages her sexuality. This is clearly a significant difference, one that engenders a potential for the emergence of deviant patterns in a number of aspects of social life. Indeed, the very significance of this difference tends to consume nearly all of the researcher's attention. What is generally neglected is the degree to which the lesbian's commitment to sexuality reflects general female patterns of sexuality, the difference in gender selection notwithstanding. It is the contention of this paper that in most cases the female homosexual follows conventional feminine patterns in developing her commitment to sexuality and in conducting a sexual career. This should not be particularly surprising considering that, despite the specific experiences that influenced gender selection, most lesbians are exposed to the numerous diffuse and subtle experiences and relations that generally serve to promote conventional sex-role identification in this society. Moreover, many of these experiences and relations occur prior to the emergence of sexuality as something explicit and salient and there is little reason to assume that these sources of sex-role learning are not assimilated in much the same way as occurs with females who are more exclusively heterosexual.

One of the major characteristics of female socialization in American society is the degree to which the general outlines of its processes are relatively simple and devoted to a single outcome, what Parsons

---

[3] Simone de Beauvoir, *The Second Sex,* New York: Knopf, 1953; Therese Benedek, *Psychosexual Functions in Women,* New York: Ronald Press, 1953; Marie Bonaparte, *Female Sexuality,* New York: International Universities Press, 1953; Sigmund Freud, "Female Sexuality," in James Strachey, translator and editor, *Collected Papers,* Vol. 5, London: The Hogarth Press, 1950, pp. 252–272; Stephen R. Graubard, editor, "The Women in America," *Daedalus,* 93, 2 (Spring, 1961), p. 579–808; Jerome Kagan, "Acquisition and Significance of Sex Typing and Sex Role," in M. L. Hoffman and L. W. Hoffman, editors, *Review of Child Development Research,* Vol. 1, New York: Russell Sage Foundation, 1904, pp. 137–167; Rheingold, *op. cit.*
[4] William Simon and John H. Gagnon, "The Lesbians: A Preliminary Overview," in John H. Gagnon and William Simon, editors, *Sexual Deviance,* New York: Harper & Row, 1967.

has called, after Burgess, the domestic pattern.[5] Whatever the desires of females for glamor, careers, or companionship patterns, the most pervasive commitment of the society is the production of wives and mothers among all females. Much like the military's inability to conceive of a soldier who is not modeled on the rifle-carrying infantryman, the society does not conceive of, nor does it train except by inadvertence, females who will have more complex roles than those of wife and mother. In the process of socialization, patterns both of aggression and assertion, as well as those of sexuality, are inhibited among female children, so that they will be labile and conforming to the needs of the male.[6] As Parsons points out, there is really no equivalent for the male term "bad boy" (except in the sexual domain during adolescence).

The single-model system of reproducing women has other basic consequences that are more discernible from the psychoanalytic literature. It is here that the enigma not only of female sexuality but of femininity and womanness is most profoundly confronted. In contrast to an author like de Beauvoir, the psychoanalyst Rheingold discusses the substantial influence that sheer biological differences play in the development of femininity and the commitments of women. As he suggests, "The denial of the body is a delusion. No woman transcends her body."[7] In addition to the biological fact of childbearing and consequently the social fact of childrearing,[8] the female is subjected to the training processes of this society focusing their energies on molding women to be "mother of the family" rather than into another role. Indeed, the alternative roles available for women, especially that of "career"—whether professional or glamorous—are almost as deviant for the society as is the role "lesbian."[9]

---

[5] Talcott Parsons, "Age and Sex in the Social Structure of the United States," *American Sociological Review*, 7, 5 (October, 1942), pp. 604–616.
[6] This may account for the Kinsey finding that there were no differences in the sexual patterns of females when socioeconomic status was held constant except for age at marriage and therefore age at first coitus, a fundamentally dependent variable in this case. Female sexuality is designed to conform to a relatively wide range of male sexual performance without major upset or anxiety.
[7] Rheingold, *op. cit.*, p. 215.
[8] Alice Rossi, "Equality Between the Sexes: An Immodest Proposal," *Daedalus*, 93, 2 (Spring, 1964), pp. 607–652. The author points out that for the first time in history there is a situation in which child-rearing is the full-time business of the woman rather than being simply one of her many duties as in the past.
[9] Changes in the technology and social organization of work have considerably lessened the strain of choosing between family roles and work for middle-class females. However, the problems of managing a strong career commitment, including

Previous research clearly supports the contention that the patterns of overt sexual behavior of homosexual females tend to resemble closely those of heterosexual females and to differ radically from the sexual activity patterns of both heterosexual and homosexual males.[10] Exceptions to this generalization result either from prison experience or certain other limited group situations where the constraints operating upon sexual performances and role assignments are basically different from those observable in the rest of society.[11] The homogeneity among women (regardless of sexual object choice) and the differences between women and men begin, overtly at least, in the different introductions of males and females to sexuality. Many of the most important differences become evident when we consider the phasing of entry into sexual activity. For males the major organizing event in their sexual lives is clearly puberty. Within two years after puberty the vast majority of males have their commitment to sexuality reinforced by the experience of orgasm.[12] This is largely the result of the fact that masturbation occurs among males at fairly high rates during early adolescence. Females, on the other hand, tend to begin overt sexual activity—that is, behavior that has a reasonable probability of culminating in orgasm—much later, during late adolescence or the early years of adulthood. Moreover, for females the initial experience of orgasm is nearly as likely to occur during sociosexual activity (pre-coital petting or coitus) as it is likely to be a result of masturbatory activity. Indeed, half or more of the women who report masturbation as a source of sexual outlet "discovered" this outlet after achieving orgasm in sociosexual activity. In this pattern of male-female difference, female homosexuals do not appear to differ significantly from heterosexual females.

---

aspirations levels appropriate for a given career, appear to remain problematic. As Mervin Freedman observed in describing his study of Vassar students: "The interviews also reveal some reluctance on the part of women to assume leadership in various professions or fields except for those which possess considerable female connotation—for example, social work. They are likely to retreat from any exceptional accomplishment which may threaten the security of men. . . . All in all, as I see it, most women today are striving to maintain the integrity of the family and, at least to some extent, the continuity of traditional sex roles." In *The College Experience,* San Francisco: Jossey-Bass, Inc., 1967, pp. 119–120.

[10] A. C. Kinsey, *et al., Sexual Behavior in the Human Male,* Philadelphia: Saunders Co., 1948; A. C. Kinsey, *et al., Sexual Behavior in the Human Female,* Philadelphia: Saunders Co., 1953.

[11] Rose Gialombardo, *Society of Women,* New York: Wiley, 1966; D. A. Ward and Gene G. Kassebaum, *Women's Prisons: Sex and Social Structure,* Chicago: Aldine Press, 1965.

[12] A. C. Kinsey, *et al., op. cit.,* 1953, Figures 148–50, p. 717.

Two factors significant in the management of sexual life appear to derive from this differential male-female introduction into sexuality. The first of these is the fact that males usually develop commitments to sexuality prior to involvement in complicated, emotionally charged inter-personal relations—that is, prior to developing a commitment to the rhetoric of love. For females, most lesbians included, the reverse appears to be true: training in love precedes training in sexuality. As a result, sex as an interest and an activity appears to possess greater autonomy for males. It is an activity that can be engaged in with relative detachment from other areas of life. For most women—including most lesbians—the pursuit of sexual gratification as something separate from emotional or romantic involvement is not particularly attractive; indeed, for many it may be impossible. This is in part reflected in the number of sexual partners an individual reports. In the original work of Kinsey and his associates it was observed that of the lesbians interviewed only 29 per cent had sexual relations with three or more partners, and only 4 per cent had contact with ten or more partners. These figures are extremely close approximations of proportions for females *per se,* whether homosexual or heterosexual.[13] This is far below comparable statistics for heterosexual males and dramatically below that for male homosexuals.

The second significant factor is that differences in the early management of sexuality suggest that the repression of sexuality is an essential part of learning to be a female in our society and is learned by heterosexual and homosexual women alike. Unlike males, females during adolescence and the early adult years typically tend not to report a feeling of sexual deprivation during periods of sexual inactivity. Similarly, sexual arousal by such things as dreams, fantasy, visual stimulation, and exposure to pornography is a substantially less common experience for females than for males. Sexual arousal in females—of all indirect sources—is highest from non-pornographic fiction and movies or precisely where sex, if significant as an element, appears in the context of a legitimizing emotional setting.[14] The reported rates of sexual stimulation without emotional contexts tend to be somewhat higher for lesbians than for heterosexual women but far lower than those reported for both heterosexual and homosexual males, and far lower than one might suspect given

13 A. C. Kinsey, *et al., op. cit.,* 1953, p. 475 and Table 78, p. 336.
14 A. C. Kinsey, *et al., op. cit.,* 1953, pp. 642–689.

the obviously greater salience of sexuality for the lesbian. Sexuality for the lesbian should be more self-conscious, if only because it becomes the basis for her commitment to deviant patterns; however, the more general character-molding processes of society appear to be the dominant factors. Despite a generally oversimplified and widely current image of the lesbian as a "counterfeit man," the gender of the object of her sexual desires may be one of the relatively few attributes that she shares with males.

The social careers of lesbians and, more particularly, the patterns of group life that emerge can only be understood in the light of considerations such as those that have just been raised. These considerations have substantial ramifications for an appraisal of the lesbian community when it is contrasted with the male homosexual community.

For both male and female homosexuals it is possible to talk about the existence of a community, at least in most relatively large cities.[15] In the same manner as many ethnic or occupational groups, which also can be said to have a community, this subcommunity does not require a formal character or even a specific geographical location. It is, rather, a continuing collectivity of individuals who share some significant activity and who, out of a history of continuing interaction based on that activity, begin to generate a sense of a bounded group possessing special norms and a particular argot. Through extensive use such a homosexual aggregate may identify a particular location as "theirs," and in almost all large cities this includes one or more taverns that cater exclusively to a particular homosexual group. In these bars the homosexual may act out more freely his or her self-definition as compared with less segregated situations. Several homophile social and service organizations have recently appeared which offer a more public image of the homosexual. These various social activities reinforce a feeling of identity and provide for the homosexual a way of institutionalizing the experience, wisdom, and mythology of the collectivity. A synonym for

[15] Studies of male homosexual communities are E. Hooker's "The Homosexual Community," in James O. Palmer and Michael J. Goldstein, editors, *Perspectives in Psychopathology,* New York: Oxford University Press, 1966, pp. 354–364; Maurice Leznoff and William Westley, "The Homosexual Community," *Social Problems,* 3 (1956), pp. 257–263; a more specialized study is Nancy Achilles' *The Homosexual Bar,* unpublished M.A. thesis, Department of Sociology, University of Chicago, 1964.

this community, one not untouched by a sense of the ironic, is "the gay life."

For the individual homosexual, both male and female, the community provides many functions. A major function is the facilitation of sexual union; the lesbian who finds her way to the community can now select from a population that, while differing in other attributes, has the minimum qualification of sharing a lesbian commitment. This greatly reduces what is for the isolated lesbian the common risk of "falling for a straight girl," i.e., a heterosexual. The community provides a source of social support; it is a place where the lesbian can express her feelings or describe her experiences because there are others available who have had feelings and experiences very much like hers. It is an environment in which sexuality can be socialized and ways can be found of deriving sexual gratification by being admired, envied, or desired while not necessarily engaging in sexual behavior. Lastly, the community includes a language and an ideology which provide each individual lesbian with already developed attitudes that help her resist the societal claim that she is diseased, depraved, or shameful.

Everything said about the community to this point can obviously apply to both male and female homosexual communities. Indeed, in certain ways, it is difficult to establish the fact that two separate communities exist as there is considerable overlap and sharing of facilities. However, marked differences arise when the community is examined more closely in the light of the differing sexual commitments of male and female homosexuals.

First, quite clearly, from any acquaintance with homosexual communities, the proportion of lesbians utilizing the gay world is markedly smaller than that of male homosexuals—though in both cases the visible gay world is an inadequate sampling of the respective homosexual populations. There are homosexuals of both sexes who completely avoid contact with public forms of the gay life (more true of females than males), others whose use is episodic (more true of males than females), and still others whose contact is indirect (maintaining social contact with other homosexuals who participate in the gay life). This lower rate of use by lesbians may be attributed to two related factors. One, the lesbian's sexual commitment is not as immediately alienating from the conventional society. The lesbian may mask her sexual deviance behind a socially prepared asexual role. Not all categories of women in our society are necessarily defined as sexually active. For example, spinsters are not assumed to be more sexually active than are married women by the fact of their spinsterhood. To the contrary, they are assumed to be less active sexually. In line with this, the image of two spinsters living together does not immediately suggest sexual activity between them, even when there is a public display of affection. The same is not true for men. The bachelor is presumed to be even more sexually active than the married man, and the idea of two males living together—past the years of young adulthood—strikes one as strange. This makes it more likely that the lesbian will find sources of social support or compensation in the larger society than will the male homosexual, thereby lessening her need for the subcommunity. What is involved in this socially provided asexual role for the female is society's assumption that women can manage careers of sexual inactivity with success while the male cannot.

The second factor directly involves the learning of techniques for the management of sexuality. It is possible that the same techniques of repression that lead to differences between males and females in the ages during which sexual activity is initiated allow the female to handle subsequent sexual deprivation more easily. More females than males should therefore be able to resist quasi-public homosexual behavior which increases the risks of disclosure; further, lesbians should be better able to resist relations that involve sexual exchange without any emotional investment. It is hardly a novel observation that training in the repression of sexuality is far more thorough and systematic for females than it is for males in our society. One reason for this is suggested by Rheingold when he observes that females run a double risk in the management of sexuality, while there is only a single risk for most males. "The woman's adjustment is precarious, for each new biologic event or social role evokes the fear of consequences. A man fears that he may fail; a woman fears both that she may fail and that she may succeed." [16] What is implied by success is the ability to express and pursue sexual interest and a competence in performance. This may also involve a sense of the sexual as something at least partially autonomous, as a form of behavior that need not *always* be justified in terms of service to some non-sexual end. It is the linking of sexual activity with the non-

---

[16] Rheingold, *op. cit.*, p. 213.

sexual that makes ours a society where both the non-sexual and fully sexual adaptations for women are viewed as deviant.

These factors should produce not only differences in the relative proportions of each sex utilizing the visible homosexual subcommunity, but also should produce differences in the quality or content of community life. Thus, camp behavior—behavior that is both outrageous and outraging—appears to be essentially a product of the male homosexual community. In terms of general social and political values the lesbian community is far more traditional—indeed, one might say conservative. There is little visible avant-gardism in the lesbian community; to the contrary, its collective taste appears highly traditional, perhaps stodgy. Partly this may be a function of the fact that lesbians are more likely to "come out"—that is, acknowledge their homosexuality—at later ages, at ages when other constraining commitments to the larger society are already established. Also, the lesbian is more likely to become available to the community only after a relatively isolated affair or series of affairs. The lesbian community, then, is far less often the scene of "coming out," and consequently less often the scene for the acting-out behavior frequently associated with this stage in the male homosexual community, where the discovery of self as homosexual and the discovery of the homosexual community more often coincide.

If two of the major functions of a homosexual community are the facilitation of sexual activity and the socialization into sexual roles, the relative emphasis given these by the two sexes should also differ. For males the emphasis upon the facilitation of sexual activity should be greater, while emphasis upon the socialization process should be greater among females. If nothing else, the lesbian community should contain a higher proportion of members existing in relatively stable, dyadic relationships, relationships that are more than sexual alliances. The use of the community by this segment of its membership is more exclusively social, providing contextual constraints against the tradition of aggressively seeking sexual partners that tends to typify the male homosexual community. However, it is possible that the extent of participation within either community may have opposite effects upon males and females. As a male homosexual becomes more integrated into the homosexual community, it becomes more possible for him to develop extensive forms of gratification that feed a homosexual identification without necessarily being sexual, while the lesbian, as she becomes more integrated into the lesbian community, may find the experience deinhibiting, freeing her somewhat from the constraints of her feminine socialization and allowing her to be sexual in more direct ways.

Both male and female homosexual communities generally share an important characteristic: both give rise to appearances that reinforce the societal image of the respective homosexualities. That is, the appearances of the male homosexual community tend to project an essentially feminine image of the male homosexual, while the appearances of the lesbian community may well reinforce the social image of the lesbian as masculine. And, of great importance, such collective appearances reinforce the notion that pseudo-masculinity or pseudo-femininity (as the case may be) are essential to the sexual commitment and performance of the homosexual. A counterargument is that, in the case of the lesbian, the community constrains *most* participating lesbians to appear more masculine than they would ordinarily desire. Firstly, this promotes a sense of group identity and participation and helps create a sense of distance between the group and the outside majority. Secondly, it reflects the activity of a relatively small proportion of lesbians for whom feminine socialization processes failed more thoroughly and/or whose sense of alienation from conventional society is fairly intense, and who self-consciously pursue a masculinized role of the "butch." It is this group that is both the most visible and, because of the extreme nature of its deviant performance, has the greatest need for the community. Thirdly, it reflects the presence of a larger proportion of lesbians who pursue a masculinized role during a limited amount of time in their homosexual careers—a stage through which many lesbians may pass, but one in which relatively few remain. This is largely a phase during which the acceptance of private homosexuality is being transformed into an acceptance of social homosexuality, a period Erikson would describe as an identity crisis with experimentation with masculinized roles being one expression of this transitional crisis.

Like many other discussions of deviant behavior, too much of the social landscape has been left out; however, it is a preliminary attempt to bring the exotic to terms with the pedestrian. One goal of this paper has been to argue the need for viewing female homosexuality in terms of both its discontinuity and continuity with conventional behavior and conventional determinants, the need to balance a sense of the degree to which the lesbian departs from standard definitions of appropriate sex-role behavior with a sense of how much of her behavior derives from the embodiment of standard definitions of sex-role behavior. Perhaps more importantly, this is an attempt to demonstrate that an understanding of homosexuality can only follow from an understanding of sexuality itself. With regard to the lesbian, we begin to come close to this when we approach more closely an understanding of the complex interweaving of sociocultural and biological forces that produce the varied forms of female sexuality.

Coming Out Among Lesbians
by Denise M. Cronin

The experience of *becoming homosexual* is frequently referred to by homosexuals as *"coming out."* It is that period in one's life when a homosexual identity is first acquired. Gagnon and Simon (1968: 356) refer to "coming out" as ". . . that point in time when there is self recognition by the individual of his identity as a homosexual and the first major exploration of the homosexual community." Hooker (1965:99) refers to the process as a "debut . . . of a person who believes himself to be homosexual but who has struggled against it." For Hooker (1965:99) "coming out" occurs when "he identifies himself publicly for the first time as a homosexual in the presence of other homosexuals by his appearance in a bar." Dank (1971:181) uses "coming out" to mean only "identifying oneself as being homosexual." In this study, most women used the expression to describe the conditions under which they came to decide that they were homosexual. Thus, within the confines of this paper, "coming out" will be used to mean *unequivocably identifying oneself as homosexual.*

RESEARCH METHOD

The present study was initiated in the summer of 1972 in order to obtain information on a large sample of female homosexuals in a northeastern city.

The homosexual women were selected from two distinct areas within the Lesbian community: Lesbians who were introduced to the investigator by homosexual friends, and Lesbians who were members of a homophile organization (The Daughters of Bilitis). The first sample consisted of 65 self-admitted Lesbians, ages 19–46, with whom I conducted 3–4-hour interviews. I was introduced to approximately two-thirds of these women in bars catering to homosexuals or at private gatherings of Lesbians, and was presented as someone who was interested in doing a study of Lesbians. These initial contacts introduced me to still other Lesbians who later became engaged in the study. The second sample was composed of 137 self-acknowledged Lesbians, ages 17–38, who were attending a Daughters of Bilitis meeting. I distributed 137 questionnaires at that time and 89 questionnaires were returned. Prior to collecting the data, the questionnaire was pretested on 23 female respondents who were not included in the study.

The data from both homosexual samples will be presented as if they comprised one group, except on those rare occasions when the two samples differ significantly from one another. These differences will be noted in the text.

It is not possible to determine the degree to which this sample is representative of the total universe of Lesbians. Nearly all of my respondents live within the inner city of a large northeastern city.

CREATING A LESBIAN SELF

The central mechanism through which women become Lesbians is shaped by the larger society's definition of sex roles. As Gagnon and Simon point out, the mode of discovery or entry into a homosexual "career" for women is a totally feminine one. "The discovery of their homosexuality usually occurs very late in adolescence, often even in the years of young adulthood, and the actual commencement of overt sexual behavior frequently comes as a late stage of an intense emotional involvement" (Gagnon and Simon, 1967:251). I asked the women in my study the age at which they first became aware of any sexual desires toward other women, in addition to the age at which they came out. The average time interval between first sexual desire for a member of the same sex and the decision that one is homosexual is five years. Most Lesbians reported that they first became aware of their sexual feelings between the ages of fifteen and nineteen, but that they did not develop a Lesbian identity until their early twenties.

Clearly, then, the fact that a woman is aware of her feelings toward others of the same sex does not necessarily mean that she thinks of herself as a Lesbian. The development of a Lesbian identity seems to be tied in a very dramatic way to the development of an intense affectionate relationship with another woman. It is within such a relationship that a woman progresses from a friendship in which tokens of intimacy are seen as lacking in sexual intent to a relationship of great mutual affection and erotic arousal. In this context, each woman learns to associate the tokens of intimacy and endearment that each confers on the other with sexual intent, and thus gradually recognizes the sexual significance of the relationship. I asked the women in the study to describe how they came to see themselves as Lesbian. In three-quarters of the cases, they reported that they arrived at this conclusion only as a consequence of an intense affectionate relationship with another woman. One of my respondents described her growing intimacy with another woman and the subsequent development of her homosexual identity in the following way:

> When I first came to school we were on the same hall. We both had singles. A lot of us used to hang around the floor lounge and talk, and Helen and I got to know each other pretty well. We always used to do things together, go to shows and concerts. She was a movie freak. The next term we got a doublet together, but nothing happened for a long time. She was just someone I got really close to and we shared a lot of our personal feelings with one another. Sometimes we used to hug each other if we were happy or if something really good happened, but that's all and neither one of us thought anything of it. Then it just happened. We'd hold hands and feel really close to each other. It was nice. I stayed in the city that summer and got a job. We decided to still live in the dorms . . . I really didn't think much about what I might be [sexually]. We never talked about being gay or anything. Anyway nothing really big [i.e., sex] happened for a long time. We just kept getting closer and we were really important to each other. When it did happen, it was nice and seemed natural. We knew we were [Lesbian] then, and that was nice too.

Another woman described her relationship in the same manner. Again, the close, mutual friendship and a gradual progression to sexuality dominated the development of the Lesbian identity.

> Before Harriet even got the secretarial job, I'd been thinking about

moving into the city. It'd be a lot more convenient to be able to walk to work, plus I'd save some money. Anyway, September came around and . . . Harriet was looking for a nicer place and I was still thinking about moving in. So we decided to go it together. I'd known her for about two months then. After we started living together things were different. I don't mean really changed. I guess I mean that before we were good friends and we saw each other outside of work, but not a lot. Afterwards though, we seemed to spend all of our time together. I got to know her really well . . . , her family, friends, what she really wanted to do. You know, everything, and she knew the same about me. We did everything from going to the market to picking out clothes. At work we used to plan what we'd do that night or on the weekend. Anyway, we were really close people. In the beginning it was nothing much [sexually]. I remember when she touched me on the cheek. Everything at work had gone wrong, and I screwed up a bunch of charts. She just touched me and said "Forget it." And, on my birthday when I was depressed about being so old, she made me a cake with surprises in it, and I cried. Then she kissed me. I mean you really had to love this girl. It pretty much went on that way for a while. Nothing sexual went on for a while. At first we touched each other, just casually on the arm. . . . Later it was more, and then we had to think about it, but I knew how I was about her and she knew it—even if we didn't say it. We needed to need and be with each other. After that, the rest has just been better for the both of us.

This romantic "drift" into homosexual behavior is typical of most of the women in our sample, and is often preceded by such activities as touching, kissing and holding hands without perceiving them as being specifically sexual in intent. In contrast with male homosexuality, initial Lesbian relations tend to be more romantic, more affectionate, relatively long-lasting and monogamous.

Although most (76 percent) women came to acknowledge their homosexuality through a love relationship such as those described above, others came to the realization on their own (11 percent). That is, they recognized their sexual feelings for other women, but did not search out other homosexuals or engage in overt homosexual activities. Katherine, a woman who has been overtly homosexual for almost six years, describes what it was like for her in the beginning:

When I was in high school I knew I was different from other people, but I really didn't know how for a long time, and then I didn't like to think much about it. I guess I was really messed up. I didn't know what I was. I didn't avoid guys, but I never went out with them or anything, but I would rather just hang around with my girlfriends. I used to think about them a lot, and dream about them and be, oh God, so scared for myself, 'cuz I could never tell anyone what I was thinking of. Sometimes I'd even pretend that I never dreamed that stuff. I hated myself for a while, thought I was sick and needed help. But when I think about it, I really didn't want anyone to tell me I was sick. I just wanted to know what I was. I used to read everything I could get on gays, but I never knew anyone then who was, and I never went to bars or had anything going with anyone. That's why I feel I did it by myself. I just decided to accept what I felt, and decided that it was okay, decided that it was better to be something that you were than something that you weren't. It wasn't till a lot later, when I went to school, that I tried to find other gays.

Still other women reported that supportive discussions with close friends helped them to verbalize their sexual feelings and see themselves as homosexuals (7 percent). One woman explained it in this way: "I think Carol really helped me out quite a bit. She was the only one I dared to talk to. She never thought I was disgusting or pathetic, and that's what I needed then. I had to decide for myself without having to feel ashamed. She helped me get myself together." A second explained the role of close friends in developing her sexual identity in the following words: "Patty was hip to any scene you know. She knew a lot of gays . . . she wasn't [gay herself], but she knew them, and knew where their heads were at. I was lucky to have her around, I mean to talk to. She cared about people, and got me to believe in her way of life—if you feel something, you've got to act on it. You can't just wait around pretending you don't or wishing you didn't. Talking to her helped the most . . . to accept myself." A third respondent put it this way:

I used to have one great friend and I used to have long talks with her. Sometimes when she stayed overnight, we'd stay up all night and talk. I used to talk about it [homosexual desires], not saying much but sort of talking about it, just to feel her out. I didn't know how she'd react. She knew I was getting at something, but she never pressed me. She let me talk about dates, and guys, and sex. . . . When I started telling her about how I felt, that I didn't know how I felt, well, I thought she thought I was insane, but she never let me know it, never stayed away from me or told anyone. I knew she couldn't handle it for her. But she never said it was bad or sick or that I shouldn't even think about it. She let me talk it out, and that's what got me where I am.

The striking feature of nearly all these reports is the crucial role a close relationship plays in the development of a Lesbian identity. Occasionally, the relationship which helps the Lesbian recognize and accept her sexual desires is a close supportive friendship. More often, however, the relationship is one of great mutual affection between two women, and is characterized by a slow-moving series of endearments. It is within such a relationship that a woman interprets the meaning of her own sexual feelings to herself, recognizes the relationship's sexual significance and develops a homosexual identity. The majority pattern appears to be one in which self-identification as a Lesbian develops before or during genital contact itself, and as a late stage of a close, affectionate relationship.

SEXUAL STEREOTYPES AND THE DRIFT INTO LESBIANISM

It is not surprising that such an unconventional sexual identity is developed in such a conventional, intimate and slow-moving way. In fact, the pattern of the majority of homosexual women seems to be guided by many of the stereotypes which govern the way men and women relate to each other in Western society. In the West, for example, men are assumed to be easily aroused, and thus nearly all tokens of intimacy take on immediate sexual interpretation. Women, however, are not assumed to have such a low threshold of sexual arousal. Rather, they are seen as requiring a slow building up to sexuality; one which usually takes the form of a graduated series of endearments, vague hints, precoital petting, etc. Some intimacies on the part of women, then, are not necessarily taken to indicate sexual intent, nor are they thought inevitably to lead to sexual arousal.

It may be that such stereotypes of male and female sexual behavior are largely self-fulfilling prophesies. Both men and women may tend to think of themselves and relate to one another in terms of such stereotypes. Men are quick to take each other's shows of intimacy as sexually intended. Women are slow to perceive sexual meaning in each other's shows of affection but first develop a relation of affection and then, only later, come to see each other as sexual partners.

Since males are likely to be quick in attributing sexual intent to gestures, speech, etc., it would be difficult for them to establish mutual friendship relations without concurrent sexual interpretations. Only when women have advanced to kissing and petting are they likely to recognize the sexual content of their relationship. Coming out for women, then, is likely to occur in a traditionally feminine fashion and within the privatized continuity of a single affectionate relationship.

The individual who is to become a Lesbian is socialized in the same manner as any other member of society. The attitudes and beliefs that she acquires are those dictated to her by heterosexual society. It seems that without an explicit awareness on the part of either parent or child, the next generation is taught to think of itself and others as "naturally" heterosexual, and to adopt socially appropriate sex roles. The child who is eventually to become a Lesbian has had no preparation for the role—but she has received images of it through heterosexual stereotypes. She has not been instructed in how to be a homosexual, nor does she command a vocabulary that will help her to interpret the meanings of her emerging sexual feelings. For women, the task of learning about Lesbianism does not usually present itself until late in adolescence.

For most women, homosexuality has been associated with mental illness, sexual deficiency or decadence. This notion of homosexuality is one which heterosexual society dictates, and is one which the Lesbian herself has previously held. Since it is highly negative and characterizes women in a way in which they are not likely to view themselves, women who are to become Lesbians must first struggle against and alter this view if they want to comfortably place themselves within the category "homosexual." Thus, identifying oneself as a Lesbian almost inevitably entails a period of redefining homosexuality. It is a period in which the Lesbian uses techniques of neutralization to reject the dominant view. When asked how she had viewed homosexuality before coming out, one woman responded: "Before I thought like anybody else, I guess—that they were sick people. I think that's why I had such a hard time. Afterwards, I didn't think I was sick or anything, just different." Another woman explained that: "People who think gays are social rejects are just speaking out of ignorance. I was like that—having opinions on the basis of no experience with gays. Once you've been there, you know that gays aren't all flamers or crazies, they're regular people. I mean I was never like that, and most gays aren't."

Two things which appear to play an important role in facilitating the woman's redefinition of homosexuality are her rather stable and typically monogamous relationship with another woman, and her knowledge of and subsequent interactions with other Lesbians. Lesbians' mutual affectional relationships have been likened to the stereotypical, conventional, idealized heterosexual marriage, in which each partner is intent upon seeing that the other's emotional, physical and sexual well-being is secured. In the Lesbian relationship the roles and responsibilities traditionally delegated to men and women in marriage are taken up and often shared cooperatively by members of the same sex. Thus, even though the Lesbian has chosen a socially "inappropriate" partner, she may see herself as participating in a perfectly normal relationship between lovers.

The Lesbian's knowledge of and interactions with others like herself may also play an important role in the process of redefinition. As the Lesbian enters the homosexual community, she encounters women like herself who hold jobs, have families and participate in a variety of social experiences. These individuals do not fit society's negative stereotype of the homosexual as mentally ill, and thus permit the Lesbian to reject the conventional definition of homosexuality and redefine it in such a way as to place herself comfortably within the category.

SEXUAL BEHAVIOR

Psychiatrists often cite the "promiscuity" of male homosexuals as evidence of the inherent inauthenticity of homosexuality as a way of life. Even ignoring the question of whether this does, in fact, accurately characterize male homosexuals, it is clear that Lesbians are very rarely "promiscuous." They almost never "cruise" for sexual partners in the way that males are reputed to do. They very rarely report searching out sexual partners publicly. In fact, the female homosexual's pattern of coming out closely parallels her later pattern of sexual activity.

Women typically report that they meet under private, rather than public circumstances, where the slow-moving, affectionate relationships they seem to require can take place. Lesbians are often introduced to one another by close friends. They tend to develop their identity within the confines of an exclusive relationship. Even their entry into and continuing adherence to, an unconventional sexual role seems to be guided by dominant sexual stereotypes. Male homosexuals tend to have far more sexual partners than Lesbians. One study (Saghir and Robins, 1973:229) reports that only 15 percent of their homosexual women but 94 percent of their homosexual men had had sex with more than fifteen homosexual partners. With women, an emotional relationship exists prior to sexual activity, and the exclusiveness of this relationship inclines her to remain with one partner over long periods of time. The opposite seems to be true for men.

These male-female differences seem to extend into a number of different areas. Males are more likely to employ flagrant displays of their homosexuality to solicit additional sexual partners. Lesbians, in contrast, rarely adopt the dress and mannerisms which signal their sexual intentions. Our findings indicate that, upon becoming homosexuals, very few women alter their style of dress to solicit further sexual partners or to fit homosexual stereotypes. Nor do most Lesbians report adopting the "butch" (so-called masculine) or "fem" (feminine) mannerisms.

The woman's less ostentatious display of her homosexuality probably means that her commitment to homosexuality will involve considerably less change in her life-style than is true for her male counterpart. Undoubtedly she must make adjustments, but as compared with males, she is more likely to live among heterosexuals and to partake in many of the same conventional social activities as do heterosexual women. Adopting a homosexual identity does not seem to have such a drastic effect on the lives of our respondents as with male homosexuals. Lesbians tend to remain less involved in the more public forms of the homosexual community, and participate mainly in private gatherings of homosexuals. The Lesbian's tendency to privatize her sexual relations and to lead a rather conventional life has made her to some degree invisible to social science researchers. Only a few studies of Lesbians exist. The more overt and highly visible forms of male homosexuality, however, have made far more male homosexuals available for study.

The point that was made earlier about the uniquely and specifically feminine character of Lesbians—their own style of coming out, their distinctive patterns of love and sexuality—should alert the observer to a seemingly obvious, yet oft-ignored fact: Lesbians are women first and homosexuals second. They have far more in common with their heterosexual sisters than with their male counterparts.

References

Dank, Barry M., "Coming Out in the Gay World," *Psychiatry* 34 (May 1971): 180–197.

Gagnon, John H. and Simon, William, "The Lesbians: A Preliminary Overview," in John H. Gagnon and William Simon (Eds.), *Sexual Deviance,* New York, Harper and Row, 1967, pp. 247–282.

——— "Homosexuality: The Formation of a Sociological Perspective," in Mark Lefton et. al. (Eds.), *Approaches to Deviance,* New York, Appleton-Century-Crofts, 1968.

——— *Sexual Conduct,* Chicago, Aldine Publishing Company, 1973.

Hooker, Evelyn, "Male Homosexuals and Their Worlds," in Judd Marmor (Ed.), *Sexual Inversion: The Multiple Roots of Homosexuality,* New York, Basic Books, 1965.

Saghir, Maurice and Robins, Eli, *Male and Female Homosexuality: A Comprehensive Investigation,* Baltimore, Williams and Wilkins, 1973.

Lesbianism and Bisexuality
by Philip W. Blumstein and Pepper Schwartz

The analysis of human sexuality continually encounters evidence contradicting what we have always "known to be true." Our own research on sexual identity has provided dramatic evidence that the way an individual organizes his or her sexual life often fails to possess the coherence and continuity that have always been taken for granted. For example, a person may think of himself or herself one way (e.g., as being heterosexual) and yet act another way (having sexual relations only with members of the same gender). Or a person may shift basic sexual orientation several times in a lifetime. For example, the woman who has been married twice *and* has been involved in long-term relationships with other women; or the man who considered himself homosexual until he was twenty, then was married for fifteen years, and is now dividing his time between male and female lovers. The diversity is impressive, especially since most of us—including the people in the examples—have been thoroughly trained to think in terms of polarities (male or female, heterosexual or homosexual), and it is exceedingly difficult to reanalyze sexuality in a manner that captures the variations we have observed.

We may begin to reconsider the relationship between sexual identity and sexual behavior with the subject of homosexuality. When is someone a homosexual? A commonsense definition would say, when he or she is erotically attracted to, and has preference for sexual contact with, others of the same gender. But this definition has all the problems suggested in the examples above. How do we classify those people who have sexual relations with others of the same gender but who identify themselves as heterosexual (for example, the many men who have impersonal sexual contacts in public restrooms, but who are married and never become emotionally involved with their contacts?)[1] Or those with the reverse pattern, whose sexual behavior is often directed toward the opposite gender but who insistently call themselves homosexual? Or, more relevant to the women we will discuss in this paper, those people who combine elements of homosexuality and heterosexuality (*ambisexuals*—or, in the more popular but somewhat misleading terminology, *bisexuals*)?

We know that a great many people have sexual relations with members of both sexes. Seldom do they claim to divide their attention and commitment absolutely equally (hence the misleading quality of the term bisexual), but both types of sexual experience have independent importance for them. Despite the documented existence of large numbers of such people, one is hard-pressed to find much systematic scientific literature on the topic of bisexuality. Psychoanalysis, for example, has already declared itself on this issue: it is irrelevant. Orthodox Freudian analysts feel that bisexuality does not exist as a clinical entity; a person is either heterosexual or homosexual. The person's expressed self-identification is of no consequence, except as a symptom of inability to come to grips with his or her true sexuality. Irving Bieber has stated: "I conceive of two distinct categories—heterosexual and homosexual. . . . The two categories are . . . mutually exclusive and cannot be placed on the same continuum. . . . A man is homosexual if his behavior is homosexual. Self-identification is not relevant." [2]

As we have noted, our observations directly contradict those of Bieber. In fact, the disparity between behavior and self-identification is a major and crucial issue in research on human sexuality. Perhaps, then, the phenomenon of bisexuality is the place to begin to unravel this question, since the number of people whose behavior might be construed as bisexual far exceeds the number of people who attach that label to their sexual selves.[3]

Often it is difficult to know exactly what people mean when they identify themselves as bisexual. For example, one female respondent said that she is mainly heterosexual in her behavior, but feels herself to be bisexual. Upon further questioning, however, we found that she has had only two homosexual experiences, one casual night with a close friend and a later affair lasting three months, both experiences having occurred ten years ago. She felt the ten-year lapse to be irrelevant, since, in her eyes, the only reason she has not been involved sexually again with a woman is because the right one has not come along. She felt that she could easily enter such a relationship even though she has not wanted to during the ten-year abstention. She believes herself to be a bisexual, but it is also possible that there may be an ideological underpinning to her self-definition. That is, she may identify herself as a bisexual not because she has a strong need to sexualize women, but rather because she believes it to be right and proper to be a bisexual, that she ought to be a bisexual, and that she has at least some past experience to justify her adoption of bisexual credentials. While we accepted her own self-description at face value, we also felt, because of examples like hers and others, that there is no simple way to classify persons on the basis of their sexuality.

Instead, we need a systematic scheme for understanding the various combinations of identity and behavior we have observed. We know, of course, that no such scheme can exist without seriously distorting the evidence, and that any attempt to create such a system could ignore many of the important variations we have observed. Nevertheless, let us suggest some patterns in sexual life-style that have appeared with some regularity in our sample. We will begin where our respondents begin, with their self-identification, and observe its relationship to their behavior.

We have been guided in this effort by the heterosexual-homosexual rating scale used in the Kinsey studies. Respondents were asked to identify themselves as one of the following:

0 exclusively heterosexual

1 mainly heterosexual with a small degree of homosexuality

2 mainly heterosexual with a substantial degree of homosexuality

3 equally heterosexual and homosexual

4 mainly homosexual with a substantial degree of heterosexuality

5 mainly homosexual with a small degree of heterosexuality

6 exclusively homosexual.

They could use the scale to identify both what they thought they were and how their current behavior would be classified by others. Most of the respondents, though not all, differentiated between the two responses. Some respondents refused to use the scale, claiming that they were both totally homosexual and totally heterosexual, depending on the gender of their sexual partner.

HETEROSEXUAL IDENTITY—
HOMOSEXUAL BEHAVIOR

Given this background, we may begin with women who identified themselves as closer to the heterosexual end of the scale. Many of these women coordinated their erotic and affectional reactions, and thus generally had sexual activity only within the context of a relationship of some durability. There was, however, a significant minority who were able to have "sex for sex's sake." Some of these were "swingers," women who enjoyed uninvolved sexual contact with people who shared their sexual rules and perspectives; others were able to have sex with casual friends or in a threesome where only one of the partners was a prior intimate. No women in our sample had impersonal sexual experiences equivalent to those found in parts of the male homosexual culture, i.e., having sexual contact in an anonymous situation, such as a steam bath or public restroom, without exchanging names or interacting on any level other than sexual. The nearest equivalent to this pattern in women consisted of those who could be predatory and were unabashed about identifying other women as sexual objects, to be evaluated on purely sexual and physical grounds. For example, one woman who identified herself with the number 2 on the Kinsey scale spoke of her behavior when "cruising" for other women:

> Almost everywhere I go I am looking for people and approaching them. I approach different women in different ways: I may say, "What an incredible dress you're wearing," or "God, you have pretty hair." I include all kinds of behavior and places, like cable cars, wolf whistles at leggy ladies in Joseph Magnin's, smiles, nude beaches, and almost everywhere there are people. I say *almost* because I have yet to find someone at a church group.

Within the group of women who identify themselves as heterosexual there are a sizable number who under certain special circumstances have sexual relations with women. There are prostitutes who will "party" (have sex with women or engage in threesome for the pleasure of, and at the request of, the male client), and female prisoners who enter emotional and sexual relations with other prisoners, but who return to a purely heterosexual pattern upon release from prison.[4] We have also encountered respondents who, in retrospect, recall periods of their life during which their behavior was overtly homosexual, but they did not recognize it as such at the time and therefore did not find it necessary to question their heterosexuality. For example, one respondent would routinely return to her college dormitory from a heterosexual date in a state of high sexual tension and slight inebriation and would allow her roommate to make sexual contact. The incident would be forgotten by morning and never discussed.

HETEROSEXUAL IDENTITY— EXPLORATORY HOMOSEXUAL BEHAVIOR

Another important group of self-identified heterosexual women who engage in sex with both men and women consists of those who are just entering the bisexual arena but have not accepted the self label, or those who are not willing to accept a total Lesbian self-definition. Here we found many women who gave curiosity and experimentation as their primary reasons for entering homosexual relations. It was very common for these women to have had their first experiences as a consequence of male orchestration, i.e., where they found themselves in a "spontaneous" threesome in which the man would have intercourse with both women and, by his presence and encouragement, legitimate sexual intimacy between the two women. In some of these cases the women reported that because there was generalized sexual tension in the episode, it was only appropriate that they turn to one another. On some occasions homosexual relations were treated as an experiment between two heterosexually identified women as a consequence of a rational and explicitly discussed need to know the whole spectrum of sexuality. Sometimes these experiments became routine, but often they were not repeated.

BISEXUAL IDENTITY—HOMOSEXUAL BEHAVIOR

What about women whose identity is bisexual? Some of our respondents regard bisexuality as their only sexual identity, or, as one woman described it, their sexual "place." They do not see it as a broad area in the middle of the Kinsey scale, but as a unique sexual pattern that cannot be understood as an amalgam of homosexuality and heterosexuality. They strongly feel that the unique problems and pleasures of being bisexual compel them to search out and affiliate with other bisexuals in order to defend the uniqueness of their way of life. This is often a frustrating situation. For example, as one of our respondents put it, "I am not heterosexual but I'm not Lesbian either. I am one of those strange creatures, a bisexual. No one believes I exist." [5]

While we will return to this type of bisexual woman below, let us first discuss the women who identify themselves as bisexual, but who presently direct their sexual energies toward women. Some of these use the label *bisexual* rather than *gay* in order to avoid the homosexual stigma (e.g., "I fell in love with a woman, but I didn't really meet other Lesbians and was not part of the Lesbian subculture at all. I would, in fact, definitely consider myself not like them, and I would actively reject the label"). Others choose the bisexual label because of their pleasurable memories of extensive heterosexual experience in the past, and the implication that it would not be impossible for them to enter a sexual relationship with a man in the future, even though they now have no desire to, or realistic expectation of, doing so. Another group is in transition, i.e., its members are living with a woman but continue to think sexually about men and reserve the freedom to move to a heterosexual relationship if their current homosexual commitment were to dissolve.

This last group is often the target of highly charged negative feelings from many members of the Lesbian community who see bisexuals as "fence-sitters," women who are liable to end a Lesbian relationship when a heterosexual opportunity arises. As one Lesbian respondent described the situation:

> I really resent the fact (and I think a lot of homosexuals do) that bisexuals have the advantage that they can appear to be straight when it's convenient. What I really don't like about it is that they really want to have their gay encounters or relationships, but they don't want to accept anything that goes along with it, like the emotional attachment. Also when society comes down on you or when the police come down, or when the family hits, or the friends, well, then it's very convenient to be straight, and I don't like that.

The pressures brought to bear from the Lesbian community often push women who fall into this category to commit themselves one way or the other; usually they either become totally Lesbian, or attempt to hide their bisexuality from their Lesbian friends. They might consider avoiding homosexual contacts totally, but often this is impossible because of their strong sexual and emotional feelings for women. As one woman expressed her dilemma: "I can't make it as a totally straight person. I have tried. It didn't work. I felt deprived, incomplete. I need the companionship and love of a woman, but who wants to be involved with a fence-sitter?" [6]

BISEXUAL IDENTITY—BISEXUAL AND HETEROSEXUAL BEHAVIOR

The group of women who are sexually involved with both men and women, and who call themselves bisexual, is enormously varied. Some feel that they have absolutely no preference for partners of one gender or the other, but rather evaluate each experience as a unique personal relationship. Others state a preference, but allow that it could be completely modified by future events. There were also women who had had only exploratory or limited sexual experiences with members of the same sex, yet they invested those experiences with enough positive emotion that they felt their bisexuality and its potential for future relationships to be irrevocably part of their identity.

Finally, we should include here women who identify themselves as bisexuals but, in fact, have had no postadolescent sexual contact with women. Some of these women are *ideological bisexuals,* i.e., they feel that all people are inherently bisexual and that they themselves have simply not been able to actualize their basic human potential. Often they have come to this position either through the Women's Movement or through educational sources (e.g., "Of course I knew these feelings were normal—I was an undergraduate psychology major"). The Women's Movement has in some measure endorsed the notion that Lesbianism is a valid form of sexuality and that it would be appropriate to be able to be sexually involved with one's sisters. Often our respondents cite how affectionate they have come to feel toward other women whom they have known in the Movement, and have agonized over the "blocks" they felt which stopped them from sexualizing these friendships. These women worried about the contradiction between the new legitimacy of homosexual behavior, the strength of their emotional ties to other women, and their inability to integrate these into a proper sexual script.

LESBIAN IDENTITY—HETEROSEXUAL AND HOMOSEXUAL BEHAVIOR

Finally, we have interviewed women with a Lesbian identity, some of whom have sexual relations with men, others of whom do not. Most of the latter have had some heterosexual experience, which they felt to have been unsatisfactory. In rejecting those relationships they often rejected any appeal men held for them. Nevertheless, while these women are strongly committed to a Lesbian identity, many recognize that they have been capable of heterosexual relationships in the past.

The group of women who are self-identified as homosexual, but whose sexual responsiveness includes both genders, is also highly varied. It includes some married women and some prostitutes whose heterosexual behavior is exclusively for financial support, as well as Lesbians who occasionally have sexual relations with a man with whom they feel an emotional rapport. Some might choose a man in order to test and reaffirm their Lesbian identity. As one respondent told us, "This one gal would not believe that I was gay, wouldn't go with me unless I knew for sure. So I rounded up a fellow that I had met, and after I went to bed with him I said, 'Yuck, leave me alone.' " Another respondent, now a politically active Lesbian, recounted:

> I was still faced with some of those unanswered questions. Why am I a Lesbian? And the only thing left—this is when I was twenty—as far as I could tell, would possibly be that I was afraid to go to bed with men. So I went out and fucked three men and decided, "No, that's not the answer. I'm not afraid to go to bed with men, I don't get off on it, I don't enjoy it at all." Whatever there is that makes it an emotionally enjoyable experience to other women is simply not there. That was like the end of the questions as far as I was concerned.

THE INTRODUCTION OF HOMOSEXUAL BEHAVIOR

The wide differences between behavior and self-identification illustrated by our respondents raise several important questions. First, why do women engage in homosexual behavior when they are not committed to a Lesbian identity? What are the mechanisms that allow the heterosexually defined woman, or the woman who is beginning to consider a bisexual identity, to begin to explore the world of tabooed homosexual relations? The first reason we might suggest is the set of institutional arrangements in Western society that set a foundation for sexual attraction between women. Women are sexualized in American society by advertising, fashion, and literature. A woman's self-evaluation is in great part based on her value as a sexual object for men. In coming to a self-evaluation she incorporates not only the positive or negative reaction of males, but also takes a male's perspective when comparing herself in value to other women. She must learn in great detail what constitutes a beautiful, sexually arousing female. She becomes expert at knowing her own worth by knowing other women's market value. Thus, women watch each other much as men watch women, and attribute sexual qualities to women who fit certain cultural standards. They may also treat other women as models for developing their own attractiveness, learning from watching them what cues are sexual to men. Women also often develop strong emotional responses to physically attractive women, and while this emotional arousal may be defined and experienced as envy, jealousy, great affection, or vicarious identification, it is nevertheless a strong emotion. Once certain barriers are broken down, *erotic* attraction becomes an additional potential emotion. So, for example, current involvement in the Women's Movement often causes women to eschew feelings of envy or jealousy, and focus on the positive side of their feelings. These positive feelings, given the intensity of the emotions engendered, seem to translate comfortably into the sexual.

Norms in our society also allow women physically to touch one another and to be emotionally vulnerable with one another. If they are curious about one another's sexual behavior and sexual feelings, they might be tempted to discuss their curiosity, because this has become part of proper female sociability. Occasionally, we have found, such discussions, along with close personal friendships, may lead to experimentation. For example, two well-educated respondents, who had a history of close friendship and heterosexual activity, began sharing discussions of sex and sexual fantasies. This eventually led them to feel it was appropriate to experiment with sex together, "regardless of how silly it might turn out."

One reason for sexual experimentation may again be membership and commitment to the ideology of the Women's Movement. We have already suggested that Women's Liberation has been an important influence on women's ideas about sexuality. It has reduced the stigma surrounding formerly counternormative sexual behavior, especially homosexual behavior, and at the same time it has increased women's nonsexual positive feelings toward one another. It has suggested that not only female-female emotional bonding, but also sexual bonding might be a welcome alternative to unsatisfactory heterosexual relationships. While feminists once looked down on Lesbians, ideology has now shifted and there is a great deal of support for homosexuality.

The new ideology is that women should be allowed the same set of feelings toward one another that they previously could legitimately hold toward men. That women could love one another emotionally in a sisterly fashion laid the foundation for them to be permitted to love one another sexually. Indeed, among women strongly identifying with the more liberal or radical edges of the Women's Movement, sexual involvement with another woman (or at least ideological commitment to its appropriateness) has become an important and expected political position. Thus, many women are anxious to have at least one experience with another woman and thereby extend their sexual and political liberation. Two quotations from heterosexual women show the dimensions of these factors:

"I went to bed with a radical Lesbian; I just had to know what it was like."

"The Women's Movement was critical in that it allowed me to express my feelings for women. I knew other women were trying things, so it didn't seem so weird and far out. And how can you live in New York and have friends and go to bars and know everybody's doing it and not want to try it yourself?" [7]

Some introductions, however, to homosexual behavior were more a part of the general libertarian climate for nonmarital sex than a result of feminist awareness. The liberalization of attitudes toward sexuality in the 1960's and 1970's (realization of the injustices of the double standard and acknowledgement of sexual desires and experience as appropriate for "good" women) contributed to the idea that one should satisfy one's curiosity in sexual matters. Part of that curiosity was expressed in experimentation with group sex and threesome, which provided a perfect ambience for excursions into homosexual experiences. The risk of rejection or stigma was low, since initiating gestures could be defended as accidental or random sexual moves if they met with antagonism. Once initial gestures proved acceptable, more committing behavior could be attempted. Further, as we suggested earlier, the homosexual component was muted and legitimized for the women by the presence of a male figure whose purposes were presumably being served. The men found the experience highly arousing and unthreatening to their sense of sexual property—since many gave credence to the idea that "a woman cannot compete with a man for a woman's favors." In many cases this was a meaningful introduction to homosexual conduct between the women, often culminating in the adoption of a bisexual identity. It also frequently occurred that after the event the woman decided (with varying degrees of soul-searching) that while the behavior was not anxiety-provoking, she was not interested in pursuing it further. Then at some later point in her life, other circumstances arose (e.g., a strong nonsexual friendship for a woman, disillusionment with a heterosexual relationship, being propositioned by another woman) which precipitated entry into a purely homosexual relationship, one that prior to the threesome would have been impossible.

This same ideology can also foster a bisexual identity when the individual has been disappointed with her previous sexual experiences. Women often expressed to us that structural reasons for their unhappiness with sexual and/or interpersonal relations with men tended not to be present in their dealings with women. Heterosexual marketplace standards often do not value the personal qualities a woman may wish to apply for her self-evaluation, but in the world of women she may achieve high status and desirability. Thus, she may be tempted to quit the dating scene and enter the female culture where she is appreciated. As one predominantly Lesbian respondent answered a question concerning her attractiveness:

> If you're speaking heterosexually, I guess I would say I don't feel I'm attractive. I say that because when you compare yourself with all these movie stars, people on TV, you're fed what you're supposed to look like, what you're supposed to wear, all the makeup, the hair . . . then I don't feel attractive. But if you're talking about my homosexual peers, I would have to say I am. Among gay women I definitely have a different kind of attractiveness and it's more appreciated.

It has already been indicated, however, that most Lesbians have had some past sexual experience with men. Estimates of the numbers who have had dating experience vary between 90 and 95 percent, and of those who have had sexual intercourse between 50 and 80 percent.[8] So even at the point where a woman decides she is neither heterosexual nor bisexual, she has some part of her past history to account for. She may remember earlier sexual experience as unexciting or unpleasant, or performed only because she had to conform to peer expectations. As she tries to analyze her past sexual history, she may come to the conclusion that her sexual awakening began with her introduction to homosexuality.

THE INTRODUCTION OF HETEROSEXUAL BEHAVIOR

While these Lesbian women are often adamant that they will never return to heterosexual behavior, our data indicate that some of their predictions of the future might be inaccurate. One woman, who in our initial interview expressed total contentment with her homosexual relationship and expected it to last forever, was found a year later to be cohabiting with a man and contemplating marriage. Another respondent, after more than ten years of exclusive Lesbianism reported:

> With the fellow I'm involved with now, the only reason that we're involved sexually is there is an emotional thing that I've never felt before. . . . This is very new. And consequently, it's the first time that the sexual part has been rewarding, or fun, or exciting.

Thus, again, we must acknowledge the potential for fluidity of sexual response and identification over the life-span, as well as the tendency among many people to see their sexual history as much more unchanging and unilinear than perhaps it is.

How these women who have committed themselves to a Lesbian identity can enter a phase in which they have sexual involvements with men is a question deserving our attention. First, one must consider societal pressures, especially those exerted by family. A woman who chooses not to marry and bear children is traditionally seen as failing at the major purposes for being a woman in our society. The problem is exacerbated because women have been so thoroughly socialized to *want* children. Aided by these cultural pressures, significant life experiences may weaken the woman's commitment to exclusively homosexual behavior. Often an unhappy experience with a female lover precipitates a feeling that the perils of a love relationship with a woman may be greater or at least as great as those with a man, while the latter provides many benefits (such as children, physical security, and respectability). We have found that it is during periods of sexual uninvolvement that self-identified Lesbians are more prone to heterosexual behavior than during periods of involvement.

SEXUAL BEHAVIOR AND SEXUAL COMMUNITIES

In contemplating entry into a heterosexual relationship, the Lesbian must not only overcome any antipathies toward men remaining from earlier heterosexual experiences, or *create* sexual interest where little or none has existed, but she must also overcome the negative feelings toward bisexual behavior found in her Lesbian peer group. While the Lesbian subcultural position supports the negative side of her own ambivalence about heterosexual involvement, a more potent concern is the ridicule and ostracism she is likely to encounter if she is open about her ambivalence.

Bisexuality meets with antagonism and suspicion in most, although not all, Lesbian communities. Politically organized Lesbians actively fight a societal ideology that a woman is a less compelling long-term partner than a man. Naturally, they reject the notion that because of anatomy, sex between women is some form of makeshift or make-do activity, and that its sexual fulfillment can never reach the heights of heterosexuality.

On the personal level, Lesbian women fear that a partner who is not totally committed to Lesbianism, even if she claims commitment to the particular relationship, will feel that she eventually has to return to a man. As one of our respondents characterized the position of the Lesbian community: "The [Lesbian] subculture says, 'Better be careful of those switch-hitters, because they can really fuck your head over and go off and be with a man.'" Bisexuality is seen as a failure to accept the emotional responsibility of a homosexual relationship, and the emotional burden of homosexual stigma.

Many of our Lesbian respondents describe love affairs with bisexuals in which they attribute the painful dissolution to lack of a homosexual commitment:

> I wouldn't get mixed up with a bisexual for ten million dollars. I don't want to be with somebody who goes to bed with men because obviously they won't be happy with me, because they're still going to need men. . . . In fact, I went with this gal. At the time she had not really made up her mind that she was going to be gay. And so she did see guys and went to bed with guys, and it's a very degrading feeling. It made me very angry. If you are a Lesbian, trying to live with someone who is bisexual, you can't—you either have to accept a totally miserable life, or you have to get out of the relationship.

Since most Lesbians have had some heterosexual experience, and all have suffered some emotional strain from the process of "coming out" as homosexual, it is widely believed in the Lesbian community that a "bisexual phase" is really only a manifestation of the ambivalent feelings associated with "coming out." Hence, a bisexual is often defined simply as a homosexual who has not yet been able to accept her true identity. In the extreme, some Lesbians refuse to believe that true bisexuality (or even ambisexuality) exists. Most of our respondents, however, believe that bisexuality exists in the abstract and in a few rare instances, but that most people claiming bisexuality will ultimately be gay. Hence, women who claim a bisexual identity receive not only hostility from their Lesbian peers, but are in a sense told that the identity they are claiming is not real, but rather a fantasy or a phase which will not endure experience. Lesbians who have spent a long time in the homosexual community often socialize younger ones to treat any heterosexual feelings as delusions.

While these sentiments have a long history in Lesbian circles, recent developments have given a political edge to the argument. A significant part of the community, especially those women active in radical feminist organizations, feels that bisexuality is dangerous and that the bisexual is consorting with the enemy. The existence of women claiming to be bisexual creates the specter that homosexual relations among women are not sufficient, that dependence upon men remains, and that separatism (or at least autonomy) is therefore not a viable political form. As one feminist writes, "Women who practice bisexuality today are simply leading highly privileged lives that do not challenge male power and that, in fact, undermine the feminist struggle." [9] Women whose peer associations are mainly among Lesbian separatists report almost total castigation once they become sexually or emotionally involved with men. In order to avoid confrontation, many such women make great efforts to conceal their heterosexual activities from their Lesbian friends or sexual partners.

Clearly, then, bisexuality is not considered liberating, or "better" or "more advanced" among a large number of Lesbian women. The advent of the slogan "If gay is good, bi is better" was not received with good humor. The Lesbian community cannot deny the existence of bisexual behavior, but its members do not encourage it, and they do not easily accept women with a bisexual identification.[10]

Response to bisexuality—and the amount of individual encouragement it receives—among heterosexuals is quite different. Among the sexually conservative, extensive bisexuality is equated with homosexuality. Only very sporadic homosexual behavior, and only under special circumstances (e.g., in an adolescent "phase," in prison, when occasionally drunk, etc.) may be practiced among heterosexuals without the homosexual label being applied, both by others and by the person herself. The homosexual label implies among most Americans either moral failure or mental and emotional maladjustment, both of which are negatively sanctioned.[11]

In the most liberal part of the heterosexual community—what we call the *libertarian community*—bisexuality may in fact have positive status. With the development of an ideology of sexual libertarianism (one should do one's own thing) has come a greater tolerance of sexual eccentricities. It is considered inappropriate to show adverse reaction to the unorthodox sexual life-styles of others. At one time it was appropriate in libertarian circles to show tolerance toward any sexual practice or sexual orientation that was not explicitly repugnant to one of the sexually involved partners. But the norm has been moving away from the ability to be undisturbed by the idiosyncrasies of others, and toward positive sanctions for an individual's ability to develop his or her sexual repertoire. Liberality is no longer established merely by declaring, "It's not for me, but I defend everyone's right to have the sexual life he or she wants." One's mettle is demonstrated by the diversity of experiences one has had.

COMMUNITY SANCTIONS AND
SEXUAL IDENTIFICATION

These sociosexual communities (the Lesbian community, the conservative straight community, and the libertarian community) are particularly important in either encouraging or discouraging bisexual behaviors and labels. In the case of the libertarian community, for example, there has probably been a complex interaction. Ideology permitted sexual experimentation, which allowed women to enjoy homosexual contacts while preserving a heterosexual identity. With greater toleration of homosexuality as part of the emerging ideology came a greater willingness to integrate these homosexual interests into one's sexual self-identity. But both ideology and the history of gratifying experiences with men allowed many of these women to adopt the label bisexual; they felt little pressure to see themselves as Lesbians. Our respondents say they felt too well-established in their heterosexuality to consider adoption of a Lesbian identity. Interestingly, they found such a label both inappropriate and highly undesirable, although they expressed few qualms about the bisexual label.

The Lesbian community provides a perfect counterpoint. In it, claiming a bisexual identity receives no community validation, but rather a great deal of negative response. More important, it is precisely in this community that women learn how to "understand" their own sexuality, the motivations to attribute to themselves, and the boundaries of the sexually possible, the sexually likely, and the sexually impossible. In this context one learns that bisexuality is possible, but uncommon, and that bisexuality is really an inability to come to grips with "true" underlying Lesbianism. These definitions of how one may and ought to see oneself have phenomenal impact on how people actually do see themselves.[12]

Given these observations, it seems clear that bisexuality will continue to be a difficult issue among confirmed Lesbians or among women whose experimentation with homosexuality brings them in close contact with the Lesbian community. It also seems likely that the libertarian community and the Women's Movement are potent forces in legitimizing bisexual behavior and bisexual self-identification among a sizable number of women. How many women are involved or how many will become involved in the near future is impossible for us to specify. Bisexual behavior is still contrary to a powerful set of social rules that have been well inculcated, and the likelihood that these prohibitions will drastically change in the near future remains quite small.

What seems likely for the near future is an increase in sexual experimentation, triggered in individual lives by some of the factors we have indicated. It also seems likely that among some of those experimenting, the new behaviors will be incorporated into a bisexual identity. It is our feeling that as peer environments become more receptive to bisexuality, and define it as a viable sexual form, there will develop a set of "common understandings" for members to guide their experiences and their feelings. In fact, in several parts of the country we have noticed the recent emergence of a "bisexual community," persons who form organizations and interact informally for precisely the purpose of offering one another support for a novel identity, to "compare notes," and to develop a body of knowledge on how to live a life as a bisexual. It is our feeling that as such subcultures proliferate, a true bisexual life-style will emerge.

Footnotes

The observations in this article are based on interviews with 150 females and males who have had more than incidental sexual experience with members of both sexes. The study was conducted in Seattle, New York, Chicago, San Francisco, and a few other locations during 1973–1975. The authors are assistant professors in the Department of Sociology, University of Washington. The order of authorship is alphabetical and in no way characterizes the division of labor in preparing this article.

1. See Laud Humphreys, *Tearoom Trade: Impersonal Sex in Public Places.* Chicago, Aldine, 1970.
2. "Playboy Panel: Homosexuality," *Playboy* magazine, April 1971, pp. 63, 67.
3. According to Kinsey and associates, 25 percent of the male population of the United States in 1948 had had "more than incidental homosexual experiences or reactions for at least three years between the ages of 16 and 55." See Alfred C. Kinsey, Wardell B. Pomeroy, and Clyde E. Martin, *Sexual Behavior in the Human Male.* Philadelphia, W. B. Saunders, 1948, pp. 650–651. Among females studied by Kinsey and associates, the percentage with more than incidental homosexual experience in each of the years between the ages of 20 and 35 were as follows: between 6 and 14 percent for unmarried women, 2 to 5 percent for those married, and 8 to 10 percent for those previously married. See Alfred C. Kinsey, Wardell B. Pomeroy, Clyde E. Martin, and Paul H. Gebhard, *Sexual Behavior in the Human Female.* Philadelphia, W. B. Saunders, 1953, pp. 473–474.
4. See David A Ward and Gene G. Kassebaum, *Women's Prison: Sex*

and Social Structure. Chicago, Aldine, 1965; and Rose Giallombardo, *Society of Women.* New York, Wiley, 1966.

5. From an anonymous essay called "Up Shit Creek," in *So's Your Old Lady,* published by the Lesbian Resource Center of Minneapolis, April 1973, p. 32.

6. *Ibid.*

7. Interviews quoted in Barbara Grizzuti Harrison, "Sexual Chic, Sexual Fascism, and Sexual Confusion," *New York Magazine,* April 1, 1974, pp. 31–36.

8. The more conservative estimates are based on a sample of 65 homosexual women reported in Jack H. Hedblom, "Dimensions of Lesbian Sexual Experience," *Archives of Sexual Behavior* 2 (December 1973): 329–341; the other data are based on a sample of 57 homosexual women discussed in Marcel T. Saghir and Eli Robins, *Male and Female Homosexuality.* Baltimore, Williams and Wilkins, 1973.

9. Loretta Ulmschreider, writing in the March, 1974 issue of *Furies.*

10. While our characterization of the Lesbian community is totally consistent with our interview material, it should be noted that some politically active Lesbians have expressed positions more accepting of bisexuality, i.e., while they would hesitate to become personally involved with a bisexual, they would defend a woman's right to choose such a life-style.

11. A survey representing the attitudes of the American population in 1970 found that 59 percent felt there should be a law against homosexual acts, 65 percent felt homosexuality to be very obscene and vulgar, and 49 percent endorsed the statement "Homosexuality is a social corruption which can cause the downfall of a civilization." See Eugene E. Levitt and Albert D. Klassen, "Public Attitudes Toward Sexual Behaviors: The Latest Investigation of the Institute for Sex Research," paper presented at the annual convention of the American Orthopsychiatric Association, 1973.

12. We are not trying to portray Lesbianism as standing in the way of emerging societal strains toward bisexuality. Rather we are using Lesbianism as an example of how definitions of sexuality that are institutionalized in a subculture come to affect individual experiences of members.

VI
Rape

What is or is not rape is *partly* a matter of definition. Two people could watch exactly the same behavior, and one would call it rape, while the other wouldn't. So there are social and cultural variations in conceptions of the nature of rape. And to make matters worse, there is also the *legal* definition, which may be something altogether different. The issue of *statutory* rape further confuses matters. The law assumes that below a certain age—which differs from one state, country and jurisdiction to another—a woman is considered not competent to consent to sexual intercourse. Thus, by definition, any sex with her is rape. In this chapter, we will concentrate only on what is called "common law" or *forcible* rape, and ignore statutory rape. Rape is sexual intercourse with a woman *by force and against her will and consent*. The debatable part of the definition is, of course, what exactly "by force" and "against her will and consent" actually mean.

There is an element of aggression in much of heterosexual intercourse; just how much aggression constitutes rape can be contested endlessly. In addition, women grow up in this society learning two contradictory messages: be attractive and enticing to gain the attention of men, but also be chaste until you are married. Moreover, submissiveness to male authority still has something of a hold on many women's minds. Even today, some men believe that it is impossible for one man to rape a conscious, struggling woman. But few women who do not wish to have intercourse want to avoid it *at any cost,* including serious injury, mayhem or death. (The notion that to a virtuous woman death should be preferable to rape was a popular theme in the history of Christian thinking and writing.)

Unwanted intercourse is no less lacking in consent if a woman submits in preference to being killed or maimed. Violence is not necessary for either a legal or a social definition of rape. Having intercourse with a woman who is unconscious or asleep constitutes rape, since she did not grant consent. If the *threat* of violence is used to obtain intercourse, rape has occurred. Most women will (wisely) not struggle with a knife at their throat. In these cases, no overt violence has taken place, but they are all cases of rape by any reasonable definition.

Many men are genuinely astonished when accused of rape by a woman with whom they have had intercourse. This fact, perhaps more than any other, emphasizes the sexism which is deeply entrenched in our society. *Rape grows out of masculine contempt for women.* As with prostitution, men use a woman's body for their own private sexual gratification without regard for the woman's desires. Very few prostitutes enjoy sex with their customers, and no woman enjoys being raped. (A vigorous male fantasy is that most women do in fact "enjoy it.") In prostitution, the woman is a marketed commodity. In rape, she is also an object to be used—and abused. Many men feel that sexual aggression against women is justified because they see them as objects of exploitation. *These men do not see what they do as rape because, for them, the mistreatment of women is routine and deeply ingrained.*

Rape is one of the most difficult of all human activities to study because most of the time it isn't reported, even in cases which are clear-cut, in the sense that if they were observed, nearly everyone would consider them rape. A much larger number of cases would fall into a gray area in between where many observers would call them rape, and many others would feel that compliance occurred. So two basic questions anyone has to answer who wants to understand rape are, first what are the characteristics of officially *known* rape cases, and, second, how would we go about finding out the ways that *hidden* cases of rape differ from those that are known?

Only a very tiny number of systematic studies have been conducted on rape. As Susan Griffin points out, this in itself points to the male-centered nature of the enterprises of science and medicine. Why should men study something that is a problem almost entirely to women? And why should they want to study a phenomenon about male victimization of women? In the past, rape was often seen as irrelevant and peripheral, committed by a few insane, sexually maladjusted men. Even when rape was considered a problem, it was couched in the form of being a threat to "our" women—that is, to the property of men. It has been only in the past few years that a more accurate perspective has been developed, and more accurate facts unearthed. It turns out that the image of the lone, mad, isolated and rare stalker of women as the *typical* rapist is fallacious.

To begin with, rape is much more frequent than official records indicate. In a study of victimizations of all kinds, conducted by the President's Commission on Law Enforcement and Administration of Justice in the late 1960s, women were *about four times* as likely to report to an interviewer that they had been raped in the previous year than had reported being raped to the police. The likelihood of being subjected to forcible rape during the previous year for women of all ages in this study was 83 out of 100,000. For women who were between twenty and twenty-nine, this figure was 238. If these figures are accurate, and the incidence of rape were to remain stable over time, this indicates that about 1 woman out of 25 is going to be raped in the United States over the fifty-year span during which she is likely to be a target.

This one in twenty-five figure is probably very conservative, however. Since everyone usually tends to understate their participation in painful, shameful activities, the incidence of rape was probably a good deal *higher* than even these victimization interviews showed. It should be clear why women are so hesitant to report being raped to the police: *rape is one of the very few forms of deviance in which the victim is stigmatized almost as much as the perpetrator.* The police are suspicious whenever a woman reports being raped; they subject her to humiliation and harassment. The character of the victim herself is called into question. Perhaps—the police, many men and more than a few woman will think—she encouraged the assailant, perhaps she wasn't really raped or perhaps she "deserved" it. There is a tendency on the part of many conventional people to *blame the victim,* to taint *her* with the stigma of the crime perpetrated *against her.* This reaction is summed up in the comments of Charles Hayman, a physician and Associate Director for Preventive Services in the Health Services Administration in Washington, in reacting to reading a study by Menachem Amir, author of *Patterns of Forcible Rape;* Hayman writes that Women's Liberation has contributed to the increase in rape over the past few years "in that many women and girls have put themselves in more dangerous positions; for example being alone on streets and in bars at night, and have acted more provocatively in matters of (un) dress." Hayman also puts the blame on women who hitchhike. These statements appear to be saying that women *have no right* to the physical freedom and mobility that men enjoy. If they attempt to exercise this right, they will understandably be punished, as they should expect.

It is probable that rape is increasing in the American population. However, it is really impossible to test this proposition on the basis of the information that is available. There is, of course, a rise in *official* and *reported* cases of rape. But the rise may be in part due to a *greater willingness to report rape* than in the past, which is another way of saying, *a growing refusal on the part of women to be passive victims of male aggression.* In other words, many more women are willing to subject themselves to the humiliation that reporting rape to the police entails. Perhaps, too, less stigma attaches to being raped today than in the past. Perhaps the police are a bit more sympathetic to a woman's report of being raped. (Some departments have set up "rape squads" which permit victims to tell their account to policewomen.) Perhaps women's definition as to what is rape has changed. Perhaps they are far less likely to walk away from masculine sexual aggression directed against them and think: "Was I raped? I'm not sure. Maybe I did provoke it." It is likely that women's conceptions as to what constitutes rape have changed, making rape more common *because more male sexual behavior is seen—and experienced—as rape.* In other words, the greater the pride and self-confidence that exists among women, the more likely it is that male sexual aggression against them will be reported and recorded officially; the lower this feeling is, the more hidden from view rape will be, and the lower its officially recorded incidence. But it may also be that male sexual aggression itself is increasing; no one knows for sure.

The image of the lone, mad and uncommon stalker of women as the typical rapist is false for a number of reasons in addition to its understatement of how frequently rape takes place. Another reason is that it assumes that the rapist typically selects a stranger for a victim, that rapist and victim are unknown to one another. This does happen, but it is far from representing the characteristic picture everywhere. The relationship between the victim and the rapist has not been thoroughly and sufficiently examined. The few studies that are available show inconsistent data on this issue. In the study conducted by the Institute for Sex Research, a majority (72 percent) of the men who were convicted for heterosexual aggression against adult women—which included assault and attempted rape, as well as completed rape—were strangers to their victims. But in another study, conducted by the District of Columbia Crime Commission, only one-third (or 36 percent) of the assailants were complete strangers to their victims. In the study conducted by the National Commission on the Causes of Violence, 53 percent of the rapists and victims were strangers to one another. And in the Amir study, 52 percent were strangers. Thus, all of these studies document at least one thing: "Rapists by no means always choose unknown women as objects of attack," to quote Amir. But these are either officially reported figures, or were obtained by means of interviews; they grossly overstate the stranger relationships, and understate the friend and acquaintance relationships. Stranger rapes are far more likely to be reported and admitted than friendship and acquaintance rapes. As the Kinsey Institute writes:

> These percentages of strangers, acquaintances present . . . a false picture of rape. . . . It is known that many rape cases go unreported, especially if the two people concerned have been dating. No girl likes to advertise her misfortune through court action, and she is especially loath to do so if the defendant is someone with whom she has been friendly, lest there be some question about the validity of her charge. To be raped by a stranger makes one a martyr; to be raped by a friend makes one an object of suspicion.

This follows more or less the same pattern as assaults and murders: it is those who are closest to you who are most likely to do harm to you. Strangers murder strangers in only 10 to 20 percent of the cases; something like one-quarter to one-third of all murders are committed by a member of the family. We don't have to invoke any psychoanalytic reasons for this. The people closest to you are those you have the most to do with. They are more likely to do everything to and with you—good *and* bad. But in the case of rape, there is a crucial difference: by law, a man cannot rape his wife. He is legally "entitled" to have intercourse with her any time he wishes, in spite of what she wants. It is very likely that the greatest number of rapes that fall within our original definition—"sexual intercourse with a woman by force and against her will and consent"

—take place between married couples and lovers. When the couple is married, rapes never appear anywhere in official or unofficial figures because, according to the sexist legal definition, a man cannot rape his wife, even though anyone watching sexual aggression between man and wife would *see* the act as rape. Rape between lovers almost never gets reported because the police think along the lines of, "If you had intercourse with him once, why can't he do it anytime he wants?" It is easy to understand from these examples that behavior isn't simply something that happens; it also has to be judged, evaluated and put into categories. And there will always be dispute as to what categories different types of behavior belong to. In the case of rape, the view that the woman should have the legal and cultural right to be the equal of the man determines how frequently one will see acts of sexual aggression against women as rape.

A third myth which recent research destroys—along with the myths relating to the rarity of rape and the typicality of stranger rapes—has to do with race. In spite of the fears of white racists (along with the boasts of a few Black militants for whom raping a white woman is a revolutionary act), and in spite of a long history in America of white male brutalization of Black women, today the overwhelming majority of all rapes occur between men and women of the *same* race. In technical terms, most rapes are *intra*racial rather than *inter*racial. If the victim is Black, her assailant is most likely to be Black. If the victim is white, her assailant, in all likelihood, is white. There are exceptions to any generalization, but this seems to be the most typical pattern. In addition, Black women appear to be the victims of forcible rape about four times as frequently as white women. This also fits in with the general victimization picture: Blacks are far more likely to be the victims of crimes of all kinds than are whites.

These three myths—that rapes are rare, that women are usually raped by strangers and that rapes are typically interracial—are cut out of the same cloth. And so is the truth, their precise opposite. The mythology is this: that rape is a distant, freakish, extremely rare, psychotic act committed by "outsiders."

The truth is this: rape is much closer to home; it is an exaggerated form of "normal" relations between the sexes; it is not something that happens to others, over there somewhere; it grows out of the fabric of our civilization. The nature and character of relations between men and women in a society determine the form and incidence of rape. As Susan Griffin points out, in some societies rape is almost unknown; males simply do not force women to submit sexually against their will and, indeed, men would find rape an incomprehensible act. In other societies—and here we would have to count our own—rape is common; this tells us that in such societies, male aggression and dominance are deeply felt cultural values. Probably the society in which rape is most common would be the one in which men still hold sexist, chauvinistic beliefs. Today, however, even in such societies, many women are asserting their equality, and refusing to be victimized by men.

Anal rape of men by other men is far less frequent than the rape of women by men. It is not uncommon in prison, however. The rapist in this case is almost never homosexual in the outside world, and is never thought of as a homosexual in the prison as a consequence of his behavior. In fact, prisoners would consider the rape of a slender, young, attractive inmate an act indicating supreme masculinity, because it is violent, aggressive and dominant—in an environment in which such expressions are severely punished. As in heterosexual rape, the conquest and degradation of the victim is sought, and not simply sexual release. In one study of rape in prison in the late 1960s, "Sexual Assaults in the Philadelphia Prison System" by Alan J. Davis, an estimate was made that of the approximately 60,000 inmates who passed through the Philadelphia prison system in a two-year period, about 2,000 were raped, by approximately 4,000 of their fellow inmates. Unlike heterosexual rape, homosexual rapes in prisons are closely linked with race; 80 percent of the inmates in this study were Black. Of the rape incidences that were documented, in 56 percent of the cases the aggressor was Black and his victim was white. (This figure would be 16 percent if rapes occurred randomly by race.) And in only 29 percent of the cases were both Black—whereas if race were not a factor, this would occur 64 percent of the time. No whites in this study raped Blacks. Davis summarizes his interpretation of the motives for these rapes in the following words:

> Most of the aggressors seem to be members of a subculture that has found most nonsexual avenues of asserting their masculinity closed to them. . . . Only sexual and physical prowess stands between them and emasculation. . . . In sum, sexual assaults . . . are expressions of anger and aggression prompted by the same basic frustrations that exist in the community. . . . These frustrations can be

summarized as an inability to achieve masculine identification and pride through avenues other than sex. When these frustrations are intensified by imprisonment, and superimposed upon hostility between the races, and a simplistic view of all sex as an act of aggression and subjugation, then the result is assaults on members of the same sex. . . . [Millions] of American men, throughout their lives, are deprived of any effective way of achieving masculine self-identification through avenues other than physical aggression and sex. They belong to a class of men who rarely have meaningful work, successful families, or opportunities for constructive emotional expression and individual creativity.

It is impossible to avoid the parallel with heterosexual rape. In addition to contempt for women, anger and frustration seem to be a major sentiment among heterosexual rapists. How and when these feelings will and can be diminished in the male population is anyone's guess. A pessimistic view would seem to be in order, however, since no large-scale social, cultural or economic changes are in the works which would change things significantly.

———◆———

Susan Griffin is a feminist novelist and author. Dr. Germaine Greer teaches English literature at Warwick University, and is the author of *The Female Eunuch*. Robert Winslow is a sociologist; he and Virginia Winslow interview "Fred," a rapist.

Rape: The All-American Crime
by Susan Griffin

I have never been free of the fear of rape. From a very early age I, like most women, have thought of rape as part of my natural environment—something to be feared and prayed against like fire or lightning. I never asked why men raped; I simply thought it one of the many mysteries of human nature.

I was, however, curious enough about the violent side of humanity to read every crime magazine I was able to ferret away from my grandfather. Each issue featured at least one "sex crime," with pictures of a victim, usually in a pearl necklace, and of the ditch or the orchard where her body was found. I was never certain why the victims were always women, nor what the motives of the murderer were, but I did guess that the world was not a safe place for women. I observed that my grandmother was meticulous about locks, and quick to draw the shades before anyone removed so much as a shoe. I sensed that danger lurked outside.

At the age of eight, my suspicions were confirmed. My grandmother took me to the back of the house where the men wouldn't hear, and told me that strange men wanted to do harm to little girls. I learned not to walk on dark streets, not to talk to strangers, or get into strange cars, to lock doors, and to be modest. She never explained why a man would want to harm a little girl, and I never asked.

If I thought for a while that my grandmother's fears were imaginary, the illusion was brief. That year, on the way home from school, a schoolmate a few years older than I tried to rape me. Later,

Reprinted by permission of the author; originally appeared in *Ramparts* magazine, Vol. 10, No. 3 (September 1971), pp. 26–35.

in an obscure aisle of the local library (while I was reading *Freddy the Pig*) I turned to discover a man exposing himself. Then, the friendly man around the corner was arrested for child molesting.

My initiation to sexuality was typical. Every woman has similar stories to tell—the first man who attacked her may have been a neighbor, a family friend, an uncle, her doctor, or perhaps her own father. And women who grow up in New York City always have tales about the subway.

But though rape and the fear of rape are a daily part of every woman's consciousness, the subject is so rarely discussed by that unofficial staff of male intellectuals (who write the books which study seemingly every other form of male activity) that one begins to suspect a conspiracy of silence. And indeed, the obscurity of rape in print exists in marked contrast to the frequency of rape in reality, for *forcible rape is the most frequently committed violent crime in America today*. The Federal Bureau of Investigation classes three crimes as violent: murder, aggravated assault and forcible rape. In 1968, 31,060 rapes were *reported*. According to the FBI and independent criminologists, however, to approach accuracy this figure must be multiplied by at least a factor of ten to compensate for the fact that most rapes are not reported; when these compensatory mathematics are used, there are more rapes committed than aggravated assaults and homicides.

When I asked Berkeley, California's Police Inspector in charge of rape investigation if he knew why men rape women, he replied that he had not spoken with "these people and delved into what really makes them tick, because that really isn't my job. . . ." However, when I asked him how a woman might prevent being raped, he was not so reticent. "I wouldn't advise any female to go walking around alone at night . . . and she should lock her car at all times." The Inspector illustrated his warning with a grisly story about a man who lay in wait for women in the back seats of their cars, while they were shopping in a local supermarket. This man eventually murdered one of his rape victims. "Always lock your car," the Inspector repeated, and then added, without a hint of irony, "Of course, you don't have to be paranoid about this type of thing."

The Inspector wondered why I wanted to write about rape. Like most men he did not understand the urgency of the topic, for, after all, men are not raped. But like most women I had spent considerable time speculating on the true nature of the rapist. When I was very young, my image of the "sexual offender" was a nightmarish amalgamation of the bogey man and Captain Hook: he wore a black cape, and he cackled. As I matured, so did my image of the rapist. Born into the psychoanalytic age, I tried to "understand" the rapist. Rape, I came to believe, was only one of many unfortunate evils produced by sexual repression. Reasoning by tautology, I concluded that any man who would rape a woman must be out of his mind.

Yet, though the theory that rapists are insane is a popular one, this belief has no basis in fact. According to Professor Menachem Amir's study of 646 rape cases in Philadelphia, *Patterns in Forcible Rape*, men who rape are not abnormal. Amir writes, "Studies indicate that sex offenders do not constitute a unique or psychopathological type; nor are they as a group invariably more disturbed than the control groups to which they are compared." Alan Taylor, a parole officer who has worked with rapists in the prison facilities at San Luis Obispo, California, stated the question in plainer language, "Those men were the most normal men there. They had a lot of hang-ups, but they were the same hang-ups as men walking out on the street."

Another canon in the apologetics of rape is that, if it were not for learned social controls, all men would rape. Rape is held to be natural behavior, and not to rape must be learned. But in truth rape is not universal to the human species. Moreover, studies of rape in our culture reveal that, far from being impulsive behavior, most rape is planned. Professor Amir's study reveals that in cases of group rape (the "gangbang" of masculine slang) 90 percent of the rapes were planned; in pair rapes, 83 percent of the rapes were planned; and in single rapes, 58 percent were planned. These figures should significantly discredit the image of the rapist as a man who is suddenly overcome by sexual needs society does not allow him to fulfill.

Far from the social control of rape being learned, comparisons with other cultures lead one to suspect that, in our society, it is rape itself that is learned. (The fact that rape is against the law should not be considered proof that rape is not in fact encouraged as part of our culture.)

This culture's concept of rape as an illegal, but still understandable, form of behavior is not a universal one. In her study *Sex and Temperament*, Margaret Mead describes a society that does not share our views. The Arapesh do not ". . . have any conception of

tne male nature that might make rape understandable to them."
Indeed our interpretation of rape is a product of our conception of
the nature of male sexuality. A common retort to the question, why
don't women rape men, is the myth that men have greater sexual
needs, that their sexuality is more urgent than women's. And it is the
nature of human beings to want to live up to what is expected of
them.

And this same culture which expects aggression from the male
expects passivity from the female. Conveniently, the companion myth
about the nature of female sexuality is that all women secretly want
to be raped. Lurking beneath her modest female exterior is a subconscious desire to be ravished. The following description of a stag
movie, written by Brenda Starr in Los Angeles' underground paper,
Everywoman, typifies this male fantasy. The movie "showed a woman
in her underclothes reading on her bed. She is interrupted by a rapist
with a knife. He immediately wins her over with his charm and they
get busy sucking and fucking." An advertisement in the *Berkeley
Barb* reads, "Now as all women know from their daydreams, rape
has a lot of advantages. Best of all it's so simple. No preparation
necessary, no planning ahead of time, no wondering if you should
or shouldn't; just whang! bang!" Thanks to Masters and Johnson
even the scientific canon recognizes that for the female, "whang!
bang!" can scarcely be described as pleasurable.

Still, the male psyche persists in believing that, protestations
and struggles to the contrary, deep inside her mysterious feminine
soul, the female victim has wished for her own fate. A young woman
who was raped by the husband of a friend said that days after the
incident the man returned to her home, pounded on the door and
screamed to her, "Jane, Jane. You loved it. You know you loved it."

The theory that women like being raped extends itself by deduc-
tion into the proposition that most or much of rape is provoked by
the victim. But this too is only myth. Though provocation, considered
a mitigating factor in a court of law, may consist of only "a gesture,"
according to the Federal Commission on Crimes of Violence, only
4 percent of reported rapes involved any precipitative behavior by
the woman.

The notion that rape is enjoyed by the victim is also convenient
for the man who, though he would not commit forcible rape, enjoys
the idea of its existence, as if rape confirms that enormous sexual
potency which he secretly knows to be his own. It is for the pleasure

of the armchair rapist that detailed accounts of violent rapes exist in the media. Indeed, many men appear to take sexual pleasure from nearly all forms of violence. Whatever the motivation, male sexuality and violence in our culture seem to be inseparable. James Bond alternately whips out his revolver and his cock, and though there is no known connection between the skills of gun-fighting and love-making, pacifism seems suspiciously effeminate.

In a recent fictional treatment of the Manson case, Frank Conroy writes of his vicarious titillation when describing the murders to his wife:

> "Every single person there was killed." She didn't move.
> "It sounds like there was torture," I said. As the words left my mouth I knew there was no need to say them to frighten her into believing that she needed me for protection.

The pleasure he feels as his wife's protector is inextricably mixed with pleasure in the violence itself. Conroy writes, "I was excited by the killings, as one is excited by catastrophe on a grand scale, as one is alert to pre-echoes of unknown changes, hints of unrevealed secrets, rumblings of chaos. . . ."

The attraction of the male in our culture to violence and death is a tradition Manson and his admirers are carrying on with avidity (even presuming Manson's innocence, he dreams of the purification of fire and destruction). It was Malraux in his *Anti-Memoirs* who said that, for the male, facing death was *the* illuminating experience analogous to childbirth for the female. Certainly our culture does glorify war and shroud the agonies of the gun-fighter in veils of mystery.

And in the spectrum of male behavior, rape, the perfect combination of sex and violence, is the penultimate act. Erotic pleasure cannot be separated from culture, and in our culture male eroticism is wedded to power. Not only should a man be taller and stronger than a female in the perfect love-match, but he must also demonstrate his superior strength in gestures of dominance which are perceived as amorous. Though the law attempts to make a clear division between rape and sexual intercourse, in fact the courts find it difficult to distinguish between a case where the decision to copulate was mutual and one where a man forced himself upon his partner.

The scenario is even further complicated by the expectation that, not only does a woman mean "yes" when she says "no," but that a really decent woman ought to begin by saying "no," and then be led down the primrose path to acquiescence. Ovid, the author of Western Civilization's most celebrated sex-manual, makes this expectation perfectly clear.

> . . . and when I beg you to say "yes," say "no." Then let me lie outside your bolted door. . . . So Love grows strong. . . .

That the basic elements of rape are involved in all heterosexual relationships may explain why men often identify with the offender in this crime. But to regard the rapist as the victim, a man driven by his inherent sexual needs to take what will not be given him, reveals a basic ignorance of sexual politics. For in our culture heterosexual love finds an erotic expression through male dominance and female submission. A man who derives pleasure from raping a woman clearly must enjoy force and dominance as much or more than the simple pleasures of the flesh. Coitus cannot be experienced in isolation. The weather, the state of the nation, the level of sugar in the blood—all will affect a man's ability to achieve orgasm. If a man can achieve sexual pleasure after terrorizing and humiliating the object of his passion, and in fact while inflicting pain upon her, one must assume he derives pleasure directly from terrorizing, humiliating and harming a woman. According to Amir's study of forcible rape, on a statistical average the man who has been convicted of rape was found to have a normal sexual personality, tending to be different from the normal, well-adjusted male only in having a greater tendency to express violence and rage.

And if the professional rapist is to be separated from the average dominant heterosexual, it may be mainly a quantitative difference. For the existence of rape as an index to masculinity is not entirely metaphorical. Though this measure of masculinity seems to be more publicly exhibited among "bad boys" or aging bikers who practice sexual initiation through group rape, in fact, "good boys" engage in the same rites to prove their manhood. In Stockton, a small town in California which epitomizes silent-majority America, a bachelor party was given last summer for a young man about to be married. A woman was hired to dance "topless" for the amusement of the guests. At the high point of the evening the bridegroom-to-be dragged the woman into a bedroom. No move was made by any of his companions to stop what was clearly going to be an attempted rape. Far from it. As the woman described, "I tried to keep him away—told him of my Herpes Genitalis, et cetera, but he couldn't face the guys if he didn't screw me." After the bridgegroom had finished raping the woman and returned with her to the party, far from chastising him, his friends heckled the woman and covered her with wine.

It was fortunate for the dancer that the bridegroom's friends did not follow him into the bedroom for, though one might suppose that in group rape, since the victim is outnumbered, less force would be inflicted on her, in fact, Amir's studies indicate, "the most excessive degrees of violence occurred in group rape." Far from discouraging violence, the presence of other men may in fact encourage sadism, and even cause the behavior. In an unpublished study of group rape by Gilbert Geis and Duncan Chappell, the authors refer to a study by W. H. Blanchard which relates, "The leader of the male group . . . apparently precipitated and maintained the activity, despite misgivings, because of a need to fulfill the role that the other two men had assigned to him. 'I was scared when it began to happen,' he says. 'I wanted to leave but I didn't want to say it to the other guys—you know—that I was scared.' "

Thus it becomes clear that not only does our culture teach men the rudiments of rape, but society, or more specifically other men, encourage the practice of it.

II

Every man I meet wants to protect me. Can't figure out what from.
—Mae West

If a male society rewards aggressive, domineering sexual behavior, it contains within itself a sexual schizophrenia. For the masculine man is also expected to prove his mettle as a protector of women. To the naive eye, this dichotomy implies that men fall into one of two categories: those who rape and those who protect. In fact, life does not prove so simple. In a study euphemistically entitled "Sex Aggression by College Men," it was discovered that men who believe in a double standard of morality for men and women, who in fact believe most fervently in the ultimate value of virginity, are more liable to commit "this aggressive variety of sexual exploitation."

(At this point in our narrative it should come as no surprise that Sir Thomas Malory, creator of that classic tale of chivalry, *The Knights of the Round Table,* was himself arrested and found guilty for repeated incidents of rape.)

In the system of chivalry, men protect women against men. This is not unlike the protection relationship which the mafia established with small businesses in the early part of this century. Indeed, chivalry is an age-old protection racket which depends for its existence on rape.

According to the male mythology which defines and perpetuates rape, it is an animal instinct inherent in the male. The story goes that sometime in our pre-historical past, the male, more hirsute and burly than today's counterparts, roamed about an uncivilized landscape until he found a desirable female. (Oddly enough, this female is *not* pictured as more muscular than the modern woman.) Her mate does not bother with courtship. He simply grabs her by the hair and drags her to the closest cave. Presumably, one of the major advantages of modern civilization for the female has been the civilizing of the male. We call it chivalry.

But women do not get chivalry for free. According to the logic of sexual politics, we too have to civilize our behavior. (Enter chastity. Enter virginity. Enter monogamy.) For the female, civilized behavior means chastity before marriage and faithfulness within it. Chivalrous behavior in the male is supposed to protect that chastity from involuntary defilement. The fly in the ointment of this otherwise peaceful system is the fallen woman. She does not behave. And therefore she does not deserve protection. Or, to use another argument, a major tenet of the same value system: what has once been defiled cannot again be violated. One begins to suspect that it is the behavior of the fallen woman, and not that of the male, that civilization aims to control.

The assumption that a woman who does not respect the double standard deserves whatever she gets (or at the very least "asks for it") operates in the courts today. While in some states a man's previous rape convictions are not considered admissible evidence, the sexual reputation of the rape victim is considered a crucial element of the facts upon which the court must decide innocence or guilt.

The court's respect for the double standard manifested itself particularly clearly in the case of the People v. Jerry Plotkin. Mr.

Plotkin, a 36-year-old jeweler, was tried for rape last spring in a San Francisco Superior Court. According to the woman who brought the charges, Plotkin, along with three other men, forced her at gunpoint to enter a car one night in October 1970. She was taken to Mr. Plotkin's fashionable apartment where he and the three other men first raped her and then, in the delicate language of the *S.F. Chronicle,* "subjected her to perverted sex acts." She was, she said, set free in the morning with the warning that she would be killed if she spoke to anyone about the event. She did report the incident to the police who then searched Plotkin's apartment and discovered a long list of names of women. Her name was on the list and had been crossed out.

In addition to the woman's account of her abduction and rape, the prosecution submitted four of Plotkin's address books containing the names of hundreds of women. Plotkin claimed he did not know all of the women since some of the names had been given to him by friends and he had not yet called on them. Several women, however, did testify in court that Plotkin had, to cite the *Chronicle,* "lured them up to his apartment under one pretext or another, and forced his sexual attentions on them."

Plotkin's defense rested on two premises. First, through his own testimony Plotkin established a reputation for himself as a sexual libertine who frequently picked up girls in bars and took them to his house where sexual relations often took place. He was the Playboy. He claimed that the accusation of rape, therefore, was false—this incident had simply been one of many casual sexual relationships, the victim one of many playmates. The second premise of the defense was that his accuser was also a sexual libertine. However, the picture created of the young woman (fully 13 years younger than Plotkin) was not akin to the lighthearted, gay-bachelor image projected by the defendant. On the contrary, the day after the defense cross-examined the woman, the *Chronicle* printed a story headlined, "Grueling Day For Rape Case Victim." (A leaflet passed out by women in front of the courtroom was more succinct, "rape was committed by four men in a private apartment in October; on Thursday, it was done by a judge and a lawyer in a public courtroom.")

Through skillful questioning fraught with innuendo, Plotkin's defense attorney James Martin MacInnis portrayed the young woman as a licentious opportunist and unfit mother. MacInnis began by asking the young woman (then employed as a secretary) whether or not it was true that she was "familiar with liquor" and had worked as a "cocktail waitress." The young woman replied (the *Chronicle* wrote "admitted") that she had worked once or twice as a cocktail waitress. The attorney then asked if she had worked as a secretary in the financial district but had "left that employment after it was discovered that you had sexual intercourse on a couch in the office." The woman replied, "That is a lie. I left because I didn't like working in a one-girl office. It was too lonely." Then the defense asked if, while working as an attendant at a health club, "you were accused of having a sexual affair with a man?" Again the woman denied the story, "I was never accused of that."

Plotkin's attorney then sought to establish that his client's accuser was living with a married man. She responded that the man was separated from his wife. Finally he told the court that she had "spent the night" with another man who lived in the same building.

At this point in the testimony the woman asked Plotkin's defense attorney, "Am I on trial? . . . It is embarrassing and personal to admit these things to all these people. . . . I did not commit a crime. I am a human being." The lawyer, true to the chivalry of his class, apologized and immediately resumed questioning her, turning his attention to her children. (She is divorced, and the children at the time of the trial were in a foster home.) "Isn't it true that your two children have a sex game in which one gets on top of another and they—" "That is a lie!" the young woman interrupted him. She ended her testimony by explaining "They are wonderful children. They are not perverted."

The jury, divided in favor of acquittal ten to two, asked the court stenographer to read the woman's testimony back to them. After this reading, the Superior Court acquitted the defendant of both the charges of rape and kidnapping.

According to the double standard a woman who has had sexual intercourse out of wedlock cannot be raped. Rape is not only a crime of aggression against the body; it is a transgression against chastity as defined by men. When a woman is forced into a sexual relationship, she has, according to the male ethos, been violated. But she is also defiled if she does not behave according to the double standard, by maintaining her chastity, or confining her sexual activities to a monogamous relationship.

One should not assume, however, that a woman can avoid the

possibility of rape simply by behaving. Though myth would have it that mainly "bad girls" are raped, this theory has no basis in fact. Available statistics would lead one to believe that a safer course is promiscuity. In a study of rape done in the District of Columbia, it was found that 82 percent of the rape victims had a "good reputation." Even the Police Inspector's advice to stay off the streets is rather useless, for almost half of reported rapes occur in the home of the victim and are committed by a man she has never before seen. Like indiscriminate terrorism, rape can happen to any woman, and few women are ever without this knowledge.

But the courts and the police, both dominated by white males, continue to suspect the rape victim, *sui generis,* of provoking or asking for her own assault. According to Amir's study, the police tend to believe that a woman without a good reputation cannot be raped. The rape victim is usually submitted to countless questions about her own sexual mores and behavior by the police investigator. This preoccupation is partially justified by the legal requirements for prosecution in a rape case. The rape victim must have been penetrated, and she must have made it clear to her assailant that she did not want penetration (unless of course she is unconscious). A refusal to accompany a man to some isolated place to allow him to touch her does not in the eyes of the court, constitute rape. She must have said "no" at the crucial genital moment. And the rape victim, to qualify as such, must also have put up a physical struggle—unless she can prove that to do so would have been to endanger her life.

But the zealous interest the police frequently exhibit in the physical details of a rape case is only partially explained by the requirements of the court. A woman who was raped in Berkeley was asked to tell the story of her rape four different times "right out in the street," while her assailant was escaping. She was then required to submit to a pelvic examination to prove that penetration had taken place. Later, she was taken to the police station where she was asked the same questions again: "Were you forced?" "Did he penetrate?" "Are you sure your life was in danger and you had no other choice?" This woman had been pulled off the street by a man who held a 10-inch knife at her throat and forcibly raped her. She was raped at midnight and was not able to return to her home until five in the morning. Police contacted her twice again in the next week, once by telephone at two in the morning and once at four in the morning.

In her words, "The rape was probably the least traumatic incident of the whole evening. If I'm ever raped again, . . . I wouldn't report it to the police because of all the degradation. . . ."

If white women are subjected to unnecessary and often hostile questioning after having been raped, third world women are often not believed at all. According to the white male ethos (which is not only sexist but racist), third world women are defined from birth as "impure." Thus the white male is provided with a pool of women who are fair game for sexual imperialism. Third world women frequently do not report rape and for good reason. When blues singer Billie Holliday was 10 years old, she was taken off to a local house by a neighbor and raped. Her mother brought the police to rescue her, and she was taken to the local police station crying and bleeding:

> When we got there, instead of treating me and Mom like somebody who called the cops for help, they treated me like I'd killed somebody. . . . I guess they had me figured for having enticed this old goat into the whorehouse. . . . All I know for sure is they threw me into a cell . . . a fat white matron . . . saw I was still bleeding, she felt sorry for me and gave me a couple glasses of milk. But nobody else did anything for me except give me filthy looks and snicker to themselves.
>
> After a couple of days in a cell they dragged me into a court. Mr. Dick got sentenced to five years. They sentenced me to a Catholic institution.

Clearly the white man's chivalry is aimed only to protect the chastity of "his" women.

As a final irony, that same system of sexual values from which chivalry is derived has also provided womankind with an unwritten code of behavior, called femininity, which makes a feminine woman the perfect victim of sexual aggression. If being chaste does not ward off the possibility of assault, being feminine certainly increases the chances that it will succeed. To be submissive is to defer to masculine strength; is to lack muscular development or any interest in defending oneself; is to let doors be opened, to have one's arm held when crossing the street. To be feminine is to wear shoes which make it difficult to run; skirts which inhibit one's stride; underclothes which inhibit the circulation. Is it not an intriguing observation that those very clothes which are thought to be flattering to the female and attractive to the male are those which make it impossible for a woman to defend herself against aggression?

Each girl as she grows into womanhood is taught fear. Fear is the form in which the female internalizes both chivalry and the double standard. Since, biologically speaking, women in fact have the same if not greater potential for sexual expression as do men, the woman who is taught that she must behave differently from a man must also learn to distrust her own carnality. She must deny her own feelings and learn not to act from them. She fears herself. This is the essence of passivity, and of course, a woman's passivity is not simply sexual but functions to cripple her from self-expression in every area of her life.

Passivity itself prevents a woman from ever considering her own potential for self-defense and forces her to look to men for protection. The woman is taught fear, but this time fear of the other; and yet her only relief from this fear is to seek out the other. Moreover, the passive woman is taught to regard herself as impotent, unable to act, unable even to perceive, in no way self-sufficient, and, finally, as the object and not the subject of human behavior. It is in this sense that a woman is deprived of the status of a human being. She is not free to be.

III

Since Ibsen's Nora slammed the door on her patriarchal husband, woman's attempt to be free has been more or less fashionable. In this 19th century portrait of a woman leaving her marriage, Nora tells her husband, "Our home has been nothing but a playroom. I have been your doll-wife just as at home I was papa's doll-child." And, at least on the stage, "The Doll's House" crumbled, leaving audiences with hope for the fate of the modern woman. And today, as in the past, womankind has not lacked examples of liberated women to emulate: Emma Goldman, Greta Garbo and Isadora Duncan all denounced marriage and the double standard, and believed their right to freedom included sexual independence; but still their example has not affected the lives of millions of women who continue to marry, divorce and remarry, living out their lives dependent on the status and economic power of men. Patriarchy still holds the average woman prisoner not because she lacks the courage of an Isadora Duncan, but because the material conditions of her life prevent her from being anything but an object.

In the *Elementary Structures of Kinship,* Claude Levi-Strauss gives to marriage this universal description, "It is always a system of exchange that we find at the origin of the rules of marriage." In this system of exchange, a woman is the "most precious possession." Levi-Strauss continues that the custom of including women as booty in the marketplace is still so general that "a whole volume would not be sufficient to enumerate instances of it." Levi-Strauss makes it clear that he does not exclude Western Civilization from his definition of "universal" and cites examples from modern wedding ceremonies. (The marriage ceremony is still one in which the husband and wife become one, and "that one is the husband.")

The legal proscription against rape reflects this possessory view of women. An article in the 1952–53 *Yale Law Journal* describes the legal rationale behind laws against rape: "In our society sexual taboos, often enacted into law, buttress a system of monogamy based upon the law of 'free bargaining' of the potential spouses. Within this process the woman's power to withhold or grant sexual access is an important bargaining weapon." Presumably then, laws against rape are intended to protect the right of a woman, not for physical self-determination, but for physical "bargaining." The article goes on to explain explicitly why the preservation of the bodies of women is important to men:

> The consent standard in our society does more than protect a significant item of social currency for women; it fosters, and is in turn bolstered by, a masculine pride in the exclusive possession of a sexual object. The consent of a woman to sexual intercourse awards the man a privilege of bodily access, a personal "prize" whose value is enhanced by sole ownership. An additional reason for the man's condemnation of rape may be found in the threat to his status from a decrease in the "value" of his sexual possession which would result from forcible violation.

The passage concludes by making clear whose interest the law is designed to protect. "The man responds to this undercutting of his status as *possessor* of the girl with hostility toward the rapist; no other restitution device is available. The law of rape provides an orderly outlet for his vengeance." Presumably the female victim in any case will have been sufficiently socialized so as not to consciously feel any strong need for vengeance. If she does feel this need, society does not speak to it.

The laws against rape exist to protect rights of the male as possessor of the female body, and not the right of the female over her own body. Even without this enlightening passage from the *Yale Law Review*, the laws themselves are clear: In no state can a man be accused of raping his wife. How can any man steal what already belongs to him? It is in the sense of rape as theft of another man's property that Kate Millett writes, "Traditionally rape has been viewed as an offense one male commits against another—a matter of abusing his woman." In raping another man's woman, a man may aggrandize his own manhood and concurrently reduce that of another man. Thus a man's honor is not subject directly to rape, but only indirectly, through "his" woman.

If the basic social unit is the family, in which the woman is a possession of her husband, the superstructure of society is a male hierarchy, in which men dominate other men (or patriarchal families dominate other patriarchal families). And it is no small irony that, while the very social fabric of our male-dominated culture denies women equal access to political, economic and legal power, the literature, myth and humor of our culture depicts women not only as the power behind the throne, but the real source of the oppression of men. The religious version of this fairy tale blames Eve for both carnality and eating of the tree of knowledge, at the same time making her gullible to the obvious devices of a serpent. Adam, of course, is merely the trusting victim of love. Certainly this is a biased story. But no more biased than the one television audiences receive today from the latest slick comedians. Through a media which is owned by men, censored by a State dominated by men, all the evils of this social system which make a man's life unpleasant are blamed upon "the wife." The theory is: were it not for the female who waits and plots to "trap" the male into marriage, modern man would be able to achieve Olympian freedom. She is made the scapegoat for a system which is in fact run by men.

Nowhere is this more clear than in the white racist use of the concept of white womanhood. The white male's open rape of black women, coupled with his overweening concern for the chastity and protection of his wife and daughters, represents an extreme of sexist and racist hypocrisy. While on the one hand she was held up as the standard for purity and virtue, on the other the Southern white woman was never asked if she wanted to be on a pedestal, and in

fact any deviance from the male-defined standards for white womanhood was treated severely. (It is a powerful commentary on American racism that the historical role of Blacks as slaves, and thus
possessions without power, has robbed black women of legal and
economic protection through marriage. Thus black women in Southern society and in the ghettoes of the North have long been easy
game for white rapists.) The fear that black men would rape white
women was, and is, classic paranoia. Quoting from Ann Breen's unpublished study of racism and sexism in the South, *"The New South:
White Man's Country,"* Frederick Douglass legitimately points out
that, had the black man wished to rape white women, he had ample
opportunity to do so during the civil war when white women, the
wives, sisters, daughters and mothers of the rebels, were left in the
care of Blacks. But yet not a single act of rape was committed during
this time. "The Ku Klux Klan, who tarred and feathered black men
and lynched them in the honor of the purity of white womanhood,
also applied tar and feathers to a Southern white woman accused of
bigamy, which leads one to suspect that Southern white men were
not so much outraged at the violation of the woman as a person, in
the few instances where rape was actually committed by black men,
but at the violation of his property rights." In the situation where a
black man was found to be having sexual relations with a white
woman, the white woman could exercise skin-privilege, and claim
that she had been raped, in which case the black man was lynched.
But if she did not claim rape, she herself was subject to lynching.

In constructing the myth of white womanhood so as to justify
the lynching and oppression of black men and women, the white male
has created a convenient symbol of his own power which has resulted
in black hostility toward the white "bitch," accompanied by an unreasonable fear on the part of many white women of the black rapist.
Moreover, it is not surprising that after being told for two centuries
that he wants to rape white women, occasionally a black man does
actually commit that act. But it is crucial to note that the frequency
of this practice is outrageously exaggerated in the white mythos.
Ninety percent of reported rape is intra- not inter-racial.

In *Soul on Ice,* Eldridge Cleaver has described the mixing of a
rage against white power with the internalized sexism of a black man
raping a white woman. "Somehow I arrived at the conclusion that, as
a matter of principle, it was of paramount importance for me to have
an antagonistic, ruthless attitude toward white women. . . . Rape

was an insurrectionary act. It delighted me that I was defying and trampling upon the white man's law, upon his system of values and that I was defiling his women—and this point, I believe, was the most satisfying to me because I was very resentful over the historical fact of how the white man has used the black woman." Thus a black man uses white women to take out his rage against white men. But in fact, whenever a rape of a white woman by a black man does take place, it is again the white man who benefits. First, the act itself terrorizes the white woman and makes her more dependent on the white male for protection. Then, if the woman prosecutes her attacker, the white man is afforded legal opportunity to exercise overt racism. Of course, the knowledge of the rape helps to perpetuate two myths which are beneficial to white male rule—the bestiality of the black man and the desirability of white women. Finally, the white man surely benefits because he himself is not the object of attack—he has been allowed to stay in power.

Indeed, the existence of rape in any form is beneficial to the ruling class of white males. For rape is a kind of terrorism which severely limits the freedom of women and makes women dependent on men. Moreover, in the act of rape, the rage that one man may harbor toward another higher in the male hierarchy can be deflected toward a female scapegoat. For every man there is always someone lower on the social scale on whom he can take out his aggressions. And that is any woman alive.

This oppressive attitude towards women finds its institutionalization in the traditional family. For it is assumed that a man "wears the pants" in his family—he exercises the option of rule whenever he so chooses. Not that he makes all the decisions—clearly women make most of the important day-to-day decisions in a family. But when a conflict of interest arises, it is the man's interest which will prevail. His word, in itself, is more powerful. He lords it over his wife in the same way his boss lords it over him, so that the very process of exercising his power becomes as important an act as obtaining whatever it is his power can get for him. This notion of power is key to the male ego in this culture, for the two acceptable measures of masculinity are a man's power over women and his power over other men. A man may boast to his friends that "I have 20 men working for me." It is also aggrandizement of his ego if he has the financial power to clothe his wife in furs and jewels. And, if a man lacks the wherewithal to acquire such power, he can always express his rage through equally masculine activities—rape and theft. Since male society defines the female as a possession, it is not surprising that the felony most often committed together with rape is theft. As the following classic tale of rape points out, the elements of theft, violence and forced sexual relations merge into an indistinguishable whole.

The woman who told this story was acquainted with the man who tried to rape her. When the man learned that she was going to be staying alone for the weekend, he began early in the day a polite campaign to get her to go out with him. When she continued to refuse his request, his chivalrous mask dropped away:

"I had locked all the doors because I was afraid, and I don't know how he got in; it was probably through the screen door. When I woke up, he was shaking my leg. His eyes were red, and I knew he had been drinking or smoking. I thought I would try to talk my way out of it. He started by saying that he wanted to sleep with me, and then he got angrier and angrier, until he started to say, 'I want pussy,' 'I want pussy.' Then, I got scared and tried to push him away. That's when he started to force himself on me. It was awful. It was the most humiliating, terrible feeling. He was forcing my legs apart and ripping my clothes off. And it was painful. I did fight him—he was slightly drunk and I was able to keep him away. I had taken judo a few years back, but I was afraid to throw a chop for fear that he'd kill me. I could see he was getting more and more violent. I was thinking wildly of some way to get out of this alive, and then I said to him, 'Do you want money. I'll give you money.' We had money but I was also thinking that if I got to the back room I could telephone the police—as if the police would have even helped. It was a stupid thing to think of because obviously he would follow me. And he did. When he saw me pick up the phone, he tried to tie the cord around my neck. I screamed at him that I did have the money in another room, that I was going to call the police because I was scared, but that I would never tell anybody what happened. It would be an absolute secret. He said, okay, and I went to get the money. But when he got it, all of a sudden he got this crazy look in his eye and he said to me, 'Now I'm going to kill you.' Then I started saying my prayers. I knew there was nothing I could do. He started to hit me—I still wasn't sure if he wanted to rape me at this point—or just to kill me. He was hurting me, but hadn't yet gotten me into a strangle-hold because he was still drunk and off balance. Somehow we pushed into the kitchen where I kept looking at this big knife. But I didn't pick it up. Somehow, no matter how much I hated him at that moment, I still couldn't imagine putting the knife in his flesh, and then I was afraid he would grab it and stick it into me. Then he was hitting me again and somehow we pushed through the back door of the kitchen and onto the porch steps. We fell down the steps and that's when he started to strangle me. He was on top of me. He just went on and on until finally I lost consciousness. I did scream, though my screams sounded like whispers to me. But what happened was that a cab driver happened by and frightened him away. The cab driver revived me— I was out only a minute at the most. And then I ran across the street and I grabbed the woman who was our neighbor and screamed at her, 'Am I alive? Am I still alive?' "

Rape is an act of aggression in which the victim is denied her self-determination. It is an act of violence which, if not actually followed by beatings or murder, nevertheless always carries with it the threat of death. And finally, rape is a form of mass terrorism, for the victims of rape are chosen indiscriminately, but the propagandists for male supremacy broadcast that it is women who cause rape by being unchaste or in the wrong place at the wrong time—in essence, by behaving as though they were free.

The threat of rape is used to deny women employment. (In California, the Berkeley Public Library, until pushed by the Federal Employment Practices Commission, refused to hire female shelvers because of perverted men in the stacks.) The fear of rape keeps women off the streets at night. Keeps women at home. Keeps women passive and modest for fear that they be thought provocative.

It is part of human dignity to be able to defend oneself, and women are learning. Some women have learned karate; some to shoot guns. And yet we will not be free until the threat of rape and the atmosphere of violence is ended, and to end that the nature of male behavior must change.

But rape is not an isolated act that can be rooted out from patriarchy without ending patriarchy itself. The same men and power structure who victimize women are engaged in the act of raping Vietnam, raping Black people and the very earth we live upon. Rape is a classic act of domination where, in the words of Kate Millett, "the emotions of hatred, contempt, and the desire to break or violate

personality," takes place. This breaking of the personality characterizes modern life itself. No simple reforms can eliminate rape. As the
symbolic expression of the white male hierarchy, rape is the quin-
tessential act of our civilization, one which, Valerie Solanis warns,
is in danger of "humping itself to death."

Seduction is a Four-Letter Word
by Germaine Greer

Once in a hot courtroom in New Zealand, I had occasion to ask a lady who was giving evidence against me for saying fuck in a public meeting whether she was as disgusted and offended by hearing the word rape used in a similar context. She wasn't. I asked her why. She thought for a moment and said happily, "Because for rape the woman doesn't give her consent."

My little linguistic inquiry opened a sudden peephole on the labyrinth of crazy sexual attitudes that we have inherited from our polyglot traditions (although it did not prevent my being sentenced to three weeks in jail). The craziness extends into our (mis)understanding of the nature of sexual communication and thereby finds its way back to behavior. Our muddled responses to the word rape have their source in the sexual psychosis that afflicts us all, especially the policemen and judges who are most vindictive in their attitudes toward those few sexual criminals who have sufficient bad luck or bad judgment to fall foul of the law.

Otherwise quite humane people entertain the notion that women subconsciously or even consciously desire to be raped, that rape liberates their basic animality, that, like she-cats, they want to be bloodily subdued and savagely fucked, regardless of their desperate struggles and cries. Women are thought to provoke the sexual rage of men who in turn may need to add blood lust to their sexual desire in order to achieve full potency. Darwin is sometimes quoted as the ideological ally of the rapist and forcible impregnator—how else but by his marauding activities could the survival of the fittest be assured?

Yet many women are afraid of rape as of nothing else. Women who have been raped may, as a consequence, be too terrified to leave their house by day or night or so distressed by male nearness that they cannot take a job or get onto a crowded train. There may be some truth in the notion that the lonely spinster who is terrified of intruders is actually longing to be violated, but her subconscious wish is of the same order as the wish of a mother to destroy her children, which is chiefly expressed in her fantasies that they may have come to violent harm. The fury that a father feels against the man who rapes his daughter might as profitably be construed as jealousy. For all practical purposes what the spinster experiences is a fascinating terror that may become an obsession. The man who actualizes her fantasy is in no way gratifying her or benefiting her, except in his own overweening estimation. The extent to which all men participate in this fantasy of violent largess can be dimly detected in their willingness to laugh at Lenny Bruce's description of his aunt going into Central Park each day for her appointment with the flashers or in the sneering assumption that older women and unattractive women are disappointed if intruders or invading soldiers don't rape them.

Many (men) believe that rape is impossible. The more simple-minded imagine that the vagina cannot be penetrated unless the woman consciously or subconsciously accepts the penetration, and so the necessary condition of rape cannot be fulfilled. The difficulty of getting a fully erect penis into the vagina is in direct proportion to the difficulty of overcoming the woman, either by physical force or by threat or by drugging her or by taking her by surprise.

The idea that rape is impossible may be an invalid extension of the view that all women subconsciously desire or provoke rape. It is certainly true that women do not defend themselves against rapists with any great efficiency. Even though they know that a sharp blow to the groin will incapacitate a man, or that a high heel smashed into the temple will have a certain effect, they seldom take advantage of what forms of self-defense may be accessible to them. The fault lies not in their suppressed lechery or promiscuity but in the induced passivity that is characteristic of women as we have conditioned them. Feminist encounter groups have developed routines in which a woman is encouraged to fight off a would-be rapist. Even strong heavy women have had to struggle to overcome the passivity that impeded the release of energy in self-defense; passionate urging from the other members of the group was needed before they could take advantage of their own strength and determination.

Without special help, most women have no idea how to defend themselves and no concept of themselves as people with a right to resist physical misuse with violence. They are like children being beaten by their parents and their teachers, or slaves being brutalized on the plantation. Their physical strength remains unexploited because of the pathology of oppression. Women are poorly motivated to be as aggressive with their assailants as their assailants are with them, and so rape is easier than it should be. But this cannot be held to justify the contemptuous attitude of the rapist. Women's helplessness is itself part of the psychosis that makes rape a national pastime. And even encounter groups have not yet developed the kind of psychic energy that can defeat a gun or a knife or the frenzy of drugs.

The fear of sexual assault is a special fear: Its intensity in women can best be likened to the male fear of castration. As a tiny child I was utterly unafraid of the derelict old men who drooped their pallid tools at my mother and me when we sun-bathed in the beach park, but I remember an occasion when much less sinister behavior provoked wild terror. A young man simply came up to me and offered me a sweet; his kind smile was the most hideous thing I had ever seen. Usually I invoked my parents' rage because I consorted so readily with strangers, but this time I recoiled from the bribe, speechless with fright. Then I was running and running until my lungs were screaming, and I fell down and cowered in the grass, desperate not to look up for fear I would see that indescribable smile. Whenever I saw that man hanging out in the lane below our apartment, looking up my six-inch skirts as I went up or down the stairs, I was terrified. When I tried to explain to the grownups why I loathed that man, I had no words for it, but I knew it was the greatest fear of all, worse than spiders or octopuses or falling off the roof. Devoted sadists might argue that my terror was simply the terror of my own innate femaleness, but it would be bad Freud, because I was presumably in my phallic phase and unaware of my vagina; and if such a view is not to be justified by the great apologist of female masochism, it is not to be justified at all. What I was afraid of was rape as Eldridge Cleaver described it, "bloody, hateful, bitter and malignant," even though I had no clear idea of what it entailed.

Sexual intercourse between grown men and little girls is automatically termed rape under most codes of law. It does not matter whether the child invites it or even whether she seduces the adult; he and he only is guilty of a felony. From the child's point of view and from the common-sense point of view, there is an enormous difference between intercourse with a willing little girl and the forcible penetration of the small vagina of a terrified child. One woman I know enjoyed sex with an uncle all through her childhood, and never realized that anything unusual was toward until she went away to school. What disturbed her then was not what her uncle had done but the attitude of her teachers and the school psychiatrist. They assumed that she must have been traumatized and disgusted and therefore in need of very special help. In order to capitulate to their expectations, she began to fake symptoms that she did not feel, until at length she began to feel truly guilty about not having been guilty. She ended up judging herself very harshly for this innate lechery.

The crucial element in establishing whether or not vaginal penetration is rape is whether or not the penetration was consented to. Consent is itself an intangible mental act; the law cannot be blamed for insisting that evidence of absence of consent be virtually conclusive, so that a woman who has not been savagely beaten or threatened with immediate harm or rendered unconscious has little chance of legally proving that she has been raped. Consent is not a simple procedure; it may be heavily conditional or thoroughly muddled, and the law cannot allow itself to be drawn into ethical conundrums. Most of us do not live according to the bare letter of the law but according to moral criteria of much greater complexity. Morally, those of us who have a high opinion of sex cannot accept the idea that absence of resistance sanctions all kinds of carnal communication; rather than rely on such a negative criterion, we must insist that only evidence of positive desire dignifies sexual intercourse and makes it joyful. From a proud and passionate woman's point of view, anything less is rape.

The law of rape was not made with a woman's pride or passion in mind. The woman is no more and probably even less the focus of the rape statutes than the murder victim is the *raison d'être* of the homicide statutes. The crime of rape is rather considered an offense not against the woman herself but against the men who made the law, fathers, husbands, and kin. It is a crime against legitimacy of issue and the correct transmission of patrimony. The illegitimate sexual intercourse constitutes the offense: what the woman who complains must do is primarily to dissociate herself from any suspicion of complicity in the outrage against her menfolk. This she must do by making a complaint immediately. She is regarded as the prosecutrix of the rapist and he has all the recourse against her accusation that any defendant has against the state prosecutor, and then some. Only a girl child escapes the ordeal, because she is automatically deemed incapable of consent. An adult woman is actually called upon to prove her own innocence in the course of a rape prosecution, as well as managing to establish that the circumstances of the man's behavior are as she alleges.

A man has to be very unlucky to be convicted of the crime of rape. He has to be stupid enough, or drugged or drunk enough, to leave a mile-wide trail of blood, bruises, threats, semen, screaming and what have you, and he has to have chosen the kind of woman about whom the neighbors have nothing but good to say, who has enough *chutzpah* to get down to the police station at once and file her complaint, and, if it results in a trial, to face down public humiliation, for hearsay evidence about her morals and demeanor is admissible. The most the court will do for her is to rule that evidence emanating from a district other than the one she actually lives in is inadmissible. Then the jury must feel confident that no element of consent entered into the woman's behavior.

Nevertheless, men do go to jail for rape, mostly black men, nearly all of them poor, and neither the judges nor the prosecuting attorneys are hampered in their dealings by the awareness that they are rapists, too, only they have more sophisticated methods of compulsion. A deprived man forces his way into a woman's body by pressing the point of a knife against her throat; a man who owns an automobile may stop on a lonely road and tell his passenger to come across or get out and walk. The hostility of the rapist and the humiliation of the victim are not necessarily different, despite the difference in the circumstances; indeed, they could both be worse in the latter case, and that sort of thing happens every day. Probably the commonest form of noncriminal rape is rape by fraud—by phony tenderness or false promises of an enduring relationship, for example.

The woman who is assaulted and raped by a total stranger may suffer less than the woman who endures constant humiliation at the hands of people she is trying to know and love. The inadequates and psychotics who are arrested for rape have been known to select their victims and lie in wait for them; other criminal rapes may involve

women who are known to or even related to their assailants, but for
the most part, the selection of the victim is as fortuitous as it might
be in an automobile accident. That element of haphazardness can
help the woman avoid permanent psychic damage, because she is not
compelled to internalize the experience, and so to feel guilty and
soiled as a consequence of it.

One of the great injustices that the victims of criminal rape
must suffer is the necessity of reliving the experience in minute detail
over and over again from the first complaint to the police to the last
phase of the trial. By attempting to prosecute the man who has raped
her, a woman dissociates herself from the crime and endeavors to
reconstitute her self-esteem, but it is a rare woman who is so independent of the evaluation of others that she can survive the contemptuous publicity that her attempt will draw upon her. If she fails to
make her accusation stick, so that people assume that she is malicious
or hysterical or that she enticed her rapist, she is in more serious
psychic trouble than before. The odds against her succeeding in her
prosecution, even after the police have reluctantly agreed to charge
her assailant, are rather worse than four to one. If a woman's only
concern is for herself and her eventual recovery from the experience,
then she is much better advised not to prosecute. Rape is a habitual
crime, however, and any woman who decides not to prosecute ought
to spare a little thought for the women who will be raped as a consequence of her decision.

It is true that women have attempted to frame men for rapes that
were never committed. Some have done so out of fear of punishment
for an illicit sexual relationship that has been discovered. Others have
done so because they needed abortions, others for revenge and other
ulterior motives, for politics or policy. Some studies of rape quote a
percentage of phony rape charges as high as 20 percent, but it is
important to remember that the essence of the frame is that it is
public, and that a good deal is left to the discretion of law enforcers
in deciding whether or not a woman has been truly offended. There
are not too many profeminists in police stations.

Criminologists believe that fewer than one in five rapes are reported, making rape the least reported crime on the books. Those
figures are, I believe, conservative, even within the terms of their
narrow legalistic definition, which refers to the second gravest crime
in the statutes—what we might call grand rape. The punishments for
grand rape are very savage, but it was not women who decided long

ago that rapists should be blinded and castrated or hanged with benefit of clergy (as they once were) or sentenced to jail for life (as they still are). Nevertheless, even from a woman's point of view there are instances in which rape is an injury just as serious as homicide, and perhaps more so. A black friend of mine spent years of passionate effort to see that the seven white youths who raped her when she was 16 years old and a virgin spent the maximum time in jail, for they ruined her life by cursing her with a child whom she could never leave and never love. (The wonder of it is, of course, that a white jockocratic court convicted on the evidence of a black girl.)

It is in the interests of everyone involved that pregnancy must not be allowed to be a consequence of rape. This means that all women claiming rape must be entitled to abortion, long before the offense can be proved. To wait for any legal process is to increase the degree of physical and mental trauma involved. Nowadays a raped woman has a pretty good chance of getting an abortion, especially if she can supply reasonable circumstantial evidence of the offense. However, the women who are most traumatized by rape are religious and sheltered women who are not likely to get over their experience by the necessity of committing what they devoutly believe to be a mortal sin as a result of an act committed upon their person against their will. In cases of scrupulous religious conscience, religion can be the woman's only consolation, but most cases of normally muddled morality would be best aided by the adoption of a protocol by medical officials confronted with rape cases. One practical solution would be to order the removal of the contents of the womb by aspiration as part of the diagnostic procedure. This would diminish the element of psychic intrusion and relieve the woman of the necessity of making a difficult moral choice arising out of circumstances beyond her control. The procedure is the same as biopsy aspiration, which is commonly practiced and need occasion very little discomfort.

The woman who is not impregnated or physically injured as a result of rape may nevertheless suffer acutely. The idea, so commonly entertained, that women somehow enjoy rape is absolutely unfounded, and a further indication of the contempt that men feel for women and their sexual functions. One might as well argue that because most men have repressed homosexual or feminine elements in their personalities, they enjoy buggery and humiliation. Women are, as a result of their enculturation, masochistic, but this does not mean that they enjoy being treated sadistically, although it may mean that they unconsciously invite it. Because of this masochism, women frequently take the whole burden of horror upon themselves. I know personally of a case in which a woman has been repeatedly raped by her mentally retarded brother for 30 years and has never sought any protection from him because of the distress that the knowledge would cause her parents. Her struggle to cope with the situation alone has had a marked effect on her psychic balance, and yet it is not beyond a law-enforcement officer to argue that she is guilty of collusion, that she is an accomplice, in effect.

Bored policemen, amusing themselves with girls who come to them to complain of rape, often kick off the proceedings by asking if they have enjoyed it. Rapists often claim in their defense that the prosecutrix enjoyed herself, that she showed evidence of physical pleasure or even had an orgasm. Most of them are lying. Some are sincere, but men are notoriously incapable of judging whether or not a woman is feeling pleasure, and women are not so unlike men that terror cannot cause something like the symptoms of erotic excitation in the genitals. Even if a woman were to have an orgasm in the course of a rape, it need not necessarily lessen the severity of the trauma that she suffers. This, it would seem, is quite understandable in the case of men raped by women, which, although not an entity in law, is still a possibility. Malinowski describes with thrills of disgusted horror the rape of a Melanesian male; if the clear evidence of the victim's sexual excitation makes any difference to his sense of outrage, it is to intensify it:

> The man is the fair game of women for all that sexual violence, obscene cruelty, filthy pollution and rough handling can do to him. Thus first they pull off and tear up his pubic leaf, the protection of his modesty, and, to a native, the symbol of his manly dignity. Then, by masturbatory practices and exhibitionism, they try to produce an erection in their victim and, when their maneuvers have brought about the desired result, one of them squats over him and inserts his penis into her vagina. After the first ejaculation he may be treated in the same manner by another woman. Worse things are to follow. Some of the women will defecate and micturate all over his body, paying special attention to his face, which they pollute as thoroughly as they can. "A man will vomit, and vomit, and vomit," said a sympathetic informant.

For Malinowski the trauma is directly connected with loss of dignity and obliteration of the individual's will, at which his body actually connives. Women, too, have been known to vomit and vomit, to wash themselves compulsively, to burn their clothes, even to attempt suicide, after a rape. Nightmares, depression, pathological shyness, inability to leave the house, terror of darkness, all have been known to develop in otherwise healthy women who have been raped.

Malinowski was writing from the point of view of the rapee. The injury for him lay not in an outrage to his tutors and guardians, nor in injury to his body, nor in an unwanted pregnancy, but somewhere even more fundamental, in his will, and thence in his ego, his dignity. In this perspective the legalistic category of grand rape fades into unimportance. Sexual rip-offs are part of every woman's daily experience; they do not have the gratifying strangeness of disaster, with the special reconstructive energies that disasters call forth. They simply wear down the contours of emotional contacts and gradually brutalize all those who are party to them. Petty rape corrodes a woman's self-esteem so that she grows by degrees not to care too much what happens or how. In her low moments she calls all men bastards; she enters into new relationships with suspicion and a forlorn hope that maybe this time she will get a fair deal. The situation is self-perpetuating. The treatment she most fears she most elicits. The results of this hardening of the heart are eventually much worse than the consequences of fortuitous sexual assault by a stranger, the more so because they are internalized, insidious and imperceptible.

The idea that a woman has merely to consent, or to give in to sexual contact, provides the basic motivation for petty rape. Silence or failure to resist is further misconstrued as consent. Then, by a further ramification of blunder, passive silence is thought to indicate pleasure. The breakdown in sexual communications occasioned by acceptance of these related vulgar errors can be illustrated by an example.

A young Cambridge undergraduate at a party in London missed his last train back to Cambridge and so asked around the party for a bed for the night. A female guest, who lived nearby, said he might use her spare room, unconcerned by the fact that her husband was away, for the young man and all his family were well known to them. She duly drove him to her apartment, where clean towels and pajamas were laid out for him, and he was wished a good night's rest in the spare room. She had had a lot to drink at the party and was feeling giddy and rather ill, so she was grateful to slide between the sheets and pass quietly out.

It was beneath young Lochinvar's dignity to stay in his room, though, and his hostess was just slipping through rather swirling veils of sleep when he climbed into the bed beside her. She resisted, but there was little point in making much to-do; having the police called to the apartment would have made a scandal, upset everybody and left her in a ridiculous situation. The law would take only one view of an unaccompanied married woman's invitation to a young man to stay the night, regardless of the fact that Victorian sexual paranoia is gradually ebbing in other areas. She scolded and pleaded, exaggerated the degree of her drunkenness and even resorted to being sick, but the young man's ego would give no quarter. Like a Fascist guard in Mussolini's Italy, he woke her every time her eyelids began to close. Then he made his little show of force. She offered only passive resistance and so got fucked.

It was, of course, a terrible fuck. She was exhausted, distressed and mutinous; he was deeply inconsiderate and cruel, although he fancied himself a nipple twiddler and general sexual operator and believes to this day that he gave her the fucking of her life. He has boasted of his conquest just often enough so that his talking about it has come to her ears and reduced her to a state of misery. She has never told her husband what happened because of the sheer unlikeliness that he would exonerate her from any taint of desire for the little shit, however nobly he decided to behave. Worst of all, she must see her enemy frequently at dinners and parties in friends' houses and endure his triumph over her time and time again. She has not allowed the circumstances to corrode her self-esteem to any serious extent, but her enemy cannot lay the fact to his credit.

What happened is just one of the zillions of forms of petty rape. There is no punishment and no treatment for offender nor victim in a case like this. It just has to be crossed off as another minor humiliation, another devaluation of the currency of human response. The woman in this instance revenged herself by striking the man from her list of friends, but he hardly noticed. His account of the affair, needless to say, is very different from hers.

The attitude of the rapist in such an example is not hard to interpret in terms of the prevailing sexual ideology. A man is, after all, supposed to seduce, to cajole, persuade, pressurize and eventually overcome. A reasonable man will avoid threats, partly because he has a shrewd idea that they will not produce the desired result. A psychotic rapist is quite likely to desire fright and even panic-stricken resistance and struggle as a prerequisite to his sexual arousal or satisfaction. But not your everyday pusillanimous rapist. He simply takes advantage of any circumstances that are in his favor to override the woman's independence. The man who has it in his power to hire and fire women from an interesting or lucrative position may profit by that factor to extort sexual favors that would not spontaneously be offered him. A man who is famous or charismatic might exploit those advantages to humiliate women in ways that they would otherwise angrily resist. In cases like these, mutual contempt is the eventual outcome, but what the men do not realize is that they are exploiting the oppressed and servile status of women. The women's capitulation might be ignoble, but it is morally more excusable than the cynical manipulation of their susceptibility.

One of the elements that is often abused in the petty-rape situation is the woman's affection for the rapist. This might not even be a completely nonsexual affection: There is a case on record in Denver in which a woman who was brutally raped explained to the judge that she would have been quite happy to ball with her assailant if he had asked her nicely, but as soon as they got into her apartment, he beat her up and raped her. The parallel in petty rape is the exploitation of a woman's tenderness, which would involve eventual sexual compliance, for a loveless momentary conquest. Because a woman likes a man and would like to develop some sort of relationship with him, she is loath to make trouble when he begins to prosecute his intentions in an offensive way. Her enemy takes cold-blooded advantage of that fact. For lots of girls who slide into promiscuity, this is the conflict in which they are defeated time and time again.

In all but the most sophisticated communities, a young woman who wishes to participate in the social life of her generation must do so as a man's guest. Dating is a social and economic imperative for her. This situation is the direct result of her oppressed condition, and however venal her motives may seem to be, she is not totally responsible for them. For her the pressure is disguised as pressure to fall in love and go steady; he may see it as a kind of being on the make, corresponding to his own fairly impersonal desire for sexual gratification. If she gets raped as a result of her dependence upon a man as an escort, neither party thinks that she has anything grave to complain of, and yet a great wrong has been done.

For most young women who set out on the dating road to marriage, petty rape is a constant hazard. The fact that a man pays for the night's entertainment, that he owns and drives the car, that he has initiated all that has happened means by extension that he is also entitled to initiate and to set the pace of the physical intimacies that will occur. She would probably be disappointed if he manifested no desire for her, but she also has the problem of not seeming easy while keeping him interested. His self-esteem prompts him to achieve as much intimacy as he can before she draws the line. The element of petty rape appears when he threatens to throw her over if she doesn't come across or whenever he decides that he does not like her well enough to move gradually through the stages of intimacy as she desires them, but will force the pace to get as much as possible out of an otherwise unsatisfactory encounter. His use of the vocabulary of tenderness becomes fraudulent. He may even fake an excess of sexual desire.

A group of law students at the first university I attended had a competition to see who could fuck the most women in one semester; one ploy that they all had in common was a trick of heavy breathing and groaning, as if they were writhing in torments of desire. As they were after quantity and not quality, this was not often the case. It worked very well, in the main, but partly because they were exercising the class prerogative of the rich bourgeois and wantonly disrupting the lives and expectations of women situated in less fortunate circumstances, like the hero of *My Secret Life,* but more callously.

The man who won that competition was an expert in exploiting women's fantasy and vanity, and their tendency to delude themselves that the contact they were experiencing was a genuine personal encounter and not a crass sexual rip-off. He and his friends were proud of their mastery of the gestures of tenderness, but their use of them was utterly self-centered. They were simply exercising a skill like angling, drawing silly women to their own humiliation. The only way to earn their respect, and friendship was to resist them, so they wantonly encouraged toughness and suspicion in this cold world. The girls they had had never realized they'd been victims of petty rape until they grasped the fact that the first time was also the last.

For such rich and handsome young men, petty rape was a sport that by virtue of their privileges they played with great success. There were occasional uglinesses that marred the lightheartedness of their proceedings. One of them was threatened with a paternity suit, but all his friends turned up in court and testified that they had had carnal knowledge of the plaintiff, and so he got off. In fact, they committed perjury, but it did not disturb their sleep.

The group-bonding skills of males will always defeat the interests of isolated women. Men will conspire to see that acts of petty rape are successful. Many women would be appalled to learn just how their most intimate behavior and physical peculiarities are discussed by men, and this supplies a further dimension of petty rape by blackmail. There is no point in resisting a man's advances if he is going to talk about how he had you in any case, especially when your word is generally less respected than his. I was once pestered for three or four days by a detestable male chauvinist who explained my consequent dislike of him as pique because he refused to fuck me. When sex is an ego contest, women get fucked over all the time.

Petty rape is sometimes called seduction, which is not regarded as a contemptible or particularly damaging activity. A woman who capitulates to a seducer is considered to do so because she really wanted to or because she is too silly or too loose to know how to resist. It might even be thought to be in her interest to overcome her priggishness about sex. The man who excuses his unloving manipulation of women's susceptibilities in ways such as these cannot honestly claim to have the women's interests at heart. His assumption that he knows what is good for them is overweening even if it is sincere, which it usually is not.

Some men decide that it is their prerogative to punish a woman in a sexual encounter, either for her looseness or for teasing or for lying and evading the issue. The distortion of an erotic response into a chastisement is pathological, but not uncommon. An economics student, son of a high-ranking public official, boasted to me once that because a girl had lied to him that she was menstruating, he punished her by raping her, buggering her and throwing her out of his rooms in Cambridge in the small hours of the morning, knowing that she would find no kind of transport to take her back to her home in the country. He had absolutely no understanding of her motives for lying to him. He believed she was stalling him; in fact, all she needed was time to build up a desire for intimacy that he was forcing on her. She could have walked out earlier, or screamed and brought the housekeeper to her rescue, but that would have meant rustication for him and a summary end to any developing relationship. Either course would have required positive hostility, which she simply did not feel. She had very little understanding of the sexual hostility that he did feel, which underlay a good deal of his sexual response, especially in casual affairs.

The men who do cruel things to women are not a class apart; they are not totally incapable of relating to women. In nearly every case I have described, the details were told to me by the men, who explained their comparatively humane attitudes toward me as a result of my own respect for myself and my own straightforwardness in sexual matters, both results of my unusually privileged status as a woman; I was also older than most of them. But I have not entirely emancipated myself from the female legacy of low self-image, self-hatred and identification with the oppressors, which is part of the pathology of oppression. The girls who have been mistreated in the ways that I have described take the fault upon themselves. They think they must have made a mistake somewhere, that their bodies have provoked disgust, that they were too greasy in their conversation. The internalization of the injury is what makes petty rape such an insidiously harmful offense against women. What the men have done is to exploit and so intensify the pathology of oppression.

Many petty rapists do not wittingly dislike women or hate them; they do not revenge themselves upon their mothers through other women's bodies in any conscious way. Group-therapy sessions at treatment centers for sex offenders are producing results that seem to indicate that repressed hostility toward the mother is one of the most common unconscious motivations for violent rape. But these conclusions ought not to be regarded as particularly enlightening; if an analyst is seeking evidence of an infantile trauma involving women, it is almost inevitably going to involve a mother or a mother surrogate. It is small wonder that our civilization manifests a psychotic attitude to women, when children are thrown upon the mercy of one woman almost exclusively during the formative years between one and five. Women's hostility to one another may be explained by the same phenomenon, at least partially. Teachers anywhere, women in authority over men in any capacity attract a good deal of antagonism, some of which masquerades as affection.

There are other discernible motives for active sexual hostility in the male. Religions that rely upon guilt mechanisms for their hold upon the faithful build up an image of the female as an occasion of sin. The nuns at my Catholic primary school prepared the children for raping and being raped by treating even the littlest girls' bodies as dire inducements to lasciviousness, to the point of forbidding us to bare our upper arms or our collarbones, and begging us all not to look at our "private parts" even when we were washing them as perfunctorily as possible in the bath. This wanton stimulation of sexual tension still goes on in religious schools. If scientology and other forms of psychic manipulation for eventual control can be declared illegal, then some attention should be paid to this process, enacted without fear of reprisal upon the very young.

Undue aestheticism in representing sexual behavior can also have harmful effects. The inauthenticity of sexual fantasy as it is stimulated by commercial representations of the woman as sex object leaves many immature men unable to cope with the eventual discovery that women do not feel smooth and velvety all over, that their pubic hair exists and is not swan's-down or vine tendrils, that a woman in heat does not smell like a bed of roses. (Most convicted rapists who have been subjected to any degree of analysis have shown an exaggerated dislike of menstruation.) For most men, sexual experience begins and persists throughout the years of most intense libidinous activity, the teens, as fantasy and masturbation rather than actual physical confrontation with the object of their desire. It is not surprising, then, that the imagery of their puerile fantasies continues to interpose itself between the ego and the reality long after their active sexual life has begun in earnest. What the permissive society has achieved, in fact, is merely the proliferation of inauthentic sexual fantasy, with virtually no degree of emancipation of the sexes into genuine communication and mutual understanding.

Women are not yet consumers of commercial soft-core pornography; they do not have the same fetishistic attitude toward men's bodies that men have toward women's. Instead they are further alienated from the area of male sexual orientation by their own culture of romantic fantasy. Attempts to duplicate the marketing of images of women's bodies have been made with men's bodies without much success, and similar inauthenticities were represented. When my husband, Paul du Feu, posed for the gatefold in the British edition of *Cosmopolitan,* it was found necessary not only to cover him with body make-up and hide his penis behind his upraised thigh but also to airbrush his navel and the wrinkles on his belly clean out of the picture. Men trying to understand feminists' reactions to the commercialized stereotype of women ought to study their own reactions to the degradation and desexualization of Paul du Feu.

Those who hate women most are often the most successful womanizers. The connection used to be recognized in common parlance by the expressions lady-killer and wolf. Sylvia Plath describes a crucial encounter with one such in *The Bell Jar,* leaving it to the reader to estimate the role that this humiliation plays in Esther Greenwood's eventual collapse.

> Marco's small flickering smile reminded me of a snake I'd teased in the Bronx Zoo. When I tapped my finger on the stout cage glass the snake had opened his clockwork jaws and seemed to smile. Then it struck and struck at the invisible pane till I moved off.
>
> I had never met a woman hater before. I could tell Marco was a woman hater, because in spite of all the models and TV starlets in the room that night he paid attention to nobody but me. Not out of kindness or even curiosity, but because I'd happened to be dealt to him, like a playing card in a pack of identical cards.

Young Esther has no hope of beating Marco at the game he has been perfecting most of his adult life. He sweeps aside her tremendous attempts to remain independent. On the dance floor he forces her to give up all idea of independent locomotion:

> "What did I tell you?" Marco's breath scorched my ear. "You're a perfectly respectable dancer."
>
> I began to see why woman haters could make such fools of women. Woman haters were like gods: invulnerable and chock-full of power. They descended and then they disappeared. You could never catch one.

Marco's excuse for treating all women like sluts is an impossible love for his first cousin (probably a narcissistic fantasy), who is to become a nun. After he has assaulted Esther, and she has partly beaten him off and he has partly given up, saying, "Sluts, all sluts . . . yes or no, it's all the same," Esther goes back to her sexsegregated hotel, climbs onto the parapet of the roof and feeds her wardrobe to the night wind. Marco has brought her to the beginning of the end.

In all cases of petty rape, the victim does not figure as a personality, as someone vulnerable and valuable, whose responses must not be cynically tampered with. So great is women's need to believe that men really like them that they are often slow to detect perfunctoriness in proffered caresses or the subtle change in attitude when the Rubicon has been crossed and the softening up of the victim can give way to unilateral gratification. Not all woman haters can belie their feelings of hatred and contempt successfully throughout a sexual encounter. When their situation is secure—say, when they have the victim safe behind the hotel door and know that she is not about to run screaming through the lobby in a torn dress—they may abandon all pretense of tenderness and get down to the business of hate fucking, and yet still the wretched woman attempts to roll with the punches. Her enemy may use physical and verbal abuse, even a degree of force to make her comply with forms of sexual intercourse that she does not desire. Mostly he retreats into an impersonal, masturbatory frame of mind. After the loveless connection is over, he cannot wait to get rid of her, either by giving her cab fare or shutting her out of his mind by going to sleep or pretending to.

Guilt and disgust may follow. The man may be sorry that he went with such an abject creature, but he will not blame himself for the poor quality of the sex he has had, any more than when he finds the woman unresponsive because her sexual submission has been extorted from her. If he is distressed by the crassness and perfunctoriness of the love he has made or embarrassed by the willingness and generosity of the love he has been given, he will abuse the woman in his mind. She is a dog, a pig, goes with anyone, is so dumb she wouldn't know you were up her till you coughed. Like the grand rapist, he excuses his conduct on the grounds that she asked for it, by her lewdness, her willingness to discuss sex, her appetite at dinner, the money she made him spend, the dress she had on, the size of her breasts. If she has enjoyed and responded to caresses up to the point when they became brutal and then struggled to escape, then she is a tease who leads men on and then wants to chicken out when he gets to the nitty-gritty. No punishment is too severe for a tease.

Some men who are very well aware of their own preference for force fucking and their hostility to women may doubt that women's sensibilities are elevated enough to perceive their own humiliation. Feminists are at least beginning to spell it out for them, but too many men do not realize that the slogan "An End to Rape" does not so much refer to grand rapes committed on the crime-ridden streets of the cities as to the daily brutalization of contact between brother and sister, father and daughter, teacher and pupil, doctor and patient, employer and employee, dater and datee, fiancé and fiancée, husband and wife, adulterer and adulteress, the billions of petty liberties exacted from passive and wondering women. The solution is not to be found in the castration or killing of the rare rapists who offend so crazily that they can be caught and punished but in the correction of our distorted notions of the nature of sexual intercourse, which are also the rationale of the law of rape as a felony.

Women are now struggling to discover and develop their own sexuality, to know their own minds and bodies and to improve the bases upon which they can attempt communication with men. The men who continue to assume that women must be treated as creatures who do not know what is good for them, to be cajoled or coerced or punished at the will of a stiff-standing cock, seek to imprison women in the pathology of their oppressed condition. Some women are coquettish, although far fewer than the mythology of rape supposes; the only way to put an end to such fatuous guile is to cease to play the game, simply by taking women at their word. The woman who says no when she means yes and so loses a man she wants will find a way to see him again to tell him she meant yes all the time— if she really did mean yes, that is. If she didn't really mean yes, then she is better left alone.

Any man who realizes that he likes screwing mutinous women, that he is bored at the prospect of balling only women who want him, had better be aware that he finds resistance and tension essential to his satisfaction: He is a petty rapist and should look to it.

The abandonment of the stereotype of seduction, conquest, the chase and all, increases the number of erotic possibilities rather than diminishing it. Once the rigid course of sexual manipulation is disrupted, the unexpected may occur, some genuine erotic development can take place. Even the rapist author of *My Secret Life,* whose sexual activity was entirely dependent upon the possibilities of exploiting lower-class women, was aware that coercion and insistence were not in his best sexual interests, even when he had paid for the use of a woman's body and was in some sense entitled to it:

> A custom of mine then, and always followed since, is putting down my fee—it prevents mistakes, and quarrels. When paid, if a woman will not let me have her, be it so—she has some reason— perhaps a good one for me.

Nothing that I have said should be interpreted to mean that no man should try to make love to a woman unless he is prepared to marry her or to undertake a long and serious affair with her. A one-night stand can be the most perfect and satisfying sexual encounter of all, as long as there is no element of fraud or trickery or rip-off in the way in which it develops. If women are to free themselves from the necessity of deploying their sexuality as a commodity, then men will have to level in their dealings with them, and that is all we ask. There is still room for excitement, uncertainty, even antagonism in the development of sexual friendship, but *if you do not like us, cannot listen to our part of the conversation, if we are only meat to you, then leave us alone.*

As women develop more confidence and more self-esteem, and become as supportive toward one another as they have been to men, they also lose their reluctance to denounce men for petty rape. Where before they respected men's privacy a good deal more than men respected theirs (despite the phony claims of chivalry), they are now beginning to tell it how it is. A theatrical impresario well known for his randiness recently invited a leading women's liberationist to his hotel for a business meeting. To her amazement, for she had thought such gambits long out of style, he leaped on her as soon as he had her fairly inside the room. She held him off until suddenly he ejaculated all over the front of her dress. Gone are the days when she would have slunk out behind a newspaper. Her dress is a museum piece of the women's movement in her country, and the joke will be around for years.

Rape crisis centers are being set up by groups of women more interested in self-help than in vindictiveness. Here a woman who has been traumatized by a sexual experience can come for counsel, for medical and psychiatric help. She is not regarded as a culprit or challenged about the length of her skirts or the thickness of her eye make-up; her word is believed, as the first step to reconstituting an ego damaged by sexual misuse. The victim is encouraged to externalize the experience rather than to entertain feelings of guilt and shame, and she is also taught how to defend herself against future assault and brutalization, even from her husband, who by law has the right of rape over her. Menstrual aspiration will also be practiced as the technique becomes better known and the instruments more widely available. Force fucking is being phased out.

The new feeling of solidarity among women will render petty rape quite futile. Women who used to rejoice to think that their men treated other women badly cannot accept it once their consciousness is raised. A musician returning to his feminist old lady after a protracted tour abroad boasted that he managed to be faithful to her (something she had never demanded) by making the adoring groupies give him blow jobs and then get out. He was proud that he had never even kissed one of them, let alone balled one. To his amazement, his old lady walked out on him.

Women are finding, in the stirring words of women's advocate Florynce Kennedy, that "kickin' ass and takin' names, talkin' loud and drawin' a crowd is better than suckin'." Our weapons may be little more than ridicule and boycott, but we will use them. Women are sick to their souls of being fucked over. Now that sex has become political, the petty rapist had better watch his ass; he won't be getting away with it too much longer. How would you feel if a video tape of your last fuck were playing at the Feminist Guerrilla cinema? We didn't start this war, but we intend to bring it to an honorable settlement, which means we have to make a show of strength sometime. People who are fighting for their lives fight with any weapons that come to hand, so it is foolish to expect a fair fight. Sex behavior is becoming as public as any other expression of political belief: Next time I write an article like this, I'll tell you all the names. So don't say you weren't warned.

Interview with a Rapist
by "Fred," Robert W. Winslow and Virginia Winslow

Question: *You say you started out as a classic case of progressive perversion.*

Fred: Well, originally I started out as a peeping Tom at about ten to twelve years old, which is normal in that period. I was active in this with four other brothers but while they grew out of it I never did. I never got caught but it was close a lot of time. From there I went to simple assaults of women. I didn't beat them up, just reach out and feel them. Like we used to hitchhike along the road and women would pick us up. We'd feel them up and they'd say, "No, that's naughty" but we'd still continue. Young kids hitchhiking you know, older women come along and pick you up. It used to be pretty fun to hitchhike, but now I hardly ever do it anymore. For a long time I thought I was ugly; where did my sexuality go to.

Question: *How many kids in your family?*

Fred: Seven, I was in the middle. At home we were taught nothing about sex. Anything we learned we learned on our own. Most people for instance stay as peeping Toms but this lost its appeal with me and I gradually progressed. My parents were of German stock and very reserved. Sex was strictly taboo around the house. It was dirty and filthy and not to be talked about. It was strictly physical attraction with no emotion attached. That's the way I was brought up. We all know the sex act is one of the most beautiful things there is. It took me up to about three years ago to really realize this, what motivated me, etc.

Question: *What came next in your progression?*

Fred: Well, as we hitchhiked and felt women up nobody ever blew the whistle on us. They just thought we were naughty boys. I was pretty young looking when I was younger. I don't look my age now. I'm almost thirty-five now. I seldom drink anymore. Well, anyway, from that I progressed to attempted rapes. I was really afraid to have forcible intercourse with a woman. Sometimes I would beat on the woman, sometimes no. Some women like to be raped and a few times the women thanked me afterwards, that this was what they were looking for. This really bolstered my ego; I was sixteen. From there I went on to realize that I hated my mother for the way I was treated as a child and that all I wanted was to have control of the situation. My little brother used to beat the shit out of me and my mother used to sit there and laugh at me. When I was in the Army, I joined when I was seventeen, I never once stopped these activities. I went to an Army psychiatrist; blah, blah, was all he said and nothing was ever done about my situation. I later realized that I loved my mother, dad, and family, but to this day they still ostracize me and don't want anything to do with me. When I came home from the Army my dad tried to whip me and I beat the shit out of him. He never touched me again. He says the reason he never did was because I was the only one of the boys that ever stood up to him and he respected me for that. Coming from a dad that's quite a compliment. My dad was very shrewd. I was born and raised on a farm in Iowa.

I was the fastest runner in my family, which many times kept me from getting the shit stomped out of me. My dad was also a black belt in karate and he taught us all he knew when we were kids. He taught us when we were about ten. He'd use the handle from a toilet plunger to hit us quite often. To this day I have scars on my hips and on the back of my legs. He beat us until we bled. Both my parents did this; if one of us did something wrong all of us got beatings. For instance, I had been at Davenport, Iowa with my dad to pick up some supplies and had been working like a dog all day. Got back and Jack, my brother, was supposed to set the table that evening and my old man just got out the stick and started whaling away at everyone of us. It wasn't just the boys, it was the girls too, up to when they were late teenagers.

Question: *One of the things I'd like to have you cover is your relations with your peers in school.*

Fred: Well, I was what you'd call a pretty quiet fellow. I didn't date girls—girls were dirty. Mom always degraded the girl, but Dad gave us the car and money when we'd go out. I double-dated and would pick up girls in the pickup truck, but a girl I really liked and respected—well, I'd never tell my parents about her. There was never any sex play when I dated; I was afraid of intercourse. I was very sensitive and had mixed-up emotions; I thought I couldn't satisfy a woman. I had underdeveloped testicles and penis until the chief medical officer at prison gave me male hormones which helped me to have a more developed penis, but now it is a bit hyper, which presents problems. The advantages are that I now feel more relaxed with myself and trust myself. This new confidence was the thing that got me over this adverse type of thinking. I progressed to simple assaults on women rather than forcible assaults.

Question: *This was in the Army?*

Fred: Yes, before the Army I would kidnap the woman and pull her out in the sticks.

Question: *Did you have sexual intercourse with her?*

Fred: No, I didn't attain orgasm. This is the thing that really shook me up.

Question: *What did you do, pull their clothes off?*

Fred: Yeah, just pulled off their clothes and touched them and kissed their nipples. There were cases where we'd have oral copulation. At knife point she'd copulate me back and I still wouldn't have orgasm. I couldn't do anything and would just let them go.

Question: *Now was this still in a small town?*

Fred: Yes, this is still in a small town.

Question: *Well, how come you never got caught at it then?*

Fred: In a small town they never said anything.

Question: *But you'd still see these people.*

Fred: Yes, you'd see them every day. They kept their secret and I kept my secret with them. Because the virgin really doesn't want to talk about it—the way it was performed and what I made them do, they don't want to retell it in court. Sometimes there was a sexual overtone, an old girlfriend who jilted me or wives who didn't want to tell their husbands. I committed my first forcible rape when I got out of the service in Tempe, Arizona. I was standing at a bus stop, not hitchhiking, when a young woman about thirty-five picked me up. I pulled a knife on her, drove out in the desert about thirty miles, raped her forcibly, took her car and clothes and left her out there—120 degrees in the sun. I never felt any guilt about it for three years.

Question: *Did you ever find out what happened to her?*

Fred: Oh yeah, I've seen her since then. I told her there wasn't any way I could undo what I'd done to her and that the best thing for me to do was never let her see me again. Ever since then I've sent her a Christmas card, she sends me one, too, and now we're good friends. That was the first time I had orgasm . . . it felt pretty good.

Question: *I can't understand why you didn't earlier. Was it fear?*

Fred: I had a gross fear of sex—I was afraid to screw the women I was raping. It was many rapes until I got down to the nitty-gritty and did it. I now realize that the sex act itself is one of the most beautiful things in the relationship between a man and a woman. Not just that but the foreplay of the sex act, too. At twelve I started peeping on other women, especially exhibitionists.

Anyway, I progressed from that to simple assaults on women, reaching out and feeling their butt, run my hand up their legs. I was about thirteen, fourteen, fifteen at that time.

Question: *How many brothers do you have?*

Fred: Four brothers and two sisters. I don't know why they didn't progress like I did. I stayed home, was a mama's boy. I was very small and slender. I feel I can take care of myself. They were dating and I was not. I was very withdrawn and nobody gave a shit about me. I felt very inadequate, not able to associate with other people. My parents were very strict. They didn't seem to care what happened to me. Later on we'd hitchhike and feel up women. I'd take women out in the woods and strip them and just look, I couldn't have an orgasm; this shook me up pretty bad. My mother took me to a family doctor when I was about fifteen and found I had a slight case of large nipples. He poked around and made me feel very embarrassed and I ran out of his office crying. I hated my mother for this and didn't talk to her for a year.

In the Army I went to Ranger school, survival school and learned how to be very, very sneaky. We specialized in guerrilla warfare and I specialized in hand-to-hand combat. I was a bayonet instructor for four years. Taught judo and now have learned Kung Fu. This training has enabled me to trust and feel in control of myself. This is something I never felt before. I've been out of prison about seven months now and I've had no trouble functioning in all ways. I think and thoroughly feel like a real man. This to me is an important part of being a mature human being. The only one I feel has ever been a complete human being is Jesus.

I progressed from forcible assaults to forcible rapes. The first rape I committed was when I was twenty-three years old. It was the first time I attained an erection and experienced orgasm. Before this it always shook me up bad not to attain erection and have orgasm.

I've been in prison twice, four years each. The reason I went the second time was for a simple assault on my sister-in-law. My older brother is a Ph.D. in psychology and the night I assaulted his wife we sat and talked. He was my parole officer, by the way, which made it pretty rough at home. I was living with them and found myself falling in love with my sister-in-law. I felt pretty bad about this. In prison I kept getting in fights and they'd keep shipping me around. I lost this tooth in a fight. I learned to keep my mouth shut, pay attention to the therapy and talk about myself. Really started to learn about myself. I realized that if I wanted to be treated like a human being I had to start acting like a human being, not like an animal. I had also before assaulted my mother. I raped both my sisters and felt very guilty about it. I thought about suicide many times and tried to take my life once; hung myself and my eyes were starting to pop out when my mother found me. She cut me down and saved my life. She asked me why I did it and I told her to go screw herself, so she kicked me out of the house. I've never been back, for fifteen years. No one in my family will even talk to me. My mother pretty well controls the family but I love them all and miss them all. Those rapes on my sisters were the worst things I'd ever done. In 1960 I assaulted two police officers, ambushed them, broke their knees with a two by four. I was never convicted of that one. I pulled a few armed robberies and rapes simultaneously. Never was convicted. I went into a bank late in the afternoon when just a man and woman were there. I made the man lay down and I screwed the woman. They chased me all over town for fourteen hours before they caught me. They weren't sure I was the right guy 'cause I rubbed mercurochrome on my face and the camera film from the bank camera came out blurred. Forcible rape in Arizona calls for the death penalty, which is the gas chamber; I helped build the one in Arizona. Anyway, I was found not guilty for lack of evidence.

When I assaulted my sister-in-law I had intended to rape her but I just couldn't do it. I broke down and cried. She was very susceptible to rape. She was very open-minded, nothing shook her up. I told her the problems I was having with myself. As gross as it may sound, going to the joint was the best thing that ever happened to me. I have an AA degree and a BS in horticulture science. Got 'em in prison. In two weeks I'll begin work at [names firm] as a landscaping maintenance supervisor, paying $6.10 an hour, and that's a hell of a job. I love working with plants and have been able to channel my emotions constructively by growing plants.

I've been able to function as a man. In CMC, California Men's Colony, a doctor started giving me testosterone proof 100—100 milligrams of this hormone every two weeks. This male hormone is made from bulls' testicles. My testicles and penis are fully developed now and I'm able to function successfully and completely; it's a hell of a feeling. I feel like a human being again.

Question: *Did you continue with your sexual activities when you were in the service?*

Fred: Yes, I did. I committed an average of three rapes a week, never attaining orgasm until I got out of the Army, and that was in 1959.

Question: *Do you think that most of the Rangers and Green Berets that you knew were compensating for any sexual inadequacies they might have had?*

Fred: Well, most of my outfit were criminals or ex-cons. They were willing to serve in the Army to keep from going to prison, such as I did. I can't say really that there were any questionably masculine men in the Green Berets. I will say that most of the guys were always trying to prove something. We pulled some pretty vicious raids. We spent many a day in the stockade for some of the things we pulled.

Question: *I'd like to know how you can tell if women are susceptible to rape and how they respond.*

Fred: All right, I'd say most of the women that are susceptible to rape are pretty broadminded and pretty sexy. Sometimes a woman who tries to hide sexuality is very susceptible to rape. What she's really saying is, "I'm a woman but I'm not gonna let anybody know about it, but I dare you to find out." So you find that she is a woman and most of the time she's the best lay. A woman who's very broadminded such as you, and a few others in here that are smiling. This type of a woman tries to be nice to everybody and sometimes it comes out the wrong way. You sort of sense this. It's just a feeling you have. With me it was being familiar with women for so many years.

Question: *If you hadn't been successful in raping a woman do you ever think you would have gone as far as to kill the woman?*

Fred: Yes, the first time I went to prison I went to a mental institution in California. This is a maximum security hospital for sex offenders. I was there four years and eight months. The reason I went there was that I committed a rape in Arizona where I cut her nipple off with a knife. I had the knife under the nipple and she jerked away and cut it off. I thought then about killing her, but I didn't. I was deathly afraid of murder. I asked the court to send me to [the hospital]. I knew that if I killed somebody I would take my own life. I didn't want to do that. [The hospital] is a real hellhole.

Question: *How do you spot a developing sex offender?*

Fred: There's really no clear-cut way. A person who fights constantly for no particular reason, shoplifts, or runs away all the time. Likes to bully people. A person who wants to be noticed but goes about it in an assaulting way. I was in trouble in school all the time. We used to pull all kinds of tricks. I got kicked out of a typing class 'cause I dropped a typewriter on the teacher's toe.

Question: *You mentioned that you were in Alcoholics Anonymous because you were having a drinking problem. Why is this?*

Fred: Well, I was drunk a few times when I pulled my last crimes. I was drunk the night I assaulted my sister-in-law. My granddaddy had a still and I started drinking when I was a kid. It has aggravated my crimes. He was a great bootlegger, drunk all the time. He even used to give it to the babies. If you've ever seen a baby drunk it's as comical as all hell. It's pathetic, too. Liquor makes me sicker than a dog.

Question: *Are you married?*

Fred: No. Interested?

Question: *What provoked you to ambush the police officers?*

Fred: Well they accused me of something I didn't do; going 50 in a 35-mile zone. I was in reality going 25. They were drunk when they gave me the ticket. I defended myself and they were suspended for ninety days. The harassment really started after that. I was living up in Linda Vista at the time. There were sixteen cops living in a five-block area near my house, so relations weren't too friendly. I had a civil bond put on them which is when the courts say the law or police can't mess with somebody. They kept it up though. I went to each of their houses one night and told them to quit it, to get screwed. It got worse after that. About two weeks after that I ambushed them on two separate occasions. I spent about four hours apiece on them, really worked them over. One of them I saw about three days later at the police station when I went to reregister my change of address.

During one rape a woman actually thanked me. How about that? But then there were times when they called me every kind of name. That's okay, I'm a crazy bastard but I'm at least enjoying myself. Average age was about twenty-five. For instance a woman picked me up at the bus station when I was waiting for a ride to Phoenix; this is the same one that writes me Christmas cards. I pulled a knife on her. She had a low-cut summer dress on, no bra or panties. Her nipples were up at this time so I knew she was sexually excited. She looked like she just came from being seduced. She was still sweating, hair matted down and kind of messed up. Her bra and panties were laying in the back seat so I don't know where she'd been. She was thirty-five years old, married with a daughter thirteen years old. I pulled a knife on her and she said, "What do you want, the car?" and I said, "Yeah, among other things." "I don't have any money; do you want sex?" she said. I told her I was gonna rip her off. She said she'd let me. I put the knife down on the seat and never took it out again until we got out on the desert. I raped her out on an Indian reservation which made it a Federal crime; kidnap and rape. When we got out there she told me her husband was an invalid in a wheelchair and I undressed her in the car as we were driving along. She didn't have a stitch on as we went down that freeway; people would drive by and really stare. Even though she was willing, because a knife was involved it makes it forcible. All you have to do is indicate that you have a weapon and it makes it forcible.

Question: *Did she report you?*

Fred: No, I got caught on another attempted rape about two weeks later. That's the one where I beat up the woman and accidentally cut off her nipple. I got shook up and told her I was gonna kill her. Cut her a few more times on the breast and in the pubic area. Then I decided I wasn't gonna kill her. She was down on her hands and knees looking for her nipple, said she was gonna put it back on. She was crying and carrying on about it so I just took her clothes and left her there. Ditched her car later. There was an article in the paper about a car being stolen but nothing about the assault at all.

I don't know how she got home, but I saw her about two weeks later and she was still blistered up bad. We later became very good friends. At that time I didn't give a damn whether she lived or died. I would've preferred that she died 'cause it would've left me clear. By the way, I wore disposable gloves every time I pulled a rape. No prints.

Question: *If you had a choice between a passive and aggressive woman, who would you rape?*

Fred: Probably the passive one first. The aggressive one would be second choice. I'd be reluctant to rape the aggressive one because I want control of the situation unlike the way it was at home. There I was pretty much the scapegoat. The best thing to do if you get raped is to go along with it and let the man rape you. Those that get murdered usually resist. The more violent you resist, the more violent the attacker becomes.

Question: *Have you ever had a girlfriend?*

Fred: Yes, When I was nineteen I was going to get married. I was home on a forty-eight-hour leave from the Army to get married and the day before the wedding my fiancee got killed. If she was alive today I'd marry her. . . .

Question: *Did you love your fiancee?*

Fred: I loved her very much. If she was alive today I'd marry her. She was the only girl my mother ever approved of, too. . . .

VII
Kinky Sex

Kinky sex, or just plain "kink," has been with us for centuries. Descriptions of unusual sexual practices abounded in ancient Greek and Roman times; even Victorian England produced novels and autobiographical accounts—usually published anonymously or under a pseudonym—of sadism, masochism, flagellation, fetishes, fixations, exhibitionism, voyeurism, and pedophilia and pederasty. "Kinky" and "kink" are words which were used, until a few years ago, mostly by British prostitutes to describe sexual acts requested by their clients which were extremely unusual and bizarre, and for which their clients paid considerably more than the usual fare. Now the terms have common currency among the public. This is in part due to the fact that what was shameful a few years ago has become almost respectable today. Acts which a sexual partner would consent to perform only if paid ten years ago are now standard fare in our most popular sex and marriage manuals. Consider the following suggestions, offered in a section entitled "Sauces and Pickles for Special Occasions" in *The Joy of Sex,* by Alex Comfort, a book which appeared on all best-seller lists between 1972 and 1974:

"Leather: Probably the most popular super-skin turn-on. . . . Some men like women encased in it. . . . This is one object turn-on which women respond to as well as men . . . (p. 197).

"Masks: These excite some people: if this seems odd, remember that they are the oldest human device for getting mystical as well as sexual inspiration, by making the wearer menacing, other than themselves, and 'possessed' by the mask . . . (p. 197).

355

"Boots: Notorious turn-on for many people—the longer the
            better. Complicated symbolism here involving ag-
            gression (jackboots and so on), phallicism and fe-
            male lower extremity. Used to be the badge of the
            prostitute . . . (p. 172).

"Armpit: Axillary intercourse in an occasional variation.
            Handle . . . with your penis under her right
            arm. . . . Not an outstandingly rewarding trick
            but worth trying if you like the idea (pp. 158, 159).

"Bondage: Bondage . . . is the gentle art of tying up your
            sex partner—not to overcome reluctance but to
            boost orgasm. It's one unscheduled sex technique
            which a lot of people find extremely exciting but
            are scared to try, and a venerable human resource
            for increasing sexual feeling. . . . Games of this
            sort are an occasional optional extra to all sorts of
            sex-play and intercourse, since the tied partner can
            be kissed, masturbated, ridden, or simply teased to
            orgasm . . . (pp. 165, 167)."

One of the largest-circulation magazines in the country, *Pent-house*, publishes in each issue a number of letters from readers describing their kinky sexual practices. (A sibling publication of *Penthouse, Forum*, devotes many pages to such letters.) Here are a few:

For my husband (a superstrong construction man who can deliver a strong wallop) and me, spankings have been an addition to our love-making for the four years of our marriage. . . . We have a little paddle . . . hanging in the den. . . . He puts me on his knee, pulls down my panties, keeps one hand feeling my cunt, the other slamming my ass. No matter how long or hard I get it like that I love every second . . . (December 1973).

For the shoe and foot fetishist, my husband has an erotic fantasy which involves me. It's the sexiest foreplay I've ever known. He ties me up on the floor, stretching me out. I'm nude except for red, three-inch spike-heeled shoes. After teasing my clitoris with his tongue for a few minutes, he removes my shoes. Then, with his fingers or with some soft feathers, he tickles my feet (a little sadistically), especially on my soles, and between my toes, for up to half an hour. My feet are highly ticklish, but this is a pleasurable punishment to endure. It drives me crazy, but nothing gets me hotter (July 1973).

While spending a hot summer day in upstate New York . . . I suggested to my girlfriend that we completely undress and feel the cool breeze against our hot bodies while cruising on my motorcycle. . . . A little later that day, I told my chick to sit on the gas tank and bend over. I sat behind her . . . and stuck my penis into her asshole while downshifting to second gear. As we came around a bend in the road, we were pulled over by a state trooper who forced my chick to blow him or he would arrest us for sodomy (September 1973).

What is remarkable about these experiences from *Penthouse* readers, and the suggestions in *The Joy of Sex,* is not that they occur, but that they are respectable enough to a large enough group of people to be given mass circulation. (The letter writers, it might be qualified, usually prefer to remain anonymous.) What is or is not considered kinky has undergone, and will continue to undergo, transformation. Several generations ago, anything but face-to-face, male-above, marital, genital intercourse was considered abnormal, perverse and kinky by respectable people. Only half a century ago, physicians warned of the pathological effects of the "perverted lusts" of cunnilingus and fellatio. The couple marrying today that does not take part in these practices is statistically in the deviant minority. It was not long ago in historical time that a man who wished fellatio to be performed on him had to seek the services of a prostitute. What was once kinky has become routine, and is now considered normal, natural, and healthy. The shifting definition as to what is kinky and "perverted" also points to another major point: *it is impossible to draw a clear-cut line between kinky and "normal" sex.* Sexual behavior forms a kind of spectrum, from acts which are widespread, and which nearly everyone would think of as normal, all the way over to behavior rarely practiced which nearly everyone would feel is bizarre and perverted. Acts can't be neatly pigeonholed into kinky and normal. One act shades over into another; there are *degrees* of kinkiness.

What's the difference between kinky sex and "perversions"? Kink is a popular, nontechnical term; perversion is both a popular and a psychiatric term. Used by the man and woman in the street, a perversion can be any sexual act that the person using the term doesn't like. While psychiatrists do not agree completely as to what acts are perversions, they are far less generous today in applying the term. While in an earlier historical era, *specific acts* were termed perversions, today the term is usually applied to *patterns* of behavior rather than to isolated acts. Thus, to engage in one single instance, say, of anal intercourse, would not qualify, but if that were the *exclusive* mode of intercourse, then it would be seen by most psychiatrists as a perversion. The following rules appear to be used by the psychiatric profession in determining what forms of behavior are to be considered perversions:

(1) if they are practiced to the exclusion of heterosexual coitus; or

(2) if one partner, or both partners, are physically injured in the sex act, and if this was the motivating goal of one or both partners; or

(3) if nonhumans, the dead or the prepubescent are the sexual object; or

(4) if the sexual behavior involves a fetish, a fixation or a partialism so powerful and obsessive that intercourse cannot be achieved without it.

Kinky sex encompasses a much broader area of human behavior; the exact boundaries cannot be delineated with much accuracy. Wherever we draw the line between kink and ordinary sex would be arbitrary. Kink is in the eyes of the beholder. While all psychiatric perversions are kinky, not all kink would qualify as a perversion. First of all, specific acts may be termed kinky. To engage in bondage once a month with your spouse would be to engage in kinky sex, at least today—but almost no psychiatrist would call that a perversion. It is "normal" but not *ordinary* sex. Perhaps kink is simply that which strays a fairly great distance from ordinary, routine, everyday sex; kinky sex is *unusual* sex. But in addition, there is the element of the *forbidden* as well: kink breaks outside the boundaries of propriety. It is sex with a dash of evil and decadence.

Which leads us to another point: *The smaller the deviation from what is considered normal, the more common the behavior is; the "kinkier" the sexual act, the rarer it is.* Perversions do not form a clinical entity, magically removed from the parent body of common sexual behavior. The cases of baby rapes, "lust murders," necrophilia (intercourse with human corpses), and so on described in psychiatric textbooks are a statistically minute fragment of unusual sexual practices. They represent the polar extreme of a tendency that exists *in miniature* in us all. But in most of us, our deviation from the norm is small. The greater the distance from what is considered ordinary sex, the greater the likelihood that a given form of sexual behavior

will be called a perversion, the less frequently it has to be repeated
to be termed a perversion, and the rarer it will be practiced. On the
other hand, plain old kinky sex, in its milder forms, will always be
with us in abundance.

To sum things up, then: kink is statistically unusual sex which
is exciting because it is unusual, bizarre, forbidden, or immoral, and
which is desired by the participants for that very reason. A *partialism*
is usually defined as the strong erotic desire toward an unusual and
highly specific nongenital part of one's partner's body: the hair, the
feet, perhaps the armpits, etc. A *fetish* is a fixation on an inanimate
object—silk, fur, rubber, overcoats, undergarments, and so on.
Sometimes the term "fetish" is used to indicate any unusual sexual
practice. Often, erotic desires run toward some highly specific sexual
routine, such as bondage, sadomasochism, exhibitionistic sex. It is
not uncommon for sexual excitation to occur toward objects, acts,
or partners which do not excite most people. Most people, for instance, would feel disgust at the thought of receiving an enema. As
one of the selections which follows indicates, some actually seek out
enemas—and become intensely aroused by them sexually. Often it is
the choice of *partner* which determines that an activity is "kinky."
Disfigured men or women are not sexually exciting to most of us—
but some people do have strong desires specifically toward the
physically disfigured. The desire to have intercourse with prepubescent children has probably entered the mind of most of us, but only
a statistically minuscule proportion of us ever act on this thought.
Some sex is kinky because of the *situation* in which it occurs. To
haxe sex in public probably qualifies as "kinky"; certainly, exhibitionism is among one of the many psychiatric "perversions."

Kinks, fetishisms, partialisms, or fixations can be divided, more
or less, into three types. First, they may be "an erotic stimulus to
sexual intercourse," to quote Eustace Chesser, author of *Strange
Loves: The Human Aspects of Sexual Deviation.* That is, kink would
be any unusual sexual practice which spices up, and is an enhancer
of and adjunct to, ordinary sexual intercourse. This is by far the
most common type of kink. It is the type recommended in *The Joy
of Sex.* Mild bondage scenes, for instance, make the sex lives of many
married couples a little more interesting and exciting. Occasional
"swinging" will sometimes make one's partner more desirable, one's
sex life a bit more exotic.

Or kink can be a *standard fixture* of intercourse: that is, it is impossible for one or both partners to become aroused without the kinky aspect, and it is *always* present during intercourse.

The third type of kink is when it becomes a *substitute* for intercourse. A man masturbates while wearing a woman's girdle, and never engages in intercourse. Or a man ejaculates at the mere sight of a woman clad in feathers. This type is the most unusual statistically, but it has always attracted the attention of psychiatrists— in part, because this type has caused the most trouble and concern, whereas the others have remained more or less hidden.

Kinky sex is instructive for a number of reasons, but sociologically, the most interesting is the point with which we opened the book: sexual arousal and behavior are not dictated by mere body plus hormones, plus another body, plus opposite-sex hormones. Sex is symbolic, and the richness of another person's symbolic life cannot be predicted with commonsense information. What turns someone on is not "rational"—whether the agent be a diamond ring, a foot, the ability to love deeply, a brilliant mind, or an ample bosom. In the first chapter, we presented the sexual customs of the people of Mangaia. Mangaian males are completely unconcerned with the female breast; what turns them on is the mons veneris—the pad of fatty tissue in the pubic area. As Donald Marshall writes:

> The Mangaian is completely flabbergasted at the American and European male's interest in the female breast, for the Polynesian considers this organ to be of interest only to a hungry baby. Yet, the Mangaian male is as fully concerned with the size, shape, and consistency of the mons Veneris as is the American male with the size, shape, and consistency of the female bust.

The point is, if sexual behavior and the agent of sexual arousal vary so enormously from one civilization to another, why can't they vary from one person to another in the same civilization?

The Marquis de Sade put it in the following words:

> Objects have no value for us save that which our imagination imparts to them; it is therefore very possible . . . that not only the most curious but even the vilest and most appalling things may affect us very appreciably. The human imagination is a faculty of man's mind whereupon . . . objects are painted, . . . modified, and . . . ideas become formed, all in reason of the initial glimpsing of those external objects. But this imagination is itself resultative of the kind

of organization man is endowed with, and only adopts the received objects in such-and-such a manner. . . . It should not by any means be cause for astonishment that what distinctly pleases some is able to displease others, and, conversely, that the most extraordinary thing is able to find admirers.

Armed with this insight—that sexual excitation originates not in the object of excitation, but in the mind—we can, perhaps, better understand sexual practices which seemed puzzling and bizarre to us previously.

Kink is, of course, a matter of degree. Perhaps the mildest and least unusual of all kinky practices—and for some, not in the least bit kinky—is swinging. Swinging is a turn-on to many couples because they think of it as naughty and far-out. It typically comes about as a means of institutionalizing and containing marital infidelity. During the first few episodes—and most couples do not continue swinging beyond the first few times—it is experienced as somewhat kinky. A kind of privatized exhibitionism is legitimated, perhaps an orgy takes place, the thought or the sight of one's spouse making love to someone else, often a stranger, are all titillating to many men and women.

The many letters to the magazine *Forum* from its readers have been collected into a book, *The Sex-Life Letters*. Most of them describe sexual practices that would qualify by almost any definition as kinky. Aside from the surprising revelation that the activities described excite some people sexually, perhaps the most instructive lesson to be gained from reading them is that many ordinary, respectable men and women engage in these activities. They do not become, in the typical case, labeled as deviants. Their practices usually do not harm anyone, including themselves. Kink, even kinky practices that seem bizarre, is not as unusual as most of us think. People are beginning to act on their sexual fantasies. Where this is taking us it is difficult to say, but the phenomenon is there, and we must be aware of its existence.

Pederasty, or pedophilia, is the strong erotic attraction to young children. Some men—and this condition seems to be overwhelmingly characteristic of men—can achieve erection only with children, while others include children among their other sex objects. The "child molester" is one of the most feared and despised of all practitioners of deviant behavior. Many pederasts are interested exclusively in young boys. Most do not attempt or achieve intercourse, but are satisfied with fondling. Some are only technically "child molesters," because of the slippery nature of definitions: after all, the age of consent is eighteen in some jurisdictions, fourteen in others, and so on. To say that an adolescent is not a legitimate sexual object for arousal, but an adult is, does not hide the fact that many adolescents are sexually desirable. Some men, on the other hand, are interested specifically in children, and lose interest as they mature. (Lewis Carroll, author of *Alice in Wonderland,* was just such a man; his passion was for photographing prepubescent English girls in the nude, although there is no indication that he ever approached any of them sexually.) It is doubtful that the scorn heaped upon them is warranted. It is our job to understand them.

———◆———

Charles and Rebecca Palson are anthropologists; they are writing a book on sex entitled *Friends and Lovers: A Study in the Use and Meaning of Sex.* Harold Greenwald is a psychoanalyst and the author of a number of books on sexual behavior, including *The Elegant Prostitute* and *The Call Girl.* Ruth Greenwald is a social worker, marriage counselor and psychotherapist, and co-editor, with her husband, of *The Sex-Life Letters.* Parker Rossman was, until 1972, dean of the Ecumenical Continuing Education Center at Yale. He is now engaged in writing a novel and a book on pederasts.

Swinging in Wedlock
by *Charles Palson and*
Rebecca Palson

Since the later 1960s, an increasing number of middle-class couples have turned to mate swapping or "swinging" as an alternative to strictly monogamous marriage. That is, married couples (or unmarried couples with an apparently stable relationship) willingly and knowingly relinquish sexual rights to their own mates so that others may temporarily enjoy these rights. This phenomenon, which is fairly recent in its openness and proportions, provides an opportunity of testing, on a large scale, the traditional theories about the consequences of extramarital sexual activity. It has often been assumed that sexual infidelity, where all the concerned parties know of it, results to some degree in jealousy. The intensity of jealousy is thought to increase in proportion to the amount of real or imagined emotional involvement on the part of the unfaithful member of the couple. Conversely, the more "purely physical" the infidelity, the less likely that there will be any jealousy. Thus it is often hypothesized that where marital stability coexists with infidelity, the character of the extramarital involvement is relatively depersonalized.

In the film *Bob and Carol and Ted and Alice*, Bob finds Carol, his wife, entertaining another man in their bedroom. Although he had previously told her that he was having an affair, and they had agreed in principle that she too could have affairs, he is obviously shaken by the reality. Nervously trying to reassure himself, he asks, "Well, it's just *sex*, isn't it? I mean, you don't *love* him?" In other words, Bob attempts to avoid feelings of jealousy by believing that

Carol's affair involves only depersonalized sex in contrast to their own relationship of love.

In the book, *Group Sex,* Gilbert Bartell offers the same hypothesis about those people he calls "organization swingers":

> They are terrified of the idea that involvement might take place. They take comfort from the fact that if they swing with a couple only once or at most twice, the chances of running into a marriage-threatening involvement are small.

These swingers, who can be described as organizational only in the sense that they tend to use swinger magazines or special swinging nightclubs to make their contacts, are mostly beginners who *may* act in ways that approximate Bartell's description. Near the end of the book, however, he mentions some couples he interviewed whom he calls dropouts. These people either had never desired depersonalized swinging or had passed through a depersonalized stage but now preferred some degree of emotional involvement and long-term friendship from their swinging relationships. Bartell does not explain how these couples continue to keep stable relationships and and can remain free of jealousy, but the fact that such couples exist indicates that depersonalization is not the only way to jealousy-free swinging.

Our involvement with the subject has been partly a personal one, and this requires some introductory explanation. In September 1969, we read an article about swinging and became fascinated by the questions it raised about sex and the American family. Did this practice signal the beginning of the breakup of the family? Or was it a way to inject new life into marriage as the authors of the article suggested? How do people go about swinging and why? We contemplated these and many other questions but, not knowing any swingers, we could arrive at only very limited answers. It seemed to us that the only way to find out what we wanted to know was to participate ourselves. In one way this seemed natural because anthropologists have traditionally lived with the people they have studied. But our curiosity about swinging at that time was more personal than professional, and we knew that ultimately our participation would have personal consequences, although we had no idea what their nature might be. We had to decide whether exploration of this particular unknown was worth the risk of changing the perfectly sound and gratifying relationship which we had built during the previous three-and-a-half years. Finally, our misgivings gave way to curiosity and we wrote off to some couples who advertised in a national swingers' magazine.

Although, like most beginners, we were excited about swinging, we were nervous too. We didn't know what swinging in reality was like or what "rules" there were, if any. In general, however, we found those first experiences not only enjoyable from a personal point of view, but stimulating intellectually. It was then that we decided to study swinging as anthropologists. But, like many anthropologists who use participant observation as a method of study, we could never completely divorce ourselves from the personal aspects of our subject.

The method of participant observation is sometimes criticized as being too subjective. In an area such as sex, where experiences are highly individual and personal, we feel that participant observation can yield results even more thorough and disciplined than the more so-called objective methods. Most of our important insights into the nature of swinging could only have been found by actually experiencing some of the same things that our informants did. Had we not participated, we would not have known how to question them about many central aspects of their experience.

This article presents the results of our 18-month, participant observation study of 136 swingers. We made our contacts in three ways. First, we reached couples through swinger magazines. These are magazines devoted almost exclusively to ads placed by swingers for the purpose of contacting other interested couples and/or singles. Many, although not all, of the couples we contacted in this way seemed to be beginners who had not yet found people with whom they were interested in forming long-term relationships. Second, we were introduced to couples through personal networks. Couples whom we knew would pass our name on to others, sometimes explicitly because they wanted our study to be a success. Third, some couples contacted us as a result of lectures or papers we presented, to volunteer themselves as informants. It should be noted that we did not investigate the swingers' bars, although second-hand reports from couples we met who had used them for making contacts seem to indicate that these couples did not significantly differ from those who do not use the bars. Our informants came from Pennsylvania,

New Jersey, New York, Massachusetts, Louisiana, California, Florida and Illinois. They were mostly middle class, although ten could be classified as working class.

Usually we interviewed couples in very informal settings, and these interviews were often indistinguishable from ordinary conversation that swingers might have about themselves and their activities. After each session we would return home, discuss the conversation and write notes on our observations. Later several couples volunteered to tape interviews, enabling us to check the accuracy of the field notes we had taken previously.

In spite of our efforts to find informants from as many different sources as possible, we can in no way guarantee the representativeness of our sample. It should be emphasized that statistics are practically useless in the study of swingers because of insurmountable sampling problems. We therefore avoided the statistical approach and instead focused the investigation on problems of a nonstatistical nature. The information we obtained enabled us to understand and describe the kinds of cultural symbols—a "symbolic calculus," if you will—that swingers must use to effectively navigate social situations with other swingers. This symbolic calculus organizes widely varying experiences into a coherent whole, enabling swingers to understand and evaluate each social situation in which they find themselves. They can thereby define the choices available to them and the desirability of each. Our research goal, then, was to describe the symbols that infuse meaning into the experiences of all the swingers that we contacted.

Unlike Bartell, we had no difficulty finding couples who either wanted to have or had succeeded in having some degree of emotional involvement and long-term friendship within a swinging context. In fact, many of them explained to us that depersonalization simply brought them no satisfaction. In observing such couples with their friends it was evident that they had formed close and enduring relationships. They host each other's children on weekends, celebrate birthdays together, take vacations together and, in general, do what close friends usually do. It should be noted that there is no way of ascertaining the numbers of couples who have actually succeeded in finding close friends through swinging. In fact, they may be underrepresented because they tend to retreat into their own small circle of friends and dislike using swinger magazines to find other couples. Thus they are more difficult to contact.

In order to see how swingers are able to form such relationships it is necessary to understand not how they avoid jealousy, but how they deal with its causes. Insecurity and fear of being replaced are the major ingredients in any experience with jealousy. An effective defense against jealousy, then, would include a way to guarantee one's irreplaceability as a mate. If, for example, a wife knows that she is unlike any other woman her husband has ever met or ever will meet, and if they have a satisfying relationship in which they have invested much time and emotion, she can rest assured that no other relationship her husband has can threaten her. If, on the other hand, a woman feels that the continuance of her marital relationship depends on how well she cooks, cleans and makes love, jealousy is more likely to occur, because she realizes that any number of women could fill the same role, perhaps better than she.

Similarly, a man who feels that the continuance of his wife's loyalty depends on how well he provides financial security will be apt to feel more jealousy because many men could perform the same function. To one degree or another, many swingers naturally develop towards a more secure kind of marital relationship, a tendency we call *individuation*. Among the couples we contacted, individuation was achieved for the most part at a level that precluded jealousy. And we found that, to the extent that couples did not individuate, either jealousy occurred or swinging had to take other, less flexible forms in order to prevent it.

We found evidence of individuation in two areas. First, we found that patterns of behavior at gatherings of swingers who had passed the beginning stages were thoroughly pervaded by individuation. Second, we found that by following changes in a couple's attitudes toward themselves, both as individuals and as a couple and toward other swingers, a trend of increasing individuation could be observed.

INDIVIDUATING BEHAVIOR AT GATHERINGS

When we first entered the swinging scene, we hypothesized that swinging must be characterized by a set of implicit and explicit rules or patterns of behavior. But every time we thought we had discovered a pattern, another encounter quickly invalidated it. We finally had to conclude that any particular swinging gathering is characterized by any one of a number of forms, whatever best suits the individuals involved. The ideal, as in nonswinging situations, is for the initiation of sexual interaction to appear to develop naturally—preferably in a nonverbal way. But with four or more people involved and all the signaling and cross-signaling of intentions that must take place, this ideal can only be approached in most cases. The initiation may begin with little or no socializing, much socializing with sex later on as a natural outgrowth of the good feelings thus created, or some mixture in-between. Socializing is of the variety found at many types of nonswinging gatherings. The sexual interaction itself may be "open" where couples participate in the same room or "closet" where couples pair off in separate rooms. In open swinging, a "pretzel," "flesh pile" or "scene" may take place, all terms which signify groups of more than two people having sex with each other. Like Bartell, we found that females are much more likely to participate in homosexuality—probably near 100 percent—while very few men participate in homosexuality. Younger people tend to be much more accepting about the latter.

All of this flexibility can be summed up by saying that swingers consider an ideal gathering one in which everyone can express themselves as individuals *and* appreciate others for doing the same. If even one person fails to have an enjoyable experience in these terms, the gathering is that much less enjoyable for everyone.

An important consequence of this "do your own thing" ethic is that sexual experiences are talked about as a primarily personal matter. Conversely they are not evaluated according to a general standard. Thus one hears about "bad experiences" rather than "bad swingers." This is not to say that swingers are not aware of general sexual competence, but only that it is largely irrelevant to their appreciation of other people. As one informant said:

> Technique is not that much. If she's all right, I don't care if she's technically terrible—if I think she's a beautiful person, she can't be that bad.

Beginners may make certain mistakes if they do not individuate. They may, for example, take on the "social director" role. This kind of person insists that a party become the materialization of his own fantasies without regard for anyone else's wishes. This can make the situation very uncomfortable for everyone else unless someone can get him to stop. Or, a nervous beginner may feel compelled to look around to find out what to do and, as a result, will imitate someone else. This imitation can be disturbing to others for two reasons. First, the imitator may not be enjoying himself. Second, he may be competing with someone else by comparing the effects of the same activity on their different partners. In either case, he is not involved with perceiving and satisfying the individual needs of his own partner. This would also be true in the case of the person who regularly imitates his or her own previous behavior, making an unchanging formula for interaction, no matter whom he is with. Swingers generally consider such behavior insensitive and/or insincere.

MODIFICATION OF ATTITUDES

Beginners tend to approximate the popular stereotype of sex-starved deviates. A 50-year-old woman described one of her beginning experiences this way:

> It was one after another, and really, after a point it didn't make any difference *who* it was. It was just one great big prick after another. And I *never* experienced anything like that in my whole life. I have never had an experience like that with quite so many. I think in the course of three hours I must have had 11 or 12 men, and one greater than the next. It just kept on getting better every time. It snowballed.

The manner in which she describes her experience exemplifies the attitudes of both male and female beginners. They are not likely to develop a long-lasting friendship with one or a small number of couples, and they focus much more on sex than the personalities involved. Frequently, they will be more interested in larger parties where individual personality differences are blurred by the number of people.

Simple curiosity seems to be the reason for this attitude. As one beginner told us, "Sometimes, we get titillated with them as people, knowing in the long run that it won't work out." It seems that because the beginner has been prevented so often from satisfying his curiosity through sexual liaisons in "straight" life, an important goal of early swinging is to satisfy this curiosity about people in general. This goal is apt to take precedence over any other for quite some time. Thus, even if a couple sincerely hopes to find long-lasting friendships, their desire to "move on" is apt to win out at first.

Bartell has asserted that both personality shallowness and jealousy are always responsible for this focus on sex and the search for new faces. For the most part, neither of these factors is necessarily responsible. First, the very same couples who appear shallow in fact may develop friendships later on. Second, as we shall see below, some couples who focus almost exclusively on sex nevertheless experience jealousy and must take certain precautions. On the other hand, some swingers *do* couple-hop because of jealousy. The Races, for example, dislike swinging with a couple more than once or twice because of the jealousy that arises each time. Very often only one member is jealous of the other's involvement but the jealousy will be hidden. Pride may prevent each from admitting jealousy for quite some time. Each partner may feel that to admit jealousy would be to admit a weakness and instead will feign disinterest in a particular couple to avoid another meeting.

This stage of swinging eventually stops in almost all cases we know of, probably because the superficial curiosity about people in general is satisfied. Women are usually responsible for the change, probably because they have been raised to reject superficial sexual relationships. Sometimes this is precipitated by a bad experience when, for example, a man is particularly rough or inconsiderate in some way. Sometimes a man will be the first to suggest a change because of erection problems which seem to be caused in some cases by a general lack of interest in superficial sexual contacts. In other words, once his general curiosity is satisfied, he can no longer sustain enough interest to be aroused.

The termination of the curiosity stage and the beginning of a stage of relative selectivity is characterized by increasing individuation of self and others. Among men this change manifests itself in the nature of fantasies that give interest to the sexual experience. The statement of one male informant exemplifies the change:

> Now, I don't fantasize much. There's too much reality to fantasize, too much sex and sex realities we've experienced. So there is not too much that I *can* fantasize with. I just remember the good times we've actually had.

Instead of fantasies being what one would wish to happen, they are instead a kind of reliving of pleasant past experiences with particular people. Also, some informants have noticed that where their previous fantasies had been impersonal, they eventually became tied to specific people with whom pleasant sexual experiences had been shared.

Increasing individuation is also noticeable in beginners' changing perceptions of certain problems that arise in swinging situations. Many male swingers have difficulty with erections at one time or another. Initially, this can be quite ego shattering. The reason for this trauma is not difficult to understand. Most Americans believe that the mere sight of a nude, sexually available woman should arouse a man almost instantly. A male who fails to be aroused may interpret this as a sign of his hitherto unknown impotency. But if he is not too discouraged by this first experience he may eventually find the real reasons. He may realize that he does not find some women attractive mentally and/or physically even though they are sexually available. He learns to recognize when he is being deliberately though subtly discouraged by a woman. He may discover that he dislikes certain situational factors. For example, he may find that he likes only open or only closet swinging or that he cannot relax sufficiently to perform after a hard day's work. Once a swinger realizes that his physical responses may very well be due to elements that inhere to the individual relationship rather than to an innate sexual inadequacy, he has arrived at a very different conception of sexual relationships. He is better able to see women as human beings to whom he may be attracted as personalities rather than as objects to be exploited for their sexual potential. In our terms, he can now more successfully individuate his relationships with women.

Women must cope with problems of a slightly different nature when they begin to swing. Their difficulties develop mostly because of their tendency to place decorum above the expression of their own individual desires in social situations. This tendency manifests itself from the time the husband suggests swinging. Many women seem to swing merely because their husbands want to rather than because of their own positive feelings on the matter. This should not be interpreted to mean that wives participate against their will, but only that as in most recreational activity, the male provides the initial impetus that she can then choose to go along with or reject. Her lack of positive initiative may express itself in the quality of her interaction. She is apt to swing with a man not because he manifests particular attributes that she appreciates, but because he lacks any traits that she finds outright objectionable. One woman describes one of her first experiences this way:

As I recall, I did not find him particularly appealing, but he was nice, and that was OK. He actually embarrassed me a bit because he was so shy and such a kind of nonperson.

This is not to say that women do not enjoy their experiences once they begin participating. The same woman remarks about her first experience in this way:

Somehow, it was the situation that made the demand. I got turned on, although I hadn't anticipated a thing up to that point. In fact, I still have a hard time accounting for my excitement that first time and the good time which I did actually have.

In fact, it sometimes happens at this stage that women become more enthusiastic about swinging than men, much to the latter's embarrassment.

Their enjoyment, however, seems to result from the same kind of psychology that is likely to propel them into swinging in the first place, the desire to please men. Hence, like her nonswinging counterparts, a woman in swinging will judge herself in terms of her desirability and her attractiveness to men much more than thinking about her own individuality in relation to others.

After swinging for awhile, however, her wish to be desired and to satisfy can no longer be as generalized because it becomes apparent that she is indeed desired by many men, and thus she has no need to prove it to herself. In order to make the experience meaningful, she arrives at a point where she feels that she must begin to actually refuse the advances of many men. This means that she must learn to define her own preferences more clearly and to learn to act on these preferences, an experience that many women rarely have because they have learned to rely on their husbands to make these kinds of decisions in social situations. In short, a woman learns to individuate both herself and others in the second stage of swinging.

Another change that swingers mention concerns their feelings towards their mates. They say that since they started swinging they communicate better than they did before. Such couples, who previously had a stable but uninteresting or stale marriage ("like brother and sister without the blood"), say that swinging has recreated the romantic feelings they once had for each other. These feelings seem to find concrete expression in an increasing satisfaction with the sexual aspects of the marital relationship, if not in an actual increase in sexual intercourse. This is almost always experienced by older couples in terms of feeling younger.

An explanation for this change, again, involves the individuation process. Marriage can grow stale if a couple loses a sense of appreciation of each other's individuality. A husband may look too much like an ordinary husband, a wife like an ordinary wife. This can happen easily especially when a couple's circumstances (job, children and so forth) necessitate a great deal of routinization of their life together. Such couples find in swinging the rare opportunity to escape from the routine roles that must be assumed in everyday life. In this setting individual differences receive attention and appreciation and, because of this, married couples can again see and appreciate their own distinct individuality, thus reactivating their romantic feelings for each other.

It is interesting to note that, those couples who do not answer in this way almost always experience jealousy, not romanticization, as a result of swinging. This is the case with one couple we interviewed, each of whom insists that the other is "better than anyone else," although it was clear by their jealousy of each other that neither was entirely confident of this.

Individuation, then, pervades the swinging scene and plays an important role in minimizing jealousy. But it alone cannot guarantee the control of jealousy—because there is always the possibility that a person will appreciate and be equally attracted to two unique individuals. Clearly, individuation must be complemented with something more if the marriage is to be effectively distinguished from other extramarital relationships.

This "something else" is compatibility. Two individuals who perceive and appreciate each other's individuality may nevertheless make poor living mates unless they are compatible. Compatibility is a kind of superindividuation. It requires not only the perception and appreciation of uniqueness, but the inclusion of this in the solutions to any problems that confront the relationship. Each partner must have the willingness and the ability to consider his or her mate's needs, desires and attitudes, when making the basic decisions that affect them both. This is viewed as something that people must work to achieve, as indicated by the phrase, "He failed in his marriage."

Unlike swinging, then, marriage requires a great deal of day-to-day giving and taking, and an emotional investment that increases with the years. Because such an investment is not given up easily, it provides another important safeguard against jealousy.

The dimension of marital compatibility often shows itself in swinging situations. If and when serious problems are encountered by one marriage partner, it is expected that the other partner will take primary responsibility for doing what is necessary. One couple, for example, was at a gathering, each sitting with their swinging partners. It was the first time they had ever tried pot, and the wife suddenly became hysterical. The man she was with quickly relinquished his place to her husband, who was expected to take primary responsibility for comforting his wife, although everyone was concerned about her. Another example can occur when a man has erection problems. If he is obviously miserable, it is considered wrong for his wife to ignore his condition, although we have heard of a few cases where this has happened. His wife may go to his side and they will decide to go home or she may simply act worried and less than completely enthusiastic, thus evincing some minimal concern for her husband. In other words, the married couple is still distinguished as the most compatible partners and remains therefore the primary problem-solving unit.

The importance of compatibility also shows up in certain situations where a couple decides that they must stop swinging. In several cases reported to us, couples who had been married two years or less found that swinging tended to disrupt their marital relationship. We ourselves encountered three couples who had been married for under one year and had not lived together before marriage. All three had difficulties as a result of swinging, and one is now divorced. These couples evidently had not had the time to build up the emotional investment so necessary to a compatible marriage.

It is clear, then, that to the degree that couples individuate and are compatible, jealousy presents no major problems. Conversely, when these conditions are not satisfied, disruptive jealousy can result.

There are, however, some interesting exceptions. For a few couples who seem to place little emphasis on individuation, marital compatibility is an issue which remains chronically unresolved. Compatibility for them is a quality to be constantly demonstrated rather than a fact of life to be more or less taken for granted. Hence, every give-and-take becomes an issue.

These couples focus on the mechanics of sexual competence

rather than on personal relationships. These are the people who will talk about "good swingers" and "bad swingers" rather than good and bad experiences. One of these husbands once commented:

> Some people say there's no such thing as a good lay and a bad lay. But in my experience that just isn't true. I remember this one woman I went with for a long time. She was just a bad lay. No matter what I did, she was just lousy!

In other words, his bad lay is everyone's bad lay. One of his friends expressed it differently. He didn't understand why some swingers were so concerned with compatibility; he felt it was the sex that was important—and simply "having a good time."

Because they do not consider individuation important, these couples tend to approximate most closely the popular stereotypes of swingers as desiring only "pure sex." Swinging for these couples is primarily a matter of sexual interaction. Consequently, they are chiefly interested in seeing how sexually competent a couple is before they decide whether or not to develop a friendship. Competence may be defined in any or all of a number of ways. Endurance, size of penis, foreplay competence—all may be used to assess competence during the actual sexual interaction whether it be a large open party or a smaller gathering.

It is clear, then, that such couples perceive sex in a way that individuators find uncongenial or even repugnant. When we first observed and interviewed them, we interpreted their behavior as the beginning stage of promiscuity that new couples may go through. But when we asked, we would find that they had been swinging frequently for a period of two years, much too long to be considered inexperienced. How, we asked ourselves, could such couples avoid jealousy, if they regularly evaluated sexual partners against a common standard? It seemed to us that a husband or wife in such a situation could conceivably be replaced some day by a "better lay," especially if the issue of marital compatibility remained somewhat unresolved. Yet these couples did not appear to experience any disruptive jealousy as a result of swinging. We found that they are able to accomplish this by instituting special, somewhat less flexible arrangements for swinging. First, they are invariably exclusive open swingers. That is, sexual interaction must take place in the same room. This tends to reduce any emotional involvement in one interaction. They think that closet swinging (swinging in separate rooms) is "no better than cheating." They clearly worry about the possibility of emotional infidelity more than individuators. An insistence on open swinging reduces the possibility of emotional involvement, and with it, the reason for jealousy. Second, they try to control the swinging situation as much as possible. So, for example, they are much more likely to insist on being hosts. And they also desire to state their sexual preferences ahead of time, thereby insuring that nothing very spontaneous and unpredictable can happen. Third, the women are more likely to desire female homosexuality and more aggressively so. This often results in the women experiencing more emotional involvement with each other than with the men, which is more acceptable because it does not threaten the marital relationship.

SEXUAL REVOLUTION

We are now at the point where we can answer some of the questions with which we began our research. Contrary to many who have assumed that any extramarital activity results in at least some jealousy and possibly even marital breakup, especially when there is emotional involvement, we have found that swinging often succeeds in solidifying a marriage. It does this by reromanticizing marriage, thereby making it tolerable, even enjoyable to be married. In a very important way, then, swinging is a conservative institution.

It is usually assumed that the present "sexual revolution" of which swinging is a part will continue. Bartell, reflecting this view, points out that an increasing number of people are becoming interested in swinging. Basing his prediction on a projection of present trends, he believes that swinging will probably grow in popularity and become in some way a permanent part of American culture. A similar view is expressed by James and Lynne Smith. Although they do not believe that it will become a universal form in marriage, they believe that eventually as many as 15 to 25 percent of married couples will adopt swinging.

But predictions based on projection are inadequate because they do not consider the causal processes involved and therefore cannot account for future deviations. In other words, in order to predict increasing sexual freedom, one must first understand what caused it to appear in the first place.

Although we cannot at this time make rigorous scientific statements amenable to disciplined criticism, a glance at American history in this century reveals trends that suggest some tentative answers. Since the 1920s, greater sexual freedom has always been followed by periods of relatively greater sexual repression. The flappers of the 1920s were followed by the more conservative women of the 1930s, and the freer women of World War II were followed by an era where women flocked back to conservative roles in the home. And finally, of course, we have the counterculture which expresses an unprecedented height of sexual freedom in this century. An important factor present in all of these periods seems to be the economic ebb and flow. Economic depressions and recessions have preceded all years of more conservative sexual norms. And it is probably no accident that the present summit of sexual freedom has taken place in the longest run of prosperity this country has ever experienced. With increased economic independence, women have gained sexual privileges more nearly equal to those of men. Even homosexuality has become more acceptable. Further evidence that economic ebbs and flows may directly affect sexual norms can be seen by comparing class differences in sexual behavior. For example, working-class attitudes towards sex tend to be more conservative than those of the middle and upper classes. In general it would seem that as economic resources become more plentiful so do acceptable alternative norms of sexual behavior.

If this is so, given the present decline of economic prosperity, we should find the numbers of acceptable alternative norms shrinking. One of the more obvious indications of this is the back-to-Jesus trend which is attracting increasing numbers of young people who would have formerly been drawn to the rock-drug counterculture.

It is possible, then, that swinging and sexual freedom in general is a function of factors that are beyond the immediate control of individuals. Such factors as investment flows, limited resources, fluctuations in world markets and so forth, all events that seem isolated from the arena of intimacy which people carve out for themselves are in fact very much a part of their most personal relationships. These superstructural events are critical in that they regulate the resources at the disposal of groups of people, thereby limiting the alternatives available to any one individual in his social relations including his sexual relations.

Given economic prosperity as a necessary condition for increasing sexual freedom, it is quite possible that with the economic difficulties this country is now facing the number of available acceptable sexual alternatives will decline and swinging may all but disappear from the American scene.

The Sex-Life Letters
Edited by Harold Greenwald and Ruth Greenwald

VENUS IN FURS

The thing that really sends me is fur. Fur works me up to such a degree that I often masturbate looking at photos of models clad in furs.

I am wondering if this is passed down from father to son because I have, when I was very young, entered my parents' bedroom in the early morning and seen my mother's silver fox fur on the bed.

I also remember on a couple of occasions my mother tickling my father's chin and neck with the tail of this particular fox. Although I thought nothing about it at the time, I am sure it has had some bearing on my life.

When I got married, which was only three years ago, I was able to discuss with my wife my likes and dislikes about sex. She asked me one night, "What really makes you feel sexy; would, in fact, a nude woman appeal to you?" I said it would, but if she was lying on a bed of fur or was wearing a fur of any kind it would be more attractive to me.

"I had better get myself a fur then," she said, laughing, "and after that a wheelchair to wheel you about in, because they say too much sex makes you weak." I then told her that even talking about furs made me feel very sexy.

That night she commented on the fact that I felt much bigger in her than usual and she had three orgasms.

Reprinted by permission of J. P. Tarcher, Inc., from Harold Greenwald and Ruth Greenwald, Eds., *The Sex-Life Letters*, New York, Bantam Books, 1973, pp. 6–7, 23–24, 52–54, 67, 70–71, 116–117, 122–123, 137–139, 144–145, 170–171, 205, 230–231, 250–251, 264–265, 344.

A week later, just after we got into bed, she said, "Do you feel like intercourse?" I said that being married to such an attractive woman I always fancied it.

"I bet you I could finish you, even without touching you with my hands," she replied. She then stripped and went to the wardrobe where she took out the most beautiful pair of silver fox furs I have ever seen. I could not believe my eyes as she stood there wearing nothing but silver foxes, moving the furs over her body so that they stroked her breasts lovingly. Next she took a fox tail in each hand and slowly tickled my body, starting at my neck and working down to my knees until I could contain myself no longer and grabbed her. We really had a night of loving after that, only stopping for a short time between bouts.

I am happy to say that since then furs have always been a part of our loveplay and intercourse up to this day.

I bought a book called *Venus in Furs* just recently which we both enjoyed very much. Also we both went to see the film "Midnight Cowboy" and were thrilled to see one of the actresses making love in a beautiful red fox coat. My wife tossed me off when we saw this in the pictures, as I was so worked up, but seeing this action without the furs would not have had the same effect.

Surely there must be many other people who are as affected by fur as I am?

B.R.

SADDLES HUSBAND

My husband thinks he's a horse. Well, not all the time and he certainly has no aspirations to win the Grand National. But he's a horse alright. At least five nights a week. He'll strip naked, get down on all fours and having already dressed in jodhpurs and riding cap I'll throw a saddle over him, straddle his waist, and duly mounted we ride around the room. I'll also cut his flanks with a riding crop and it is all a prelude to sexual intercourse when in fact I am mounted by the "horse."

I'll admit to enjoying this which gives me sexual satisfaction but until I read *Forum* I was worried about the deviation. Is it normal for male partners to associate themselves with animals? Perhaps my husband carries it too far for he'll ride around the room for perhaps an hour whinnying to the whip. Lately he's also asked permission to build a special stable in a corner of the bedroom in which to store his equipment and stock. But the real fly in the ointment is, am I doing wrong by jockeying along?

Mrs. J.R.

TALLYHO

It is difficult to fully understand the motivations of these men who prefer flagellistic practices as a prelude to intercourse instead of the highly erotic and stimulating art of female adornment. I find this to be an anomalous situation, inasmuch as the wearing of pretty or provocative clothing is so much more sexually stimulating than being laid into with a whip.

As for me, I find my wife's wearing of riding clothes to be a most powerful sexual stimulant. My wife took up this worthy sport sometime ago and for the purpose, bought herself a skintight pair of fawn breeches and a pair of long black leather boots. She wears these with a white shirt, appropriately close fitting over her breasts and, beneath all, a pair of long stretch nylon panties of a charming light blue color.

The immediate fear of bankruptcy due to the high cost of getting astride the noble beast was at once mitigated by the sight of my wife, a comely woman with an hourglass figure and deep breasts, clad in this sheath-fitting attire which was enough to set my eyeballs bulging. In fact, it so much enhanced our lovemaking, she only has to dress the part, whether to ride or not, and we have achieved a new and exciting relationship, and this after 17 years of marriage! From my wife's point of view, the stimulation of opening her thighs to get astride a horse and the subsequent jogging motion often arouses her desires to the pitch where only a long session of lovemaking can assuage them.

Thus, the innocent sport of horse riding has stimulated our desires in a way we find wholly delightful.

J.K.

PLEASURE BY ENEMA

Since I was a girl of nine (I am now a widow of 39) I have held the view that an enema is a pleasurable experience. When I was a schoolgirl I spent a week in hospital after an operation. During that week I received several enemas. Although I felt embarrassed and humiliated, I actually enjoyed the experiences in a manner that is now difficult to recall precisely.

So lasting was the impression that I have never forgotten it and I have tried to relive it many times since. Between nine and 19 I used to dwell on every detail and it was my principal fantasy when I masturbated. The mere sight of an enema syringe in a surgical store was enough to excite me.

I purchased a syringe when I was at college but self-administraiton was quite unsatisfactory. I had a girlfriend who was a nurse and the first person to whom I confessed my unusual interests. When she offered to repeat the treatment, I accepted willingly and I found the experience very satisfying. After several occasions she proposed we switch roles so that I became the "nurse." I found this so very satisfying that I surprised myself and began to wonder what was wrong with me.

By now I was enjoying normal sexual relationships with men and I began to realize that I had still one step to go to achieve my real desire. I wanted a man to administer the intimate enema treatment, but I could not bring myself to discuss it with a male friend. Then, one evening I was at a party where there was a fair amount of sexual activity going on. I found myself in a bedroom with a partner who put me across his knee, took my panties down and gave me a playful spanking which I enjoyed very much. He became more intimate, separated my buttocks and inserted a vaselined finger up my anus. I could not disguise my intense sexual pleasure and when he asked if I was enjoying it I admitted I did, "because it felt like being given an enema."

He proceeded to cross-question me and extracted my first full confession to a man. To my delight he was completely understanding and offered to provide me with the full treatment just as I had described it.

I could scarcely wait till the following evening when I visited his apartment. The anticipation was almost unbearable. After a fantastic half-hour across his knee we went into the bedroom where he gave me a large, warm, soapy enema just as the nurse had done when I was a child. The only difference was that as he syringed me he masturbated me. The sensation was indescribable, I came almost immediately and by the time the enema was finished I had had several orgasms.

He was very experienced and I learned for the first time that other women derived sexual satisfaction from the same treatment though very few care to admit it. We subsequently had intercourse and before I left I had a second enema, even more exciting than the first.

I continued to visit him about once a week and on the third occasion we reversed the roles of "nurse" and "patient." He enjoyed both roles but his preference was for the active role and mine for the passive.

Two years later I married another man who had no interest in my "special" activities. We had a normal relationship and were happy. I was never unfaithful in the accepted meaning of the word but I did very occasionally visit my former partner only to repeat the treatment that had affected me so profoundly.

My husband was killed in an automobile accident and I am now a widow with no children. I indulge in my former pursuit when the opportunity arises, which isn't often, but I still get tremendous anticipation whenever the day arrives. The same acute, mixed, bittersweet sensations are always there; being undressed, intimately examined, having my buttocks separated and my anus vaselined and finally being thoroughly syringed and masturbated simultaneously until I don't know which urge to obey first.

Although I now know that my reactions are not unique, I always wonder how many other women have and enjoy similar experiences. And when I hear someone say they dread the prospect of an enema I feel they just don't know what they're missing!

Mrs. E.G.

KICKS FROM BOOTS

Why does a person suddenly, out of the blue, become hyper-addicted to a particular article of clothing? And is there any chance of such a fixation getting out of hand?

My reason for asking is that I have developed what seems to me to be an exaggerated and quite unreasonable attraction toward girls in white boots, not the short Courrèges type but specifically the tall, tight-fitting variety that are beginning to be fashionable again. My addiction goes back to last winter, and the fact that I can find no logical reason for this passion shames and troubles me greatly. I find girls in white boots completely distracting and utterly irresistible. I have taken to following women wearing white boots (even long white socks that look like boots until you get up close) and after losing sight of them I often have to duck into the toilet to relieve myself. I sat opposite a girl wearing a pair the other day in the tube, and by the time she got off I had an erection and was weak with emotion. I have a scrapbook full of newspaper cuttings of girls in white boots and spend hours looking at them and masturbating.

How does a kink like this begin? Although I naturally appreciate miniskirts and am wild about black boots, no other article of female attire has this effect on me. I have never suffered from such an obsession before and it strikes me as distinctly unhealthy. I just hope I am not turning into a fetishist. I have never been to a prostitute, but I think if I did I would reach orgasm simply by touching her white boots. Is my addiction unusual?

A.M.

BONDAGE

A great deal has been, and is being, written about the sexual act—particularly in reference to its surroundings, its performance, and so on—but, as some of your correspondents have remarked, the act is the fulfillment of a longer or shorter period of preparation. And to my mind, it is this preparation which is by far the most important aspect of lovemaking.

My wife and I have been married now for nearly 16 years, and we find that bondage is the most exciting parcel in which to wrap the center.

New and exciting ways and means were tried, to be discarded or improved upon, during the early days of our marriage, and over the course of the years we have built up a store of varying equipment, dress, etc., which almost fills a complete chest of drawers. What we did find in our early days was that cords, however soft they were, were not satisfactory. Apart from the fact that the wearer may be able to manipulate a sharp blade to cut herself free, we found that if the cord was tight enough to be really effective, it was too tight to leave for any length of time; while if I tied it loosely enough not to interfere with the circulation, then it was completely ineffective and my wife would be free in a trice.

So, in our wanderings, we picked up a couple of pairs of police regulation handcuffs and two pairs of leg irons, and these—together with any number of lengths of chain and padlocks—have been our standby for a number of years. Without the keys, they are completely inescapable, and they are "comfortable" enough to wear for days at a time, if the occasion warrants it—certainly for many hours. And the time was when we would never go out in the car for a picnic, or evening drive, without at least one pair of handcuffs in the glove compartment.

However, we have now found that our old cord technique was all wrong, and we have gone back to the occasional use of cords but applied differently. This business of the heroine in books being "bound cruelly hand and foot so that the cords dug deep into her tender flesh" may be alright in fiction but is quite unnecessary. I can now tie my wife's wrists together, first of all "acrossward" and then "up and down" (at right angles to the first)—as loose as you please. The trick comes in winding the rest of the cord between the wrists in the "third dimension," thus drawing the other cords into some degree of tightness. When the last bit of the cord is pulled as tight as you want and knotted on top of the bound wrists, and thus away from prying fingers, I can assure you it is absolutely secure.

If the ankles are also to be tied, then again wind the cords between the legs as well and tie the knot in front, so that the bound hands cannot reach it. What you do in each case, in fact, is to make two quite effective cord handcuffs! Tied in this way, my wife has literally spent hours and hours in helpless bondage without undue discomfort.

My wife and I can both thoroughly recommend this pre-act bondage play, which, if reasonable care is taken, may transport a mere "rush job," as it so often is, into a whole evening's wonderful delight.

M.R.

BONDAGE SHARING

My wife and I are bondage enthusiasts, and in our frequent talks we have tried to analyze the motives which attract us to it.

There is no doubt that the majority of women really enjoy being dominated by the men they love and thoroughly enjoy uninhibited sex with their partners. Being subjected to bondage can add tremendously to their pleasure, especially as they can fantasize freely, even imagining that they are being raped and helpless to prevent it. This my wife has freely admitted to me.

But equally so, since a partnership based on genuine love requires that all pleasures and responsibilities should be shared, it is essential that the male partner accede freely to any demands made on him. Thus, to willingly submit himself to bondage indicates no sense of inferiority on his part. Rather, it is further evidence of his affection for her and his desire to share equally. There are often occasions when a woman likes temporarily to adopt the dominant role, in which she can be free to do anything possible to please and satisfy her male.

During our weekend bondage sessions we take it in turn to accept the dominated role and this most assuredly maintains our ardor and prevents any risk of boredom. And I find that for me to adopt this role is no way contrary to normal male status. Instead, I am allowing my partner to express her passion and sexuality to the utmost extent, and with complete freedom to let her imagination run riot. I cannot think of anything more exciting than to be trussed up helpless by my wife and to gaze on her naked body as she goes to work on me, fully aware that she is in complete control, so that even though I am in desperate need of an orgasm, I cannot achieve this until she brings it about by one means or another.

The same is equally true when it is her turn to submit to bondage. Every part of her lovely body is at my disposal and she revels in being excited by my caresses almost to the point of screaming. The frequency and intensity of her orgasms are far greater than during normal lovemaking.

The combination of fellatio, cunnilingus and bondage has had fantastic results, and the restricted partner quickly reaches a peak of ecstasy beyond words to describe.

Recently we have acquired several additional items of equipment, notably two vibrators, a dildo, and a leather gag. We have tremendous fun with the vibrators, especially when my wife is trussed up and I can use both of them simultaneously on two highly erogenous zones. The dildo has a variety of uses, and when she has me immobilized she takes a delight in inserting it in my rectum while using her hands to manipulate my penis and scrotum. The gag is most effective, but is used only when severe restriction is imposed, and only for limited periods of time. It certainly adds to one's sense of helplessness, especially when the wearer is made to walk about the house and is unable to make any protests against unexpected attacks.

We are fortunate in that we are both equally interested in bondage—it's not something a husband or wife should force on an unwilling partner—and the stimulation it gives us plays an important role in keeping our love for each other fresh and exciting.

A.L.

APPETITE ENHANCER

I have discovered a most delicious technique of satisfying my husband's physical and sexual appetites at the same time, and believe me, it's made our marriage more exciting than ever. My husband is one of those men who has a sweet tooth and insists on a dessert after his meals. One night, suddenly "inspired," I hit upon the idea of serving him his dessert (strawberries) in a most unique manner— instead of a bowl, I substituted my vagina, and if he wanted his dessert, which he did, there was only one way to get it.

Fortunately, my husband is a good sport and he soon got into the spirit of things. Not only did he eat every strawberry, but being quite worked up, he brought me to orgasm cunnilingually (is that the word?) followed by a terrific session in bed.

Since then, he's enjoyed every conceivable type of dessert by means of what he calls the "cuntainer"—cheesecake, chocolate mousse, eclairs, apple pie, jelly and his favorite, a chocolate sundae with nuts. Cold ice cream on the vagina can be pretty excruciating, but by the time my husband licks up the last bit of the sundae, I am anything but cold.

From time to time, I have my dessert on his private parts, and there have been occasions when we both had our desserts at the same time. What a glorious ending to a dinner! Someone told me that *The Sensuous Woman* became a best seller because it described how the author placed whipped cream topped by a cherry on her lover's penis. Frankly, I have found that doughnuts go much better with a man's organ than whipped cream.

There's no doubt in my mind that if a wife uses her imagination, she won't have to worry about her marriage getting stale or her husband fooling around with other women. As long as her husband is not a stick-in-the-mud and has a good appetite, there's no limit to what an imaginative wife can cook up for him.

Mrs. J.S.

A CONFORMED MASOCHIST

I have been married for twelve years and am still very much in love with my husband. Even before we were married, I was aware that he had slightly unusual sexual inclinations: to be specific, he liked me to ill-treat him before we made love. At first it didn't amount to much and I was happy to indulge him.

During the last few years, however, my husband's craving for physical maltreatment has become more intense. For some reason he is no longer able to accept any kind of success without wanting to suffer for it by being punished by me. Whenever, for instance, he lands a new contract, he begs me to treat him as cruelly as I can; the greater the success, the more abuse he demands. Although I always went along with his requests as far as I could, I never really enjoyed tying him up, whipping him or subjecting him to any of the other indignities he craves. I only did it because he wanted it so badly.

About two months ago, a few days after landing an important contract he rang me up and told me to get ready for an evening out. We did a show, had a lovely meal and a marvelous time. When we got home, it was very late and my husband began to make a great fuss of me. When we were both aroused, he dropped to his knees and implored me to punish him.

I agreed, but then he produced from his briefcase a horrid little whip with a metal-tipped tail and begged me to beat him with it till I drew blood. I became a bit hysterical and said I could not possibly do what he wanted.

He got angry and accused me of not understanding and loving him, since I was denying him the intense pleasure that such a whipping would give. We went to bed and have never mentioned the subject again. Not only has he stopped asking me to whip him, but he has not made love to me at all since that evening.

A few weeks later, he had another business triumph and came home with an expensive bracelet, the sort of present he has never bought me before (and frankly not the kind of thing I'd ever wear). He said he was giving it to me as an expression of his love. It was all very puzzling, especially as he seemed so contented and relaxed, just as he used to after I punished him.

That evening, I went into the bathroom, and to my horror I saw his back and thighs were a mass of livid welts. He tried to conceal his back by turning away and using the towel and I just hoped I hadn't given myself away by the expression on my face. Someone, presumably a call girl, had given him a terrible whipping, far worse than anything he ever got from me. I suppose he had it on account of his recent business triumph.

When I confided all this to my girlfriend, who is much more mercenary and materialistic than I, she just shrugged and said, indicating the bracelet which I had shown her, "Well dear, you seem to be doing all right. After all, if he's getting it from a prostitute, it means you can leave that side of it to her."

At first I was inclined to agree, but after thinking about it, I wonder whether my husband will ever want to make love to me again. He is obviously getting all the satisfaction he needs at the hands of some professional woman. And all this because I find myself incapable of giving him the sort of brutalities he wants these days.

Mrs. S.R.

WARDROBE OF RUBBER

Even before our marriage my husband showed his interest in rubber—he called it "macking"—and although this was of no interest to me at first I have gradually become used to it. He has bought me a whole wardrobe of rubber clothes as the years have passed and now I dress in rubber much of the time.

The various magazines about this that my husband has bought seem to suggest that wearing such clothes is very uncomfortable. In fact this is not so, unless the wearer is very hot or very cold, for much of the time I'm not even aware of them.

I always wear a rubber corset or corselette, rubber panties, a rubber bra if I'm wearing a short corset, and a rubber underslip.

Only in prolonged hot weather, or after strenuous housework, do I find perspiration troublesome, and then I just slip off and bathe, putting on fresh rubber clothes after powdering.

I always wear normal clothes on top, of course, and if I have on my high-necked rubber leotard I use a polo jumper to cover it up. I have several raincoats in rubber and plastic for outside wear. When alone in the house with my husband, I use a long rubber housecoat which he likes very much. At night I wear a rubber nightdress over long rubber gloves and sometimes tight jeans or stockings.

I believe I have made my husband very contented by satisfying his needs, and our marriage is a very happy one. I still feel a little guilty though and not even my closest friends know of this practice. I have never actually met another woman who does this although, judging from the success of the rubberwear firms, there must be a great many. I should like to ask you how common this sort of thing really is?

V.S.

TRANSVESTITE SOLUTION

We were married about three years ago, and soon after my transvestite leanings made themselves felt. My wife caught me wearing her clothes as she returned from shopping one Saturday, and a most distressing scene followed. However, as we were so much in love (and still are) she was very understanding and eventually allowed me to wear female underwear occasionally when we made love. Not long afterwards we learned that so many other couples were faced with the problem of one partner being bisexual (which I believe I am).

Sometimes my dear wife will insist on me wearing one of her nighties as we go to sleep. I usually agree to this, but sometimes refuse, as I feel that a refusal must strengthen her belief that I am predominantly masculine and definitely not homosexual.

Tonight, my wife is having an evening out with some girls and she knows that while she is out I am wearing her clothes which she selected for me before leaving. When she returns she will be alone because she knows that I will be dressed as I am now, and when we have coffee together the conversation will be quite normal with only complimentary references to the clothing we are both wearing.

Anyway, I know that I can look forward to a long and uninhibited session of beautiful lovemaking which will last well into the early hours.

So, we are both happy with our new sex life, but recently my wife has expressed a desire for me to buy a vibrator and use it on her. I cannot help wondering whether she may grow to prefer the vibrator to me, and I certainly want to retain my masculine privilege of having natural intercourse with her.

R.J.

ROAD STAND

My fiancée and I have a strong need for exhibitionism. Because of our circumstances, most of our lovemaking takes place in a car which allows ample opportunity. When we are both in a particularly sexy mood, we venture out onto the road in the nude. I should explain that the road is relatively quiet with a car coming past about every quarter-hour on average. My fiancée either bends face down over the hood in which case I make entry from the rear or she sits on the hood, reclining back almost onto the windshield. I stand between her legs and make entry from the front. Of course the risk of a car coming and catching us in its headlights while we are in action is extremely stimulating. Recently when a car came, I decided to stay and be seen, but in the last few seconds, my fiancée protested, and we ducked down behind the car, I must admit to my relief, because my nerve was on the verge of breaking too!

Of course, inside the car we have much greater confidence. My fiancée does not mind exposing her naked breasts and being fondled while revealed by the headlights of a passing car.

Our experiences prompt me to enquire if it is necessary or desirable to turn sexual fantasy into fact? I believe it is not necessary to do so, but if there is not a good reason to refrain, then why not? However, my experience suggests that satisfied fantasy invariably gives way to a new fantasy.

L.W.

UNUSUAL FOREPLAY

I am surprised that none of your correspondents have so far confessed, as I do with absolutely no shame, to the predilection for being trodden on by a woman in high-heeled shoes. Although I recognize that this is a mildly deviant form of sexual behavior, it is surely quite harmless, and, if not used as an end in itself, can add a delightful piquancy to erotic foreplay.

Although by no means a rabid fetishist, I have always been strongly excited by women's shoes (which incidentally, are surely prettier today than ever before) especially shoes with stiletto heels. These have always seemed to embody the quintessence of femininity.

I first asked my wife to use hers on me when we were engaged. With a little coaxing she soon overcame her inhibitions, warmed to the idea and entered into the spirit of the game, which is how we still regard it. For the past ten years, we have invariably used this "tramping" as a prelude to lovemaking. Although my wife has never purposely hurt me during this ritual, which is really just a symbolic demonstration of our relationship, she admits to enjoying the sight of me squirming at her feet and is always threatening to "dig her heels in" . . . which only excites me more. She has this to add:—

My husband, ever since he was a little boy, has always had this "thing" about girls' shoes. The first time he asked me to use mine on him, I thought it was a bit idiotic. But the idea seemed to excite him so much I agreed to try it. When I saw what a fizz it got him in, I became very excited myself and couldn't wait to be asked again. I had never dreamed how much a pair of what seemed to me ordinary shoes could mean to a man. Now I do. Besides liking the feeling of power over him it gives me, I also welcome the chance to show off my legs to such good advantage. My husband often buys me new shoes; we choose them together, and he is very particular. I also have a variety of naughty little dresses, and slinky undies that he likes me to wear during our "sessions." It is a bit naughty, I suppose, but we find it enormously satisfying and I imagine it's a far less painful form of stimulation than the lashings and scourings described by some of your other correspondents.

Mr. & Mrs. A.I.

AIM TO PLEASE

Our "game" began a few years ago when we arrived home from an excellent evening out, both desperate to relieve our bladders and making for the toilet together. I stood aside to allow my wife to go first, but she, seeing that my need was great also, sat as far back on the seat as possible with her legs wide apart so that I could aim between them. However, after a second or two, she suddenly grabbed hold of my penis and directed the jet to the region of her clitoris. When I'd finished relieving myself I noticed that she was sitting rigid, eyes closed, almost as if having a fit. After a few moans, she relaxed and smiled. She had had a terrific orgasm without any part of her actually being touched! The evening was completed with normal sexual intercourse.

Since then, we have experimented from time to time with different methods of stimulating each other through urination, and both get a terrific kick out of it. We don't make it a regular feature of our intercourse, just occasionally for variety. Sometimes my wife holds me while I pee, trying not to get me too sexy as this stops the flow completely, or I part her lips while she pees in varying positions— squatting, sitting, standing, or bending over. Another variation is to perform together. I sit down and my wife sits astride me, facing forward. Sometimes I kiss her nipples. My penis rests against her abdomen, or else I hold it along her vulva. We both get very wet, and usually finish up with a grand climax each.

We have noticed lately that during intercourse, especially if my wife is on top, she "leaks," particularly when nearing orgasm. As she pushes in with the muscles of the vagina and abdomen, little jets of hot water squirt out along my stomach. This only increases our excitement, but does it mean that my wife's muscles or even her bladder have been weakened? They are certainly all right at other times.

Another point is, if male urine gets into the vagina, can it do any harm?

In general, do you think this practice is abnormal and could damage any part of either of us?

Mr. and Mrs. J.M.

ANILINCTUS

Having practiced cunnilingus for some time and derived a great deal of pleasure from it, I would like to tell other exponents of this art of a new variation we have discovered.

One evening after a session of anal intercourse my wife was

lying on her stomach on the bed and I noticed my seminal fluid seeping from her back passage. My curiosity was aroused and I began to lick it. The sensation I received from this came as a complete surprise, and I was further excited when my tongue ventured right up to her back passage. This aroused her and she began to respond to my advances. I then inserted my tongue fully. I became very agitated and achieved an erection without further stimulation, and after exploring with my tongue for a few moments I ejaculated and the sensation was greater than I have ever known.

Since that initial session of "anal cunnilingus" we have practiced it at regular intervals, and it seems to arouse both of us to greater pleasures both on its own and as a prelude to intercourse.

F.M.

A DOG'S LIFE

My husband and I have not come across, in your columns, the peculiarity that we share. Some might call it a perversion, but we feel that so long as we both get fun out of it, there can be no possible harm in continuing.

I love my husband to pretend to be a dog! He takes off his clothes and goes down on all fours, and I attach a collar and lead to his neck, and he follows me around the house on his knees, or, if not on the lead, behaves as any normal dog would—sometimes curling up in front of the fire, or rubbing himself against my legs while I sit quietly knitting or watching the television.

The view I get of him, especially from the back, with his penis in permanent erection, really sends me, and before long we are both making love wherever we happen to be.

I remember one hilarious and exciting evening when we persuaded a friend of my husband's to join in the fun, and he and my husband made believe they were dogs and spent a lot of time sniffing each other!

Occasionally I spank my husband's bottom with the end of the lead, and he whines and barks and strains away from me, the collar around his neck getting tighter as he goes red in the face. This, together with him rolling on his back, legs apart, is the thing that gets me most excited of all, and I can barely wait for him to enter me before I come, sometimes up to four times.

I should add that far from looking ridiculous in this position, my husband, who is a beautifully well built and muscular man, with fabulous flat stomach and very long penis and with balls that really hang down, looks to me even more desirable when I see him as a dog, than as a man.

Are we as weird as we sound, or are we as normal as most, with an interest shared by others?

Mrs. A.W.

The Pederasts
by Parker Rossman

In the early 1960s I stumbled onto a problem which seems to be largely ignored by society and where scientific research is very deficient—especially considering its deep impact on the lives of those involved. In the course of counseling some deeply troubled men, I was led to explore the world of the pederast, eventually getting acquainted with over 1,000 men who were erotically attracted to young boys. I also interviewed more than 300 boys involved with such men.

ON STUDYING THE SEXUAL UNDERGROUND

I began the study in an effort to help some men, fathers of families, responsible citizens in their communities, who were being blackmailed, having fallen into the hands of a pimp who suggested they might like to try a new sort of sexual experience. The first of these I met was a professional man from the Midwest who had come to New York City to attend a study conference and to visit the World's Fair. He had observed and participated in two "orgies," where he had gotten acquainted with several other men who were victims of the pimp. Through these men I became acquainted with several more, scattered across the country, and I was distressd to find that large numbers of children, particularly 12-, 13- and 14-year-olds, were being prostituted.

Although my first reaction was to draft proposals for better

Published by permission of Transaction, Inc.; from *Transaction/Society*, Vol. 10, No. 3 (March/April 1973), copyright © 1973 by Transaction, Inc.

guidance and supervision of children, it occurred to me that the more important question was: who are the customers? I found myself heavily engaged in counseling in an area where I knew little, attempting to deal with the problems of pederasts—not merely those being blackmailed, but those struggling with temptation and guilt. One glimpse of this anguish is well portrayed in the recent film, *Death in Venice*, where the film-maker stresses the dismay of a man who discovers that he is erotically attracted to a young boy (somewhat of a misreading of the Thomas Mann novel from which the film was made).

The pederasts I met desperately needed to talk to someone they could trust. They required help and support to stay out of trouble. So in an effort to help, I surveyed the vast literature on pederasty: legal cases, medical, analytic, psychiatric and psychological case studies; historical, anthropological, sociological and biographical material. As will be suggested in a forthcoming bibliographical article on pederasty in the *Journal of Sex Research*, some of the thinly disguised autobiographical novels may provide accurate data needed to counterbalance the existing inadequate, incomplete and subjective research on pederasty.

Without intending it and without legitimated qualifications, I was propelled into an extended research project, more comprehensive than anyone has yet attempted, the only exception being Dr. Ettore Mariotti of Naples, whose medical research was banned and burned earlier in this century. He died a broken man, and I, too, have found that research into pederasty may endanger one's career and may even endanger one's life when it leads to an exploration of child prostitution.

Because of the caution, fear and secrecy of pederasts, I do not believe anyone else has had such an opportunity. Certainly no one else has written a report on such extensive interview data. This article is not intended as a preliminary report of findings, but rather as a statement of some hypotheses for further research and as a proposal for the creation of an interdisciplinary research team which would undertake a study of pederasty and pedophilia. New insights into homosexuality also might be produced by more adequate research into the sexual experience of children and of children with adults. It is clear to me that no one discipline, no one scholar is adequately equipped to deal with the complexities which my research has uncovered.

How and where does one find pederasts? Unlike homosexuals, there are no pederast associations in the United States. Yet each pederast knows another, and across a decade one can therefore be led from person to person. If one is trusted he can in time become acquainted with the secret pederasts who never reveal themselves unless they get into trouble or go to a psychiatrist. One can begin to speak now of a "homosexual community," but pederasts are isolated from one another by fear and suspicion of each other. As G. W. Henry suggests in his book, *All the Sexes,* the number of pederasts is much larger than is commonly known or supposed.

There are mailing lists of persons who order pederast books, photographs and other materials. Before it became illegal to send unsolicited advertisements of pornography, a number of European firms sent mailings to discover potential customers. There are now (in Europe) coded mailing lists of as many as 50,000 Americans who have purchased such materials. I have sorted through a number of such lists and I found one dealer who had in his files 1,800 returned questionnaires from American pederasts who reported their activities and interests to suggest the sorts of printed materials they would be interested in buying. The majority of these were professional men: teachers, doctors, social workers—with university professors heading the list. And the questionnaires suggested that most of them ordered books and pictures as fantasy substitutes for criminal sexual activity. Those 1,800 questionnaires further indicated that such persons often went overseas, or at least far from home, if they engaged in pederast sexual acts. These questionnaires seemed to confirm what I had learned from my counseling interviews—that these pederasts tended to have sex without love with young prostitutes when away from home; and at the same time these men had affectionate, non-sexual relationships with boys at home.

This provisional answer to the question of *who* led to yet another question: why? And the pederasts I was counseling also wanted to know how unique their experience was. One of them offered to pay for sending out a questionnaire asking for autobiographical information: when did these pederasts first become aware of their temptations and desires? What was the nature of their fantasies and experience? Selecting initially 1,000 names from a commercial list, I wrote 500 persons, on five continents, to ask if they could supply me with data or bibliography on child prostitution—since it was assumed no one would admit he was a pederast. I received an astonishing volume of replies, with newspaper clippings, articles and personal experiences. Most of the persons who wrote said that they loved children and would do anything they could to stamp out abuses and exploitation of children.

I wrote again, personally typed letters on an MTST tape type-writer, to the second 500 names as well as to those who had replied to the first letter, asking for the names of persons who might be able and willing to supply data about pederasty, especially asking who would be willing to fill out an anonymous questionnaire or be interviewed. The replies were disappointing. Not many were willing to fill out even the most confidential or anonymous questionnaire. Those who finally did fill out a questionnaire were not truthful. Later, in personal interviews, many admitted that the truth was exactly the opposite of what they had written.

It should be noted that whereas an increasing number of homosexuals believe they have a battle to fight for law reform and some public acceptance, pederasts have no such illusion. Most of them are deeply fearful and resentful of any publicity, research or public notice. Some persons even threatened my life if I should pursue such a study or publish results. Many others, however, replied that they would be interested in talking to me confidentially, often adding an appeal for help. Some were very dismayed at having once engaged in a criminal act and intended never to do so again. Others were so fearful of their pederast fantasies and temptations that they would hardly shake hands with a boy. Some had felt they could not afford therapy, and others had found therapy unhelpful.

At this point I had what turned out to be a foolish notion—that one might experiment with a sort of Alcoholics Anonymous group for pederasts who needed and wanted the help and support of others to keep from yielding to temptation. So partly as a device for gathering more data into the "why," I tried convening some discussion meetings, which were useful only in revealing the overwhelming difficulties of group conversation. So, on the suggestion of several persons, I initiated a series of round-robin letters, in which pederasts wrote anonymously of their sexual fantasies, dreams and experiences. This project continued across five years, involving several hundred persons.

I began by asking the questions I had developed for a questionnaire, and essay replies were mailed to other participants for comment. In addition to personal experience and autobiographical statements, the round-robin newsletters included information on pederast books, films, articles—the equivalent finally of nearly 5,000 double-spaced typewritten pages, which drew together nearly all of the available data on pederasty from all sources, for extensive comments from pederasts themselves. Those who received and commented on this material included pediatricians (one who read and discussed it all with his wife), psychiatrists, social scientists, politicians, policemen, parole officers, clergy—including a bishop—social workers, scholars of various disciplines. Many of these persons, of course, were not pederasts, but were sex researchers and scholars of other disciplines. The plan had been to deposit all this material at the Institute of Sex Research at Indiana University.

The most substantial aspect of the research consisted of in-depth interviews, which were possible only after a basis of trust was established—even then some would talk to me only anonymously, and one man only in the dark. I would like to express public appreciation here to the many men, some distinguished in their fields of work, who not only were willing to reveal to me things they had never dared to tell anyone before, but who in many cases traveled great distances at their own expense to meet me when I was in Paris, Beirut, Tangiers, Sydney, Toronto as well as many American cities.

WHAT IS A PEDERAST?

The one contribution I should perhaps be expected to make on the basis of such extensive research would be a definition of pederasty, but the more one knows about such a subject the more difficult it becomes to establish adequate definitions, for one has learned a thousand exceptions for a thousand qualifications and complications. One cannot define pederasty without stating controversial hypotheses.

André Gide in his *Journal* wrote: "A pederast is a lover of young boys and I am one." Note that this does not necessarily define pederasty in terms of an erotic attraction to boys, nor is the pederast thus defined as one who engages in sexual acts with boys, although Gide does report such sexual activity in his autobiography, *If It Die*. Rather the pederast sees himself as one who loves boys in all the meanings of the word love.

Our difficulty with the word *pederast* is that it covers many types, some as widely different as virgin and rapist. Can one word be used to include them all? I am especially not willing to limit the word *pederast* to those who are engaging in illegal sex acts, but insist on including a large majority who have never had a first homosexual experience. Who then is a pederast? As with homosexuals, I am content to let them define themselves. A pederast is someone who accepts the label and identifies himself as such, chaste or promiscuous.

It is generally assumed that pederasty is a subdivision of homo-sexuality, pederasts being those homosexuals who prefer "chicken" (young boys). In my judgment such homosexuals are only one type of pederast. If one defines a homosexual as a person who engages in homosexual acts, then many pederasts are homosexuals. The only kind of sex act a man can have with a boy is a homosexual act. However, most homosexuals are eager to disassociate themselves from pederasty, being honestly horrified at the thought of homosexual relations with a child. Some further feel that, to accomplish legal reform to their advantage, restrictions on homosexual activity among consenting adults must be removed at the price of stricter laws against sex acts with children. Never mind the psychological damage done to children by dragging them to court on matters that should be handled medically and psychiatrically. Many homosexuals find it convenient to forget their own childhood emotions and experiences. And questioning the relationship between homosexuality and pederasty, one faces the question: who is a consenting adult? If the age of consent is 18 or 21, then many homosexuals are in fact pederasts. On the other hand, if the age of consent is puberty or age 14 as in some countries, then much pederasty becomes homosexuality, for many of the children we are discussing would then be considered adults.

More important, however, is the fact that a large percentage of pederasts are not exclusively attracted to males and are not homo-sexual if one uses the common sense definition: a homosexual is a man who is erotically attracted to an adult male. Some pederasts are admittedly homosexual; some consider themselves bisexual and should be more accurately called pedophiliacs—being equally attracted to young girls. Many pederasts relate sexually to women very well. And as researchers on homosexuality have amply shown, are married, and have children. Many of the accepted psychoanalytic theories of pederasty simply do not seem to apply to them at all. Also many pederasts have a deadly fear of "homosexual boys," for homo-sexual youngsters tend to panic at emotions they are unable to manage, or they become insanely jealous and demanding. Our understanding of pederasty must therefore be enlarged to include a much greater variety of experience, as indicated by our interviews.

FIVE TYPES OF PEDERASTY

Adequate definitions of pederasty must take account of at least five types of pederasty:

First, the smallest category is the "temporary or substitute" pederast who sleeps with a boy when women are not available. Usually he does so only infrequently, is quite cautious, and does not really consider himself to be a pederast. This type was in the past commonly found at sea; for example see Jean Bosq's *Le Vice Marin,* which helped remove young boys from French ships because of its evidence that the ship captain was accurate when he remarked that "after six weeks at sea the sodomy laws no longer apply." But ship crews no longer include young boys and most voyages are relatively short in duration. Steps have also been taken to eliminate pederasty in other traditional breeding grounds—young boys are generally not jailed in adult prisons, and women are much more available to the army.

I would also include in this category those individuals who are essentially heterosexuals who in search of new sexual kicks become the customers for young male prostitutes at home and abroad. For example, there is the tourist who patronizes the boys' brothel in Bangkok and tells his friends that for a different kick they should try young boys that are available in many tourist cities. And there is a great deal of pederasty among Americans in Vietnam, as there was among the French before them for the same reasons—not because of a lack of women.

Second is the category of "criminal or exploitative pederasts," including pimps of young boys, gangsters who run pederast hangouts, blackmailers and others on the fringes of society where many are engaged extensively with women. Some of these pederasts limit their sexual activity almost exclusively to young boys and do consider themselves to be pederasts. There is often a great deal of legal and personal risk involved in this type of activity. It is important to note that many of these people have passionate affection for boys, and they may be the most authentic survivals of the substitute type. Many of them had their definitive sexual experiences in reformatories. Across their formative teenage years and sometimes into their twenties, they had regular sexual intercourse and even passionate affairs with younger inmates. They not only developed a taste for sex with young boys, they became very skilled at seduction and learned to give and receive pleasure of a radically different kind than they have with women.

Third, some of these men who became addicted to boys in reformatories become the "promiscuous pederast" type. This category includes these men who cruise cheap motion pictures and regularly pick up the hustlers available in most cities. Many of these are lower-class men. Those I interviewed included bakers, clerks in hotels and stores, bus drivers, milk routemen, policemen.

Most men in this category are exclusive pederasts and consider themselves as such. Some have already been arrested and can no longer get good jobs. Others are careless and cynical because of fatalism. Taking risks is a part of the game. Some make sexual propositions to every boy they meet, to see which will respond. They are not likely to use drugs, alcohol or force, as some in the previous category, but many are frankly exploitative. Some are callous, others are mentally ill. There is, indeed, such variety in this category that it ought to be a dozen categories. It should be noted that the criminal and cautious types are the only ones considered in most of the theories of cause and cure.

Fourth are the "careful pederasts." These men generally do not limit themselves solely to young boys but are quite aware of their inclination toward pederasty. They generally have a good deal of money and they avoid sexual contact with boys except in carefully protected situations, thereby minimizing legal and personal risks. Some, for example, would never touch a boy in the United States, but make special trips to other countries. One man has sexual relations only with the children of call girls he befriends and baby-sits for. Another pays a sizeable monthly income to a widow whose son he is educating. I learned of two "father-son sports clubs" where fathers traded their own sons on camping trips. There have been a number of arrests in relation to one of these groups in the Los Angeles area. I found a town of 8,000 people in the Midwest where a group of men have paid for the college education of a series of boys across 20 years, in exchange for sexual favors when the boys were younger. Because of the care with which they protect themselves, these men do not usually fall into the hands of the law—unless they make careless mistakes or violate their own rules for some reason. One basic rule of the careful pederast, for example, is never to mix business with pleasure.

RESPONSIBLE PEDERASTS

Fifth, "responsible pederasts" are those men, often wealthy and of good education and position, who avoid any kind of sexual contact or involvement with children. Aware of their problem and temptations, they bend over backwards to protect themselves, some refusing to have anything to do with organizations where young boys will be present. Many of these men in their first interviews with me swore that they have never had any kind of sexual contact with a boy—at least not since they were young teenagers themselves. Later, however, many of them admitted that "some years ago," they had slipped once or twice, and they live in mortal fear that it will be discovered even yet. There are certain common factors in causing them to slip. Frequently they are not prepared to handle a seductive and seducing child, particularly one with previous sexual experience. Further the irresistible child was one who not only was aroused and demanding, but also revealed a very touching sexual hunger: "I was so fond of that child I simply could not refuse him." The third typical factor, however, is the development of strong resistance, having succumbed in this way. Being repentant, angry that he was naive and unprepared, the responsible pederast is determined to make sure that he never succumbs again.

I detected that many of them have moods that go up and down and that from time to time they do have weak moments when their resistance is low—such as some evening when in a distant and anonymous city they meet a young hustler. This is the most neglected group in pederast research and therapy. Mostly they report that analysts and psychiatrists do not take them seriously, if they report some temptations which they seem to have pretty well under control.

Finally, within each of the above categories, what we actually find is a continuum of attitudes and experiences, and many of the thousand persons who have provided data do not fit exactly into any of the above categories.

While it is useful to know how many pederasts there are, how they make contacts with boys, and the extent and type of sexual activity, there are, however, more crucial questions, revolving around the nature of the sexual experience upon life, personality, morals, values, attitudes and emotions of those who have the experience. Further, to speak of "sexual experience" points to the fact that we are concerned with more than sex acts, that is, with the meanings and interpretations given to such acts and to the emotions surrounding unfulfilled desires. For while the literature for the most part emphasizes the types and frequency of unusual sexual acts, the sexual activity of pederasts is for the most part extremely limited. Many, in fact, except for the promiscuous category, have experienced a sexual act with a boy only once or twice in a lifetime, often years ago. A high percentage of the promiscuous category are sexually active only when they are away on vacations or overseas.

PEDERAST MORALITY

At one of my early meetings with pederasts, those present pointed out that every one of them would draw a line at some point, in terms of his own moral standards:

☐ Some would never touch a boy, certainly not sexually.
☐ Others thought it was all right to hug and caress a boy, but not kiss.
☐ Others thought it was acceptable to kiss and to masturbate the boy.
☐ Others would fellate a boy, but considered anal intercourse a crime.
☐ The large majority would make the above decisions in accordance with the wishes of the boy. They would do what he desired and no more.
☐ None would touch a child not yet pubescent, because that boy would not be interested or aroused.
☐ Some would never touch a child unless there was mutual affection.
☐ Others, however, considered it a game or sport to seduce a young adolescent, especially one who wanted to play the game.
☐ Others would never seduce a boy, but would indulge in sexual acts with an experienced boy prostitute—especially away from home.

As I extended my interviews, this list grew longer and longer, suggesting an almost infinite variety of attitudes and experiences. In his ideal world, where he lives most of the time and for most of the years of his life, the pederast—except for certain criminal and promiscuous types—loves and protects boys.

What does he enjoy in sexual relations with a boy? The pederast enjoys giving the boy pleasure, perhaps in the sense of "enjoying the pleasure of the other," which Sartre in *Saint Genêt* uses to interpret the writings of that French author. They do not kiss boys, usually, because boys do not want to be kissed, so the pederast contents himself with the teasing and wrestling which a boy enjoys. Because a pederast truly wants a boy's affection, he follows the boy's sexual lead rather passively, becoming sexually active only as affection grows and as the boy wishes. Most said: "You never really have to seduce a boy. Give him time and he will seduce you." They generally agreed that those who fall into the hands of the police are the ones who have forgotten that rule.

THE CONSENTING BOYS

What do boys enjoy sexually? While I did get the chance to talk, in limited ways, to the young lovers of some pederasts—and more meaningfully and constructively with older boys and young men who had been such lovers in the past—I could not interview a truly representative sample of children. Most of my data on the attitudes and experience of boys is from interviews with boy prostitutes. In any event, some clear impressions emerge from hearing men and boys describe their experiences.

It was generally agreed that boys respond to men's overtures, or even seek men out, for four main reasons or combinations of them: 1) some boys are hungry for affection, 2) some mainly want money and gifts (and not always because of poverty), 3) some want adventure, new experiences, kicks other than sexual ones. Some at a rather young age see "playing the queers" as an exciting game to play until they are old enough for girls, 4) mostly, however much they may hide behind other reasons, boys indulge in sexual activity with men because they greatly enjoy being fellated. They are highly aroused by a sexually stimulating culture, and they want sex education and sexual kicks.

Lower-class delinquent boys are more likely to have been seduced than other youngsters. In nearly all cases the boys were first seduced by youngsters of their own age or slightly older. While this is more characteristic of the boy prostitutes (and therefore of those I interviewed), the adult pederasts I interviewed verified that this was indeed typical of most of their lovers. The sexually experienced boy is not only more available and more tempting to the pederast, but he often takes initiative in proposing sexual relations, especially in a situation of mutual trust and affection.

In most cases, the actual sexual intercourse of man with boy is much more like a game than like love-making with a woman. Indeed, a large number of boys in America, and also in England, use the term "fun and games" to talk about such activity. The boy who would react angrily to any suggestion that he had ever indulged in homosexual activity, or in sexual perversions, or love-making with males, would often admit to "fun and games." I do not know how extensive it is for adolescents to view sexual activity as a sport, but it seems to be very typical of those boys who are involved with pederasts, and seems to characterize the adolescent memories and fantasies of a high percentage of pederasts of all categories.

Therefore, instead of discussing the extent to which pederasts and boys are indulging in oral intercourse, anal intercourse or masturbation—for the first two are perhaps much more rare than commonly supposed—it might make much more sense to study the types of sexual games that are played, in which oral or anal intercourse are sometimes the penalty for the loser or the reward for the victor. There are gambling games, sporty games related to boxing and wrestling, sexual competitions and contests. There is the "hunt and chase," and there are other courtship games. One might well speak of "healthy" games and "sick" games, for some—especially as developed in juvenile penal institutions—come to involve teasing, sadistic spanking, psychological torture, prostitution, mock marriages and even rape. There are sporty games which involve very little emotion and fantasy, and there are highly charged emotional experiences in which fantasy is a major dimension of the game.

It is often pointed out that how adults react and what adults say to interpret sexual acts may be much more influential, much more crucial in the emotional development of the child than the actual sexual act in which he may have been involved. Perhaps it is even more crucial how the child interprets and fantasizes over his own sexual experience. There is an emotional point at which a homosexual affirms his identity: "All right I am a homosexual. Now I understand myself," and where the pederast says to himself: "I am a pederast. I didn't ask to be a pederast. How did it happen?" Most pederasts, if they have an opinion at all, think that it happened to them at puberty, in relation to fantasies and solitary pleasures long before they had any sexual contact with another person of either sex.

EROTIC ATTRACTION

Many pederasts reported that they were conscious of a strong erotic attraction to boys before they had any idea of the type of sexual contact they would desire. This is not true of those who actively participated in sexual games during their own adolescence. Those, who did, tend to desire the types of sexual contact which they came to enjoy during adolescent sex games. The actual nature of the games was less important than the fantasies which accompanied and interpreted the sex play, adding a pleasurable emotional dimension to the games. Interestingly enough, when one questions pederasts about the nature of those fantasies, especially the ones they remember or still repeat because of their emotional or pleasurable significance, they most often mention four types:

☐ inventing new games or elaborating upon habitual games as they might be played in the future
☐ reliving an adolescent sexual experience or elaborating an imaginary adolescent experience which was meaningful at that time
☐ fantasizing an encounter with the "ideal boy," a "love story"
☐ refantasizing an adolescent masochistic game or dream

The aim of the fantasy is genital pleasure and the accentuation of genital pleasure, and the successful fantasy is one which provides either the stimulus to masturbation or the "warm emotional glow" of sexual pleasure without masturbation. The most successful fantasies are generally a reliving of experiences of early adolescence, which grow deeper and more routine each time they are relived.

It is my hypothesis that pederasty's origin lies in the experience and interpretation of intense and exciting personal pleasure in sexual experiences at puberty and following. Wendell Pomeroy warns, in *Boys and Sex,* that adolescent homosexual play "may become so pleasurable" that a boy "will not give himself an opportunity to develop a heterosexual life." For many pederasts it may well be that the adolescent sex games were so pleasurable that he continues them alongside other types of sexual experience in later life. It seems to me that a neglected aspect of research into homosexuality and pederasty is the study of pleasure. This becomes more crucial in a time when "sex as fun" and "fun culture" take deeper root in the attitudes of the younger generation. The emphasis on the study of clinical and neurotic aspects of homosexuality, for example, as sickness, has simply understressed the role of pleasure in determining what people will do sexually.

What role do daydreams and masturbation fantasies play in the pederast's sexual pleasure, in his temptations and desires, in his self-concept of pederast and justification of his behavior? What is the difference between "man-boy love affairs" and sex games which take place in a non-love situation? How do these different experiences affect the sexual socialization and sexual behavior of various individuals? There are no clearcut answers to these questions. Indeed, some adolescents appear to engage in a great deal of sex play with little emotional impact, while the lives of others are deeply colored by one isolated sexual experience. Research is needed into the nature of sexual pleasure, especially when not in the context of a loving relationship, and into the sexual fantasies of children and young adolescents as related to the development of pederast and homosexual tendencies. We have only scratched the surface—our answers have suggested new questions. Research into pederasty has been inadequate because we haven't even known what questions to ask.